# TAKING SIDES

Clashing Views on

# Psychological Issues

SIXTEENTH EDITION

# TAKING SIDES

Clashing Views on

# Psychological Issues

SIXTEENTH EDITION

Selected, Edited, and with Introductions by

**Brent Slife**
*Brigham Young University*

The McGraw·Hill Companies

TAKING SIDES: CLASHING VIEWS ON PSYCHOLOGICAL ISSUES, SIXTEENTH EDITION

Published by McGraw-Hill, a business unit of The McGraw-Hill Companies, Inc., 1221 Avenue of the Americas, New York, NY 10020. 
Taking Sides is published by the **Contemporary Learning Series** group within the McGraw-Hill Higher Education division.

1 2 3 4 5 6 7 8 9 0 DOC/DOC 0 9

MHID: 0-07-813942-2
ISBN: 978-0-07-813942-0
ISSN: 1098-5409

Managing Editor: *Larry Loeppke*
Senior Managing Editor: *Faye Schilling*
Senior Developmental Editor: *Jill Peter*
Editorial Assistant: *Cindy Hedley*
Editorial Coordinator: *Mary Foust*
Production Service Assistant: *Rita Hingtgen*
Permissions Coordinator: *Shirley Lanners*
Senior Marketing Manager: *Julie Keck*
Marketing Communications Specialist: *Mary Klein*
Marketing Coordinator: *Alice Link*
Senior Project Manager: *Jane Mohr*
Design Specialist: *Tara McDermott*
Cover Graphics: *Rick D. Noel*

Compositor: MPS Limited
Cover Image: © Comstock/Punchstock/RF

**Library of Congress Cataloging-in-Publication Data**

Main entry under title:
Taking sides: clashing views on psychological issues/selected, edited, and with introductions by Brent Slife—16th ed.

Includes bibliographical references.
1. Psychology. 2. Human behavior. I. Slife, Brent, *comp.*
150

**www.mhhe.com**

# Editors/Academic Advisory Board

Members of the Academic Advisory Board are instrumental in the final selection of articles for each edition of *Taking Sides.* Their review of articles for content, level, and appropriateness provides critical direction to the editors and staff. We think that you will find their careful consideration well reflected in this volume.

## TAKING SIDES: Clashing Views on PSYCHOLOGICAL ISSUES

Sixteenth Edition

### EDITOR



### ACADEMIC ADVISORY BOARD MEMBERS

# Editors/Academic Advisory Board continued

# Preface

Critical thinking skills are a significant component of a meaningful education, and this book is specifically designed to stimulate critical thinking and initiate lively and informed dialogue on psychological issues. In this book I present 34 selections, arranged in pro and con pairs, that address a total of 17 different controversial issues in psychology. The opposing views demonstrate that even experts can derive conflicting conclusions and opinions from the same body of information.

A dialogue approach to learning is certainly not new. The ancient Greek philosopher Socrates engaged in it with his students some 2,400 years ago. His point-counterpoint procedure was termed a *dialectic.* Although Socrates and his companions hoped eventually to know the "truth" by this method, they did not see the dialectic as having a predetermined end. There were no right answers to know or facts to memorize. The emphasis in this learning method is on how to evaluate information—on developing reasoning skills.

It is in this dialectical spirit that *Taking Sides: Clashing Views on Psychological Issues* was originally compiled, and it has guided me through this 16th edition as well. To encourage and stimulate discussion and to focus the debates in this volume, each issue is expressed in terms of a single question that is answered with two different points of view. But certainly the reader should not feel confined to adopt only one or the other of the positions presented. These positions may fall between the views expressed or totally outside them, and I encourage you to fashion your own conclusions.

Some of the questions raised in this volume go to the very heart of what psychology as a discipline is all about and the methods and manner in which psychologists work. Others address newly emerging concerns. In choosing readings I was guided by the following criteria: the readings had to be understandable to newcomers to psychology, they had to have academic substance, and they had to express markedly different points of view.

**Plan of the book** Each issue in this volume has an issue *introduction,* which defines each author's position and sets the stage for debate. Also provided is a set of point-counterpoint statements that pertain to the issue and that should help to get the dialogue off the ground. Each issue concludes with *challenge questions* to provoke further examination of the issue. The introduction and challenge questions are designed to assist the reader in achieving a critical and informed view on important psychological issues. Also, at the beginning of each part is a list of Internet site addresses (URLs) that should prove useful as starting points for further research. At the back of the book is a listing of all the contributors to this volume, which gives information on the psychologists, psychiatrists, philosophers, professors, and social critics whose views are debated here.

In the interest of space, the reference lists of many of the original articles have been omitted or severely curtailed. Although I welcome further scholarly investigations in these issues, I assume that readers who engage in such investigation will want to look up the original articles (with the original reference lists) anyway. Furthermore, many of the articles have been heavily edited.

**Changes to this edition** This edition entails considerable revision. There are eight completely new issues: Issue 3. Does the research support evolutionary accounts of female mating preferences? Issue 5. Is homosexuality biologically based? Issue 6. Is Evolution a Good Explanation for Psychological Concepts? Issue 7. Does Divorce Have Positive Long-term Effects on the Children Involved? Issue 8. Do Online Friendships Hurt Adolescent Development? Issue 9. Are Today's Youth More Self-Centered than Previous Generations? Issue 11. Are the Recovered Memories of Psychological Trauma Valid? Issue 15. Should Psychologists Abstain from Involvement in Coercive Interrogations?

In addition to the new issues, at least one new article for four existing issues has been replaced and updated. Issue 4. Are Gender Differences in Communication Biologically Determined? Issue 12. Is ADHD a Real Disorder? Issue 16. Do Video Games Lead to Violence? Issue 17. Can Sex Be Addictive?

**A word to the instructor** An *Instructor's Resource Guide with Test Questions* (multiple-choice and essay) is available through the publisher for the instructor using *Taking Sides* in the classroom. A general guidebook, *Using Taking Sides in the Classroom,* which discusses methods and techniques for integrating the pro-con approach into any classroom setting, is also available. An online version of *Using Taking Sides in the Classroom* and a correspondence service for *Taking Sides* adopters can be found at http://www.mhcls.com/usingts/.

*Taking Sides: Clashing Views in Psychological Issues* is only one title in the Taking Sides series. If you are interested in seeing the table of contents for any of the other titles, please visit the Taking Sides Web site at http://www.mhcls.com/takingsides/.

**Acknowledgments** In working on this revision I received useful suggestions from many of the users of the previous edition, and I was able to incorporate many of their recommendations for new issues and new readings.

In addition, special thanks to the McGraw-Hill staff for their support and perspective.

**Brent Slife**
*Brigham Young University*

# Contents In Brief

# Contents

# Correlation Guide

The *Taking Sides* series presents current issues in a debate-style format designed to stimulate student interest and develop critical thinking skills. Each issue is thoughtfully framed with an issue summary, an issue introduction, and challenge questions. The pro and con essays—selected for their liveliness and substance—represent the arguments of leading scholars and commentators in their fields.

***Taking Sides: Clashing Views on Psychological Issues,* 16/e,** is an easy-to-use reader that presents issues on important topics such as *homosexuality, divorce effects, psychological trauma,* and *coercive interrogations.* For more information on *Taking Sides* and other *McGraw-Hill Contemporary Learning Series* titles, visit www.mhhe.com/cls.

This convenient guide matches the issues in ***Taking Sides: Psychological Issues,* 16/e,** with the corresponding chapters in two of our best-selling McGraw-Hill Psychology textbooks by Feist/Rosenberg and King.

| *Taking Sides: Clashing Views on Psychological Issues,* **16/e** | *Psychology: Making Connections,* **by Feist/ Rosenberg** | *The Science of Psychology: An Appreciative View, Study Edition* **by King** |
|---|---|---|
| **Issue 1:** Are Traditional Empirical Methods Sufficient to Provide Evidence for Psychological Practice? | **Chapter 13:** Personality | **Chapter 2:** Psychology's Scientific Methods |
| **Issue 2:** Classic Dialogue: Was Stanley Milgram's Study of Obedience Unethical? | **Chapter 2:** Conducting Research in Psychology<br>**Chapter 14:** Social Behavior | **Chapter 12:** Social Psychology |
| **Issue 3:** Does the Research Support Evolutionary Accounts of Female Mating Preferences? | **Chapter 1:** Introduction to Psychology<br>**Chapter 2:** Conducting Research in Psychology | **Chapter 1:** What Is Psychology?<br>**Chapter 10:** Motivation and Emotion<br>**Chapter 12:** Social Psychology |
| **Issue 4:** Must Women and Men Communicate Differently? | **Chapter 5:** Human Development<br>**Chapter 9:** Language and Thought<br>**Chapter 11:** Motivation and Emotion | **Chapter 4:** Human Development<br>**Chapter 9:** Thinking, Intelligence, and Language<br>**Chapter 10:** Motivation and Emotion |
| **Issue 5:** Is Homosexuality Biologically Based? | **Chapter 3:** The Biology of Behavior<br>**Chapter 11:** Motivation and Emotion<br>**Chapter 14:** Social Behavior | **Chapter 3:** Biological Foundations of Behavior<br>**Chapter 10:** Motivation and Emotion<br>**Chapter 12:** Social Psychology |

*(Continued)*

| *Taking Sides: Clashing Views on Psychological Issues,* 16/e | *Psychology: Making Connections,* by Feist/ Rosenberg | *The Science of Psychology: An Appreciative View, Study Edition* by King |
|---|---|---|
| **Issue 6:** Is Evolution a Good Explanation for Psychological Concepts? | **Chapter 1:** Introduction to Psychology | **Chapter 4:** Human Development<br>**Chapter 10:** Motivation and Emotion |
| **Issue 7:** Does Divorce Have Positive Long-Term Effects on the Children Involved? | **Chapter 5:** Human Development | **Chapter 4:** Human Development<br>**Chapter 12:** Social Psychology |
| **Issue 8:** Do Online Friendships Hurt Adolescent Development? | **Chapter 1:** Introduction to Psychology<br>**Chapter 15:** Psychological Disorders | **Chapter 1:** What Is Psychology?<br>**Chapter 13:** Psychological Disorders |
| **Issue 9:** Are Today's Youth More Self-Centered than Previous Generations? | **Chapter 14:** Social Behavior<br>**Chapter 15:** Psychological Disorders | **Chapter 4:** Human Development<br>**Chapter 12:** Social Psychology |
| **Issue 10:** Is the Theory of Multiple Intelligences Valid? | **Chapter 10:** Intelligence, Problem Solving, and Creativity | **Chapter 9:** Thinking, Intelligence, and Language |
| **Issue 11:** Are Recovered Memories of Psychological Trauma Valid? | **Chapter 7:** Memory | **Chapter 8:** Memory |
| **Issue 12:** Is ADHD a Real Disorder? | **Chapter 3:** The Biology of Behavior | **Chapter 13:** Psychological Disorders |
| **Issue 13:** Does Taking Antidepressants Lead to Suicide? | **Chapter 16:** Treatment of Psychological Disorders | **Chapter 14:** Therapies |
| **Issue 14:** Do Brain Deficiencies Determine Learning Disabilities? | **Chapter 5:** Human Development<br>**Chapter 8:** Learning<br>**Chapter 10:** Intelligence, Problem Solving, and Creativity | **Chapter 4:** Human Development<br>**Chapter 7:** Learning<br>**Chapter 9:** Thinking, Intelligence, and Language |
| **Issue 15:** Should Psychologists Abstain from Involvement in Coercive Interrogations? | | |
| **Issue 16:** Do Video Games Lead to Violence? | **Chapter 3:** The Biology of Behavior<br>**Chapter 14:** Social Behavior | **Chapter 3:** Biological Foundations of Behavior<br>**Chapter 12:** Social Psychology |
| **Issue 17:** Can Sex Be Addictive? | **Chapter 11:** Motivation and Emotion | **Chapter 10:** Motivation and Emotion |

# Introduction

Why does psychology need a *Taking Sides* book? The expression "taking sides" implies that there are "controversial psychological issues," as the book title states. But how can there be controversial issues in a discipline that considers itself a science? Controversial issues would seem inherent in such disciplines as philosophy and religion, but wouldn't the issues of psychology be resolved by science—by finding out what is true and false through psychology's empirical methods? If so, are the "controversial issues" presented in this book only *temporary* issues waiting for empirical resolution? And if they are only temporary, why learn or argue about them? Why "take a side"?

As this introduction will argue, there are all sorts of reasons and opportunities to take a side in psychology. Scientific findings are not only decided by data—the information produced by scientific research—but they are also decided by theoretical allegiances, industry loyalties, and philosophical assumptions that are not themselves driven or resolved by data. These allegiances and assumptions allow for and even spawn controversial issues. Indeed, they form what some call the "disguised ideologies" of science (Bernstein, 1983; Richardson, Fowers, & Guignon, 1999): implicit worldviews or philosophies that guide what variables to select for research, what methods to use in these investigations, and what sense to make of the resulting data. As we will see, these are just a few of the many places in psychological research where the researcher's bias or ideology, and thus "controversial issues," can come into play.

Some may hold that the problem of bias affects only the "soft" sciences. They may believe that "hard" sciences, such as physics and chemistry, have essentially eliminated biases and ideologies. However, as we will show, both soft and hard sciences are subject to these ideologies and controversial issues. Indeed, one of the recent conclusions of physics is that the observer's "frame of reference" always affects what is observed (Einstein, 1990; Heisenberg, 1958; Wolf, 1981). In this introduction, we will point to dramatic examples of systematic biases in both types of sciences, showing how some of the most important research—research about health treatment—is substantially driven by factors outside the data per se.

Even so, some scientists will argue that these biases are miscarriages of science, that science conducted correctly would have no systematic ideologies. As we will attempt to describe, however, nothing could be further from the truth, because the scientific method is itself based on a philosophy. It is itself based on a broad ideology in this sense. This is not to say that science is *only* bias or that science is worthless. Indeed, we will argue that science is one of the best tools we have for helping to resolve controversial issues. The main point of this introduction is that ideologies, biases, and "issues" are *never* avoided entirely and, indeed, play a *necessary* role in science. We believe this role is all the more reason to become aware of psychology's controversial issues, think them through, and, yes, even take a well-reasoned and well-informed "side."

## Allegiance Effects in the Soft Sciences

Many examples of systematic bias in psychology exist (Slife, Reber, & Richardson, 2005), but Luborsky's theoretical (or ideological) "allegiance" is surely one of the more striking and significant (Luborsky, Diguer, Seligman et al., 1999; Luborsky & Barrett, in press). It is striking because theoretical allegiance is such an impressive predictor of psychological research, forecasting an unprecedented two-thirds of the variability in treatment outcomes, with correlations as high as .85 (Luborsky & Barrett, in press). We say "unprecedented" because correlations in psychology are rarely this high. Theoretical allegiance is also significant because it concerns the pivotal question: Which psychological treatment is best? In other words, this particular systematic bias is involved in deciding what actually works in psychology.

The term *allegiance* refers to a person's conscious or unconscious loyalty or commitment to a particular ideal, philosophy, or organization. In research on psychotherapy, Luborsky views theoretical allegiance as the degree of a researcher's loyalty to a specific theory of behavior change. The most common theories of psychotherapy, and thus types of theoretical loyalty, are the broad categories of dynamic, cognitive, behavioral, and pharmacological. Luborsky and Barrett (in press) essentially showed that a researcher's preference for one of these broad categories—as rated most accurately through reprints, self-ratings, and colleague ratings—correlates with the therapy found to be the best in the researcher's comparison of several therapies. In other words, whatever therapies or ideas researchers favor *before* their investigation are, with few exceptions, what the researchers "find" their results favoring *after* the investigation.

Luborsky found this correlation through "meta-analyses." Instead of a conventional analysis of one particular study, a meta-analysis is usually an analysis of many studies—an analysis of many conventional analyses. To understand what Luborsky's meta-analysis means, consider an example. Let us say that a particular researcher favors a certain theoretical approach, such as behavioral, and sets up a study comparing behavioral and pharmacological therapies. Luborsky's analysis indicates that this study will probably favor behavioral therapies over pharmacological, even though the two might *really* be equivalent in effectiveness. According to Luborsky, "treatment benefits, as evidenced in comparative trials, are so influenced by the researcher's theoretical allegiance that in many comparisons differences between treatments lessen or become negligible when the influence of allegiance is considered" (Luborsky & Barrett, in press, p. 355).

Therefore, if we know the theoretical orientation of the researcher, we can predict with considerable accuracy the outcome of an empirical comparison among the various treatment approaches—without even making the comparison! Theoretical allegiance, in this sense, is a clear bias or ideology that is not being corrected by what is really happening in the treatment comparison.

Theoretical allegiances are occurring in spite of the controls instituted for subjective biases in these elaborate research designs. Although Luborsky believes that such allegiances *should* be controlled, conventional scientific methods are not currently doing so. In short, there are "controversial issues" that are not *currently* being resolved by the data. Also, as we will see (in the "What Is Happening?" section following), scientific research is conducted in a way that will never eliminate or resolve *all* the controversial issues.

## Allegiance Effects in the Hard Sciences

Is this also true in the hard sciences, or do they avoid the ideas and ideologies that lead to controversial issues? As mentioned, physics has long recognized Heisenberg's (1958) "uncertainty principle" and Einstein's (1990) relativity of the "inertial frame of reference" as just two of the ways in which the observer is assumed to have an important impact on the observed (Bohm, 1980; Wolf, 1981). However, the hard sciences also have meta-analyses that are similar to Luborsky's. Findings in medicine, for example, parallel those we have just described in psychology. Here, *theoretical* allegiance is less of an issue, but *industry* allegiance is widely acknowledged as a potent bias in medical research (Bhandari et al., 2004; Kjaergard & Als-Nielson, 2002; Lexchin et al., 2003). Industry allegiance refers to the high correlations between the industry sponsor of research and the pro-industry outcome of this research.

Healy (1999), for instance, suggests that much of our current conception of the effectiveness of antidepressants is molded more by the marketing imperatives of the pharmaceutical industry than by the scientific findings. There is certainly no dispute that the pharmaceutical industry is the largest funder of medical research in North America, and this, as Valenstein (1998) notes, is "overwhelmingly true" for research on psychiatric drugs (p. 187). Indeed, Valenstein claims that these companies are unlikely to fund researchers who have been negative about drug effectiveness. Still, it is one thing to point to this industry's massive funding efforts and profit motives, and quite another to claim that industry allegiance biases investigators. Is there evidence for this latter claim?

In fact, editorials in five different prestigious medical journals have all pointed to evidence that pharmaceutical funding has tainted the objectivity of these studies (Greenberg, 2001). Freemantle, Anderson, and Young (2000), for example, have recently shown in a meta-analysis of comparative studies that a sponsor's funding is the best predictor of whether studies will show the sponsor's drug to be effective. Similarly, Friedberg et al. (1999) have shown empirically that company-supported studies are more likely to report efficacy for the company's product than are independent studies of the same product. Bhandari et al. (2004) even report this effect for surgical interventions. Stern and Simes (1997) also found considerable evidence that studies that do not reflect positively on antidepressants are less likely to be published. Moncrieff (2001) reports that the problem of publication bias is even more pronounced with recent SSRI antidepressants, because the majority of trials have been conducted by the pharmaceutical industry, which has no obligation to publish negative results and may see little advantage in doing so.

## What Is Happening?

What is happening in the soft and hard sciences to produce these "allegiance" effects, either theoretical or industrial? There are issues, such as allegiance, that data never seem to determine or decide definitively. This suggests that some issues require old-fashioned discussion and debate among those in the discipline. It also indicates that scientific experiments alone will not always suffice. Why? Why can't data alone decide all the discipline's "controversial issues"? One of the primary reasons is a concept called *underdetermination,* which means that research data never *completely* determine the interpretation made of that data (Curd & Cover, 1998; Slife & Williams, 1995). The researcher always has a limited choice (within the parameters of the data) about which interpretation to use.

To begin to understand why this is true, consider that any set of data is meaningless without some interpretive framework for that data. In other words, a researcher must *add* his or her own organization or interpretation to the data for the results of any study to be meaningful findings. Even a quick scan of a (typical) data set reveals a bewildering array of numbers, especially if this scan lacks the researcher's explanation as to what specific categories of data and statistical results *mean* (or how they should be interpreted). (For an example, see Slife and Williams, 1995, pp. 5–6.) Researchers will often claim to "see" meanings in their data, but this is not because the data *inherently* "mean" something but because the researcher *already* has an interpretive framework, consciously or unconsciously, for the data in mind.

It is important to recognize that the interpretation selected must "fit" the data for the interpretation to be viable. In other words, not just any interpretation will do; meaningful interpretations must make sense of *all* the data. Nevertheless, more than one interpretation of all the data is always possible, with some potentially dramatic differences in these interpretations. This is what "underdetermination" means. (Please see Curd and Cover, 1999 and Slife and Williams, 1995, pp. 185–187, for the more technical considerations of this conception.) In this sense, a study's "findings" are never *merely* the data, because the data are not meaningful findings until the researcher organizes or interprets the data, allowing for systems of ideas, and thus "controversial issues," to enter the research picture.

Actually, data interpretation is just one of the many places where biases can creep into scientific research. Consider how researchers have all sorts of "subjective" choice-points in their studies: first—what to study (what variables are crucial); second—how to study the variables (what operationalization and method design to use); third—how to analyze the study (what assumptions are met and statistics used); fourth—what the statistical results really mean (what interpretation to use); and fifth—what limits the study has (what study problems might impede certain interpretations). These choice-points mean that subjective factors, such as allegiance, are inevitably part of any research study. Researchers, knowingly or unknowingly, are favoring their own ideologies through the decisions they make at these choice-points. Part of the purpose of *Taking Sides* books, then, is to reveal and discuss these ideologies and to help students become aware of their impact on the discipline.

## Science as Ideology

Many scientists will argue that influential ideological factors are not a necessary part of science—that the allegiance effects of psychology and medicine are examples of bad research. They may believe that good science occurs when all the systematic biases, and thus disguised ideologies, have been eliminated or controlled. However, as mentioned earlier, science itself is based on a broad ideology (or philosophy) about how science should be conducted. Moreover, this broad ideology could not itself have been scientifically derived because one would need the ideology (before its derivation) to conduct the scientific investigations to derive it. In short, *there is no empirical evidence for the philosophy of empiricism that underlies the scientific method.* Some may claim that this philosophy has been successful, but this is only a claim or an opinion, not a scientific fact. Even if we were to endorse this claim, which we would, it does not minimize the broad ideology of this philosophy of science, along with the biases and values it promotes.

Perhaps the most obvious bias or value of the philosophy of empiricism is the observability value. Because this philosophy assumes that sensory experience is the only really knowable experience, traditional science has based its doctrine of knowing on the sensory experience of vision or observability. For many students, this valuing of observability will not seem like a value (Slife, 2008). These students may have unknowingly (no pun intended) accepted this philosophy as their own, without critically examining it. In this case, the doctrine of observability will seem more like an axiom than a value.

To be a value rather than an axiom, observability must indicate not only what particular things have merit or worth but also what alternative things *could* be valued (Slife, 2008). Regarding the worth issue, it is probably obvious that traditional empiricism values, and thus selects, observable phenomena as having more merit or worth than nonobservable phenomena for scientific purposes. Perhaps the bigger hurdle for appreciating the value-ladenness of observability is understanding the possibility of alternatives—in this sense, the possibility of knowing *non*observables. Here, we could ask the empiricists if their doctrine of observability is itself observable. In other words, is the idea that "only the sensory can be known" *itself* observable? And if it is not, how then do we know that this idea is correct? Given that empiricists do not observe this idea, and given that they hold it to be correct, there must be other ways of knowing things than by observability.

We can at this point describe other philosophies (or epistemologies) of knowing that assert that many unobservable experiences are knowable, such as the feelings we have for someone or the thoughts we have about something. With the feelings of love, for example, we can surely observe someone who is "in love"—hugging and kissing or any specified observable factor (in research, these are called *operationalizations*). However, we would rarely assume that the feeling of love and these observables are identical. Hugs and kisses can occur without this feeling, and this feeling can occur without hugs and kisses. Therefore, studies of hugs and kisses (or any specified observable) are *not* studies of love. At the risk of noting the obvious, studies of observables are not studies of nonobservables. They may be studies of observables that are associated with nonobservables, but then if we cannot know the nonobservable, how can we know what is associated with them?

For this reason, traditional scientific methods selectively attend to, and thus value, one particular aspect of the world—observables over nonobservables. Indeed, this is part of the reason qualitative research methods were formulated and have become increasingly popular in psychology and other disciplines. They claim that they can investigate nonobservable experiences that are not strictly observable, such as meaning and emotion (cf. Denzin & Lincoln, 2000). If this is true, knowing nonobservables is possible, and the value-ladenness of only attending to observables is clear. Again, some may insist that only observables can be known, but this insistence is not itself a scientific claim because it cannot be decided through scientific observation (Slife, Wiggins, & Graham, 2005). It is a philosophical claim about how knowing occurs and is thus subject to comparison with other philosophical claims about knowing (other epistemologies).

Observability is not the only value of traditional scientific methods. Many of the customs and traditions of how one conducts and is supposed to conduct research originate from similarly unproven values and assumptions, including reductionism (Yanchar, 2005), instrumentalism (Richardson, 2005), naturalism (Richards & Bergin, 2005), and positivism (Slife & Williams, 1995). Indeed, the journal *Counseling and Values* (in press) devoted an entire issue to the topic of the values and assumptions of psychology's scientific methods, which are the hidden roots of some of today's "controversial issues."

The lesson here is that many values and unproven ideas are *inherent* in the system of science itself. Before a method is even formulated, the persons formulating the method must make assumptions about the world in which the method would be successful. The world cannot be known through the method, because the method has not been invented yet. Consequently, the assumptions and values used for its formulation have to be speculations and guesswork to some degree—in short, values and assumptions that are not themselves scientifically proven (Slife, 2008). Again, this does not make science wrong or bad. Indeed, these scientific values and assumptions have made science what it is, including any perceived effectiveness it has.

Still, the perceived effectiveness of the scientific enterprise does not mean that we can forget about these values. They are still unproven values, after all, and as such they can be either problematic or helpful, depending on the context in which they are used. As we described, they may be useful for observable aspects of the world but not so useful for nonobservable aspects of the world. In this sense, there will always be "controversial issues" in any scientific enterprise, hard or soft. Some will be resolved by data, but some will require other means of examination and debate.

## Application to the Issues of This Book

The issues of this book are a wide assortment of both types: "empirical questions," which are primarily decided by research, and "philosophical questions," which are primarily decided by discussion and consensus or theoretical examination in relation to disciplinary values. Psychologists typically have the most skills in resolving empirical or research issues. They have been trained since their undergraduate days with multiple courses, such as "Research Methods" and "Statistics," all in support of resolving empirical or research questions.

Psychologists are rarely as adept at philosophical questions, even though these questions pervade the discipline (as we have shown). Indeed, many psychologists may despair at such questions because they associate philosophy with irresolvable issues—issues that seem interminable. We have sympathy for this attitude, yet we need to be careful not to "throw the baby out with the bathwater." In other words, just because there are seemingly interminable problems in philosophy does not mean that decisions and judgments cannot be made about the philosophical issues of a discipline such as psychology.[1] Many decisions and judgments have, of course, already been made. Otherwise, we would not have a philosophy that guides our science or a set of values that guides our ethics. As the issues of this book indicate, however, not all of these values and assumptions have been decided. Moreover, there is a case to be made that even the decided values should be continually explicated and reevaluated, as new research arenas and topics come to the fore.

Let us close this introduction, then, by pointing explicitly to how such philosophical issues may rear their ugly heads in a discipline such as psychology, and thus in this book. One way to categorize these issues is in terms of the *production* of research and the *outcome* of research. The first involves the many ways in which controversial ideas can enter the conducting of psychological investigations, whereas the second entails the many ways in which controversial ideas can enter the interpretation of a study's data or a program of research.

In the first case, controversial issues can arise when researchers have an allegiance or agenda in formulating and conducting their programs of research. This agenda does not have to be conscious, because loyalties can be influential—political or sociological, theoretical or organizational—whether or not they are known or articulated. They can influence what researchers consider important to study, how they design the study, how they operationalize the variables involved, and how they analyze the study. All these phases of a study, as we have just described, are choice-points for researchers that allow for agendas to be revealed and loyalties to be identified. It would thus be important for students of "controversial issues" to try to discern these loyalties and agendas in the production of data. That is the reason there is often no substitute for studying the studies themselves.

Controversial issues can also result from interpretations of the existing data and studies. Perhaps the most striking example of this involves two sets of scholars—each well-trained and each looking at essentially the same data—coming to dramatically different conclusions. First, as we have noted, they can interpret the same data in two different ways (through the "underdetermination" of the data). Second, these interpretive frameworks can also lead researchers to weigh different sets of data differently. While one set of investigators views

[1]Likewise, we should not "throw out" the achievements of science just because they are not totally objective.

certain studies as pivotal, another set considers the same studies deeply problematic, and thus gives them far less weight. In both cases, the interpretive framework of the researchers is part of the reason they "take the side" they do. There is no doubt that the data of the studies are important. Nevertheless, there is also no doubt that the sides taken and the interpretations made are not solely data-driven.

## Conclusion

The bottom line is that no science can avoid controversial issues. As long as humans are involved *as* scientists, allegiances and biases will be factors. There are just too many choice-points for a scientist's ideologies, known or unknown, to seep into the methods employed. Truth be told, human beings are also the inventors and formulators of the methods of science. This means not only that these methods embody the biases and assumptions of the original inventors but also that subsequent changes in the philosophies that guide science will also stem from biased humans. In this sense, we will never be rid of controversial issues. Our job, then, is to expose them, discuss them, and take a well-informed "side" with respect to them.

## References

Bernstein, R. J. (1983). *Beyond objectivism and relativism.* Philadelphia: University of Pennsylvania Press.

Bhandari, M. et al. (2004). Association between industry fundings and statistically significant pro-industry findings in medical and surgical randomized trials. *Journal of the Canadian Medical Association, 170,* 477–480.

Bohm, D. (1980). *Wholeness and the implicate order.* London: Routledge & Kegan Paul.

Curd, M., & Cover, J. A. (1998). *Philosophy of science: The central issues.* New York: W. W. Norton & Company.

Denzin, N. K., & Lincoln, Y. S. (Eds.). (2000). *Handbook of qualitative methods.* Thousand Oaks, CA: Sage.

Einstein, A. (1961/1990). Relativity: The special and general theory. Translated by Robert W. Larson. In M. Adler (Ed.), *Great books of the Western world.* Chicago: University of Chicago Press.

Freemantle, N., Anderson, I. M., & Young, P. (2000). Predictive value of pharmacological activity for the relative efficacy of antidepressant drugs: Meta-regression analysis. *British Journal of Psychiatry, 177,* 292–302.

Friedberg, M., Saffran, B., Stinson, T. J., Nelson, W., & Bennett, C. L. (1999). Evaluation of conflict of interest in economic analyses of new drugs used in oncology. *Journal of the American Medical Association, 282,* 1453–1457.

Greenberg, R. (2001). Qualms about balms: Perspectives on antidepressants. *Journal of Nervous and Mental Disease, 189*(5), 296–298.

Greenberg, R. P., Bornstein, R. F., Greenberg, M. D., & Fisher, S. (1992). A meta-analysis of antidepressant outcome under "blinder" conditions. *Journal of Consulting & Clinical Psychology, 60,* 664–669.

Healy, D. (1999). The three faces of the antidepressants: A critical commentary on the clinical-economic context of diagnoses. *Journal of Nervous and Mental Disorder, 187,* 174–180.

Heiman, G. W. (1995). *Research methods in psychology.* Boston: Houghton-Mifflin.

Heisenberg, W. (1958). *Physics and philosophy: The revolution of modern science.* New York: Harper Books.

Kjaergard, L. L., & Als-Nielson, B. (2002). Association between competing interests and authors' concluions: Epidemiological study of randomised clinical trials published in the *BMJ. British Journal of Medicine, 325,* 249–253.

Lexchin, J., Bero, L. A., Djulbegovic, B., & Clark, O. (2003). Pharmaceutical industry sponsorship and research outcome and quality: systematic review. *British Medical Journal, 326,* 1167–1170.

Luborsky, L. B., & Barrett, M. S. (in press). Theoretical allegiance.

Luborsky, L., Diguer, L., Seligman, D. A., Rosenthal, R., Krause, E. D., Johnson, S., Halperin, G., Bishop, M., Berman, J. S., & Schweizer, E. (1999). The researcher's own therapy allegiances: A "wild card" in comparisons of treatment efficacy. *Clinical Psychology: Science and Practice, 6,* 95–132.

Moncrieff, J. (2001). Are antidepressants overrated? A review of methodological problems in antidepressant trials. *The Journal of Nervous and Mental Disease, 189,* 288–295.

Richardson, F. (2005). Psychotherapy and modern dilemmas. In B. Slife, J. Reber, & F. Richardson, (Eds.), *Critical thinking about psychology: Hidden assumptions and plausible alternatives* (pp. 17–38). Washington, D.C.: American Psychological Association Press.

Richards, P. S., & Bergin, A. E. (2005). *A spiritual strategy for counseling and psychotherapy* (2nd ed.). Washington, D.C.: American Psychological Association.

Richardson, F., Fowers, B., & Guignon, C. (1999). *Re-envisioning psychology: Moral dimensions of theory and practice.* San Francisco, CA: Jossey-Bass.

Slife, B. D. (2008). A primer of the values implicit in counseling research. *Counseling and Values, 53* (1), 8–21.

Slife, B. D., Reber, J., & Richardson, F. (2005). *Critical thinking about psychology: Hidden assumptions and plausible alternatives.* 295 pages. Washington, D.C.: American Psychological Association Press.

Slife, B. D., Wiggins, B. J., & Graham, J. T. (2005). Avoiding an EST monopoly: Toward a pluralism of methods and philosophies. *Journal of Contemporary Psychotherapy, 35,* 83–97.

Slife, B. D., & Williams, R. N. (1995). *What's behind the research? Discovering hidden assumptions in the behavioral sciences.* Thousand Oaks, CA: Sage.

Stern, J. M., & Simes, R. J. (1997). Publication bias: Evidence of delayed publication in a cohort study of clinical research projects. *British Medical Journal, 315,* 640–645.

Valenstein, E. S. (1998). *Blaming the brain: The truth about drugs and mental health.* New York: Free Press.

Wolf, F. A. (1981). *Taking the quantum leap.* San Francisco: Harper-Row.

Yanchar, S. (2005). A contextualist alternative to cognitive psychology. In B. Slife, J. Reber, & F. Richardson (Eds.), *Critical thinking about psychology: Hidden assumptions and plausible alternatives* (pp. 171–186). Washington, D.C.: American Psychological Association Press.

# *Internet References . . .*

## Resisting Authority: A Personal Account of the Milgram Obedience Experiments

This site contains information on Stanley Milgram's study of obedience as well as the personal account of one of the participants in the study.

**http://www.jewishcurrents.org/2004-jan-dimow.htm**

## Animal Research in Psychology

This site contains information published by the APA regarding the use of animals in psychological research.

**http://www.apa.org/SCIENCE/animal2.html**

## Legal, Ethical, and Professional Issues in Psychoanalysis and Psychotherapy

This site's home page offers a wealth of information about different research issues in psychology. This particular link provides access to different papers that discuss the empirically supported treatment (EST) movement.

**http://www.academyprojects.org/est.htm**

# UNIT 1

# Research Issues

*Research methods are the windows through which psychologists examine their ideas and their subject matter. Yet, the way that psychologists* view *their findings is sometimes the subject of controversy. When, for example, is the research evidence sufficient to support a particular conclusion? Is there enough evidence to support the evolutionary explanation of female mating behavior? Researchers also have a responsibility to act ethically toward the participants in their studies. Should we avoid both physical and emotional pain when dealing with research participants? Would this unduly restrict psychological researchers as they attempt to study topics like emotional pain? Is a small amount of psychological harm justified if it can reduce a large amount of pain in the future? What about studies of psychotherapy? Here, there are not only issues of ethics but also issues of the adequacy of methods that gauge the effectiveness of different therapies. Normally, traditional scientific methods are understood as "objective," and thus free of biases. But is this strictly true? If not, what effect do these biases have on psychology's quest for evidence-based practices?*

# ISSUE 1

## Are Traditional Empirical Methods Sufficient to Provide Evidence for Psychological Practice?

**YES: APA Presidential Task Force on Evidence-Based Practice,** from "Evidence-Based Practice in Psychology," *American Psychologist* (May/June 2006)

**NO: Brent D. Slife and Dennis Wendt,** from "The Next Step in the Evidence-Based Practice Movement," APA Convention Presentation (August 2006)

### ISSUE SUMMARY

**YES:** The APA Presidential Task Force on Evidence-Based Practice assumes that a variety of traditional empirical methods is sufficient to provide evidence for psychological practices.

**NO:** Psychologist Brent D. Slife and researcher Dennis C. Wendt contend that traditional empirical methods are guided by a single philosophy that limits the diversity of methods.

Imagine that one of your family members needs to see a therapist for a severe depression. Of the two therapists available, the first therapist's practices are supported by evidence obtained through traditional scientific methods. The second therapist's practices are not. The latter's practices could be equally effective or even more effective than the first therapist's practices, but we do not know. Which therapist would you choose for this member of your family?

Most people would readily choose therapists who have scientific evidence for their interventions. They think of psychotherapy much like they think of medicine, with treatments that have stood the test of science. Just as physicians can provide evidence that pain relievers actually relieve pain, so too psychologists hope to provide evidence that their practices deliver their desired results. Because not all psychological treatments come with evidence to support their use, some psychologists worry that some treatments could actually do more harm than good. It is with this potential harm in mind that many psychologists banded together to establish empirically supported treatments (ESTs). The goal was to establish a list of ESTs for specific psychological disorders. Those involved in this movement (various task forces from different divisions of the American Psychological Association) initially stressed the use of randomized clinical (or controlled) trials (RCTs)—a specific type of research design—to be sure that the scientific examination of these treatments was rigorous and thorough.

In the first article of this issue, however, the APA Presidential Task Force on Evidence-Based Practice questions whether too much emphasis has been placed on RCT research designs. This Task Force affirms the need for empirically based evidence in psychology but tries to reframe the notion of evidence-based practice so that a diversity of empirical methods, including correlational and even case study methods, are considered important for producing evidence. The Task Force calls for objectivity in gathering all forms of evidence. In fact, it still considers RCTs the most rigorous type of objective method. However, it also acknowledges that other empirical approaches to gathering information and evidence can and do have their place in deciding psychology's evidence-based practices.

In the second selection, psychologist Brent D. Slife and researcher Dennis Wendt applaud the APA Task Force for taking important steps in the right direction. Nevertheless, they argue that the Task Force's statement is "ultimately and fundamentally inadequate." The Task Force correctly champions the objectivity and diversity of methods and evidence, in their view, but they contend that the Task Force is not objective and diverse enough. They claim that just as the EST movement restricted the gathering of evidence to a single method (RCTs), the Task Force's suggestions assume, but never justify, that evidence-based practice should be restricted to a single *epistemology* of method. They acknowledge that many psychologists view this empirical epistemology as not affecting the outcome of research, but they note that most practices that are considered evidence-based fit the biases of the philosophy of empiricism.

**POINT**

- Psychological treatments should be supported by evidence.
- Evidence should include RCTs as well as other empirical methods.
- Evidence should be both objective and diverse.
- Evidence should not be limited to a single method (RCT).

**COUNTERPOINT**

- Not all psychologists agree on what qualifies as evidence.
- Traditional empirical methods are not the only methods by which evidence can be obtained.
- Including only the "empirical" is neither objective nor diverse.
- Evidence should not be limited to a single methodology.

**APA President Task Force on Evidence-Based Practice**

# Report of the 2005 Presidential Task Force on Evidence-Based Practice[1]

From the very first conceptions of applied psychology as articulated by Lightner Witmer, who formed the first psychological clinic in 1896, psychologists have been deeply and uniquely associated with an evidence-based approach to patient care. As Witmer pointed out, "the pure and the applied sciences advance in a single front. What retards the progress of one retards the progress of the other; what fosters one fosters the other." As early as 1947 the idea that doctoral psychologists should be trained as both scientists and practitioners became the American Psychological Association (APA) policy. Early practitioners such as Frederick C. Thorne articulated the methods by which psychological practitioners integrate science into their practice by . . . "increasing the application of the experimental approach to the individual case into the clinician's own experience." Thus, psychologists have been on the forefront of the development of evidence-based practice for decades.

Evidence-based practice in psychology is therefore consistent with the past twenty years of work in evidence-based medicine, which advocated for improved patient outcomes by informing clinical practice with relevant research. Sackett and colleagues describe evidence-based medicine as "the conscientious, explicit, and judicious use of current best evidence in making decisions about the care of individual patients." The use and misuse of evidence-based principles in the practice of health care has affected the dissemination of health care funds, but not always to the benefit of the patient. Therefore, psychologists, whose training is grounded in empirical methods, have an important role to play in the continuing development of evidence-based practice and its focus on improving patient care.

One approach to implementing evidence-based practice in health care systems has been through the development of guidelines for best practice. During

[1]This document was received by the American Psychological Association (APA) Council of Representatives during its meeting of August, 2005. The report represents the conclusions of the Task Force and does not represent the official policy of the American Psychological Association. The Task Force wishes to thank John R. Weisz, PhD, ABPP for his assistance in drafting portions of this report related to children and youth. The Task Force also thanks James Mitchell and Omar Rehman, APA Professional Development interns, for their assistance throughout the work of the Task Force.

From *American Psychologist,* vol. 61, issue 4, May/June 2006, pp. 271–285 (excerpts). 

the early part of the evidence-based practice movement, APA recognized the importance of a comprehensive approach to the conceptualization of guidelines. APA also recognized the risk that guidelines might be used inappropriately by commercial health care organizations not intimately familiar with the scientific basis of practice to dictate specific forms of treatment and restrict patient access to care. In 1992, APA formed a joint task force of the Board of Scientific Affairs (BSA), the Board of Professional Affairs (BPA), and the Committee for the Advancement of Professional Practice (CAPP). The document developed by this task force—the *Template for Developing Guidelines: Interventions for Mental Disorders and Psychosocial Aspects of Physical Disorders* (Template)—was approved by the APA Council of Representatives in 1995 (APA, 1995). The Template described the variety of evidence that should be considered in developing guidelines, and cautioned that any emerging clinical practice guidelines should be based on careful systematic weighing of research data and clinical expertise. . . .

Although the goal was to identify treatments with evidence for efficacy comparable to the evidence for the efficacy of medications, and hence to highlight the contribution of psychological treatments, the Division 12 Task Force report sparked a decade of both enthusiasm and controversy. The report increased recognition of demonstrably effective psychological treatments among the public, policymakers, and training programs. At the same time, many psychologists raised concerns about the exclusive focus on brief, manualized treatments; the emphasis on specific treatment effects as opposed to common factors that account for much of the variance in outcomes across disorders; and the applicability to a diverse range of patients varying in comorbidity, personality, race, ethnicity, and culture.

In response, several groups of psychologists, including other divisions of APA, offered additional frameworks for integrating the available research evidence. In 1999, APA Division 29 (Psychotherapy) established a task force to identify, operationalize, and disseminate information on empirically supported therapy relationships, given the powerful association between outcome and aspects of the therapeutic relationship such as the therapeutic alliance. Division 17 (Counseling Psychology) also undertook an examination of empirically supported treatments in counseling psychology. The Society of Behavioral Medicine, which is not a part of APA but which has significantly overlapping membership, has recently published criteria for examining the evidence base for behavioral medicine interventions. As of this writing, we are aware that task forces have been appointed to examine related issues by a large number of APA divisions concerned with practice issues. . . .

## Definition

Based on its review of the literature and its deliberations, the Task Force agreed on the following definition:

> Evidence-based practice in psychology (EBPP) is the integration of the best available research with clinical expertise in the context of patient characteristics, culture, and preferences.

This definition of EBPP closely parallels the definition of evidence-based practice adopted by the Institute of Medicine as adapted from Sackett and colleagues: "Evidence-based practice is the integration of best research evidence with clinical expertise and patient values." Psychology builds on the IOM definition by deepening the examination of clinical expertise and broadening the consideration of patient characteristics. The purpose of EBPP is to promote effective psychological practice and enhance public health by applying empirically supported principles of psychological assessment, case formulation, therapeutic relationship, and intervention.

Psychological practice entails many types of interventions, in multiple settings, for a wide variety of potential patients. In this document, *intervention* refers to all direct services rendered by health care psychologists, including assessment, diagnosis, prevention, treatment, psychotherapy, and consultation. As is the case with most discussions of evidence-based practice, we focus on treatment. The same general principles apply to psychological assessment, which is essential to effective treatment. The settings include but are not limited to hospitals, clinics, independent practices, schools, military, public health, rehabilitation institutes, primary care, counseling centers, and nursing homes.

To be consistent with discussions of evidence-based practice in other areas of health care, we use the term *patient* in this document to refer to the child, adolescent, adult, older adult, couple, family, group, organization, community, or other populations receiving psychological services. However, we recognize that in many situations there are important and valid reasons for using such terms as *client, consumer,* or *person* in place of patient to describe the recipients of services. Further, psychologists target a variety of problems, including but not restricted to mental health, academic, vocational, relational, health, community, and other problems, in their professional practice.

It is important to clarify the relation between EBPP and ESTs (empirically supported treatments). EBPP is the more comprehensive concept. ESTs start with a treatment and ask whether it works for a certain disorder or problem under specified circumstances. EBPP starts with the patient and asks what research evidence (including relevant results from RCTs) will assist the psychologist to achieve the best outcome. In addition, ESTs are specific psychological treatments that have been shown to be efficacious in controlled clinical trials, whereas EBPP encompasses a broader range of clinical activities (e.g., psychological assessment, case formulation, therapy relationships). As such, EBPP articulates a decision making process for integrating multiple streams of research evidence, including but not limited to RCTs, into the intervention process.

The following sections explore in greater detail the three major components of this definition—best available research, clinical expertise, and patient characteristics—and their integration.

## Best Available Research Evidence

A sizeable body of scientific evidence drawn from a variety of research designs and methodologies attests to the effectiveness of psychological practices. The research literature on the effect of psychological interventions indicates that these interventions are safe and effective for a large number of children and youth, adults and older adults across a wide range of psychological, addictive, health, and relational problems. More recent research indicates that compared to alternative approaches, such as medications, psychological treatments are particularly enduring. Further, research demonstrates that psychotherapy can and often does pay for itself in terms of medical costs offset, increased productivity, and life satisfaction.

Psychologists possess distinctive strengths in designing, conducting, and interpreting research studies that can guide evidence-based practice. Moreover, psychology—as a science and as a profession—is distinctive in combining scientific commitment with an emphasis on human relationships and individual differences. As such, psychology can help develop, broaden, and improve the research base for evidence-based practice.

There is broad consensus that psychological practice needs to be based on evidence, and that research needs to balance internal and external validity. Research will not always address all practice needs. Major issues in integrating research in day-to-day practice include: a) the relative weight to place on different research methods; b) the representativeness of research samples; c) whether research results should guide practice at the level of principles of change, intervention strategies, or specific protocols; d) the generalizability and transportability of treatments supported in controlled research to clinical practice settings; e) the extent to which judgments can be made about treatments of choice when the number and duration of treatments tested has been limited; and f) the degree to which the results of efficacy and effectiveness research can be generalized from primarily white samples to minority and marginalized populations. Nevertheless, research on practice has made progress in investigating these issues and is providing research evidence that is more responsive to day-to-day practice. There is sufficient consensus to move forward with the principles of EBPP.

Meta-analytic investigations since the 1970s have shown that most therapeutic practices in widespread clinical use are generally effective for treating a range of problems. In fact, the effect sizes for psychological interventions for children, adults and older adults rival, or exceed, those of widely accepted medical treatments. It is important not to assume that interventions that have not yet been studied in controlled trials are ineffective. Specific interventions that have not been subjected to systematic empirical testing for specific problems cannot be assumed to be either effective or ineffective; they are simply untested to date. Nonetheless, good practice and science call for the timely testing of psychological practices in a way that adequately operationalizes them using appropriate scientific methodology. Widely used psychological practices as well as innovations developed in the field or laboratory should be rigorously evaluated and barriers to conducting this research should be identified and addressed.

## Multiple Types of Research Evidence

Best research evidence refers to scientific results related to intervention strategies, assessment, clinical problems, and patient populations in laboratory and field settings as well as to clinically relevant results of basic research in psychology and related fields. APA endorses multiple types of research evidence (e.g., efficacy, effectiveness, cost-effectiveness, cost-benefit, epidemiological, treatment utilization studies) that contribute to effective psychological practice.

Multiple research designs contribute to evidence-based practice, and different research designs are better suited to address different types of questions. These include:

- Clinical observation (including individual case studies) and basic psychological science are valuable sources of innovations and hypotheses (the context of scientific discovery).
- Qualitative research can be used to describe the subjective lived experience of people, including participants in psychotherapy.
- Systematic case studies are particularly useful when aggregated as in the form of practice research networks for comparing individual patients to others with similar characteristics.
- Single case experimental designs are particularly useful for establishing causal relationships in the context of an individual.
- Public health and ethnographic research are especially useful for tracking the availability, utilization, and acceptance of mental health treatments as well as suggesting ways of altering them to maximize their utility in a given social context.
- Process-outcome studies are especially valuable for identifying mechanisms of change.
- Studies of interventions as delivered in naturalistic settings (effectiveness research) are well suited for assessing the ecological validity of treatments.
- Randomized clinical trials and their logical equivalents (efficacy research) are the standard for drawing causal inferences about the effects of interventions (context of scientific verification).
- Meta-analysis is a systematic means to synthesize results from multiple studies, test hypotheses, and quantitatively estimate the size of effects.

With respect to evaluating research on specific interventions, current APA policy identifies two widely accepted dimensions. As stated in the *Criteria for Evaluating Treatment Guidelines,* "The first dimension is *treatment efficacy,* the systematic and scientific evaluation of whether a treatment works. The second dimension is *clinical utility,* the applicability, feasibility, and usefulness of the intervention in the local or specific setting where it is to be offered. This dimension also includes determination of the generalizability of an intervention whose efficacy has been established." Types of research evidence with regard to intervention research in ascending order as to their contribution to conclusions about efficacy include: clinical opinion, observation, and consensus among recognized experts representing the range of use in the field (Criterion 2.1); systematized clinical observation (Criterion 2.2); and sophisticated empirical methodologies, including quasi experiments and randomized controlled experiments or their logical equivalents (Criterion 2.3). Among sophisticated empirical methodologies, "randomized controlled experiments represent a more stringent way to evaluate treatment efficacy because they are the most effective way to rule out threats to internal validity in a single experiment."

Evidence on clinical utility is also crucial. As per established APA policy, at a minimum this includes attention to generality of effects across varying and diverse patients, therapists and settings and the interaction of these factors, the robustness of treatments across various modes of delivery, the feasibility with which treatments can be delivered to patients in real world settings, and the cost associated with treatments.

Evidence-based practice requires that psychologists recognize the strengths and limitations of evidence obtained from different types of research. Research has shown that the treatment method, the individual psychologist, the treatment relationship, and the patient are all vital contributors to the success of psychological practice. Comprehensive evidence-based practice will consider all of these determinants and their optimal combinations. Psychological practice is a complex relational and technical enterprise that requires clinical and research attention to multiple, interacting sources of treatment effectiveness. There remain many disorders, problem constellations, and clinical situations for which empirical data are sparse. In such instances, clinicians use their best clinical judgment and knowledge of the best available research evidence to develop coherent treatment strategies. Researchers and practitioners should join together to ensure that the research available on psychological practice is both clinically relevant and internally valid. . . .

## Clinical Expertise[2]

Clinical expertise is essential for identifying and integrating the best research evidence with clinical data (e.g., information about the patient obtained over the course of treatment) in the context of the patient's characteristics and preferences to deliver services that have the highest probability of achieving the goals of therapy. Psychologists are trained as scientists as well as practitioners. An advantage of psychological training is that it fosters a clinical expertise informed by scientific expertise, allowing the psychologist to understand and integrate scientific literature as well as to frame and test hypotheses and interventions in practice as a "local clinical scientist."

Cognitive scientists have found consistent evidence of enduring and significant differences between experts and novices undertaking complex tasks in several domains. Experts recognize meaningful patterns and disregard irrelevant information, acquire extensive knowledge and organize it in ways that reflect a deep understanding of their domain, organize their knowledge using functional rather than descriptive features, retrieve knowledge relevant to the task at hand fluidly and automatically, adapt to new situations, self-monitor

---

[2]As it is used in this report, clinical expertise refers to competence attained by psychologists through education, training, and experience resulting in effective practice; clinical expertise is not meant to refer to extraordinary performance that might characterize an elite group (e.g., the top two percent) of clinicians.

their knowledge and performance, know when their knowledge is inadequate, continue to learn, and generally attain outcomes commensurate with their expertise.

However, experts are not infallible. All humans are prone to errors and biases. Some of these stem from cognitive strategies and heuristics that are generally adaptive and efficient. Others stem from emotional reactions, which generally guide adaptive behavior as well but can also lead to biased or motivated reasoning. Whenever psychologists involved in research or practice move from observations to inferences and generalizations, there is inherent risk for idiosyncratic interpretations, overgeneralizations, confirmatory biases, and similar errors in judgment. Integral to clinical expertise is an awareness of the limits of one's knowledge and skills and attention to the heuristics and biases—both cognitive and affective—that can affect clinical judgment. Mechanisms such as consultation and systematic feedback from the patient can mitigate some of these biases.

The individual therapist has a substantial impact on outcomes, both in clinical trials and in practice settings. The fact that treatment outcomes are systematically related to the provider of the treatment (above and beyond the type of treatment) provides strong evidence for the importance of understanding expertise in clinical practice as a way of enhancing patient outcomes. . . .

## Patient Characteristics, Culture, and Preferences

Normative data on "what works for whom" provide essential guides to effective practice. Nevertheless, psychological services are most likely to be effective when responsive to the patient's specific problems, strengths, personality, sociocultural context, and preferences. Psychology's long history of studying individual differences and developmental change, and its growing empirical literature related to human diversity (including culture[3] and psychotherapy), place it in a strong position to identify effective ways of integrating research and clinical expertise with an understanding of patient characteristics essential to EBPP. EBPP involves consideration of patients' values, religious beliefs, worldviews, goals, and preferences for treatment with the psychologist's experience and understanding of the available research.

Several questions frame current debates about the role of patient characteristics in EBPP. The first regards the extent to which cross-diagnostic patient characteristics, such as personality traits or constellations, moderate the impact of empirically tested interventions. A second, related question concerns the extent to which social factors and cultural differences necessitate different

[3]Culture, in this context, is understood to encompass a broad array of phenomena (such as shared values, history, knowledge, rituals, and customs) that often result in a shared sense of identity. Racial and ethnic groups may have a shared culture, but those personal characteristics are not the only characteristics that define cultural groups (e.g., deaf culture, inner-city culture). Culture is a multifaceted construct, and cultural factors cannot be understood in isolation from social, class and personal characteristics that make each patient unique.

forms of treatment or whether interventions widely tested in majority populations can be readily adapted for patients with different ethnic or sociocultural backgrounds. A third question concerns maximizing the extent to which widely used interventions adequately attend to developmental considerations, both for children and adolescents and for older adults. A fourth question is the extent to which variable clinical presentations, such as comorbidity and polysymptomatic presentations, moderate the impact of interventions. Underlying all of these questions is the issue of how best to approach the treatment of patients whose characteristics (e.g., gender, gender identity, ethnicity, race, social class, disability status, sexual orientation) and problems (e.g., comorbidity) may differ from those of samples studied in research. This is a matter of active discussion in the field and there is increasing research attention to the generalizability and transportability of psychological interventions.

Available data indicate that a variety of patient-related variables influence outcomes, many of which are cross-diagnostic characteristics such as functional status, readiness to change, and level of social support. Other patient characteristics are essential to consider in forming and maintaining a treatment relationship and in implementing specific interventions. These include but are not limited to a) variations in presenting problems or disorders, etiology, concurrent symptoms or syndromes, and behavior; b) chronological age, developmental status, developmental history, and life stage; c) sociocultural and familial factors (e.g., gender, gender identity, ethnicity, race, social class, religion, disability status, family structure, and sexual orientation); d) current environmental context, stressors (e.g., unemployment or recent life event), and social factors (e.g., institutional racism and health care disparities); and e) personal preferences, values, and preferences related to treatment (e.g., goals, beliefs, worldviews, and treatment expectations). Available research on both patient matching and treatment failures in clinical trials of even highly efficacious interventions suggests that different strategies and relationships may prove better suited for different populations.

Many presenting symptoms—for example, depression, anxiety, school failure, bingeing and purging—are similar across patients. However, symptoms or disorders that are phenotypically similar are often heterogeneous with respect to etiology, prognosis, and the psychological processes that create or maintain them. Moreover, most patients present with multiple symptoms or syndromes rather than a single, discrete disorder. The presence of concurrent conditions may moderate treatment response, and interventions intended to treat one symptom often affect others. An emerging body of research also suggests that personality variables underlie many psychiatric syndromes and account for a substantial part of the comorbidity among syndromes widely documented in research. Psychologists must attend to the individual person to make the complex choices necessary to conceptualize, prioritize, and treat multiple symptoms. It is important to know the person who has the disorder in addition to knowing the disorder the person has.

EBPP also requires attention to factors related to the patient's development and life-stage. An enormous body of research exists on developmental processes (e.g., attachment, socialization, and cognitive, social-cognitive, gender, moral, and emotional development) that are essential in understanding adult psychopathology and particularly in treating children, adolescents, families, and older adults.

Evidence-based practice in psychology requires attention to many other patient characteristics, such as gender, gender identity, culture, ethnicity, race, age, family context, religious beliefs, and sexual orientation. These variables shape personality, values, worldviews, relationships, psychopathology, and attitudes toward treatment. A wide range of relevant research literature can inform psychological practice, including ethnography, cross-cultural psychology, psychological anthropology, and cultural psychotherapy. Culture influences not only the nature and expression of psychopathology but also the patient's understanding of psychological and physical health and illness. Cultural values and beliefs and social factors such as implicit racial biases also influence patterns of seeking, using, and receiving help; presentation and reporting of symptoms, fears and expectations about treatment; and desired outcomes. Psychologists also understand and reflect upon the ways their own characteristics, values, and context interact with those of the patient.

Race as a social construct is a way of grouping people into categories on the basis of perceived physical attributes, ancestry, and other factors. Race is also more broadly associated with power, status, and opportunity. In Western cultures, European or white "race" confers advantage and opportunity, even as improved social attitudes and public policies have reinforced social equality. Race is thus an interpersonal and political process with significant implications for clinical practice and health care quality. Patients and clinicians may "belong" to racial groups, as they choose to self-identify, but the importance of race in clinical practice is relational, rather than solely a patient or clinician attribute. Considerable evidence from many fields suggests that racial power differentials between clinicians and their patients, as well as systemic biases and implicit stereotypes based on race or ethnicity, contribute to the inequitable care that patients of color receive across health care services. Clinicians must carefully consider the impact of race, ethnicity, and culture on the treatment process, relationship, and outcome.

The patient's social and environmental context, including recent and chronic stressors, is also important in case formulation and treatment planning. Sociocultural and familial factors, social class, and broader social, economic, and situational factors (e.g., unemployment, family disruption, lack of insurance, recent losses, prejudice, or immigration status) can have an enormous influence on mental health, adaptive functioning, treatment seeking, and patient resources (psychological, social, and financial).

Psychotherapy is a collaborative enterprise, in which patients and clinicians negotiate ways of working together that are mutually agreeable and likely to lead to positive outcomes. Thus, patient values and preferences (e.g., goals, beliefs, and preferred modes of treatment) are a central component of EBPP. Patients can have strong preferences for types of treatment and desired outcomes, and these preferences are influenced by both their cultural context and individual factors. One role of the psychologist is to ensure that patients understand the costs and benefits of different practices and choices. Evidence-based practice in psychology seeks to maximize patient choice among effective alternative interventions. Effective practice requires balancing patient preferences and the psychologist's judgment, based on available evidence and clinical expertise, to determine the most appropriate treatment. . . .

## Conclusions

Evidence-based practice in psychology is the integration of the best available research with clinical expertise in the context of patient characteristics, culture, and preferences. The purpose of EBPP is to promote effective psychological practice and enhance public health by applying empirically supported principles of psychological assessment, case formulation, therapeutic relationship, and intervention. Much has been learned over the past century from basic and applied psychological research as well as from observations and hypotheses developed in clinical practice. Many strategies for working with patients have emerged and been refined through the kind of trial and error and clinical hypothesis generation and testing that constitute the most scientific aspect of clinical practice. Yet clinical hypothesis testing has its limits, hence the need to integrate clinical expertise with best available research.

Perhaps the central message of this task force report, and one of the most heartening aspects of the process that led to it, is the consensus achieved among a diverse group of scientists, clinicians, and scientist-clinicians from multiple perspectives that EBPP requires an appreciation of the value of multiple sources of scientific evidence. In a given clinical circumstance, psychologists of good faith and good judgment may disagree about how best to weight different forms of evidence; over time, we presume that systematic and broad empirical inquiry—in the laboratory and in the clinic—will point the way toward best practice in integrating best evidence. What this document reflects, however, is a reassertion of what psychologists have known for a century: that the scientific method is a way of thinking and observing systematically and is the best tool we have for learning about what works for whom.

Clinical decisions should be made in collaboration with the patient, based on the best clinically relevant evidence, and with consideration for the probable costs, benefits, and available resources and options. It is the treating psychologist who makes the ultimate judgment regarding a particular intervention or treatment plan. The involvement of an active, informed patient is generally crucial to the success of psychological services. Treatment decisions should never be made by untrained persons unfamiliar with the specifics of the case.

The treating psychologist determines the applicability of research conclusions to a particular patient. Individual patients may require decisions and interventions not directly addressed by the available research. The application of research evidence to a given patient always involves probabilistic inferences. Therefore, ongoing monitoring of patient progress and adjustment of treatment as needed are essential to EBPP.

Moreover, psychologists must attend to a range of outcomes that may sometimes suggest one strategy and sometimes another and to the strengths and limitations of available research vis-à-vis these different ways of measuring success. Psychological outcomes may include not only symptom relief and prevention of future symptomatic episodes but also quality of life, adaptive functioning in work and relationships, ability to make satisfying life choices, personality change, and other goals arrived at in collaboration between patient and clinician.

EBPP is a means to enhance the delivery of services to patients within an atmosphere of mutual respect, open communication, and collaboration among all stakeholders, including practitioners, researchers, patients, health care managers, and policy-makers. Our goal in this document, and in the deliberations of the Task Force that led to it, was to set both an agenda and a tone for the next steps in the evolution of EBPP.

**Brent D. Slife and Dennis C. Wendt**

# The Next Step in the Evidence-Based Practice Movement

Nearly everyone agrees that psychological practice should be informed by evidence (Westen & Bradley, 2005, p. 266; Norcross, Beutler, & Levant, 2006, p. 7). However, there is considerable disagreement about what qualifies as evidence (e.g., Reed, 2006; Kihlstrom, 2006; Messer, 2006; Westen, 2006; Stirman & DeRubeis, 2006). This disagreement is not a simple scientific dispute to be resolved in the laboratory, but rather a "culture war" between different worldviews (Messer, 2004, p. 580). As Carol Tavris (2003) put it, this "war" involves "deeply held beliefs, political passions, views of human nature and the nature of knowledge, and—as all wars ultimately involve—money, territory, and livelihoods" (as qtd. in Norcross et al., p. 8).

How does one address a cultural battle of deeply held worldviews and political passions? We believe the approaches that have tried to address it so far in psychology have been well-intended and even headed in the right direction, but are ultimately and fundamentally inadequate. We will first describe what we consider the two major steps in this regard, beginning with the empirically supported treatment (EST) movement, which still has considerable energy in the discipline, and then moving to the "common factors" approach, which recently culminated in a policy regarding evidence-based practice (EBP) in psychology from the American Psychological Association (APA, 2006). We specifically focus on the latter, extolling its goals, but noting their distinct lack of fulfillment. We then offer what seems to us the logical extension of these first two steps—what could be called "objective methodological pluralism" in the spirit of one of our discipline's founding parents, William James (1902/1985; 1907/1975).

## The First Step: The EST Movement

Psychology's first step in addressing this evidence controversy involved a succession of APA Division 12 (Clinical) task forces. Beginning in 1993, these task forces have "constructed and elaborated a list of empirically supported, manualized psychological interventions for specific disorders" (Norcross et al., 2006, p. 5). In other words, this first step assumed that the battle of worldviews would be resolved through rigorous scientific evidence. "Rigorous evidence," in this case, was idealized as the randomized clinical (or controlled) trial (RCT), widely esteemed as the gold standard of evidence in medicine. The advantages of this step were obvious. Third-party payers were familiar with this gold standard from medicine, and many psychologists believed that an EST list would provide a clear-cut index of "proven" treatments, not to mention greater respect from medicine.

Unfortunately, this seemingly rigorous, clear-cut approach has manifested more than a few problems (Westen & Bradley, 2005; Messer, 2004). Much like the testing movement in education, where teachers found themselves "teaching to the test," psychologists found their practices being shaped by the RCT "test." The critics of the RCT showed how professional practices were conforming, consciously or unconsciously, to the RCT worldview in order to make the EST list. In other words, the practices being studied tended to accommodate the particular RCT perspective on treatments, therapists, and patients.

With regard to treatments, this medical-model worldview of the RCT is biased toward "packaged" treatments for well-defined, compartmentalized disorders (e.g., Bohart, O'Hara, & Leitner, 1998). This model of treatment took its cues from the pharmaceutical industry, where "one must specify the treatment and make sure it is being applied correctly" (p. 143). According to this model, every patient would receive the same thing, and it is this thing, not the therapist or patient, that is considered the agent of change. Critics have argued that this view of treatment undermined many types of therapy, such as humanistic or psychodynamic therapies, in which "treatment" does not entail a manualized set of principles (e.g., Bohart et al.; Safran, 2001).

A related argument against this packaged view of treatment concerned the role of therapists. The assumptions or worldview of the RCT, these critics contended, turned the therapist into an interchangeable part, discounting the importance of the therapist's distinctive personality, practical wisdom, and unique relationship with the patient. Many researchers have worried, to use the words of Allen Bergin (1997), that the RCT manualization of treatments turned therapists into "cookie cutters" and researchers into "mechanotropes" (pp. 85–86). This worry has been validated by research suggesting that manualization often hinders important therapeutic factors, such as the therapeutic alliance and the therapist's genuineness, creativity, motivation, and emotional involvement (Duncan & Miller, 2006; Piper & Ogrodniczuk, 1999).

Third, critics have noted that the biases of RCTs shaped one's view of the patient, assuming that researchers and clinicians work with pure patient pathologies only. According to this argument, RCTs are limited to patients with textbook symptoms of a single DSM disorder; thus, their results "may apply only to a narrow and homogeneous group of patients" (Butcher, Mineka, & Hooley, 2004, p. 563). This limitation is no small problem, critics have warned, because the vast majority of U.S. patients are not pathologically "pure" in this narrow RCT sense. Rather, they are co- or "multi"-morbid in the sense that they are an amalgam of disorders (Morrison, Bradley, & Westen, 2003; Westen & Bradley, 2005). The prevalence of these "messy" patients is corroborated by the 35%–70% exclusion rates of RCTs for major disorders (Morrison et al., p. 110).

The common theme behind the above criticisms is that the biases of the EST movement stem from its narrow framework for validating evidence. Thus, it is not mere coincidence, critics have argued, that therapies that exemplify this type of treatment (e.g., behavioral or cognitive-behavioral treatments) are the most frequently listed as ESTs (Messer, 2004). The exclusion of other types of therapy (e.g., humanistic and psychodynamic therapies) has prompted critics to contend that the EST movement constitutes a methodological bias toward behavioral and cognitive-behavioral therapies (e.g., Slife, Wiggins, & Graham; Messer, 2004). If this first step has taught psychologists anything, it has taught that what the evidence seems to say has a great deal to do with what one considers evidence.

## The Second Step: The Common Factors Movement

The second step—the common factors movement—was, in part, an attempt to learn from the shortcomings of the EST movement. Common factors advocates have argued that a focus on specific, "packaged" treatments for specific disorders is a narrow way of conceptualizing psychological research and practice (e.g., Westen & Bradley, 2005; Bohart et al., 1998). An alternative approach is to discover and validate factors of therapeutic change that are common across treatments. In this way, responsibility for change is not just attributed to the treatment, as in ESTs. Change is considered the result of a dynamic relationship among the "common factors" of therapy, which include the therapist, patient, and technique (APA, 2006, p. 275).

A common factors approach is especially appealing to the majority of practitioners, who consider themselves eclectics or integrationists. Its popularity has helped it to play a significant role in shaping APA's (2006) new policy statement on evidence-based practice. For this policy statement, evidence was liberalized not only to include studies of therapist and patient variables but also to include other methods than RCTs for conducting these studies (pp. 274–75). The main guideposts for selecting these methods, according to the underlying rationale of the APA policy, were their objectivity and their diversity. Methods should be *objective* to prevent the intrusion of human error and bias that would distort the findings (p. 276), and they should be *diverse* to prevent the shaping of practice that a focus on only one method might produce, such as the problems created by RCTs (pp. 272–74).

The problem, from our perspective, is that the APA culmination of this common factors approach is not objective and diverse enough. In other words, we applaud the goals but criticize the implementation. The APA policy is a clear step forward, in our view, but its conceptions of objectivity and diversity are inadequate. As we will attempt to show, this inadequacy means that the lessons of the EST movement have not been sufficiently learned. Recall that this first step restricted itself to a single ideal of evidence, the RCT, and thus disallowed any true diversity of methods. Recall also that several biases resulted from this restriction, obviating objectivity and shaping practice even before investigation. As we will argue, this same lack of diversity and objectivity has continued into the second approach to the evidence controversy.

Our basic criticism is this: Just as an EST framework uncritically restricts acceptable evidence to a *single method* ideal (the RCT), so does the APA policy uncritically restrict acceptable evidence to a *single epistemology.* By "epistemology" we mean the philosophy of knowing that provides the logic and guides the conduct of a group of methods (Slife & Williams, 1995). Although the EST framework is biased toward a certain *method,* the common factors framework is biased toward a certain *methodology*—a narrow brand of *empiricism.*

According to this empiricist epistemology, "we can only know, or know best, those aspects of our experience that are sensory" (Slife, Wiggins, & Graham, 2005, p. 84). This narrow conception of empiricism is fairly traditional in psychology. More liberal usages of empiricism differ substantially, such as William James' radical empiricism. James' empiricism encompasses "the whole of experience," including *non*-sensory experiences such as thoughts, emotions, and even spiritual experiences (James, 1902/1985; 1907/1975). Still, psychologists have interpreted the natural sciences to be grounded in the narrow empiricism. Historically, psychologists have wanted to be both rigorously scientific and comparable to medicine, leading them to embrace the narrower empiricism. As we will attempt to show, however, this restriction to a single epistemology is not based on evidence. Analogous to the EST restriction to a single method, the APA policy merely assumes and never justifies empiricism as the only appropriate epistemology for evidence-based practice, in spite of other promising epistemologies.

The reason for this lack of justification seems clear. Throughout much of the history of psychology, empiricism has been mistakenly understood not as a *particular* philosophy of science, but as a *non*-philosophy that makes reality transparent. Analogous to the way in which many EST proponents view RCTs, empiricism is not *a* way to understand evidence, but *the* way. Consequently, nowhere in the APA policy or its underlying report is a rationale provided for a commitment to empirical research, and nowhere is a consideration given for even the possibility of a "non-empirical" contribution to evidence-based practice.

This equation of evidence with empiricism is directly parallel to the EST movement's equation of evidence with RCT findings. Just as Westen and Bradley (2005) noted that "EBP > EST" (p. 271), we note that EBP > empirical. After all, there is no empirical evidence for empiricism, or for RCTs, for that matter. Both sets of methods spring from the human invention of philosophers and other humanists. Moses did not descend Mt. Sinai with the Ten Commandments in one hand and the principles of science in the other. Moreover, these principles could not have been scientifically derived, because one would need the principles (before their derivation) to conduct the scientific investigations to derive them.

Indeed, the irony of this epistemology's popularity is that many observers of psychology have long considered empiricism to be deeply problematic for psychological research. Again, the parallel to the dominance of RCTs is striking. Just as the majority of real-world patients, therapists, and treatments were perceived to defy RCT categories, so too the majority of real-world phenomena can be perceived to defy empirical categories. Indeed, many of the common factors for evidence-based practice are not, strictly speaking, empirical at all.

Rather, they are experiences and meanings that are not sensory, and thus not observable, in nature (Slife et al., 2005, p. 88).

Consider, for example, the efforts of APA Division 29 (Psychotherapy) to provide empirical support for therapy relationships, such as therapeutic alliance and group cohesion (Norcross, 2001; APA, 2006, p. 272). Although patients and therapists probably experience this alliance and cohesion, these relationships literally never fall on their retinas. The people involved in these relationships are observable in this sense, to be sure, but the "betweenness" of these relations—the actual alliance or cohesion themselves—never are. Their unobservability means, according to the method requirements of empiricism, that they must be operationalized, or made observable. Thus, it is not surprising, given its commitment to a narrow empiricism, that the APA policy report presumes that operationalization is a requirement of method (p. 274).

The problem with this requirement, however, is that any specified operationalization, such as a patient's feelings about the relationship (e.g., Norcross, 2002), can occur without the therapeutic alliance, and any such alliance can occur without the specified operationalization. The upshot is that the construct (e.g., alliance) and the operationalization are two different things, yet the operationalization is the only thing studied in traditional research. Moreover, one can never know empirically the relation between the construct and its operationalization because pivotal aspects of this relation—the construct and relation itself—are never observable. Thus, APA's policy runs the risk of making psychotherapy research a compendium of operationalizations without any knowledge of how they relate to what psychologists want to study.

Problems such as these are the reason that alternative philosophies of science, such as qualitative methods, were formulated. Many qualitative methods were specifically formulated to investigate unobservable, but experienced, meanings of the world (Denzin & Lincoln, 2000; Patton, 1990; Slife & Gantt, 1999). The existence of this alternative philosophy of science implies another problem with the unjustified empiricist framework of the APA policy report—it runs roughshod over alternative frameworks, such as qualitative methods. Although the policy includes qualitative research on its list of acceptable methods (APA, p. 274), it fails to understand and value qualitative research as a different philosophy of science.

A clear indication of this failure is the use of the word "subjective" when the report describes the purpose of qualitative research (p. 274). In the midst of a report that extols "objective" inquiry, relegating only qualitative methods to the "subjective" is second-class citizenship, at best. More importantly, this relegation only makes sense within an empiricist framework. In non-empiricist philosophies, such as those underlying many qualitative methods, the notions of "objective" and "subjective" are largely irrelevant because most non-empiricist conceptions of science do not assume the dualism of a subjective and objective realm (Slife, 2005).

The bottom line is that a common factors approach to the evidence controversy is a clear advancement of the EBP project, but it is not an unqualified advance. Indeed, it recapitulates some of the same problems that it is attempting to correct. In both the EST and the common factors approaches, criteria for what is evidence shape not only the studies conducted but also the practices considered supported. Indeed, we would contend there is no method or methodology that is not ultimately biased in this regard. As philosophers of science have long taught, all methods of investigation must make assumptions about the world *before* it is investigated (Curd & Cover, 1998). The question remains, however, whether there can be a framework for understanding evidence that does not *automatically* shape practice before it is investigated.

## Presaging the Next Step: The Ideas of William James

The answer, we believe, is "yes," and we do not have to reinvent the wheel to formulate this alternative. One of the intellectual parents of our discipline, William James, has already pointed the way. Consequently, we will first briefly describe three of James' pivotal ideas: his radical empiricism, his pluralism, and his pragmatism. Then, we will apply these ideas to the evidence-based practice issue, deriving our alternative to the current monopoly of empiricism—objective methodological pluralism.

James was actually quite critical of what psychologists consider empirical today. As mentioned above, his radical empiricism embraces the whole of experience, including non-sensory experiences such as thoughts, emotions, and spiritual experiences (James, 1902/1985; 1907/1975). His position implies, as he explicitly recognizes, that there are several epistemologies of investigation ("ways of knowing") rather than just one. As James (1909/1977) put it, "nothing includes everything" (p. 145). In other words, no philosophy of science is sufficient to understand everything.

Psychology needs, instead, a *pluralism* of such philosophies, which is the second of James's ideas and an intriguing way to actualize APA's desire for diversity. In other words, we not only need a diversity of methods, which the APA report (2006) clearly concedes (p. 274), we also need a diversity of meth*odologies* or philosophies underlying these methods. It is not coincidental, in this regard, that James (1902/1985) used qualitative methods to investigate spiritual meanings in his famous work, *Varieties of Religious Experiences*. His pluralism of methods dictated that he should not change or operationalize his phenomena of study to fit the method, but that he should change his method to best illuminate the phenomena—spiritual phenomena, in this case.

This approach to method implies the third of James's ideas—his pragmatism. According to James:

> Rationalism sticks to logic and . . . empiricism sticks to the external senses. Pragmatism is willing to take anything, to follow either logic or the senses and to count the humblest and most personal of experiences. [Pragmatism] will count mystical experiences if they have practical consequences. ( James, 1907/1975, p. 61)

As James implies, the heart of pragmatism is the notion that one should never approach the study or understanding of anything with fixed schemes and methods. There is too much danger that the method will distort understanding of the phenomena being studied. This is not to say that one can or should approach such phenomena without some method or interpretive framework. Yet this framework does not have to be cast in stone; psychologists should allow the phenomenon itself to guide the methods we choose to study it.

This pragmatism may sound complicated, but it is not significantly different from what good carpenters do at every job—they let the task dictate the tools they use. They have a pluralism of tools or methods, rather than just one, because many tasks cannot be done with just one tool, such as a hammer. Moreover, not every carpentry job can be "operationalized" into a set of "nails." As Dupré (1993) and others (e.g., Feyerabend, 1975; Viney, 2004) have noted, this pragmatism is the informal meta-method of physics, where the object of study is the primary consideration, and the method of studying it is a secondary consideration.

By contrast, APA's version of evidence-based practice is method-driven rather than object-driven. That is to say, psychologists have decided the logic of their investigation before they even consider what they are studying. If the object of study does not fit this logic, they have no choice but to modify it to fit this logic through operationalization. For example, an unobservable feeling, such as sadness, becomes operationalized as an observable behavior, such as crying.

The irony of this familiar research practice is that psychologists are driven more by an unrecognized and unexamined philosophy of science, as manifested through their methods, than by the objects they are studying. Indeed, they are changing their object of study—from sadness to crying—to accommodate this philosophy. We believe that this accommodation is contrary to good science, where everything including the philosophies that ground one's methods, should be subject to examination and comparison.

## The Next Step: Objective Methodological Pluralism

This description of James' three pivotal ideas—his radical empiricism, pluralism, and pragmatism—sets the stage for our proposal on evidence-based practice: "objective methodological pluralism." First, this pluralism assumes a broader empiricism, in the spirit of James. To value only sensory experiences, as does the conventional empiricist, is to affirm a value that is itself unproven and non-empirical. There simply is no conceptual or empirical necessity to value only the sensory. We recognize that many would claim the success of this value in science, but we also recognize that no scientific comparison between such philosophical values has occurred. These claims of success, then, are merely opinion, uninformed by scientific findings.

In practical terms, this move from conventional empiricism to radical empiricism means that alternative methods, such as qualitative methods, are no longer second class citizens. They are no longer "subjective" and experimental methods considered "objective," because all methods ultimately depend on experiences of one sort or another. This creates more of a level playing field for methods—a pluralism—and allows for an even-handed assessment of each method's advantages and disadvantages.

Unlike the APA policy's conception, the criteria of this assessment are not already controlled by one, unexamined philosophy of science. They are guided, instead, by the object of one's study. This is the reason for the term "objective" in our alternative, *objective* methodological pluralism. Methods, we believe, should be driven not by some philosophy of method that is deemed to be correct *before* the object of study has even been considered. Methods should be driven by consideration of the objects themselves.

This consideration is itself evaluated pragmatically, in terms of the practical differences it makes in the lives of patients. As James realized, any evaluation of practical significance begs the question of "significant to what?" In other words, any methodological pluralism requires thoughtful disciplinary discussion of the moral issues of psychology, a discussion that has begun in a limited way in positive psychology (Seligman, 2002): What is the good life for a patient? When is a life truly flourishing? Such questions cannot be derived from the "is" of research; they must be discussed as the "ought" that guides this research and determines what practical significance really means.

Obviously, much remains to be worked out with a Jamesian pluralism. Still, we believe that this particular "working out" is not only possible but also necessary. The monopoly and problems of empiricism—the lessons of our first two steps in the evidence controversy—do not go away with a rejection of this pluralism. This is the reason we titled this article "the next step"—the difficulties with empiricism and APA's desire for diversity lead us logically, we believe, to this next general step. Admittedly, this kind of pluralism is a challenging prospect. Still, if carpenters can do it in a less complex enterprise, surely psychologists can. In any case, it is high time that psychologists face up to the challenge, because ignoring it will not make it go away.

## References

APA Presidential Task Force on Evidence-Based Practice. (2006). Evidence-based practice in psychology. *American Psychologist, 61,* 271–285.

Bergin, A. E. (1997). Neglect of the therapist and the human dimensions of change: A commentary. *Clinical Psychology: Science and Practice, 4*(1), 83–89.

Bohart, A. C., O'Hara, M., & Leitner, L. M. (1998). Empirically violated treatments: Disenfranchisement of humanistic and other psychotherapies. *Psychotherapy Research, 8,* 141–157.

Butcher, J. N., Mineka, S., & Hooley, J. M. (2004). *Abnormal psychology.* 12th ed. Boston: Pearson/Allyn & Bacon.

Curd, M., & Cover, J. A. (1998). *Philosophy of science: The central issues.* New York: W. W. Norton & Company.

Denzin, N. K., & Lincoln, Y. S. (Eds). (2000). *Handbook of qualitative methods.* Thousand Oaks, CA: Sage.

Duncan, B. L., & Miller, S. D. (2006). Treatment manuals do not improve outcomes. In J. C. Norcross, L. E. Beutler, & R. F. Levant (Eds.), *Evidence-based practices in mental health: Debate and dialogue on the fundamental questions* (pp. 140–149). Washington, D.C.: APA Books.

Dupré, J. (1993). *The disorder of things: Metaphysical foundations of the disunity of science.* Cambridge, MA: Harvard University Press.

Feyerabend, P. (1975). *Against method.* London: Verso.

James, W. (1975). *Pragmatism.* Cambridge, MA: Harvard University Press. (Original work published 1907)

James, W. (1977). *A pluralistic universe.* Cambridge, MA: Harvard University Press. (Original work published 1909)

James, W. (1985). *The varieties of religious experience.* Cambridge, MA: Harvard University Press. (Original work published 1902)

Kihlstrom, J. F. (2006). Scientific research. In J. C. Norcross, L. E. Beutler, & R. F. Levant (Eds.), *Evidence-based practices in mental health: Debate and dialogue on the fundamental questions* (pp. 23–31). Washington, D.C.: APA Books.

Messer, S. B. (2004). Evidence-based practice: Beyond empirically supported treatments. *Professional Psychology: Research and Practice, 35,* 580–588.

Messer, S. B. (2006). Patient values and preferences. In J. C. Norcross, L. E. Beutler, & R. F. Levant (Eds.), *Evidence-based practices in mental health: Debate and dialogue on the fundamental questions* (pp. 31–40). Washington, D.C.: APA Books.

Morrison, K. H., Bradley, R., & Westen, D. (2003). The external validity of controlled clinical trials of psychotherapy for depression and anxiety: A naturalistic study. *Psychology & Psychotherapy: Theory, Research, & Practice, 76:* 109–132.

Norcross, J. C. (2001). Purposes, processes, and products of the task force on empirically supported therapy relationships. *Psychotherapy: Theory, Research, Practice, Training, 38,* 345–356.

Norcross, J. C. (2002). Empirically supported therapy relationships. In J. C. Norcross (Ed.), *Psychotherapy relationships that work: Therapist contributions and responsiveness to patient needs* (pp. 3–32). Oxford, NY: Oxford University Press.

Norcross, J. C., Beutler, L. E., & Levant, R. F. (Eds.) (2006). *Evidence-based practices in mental health: Debate and dialogue on the fundamental questions.* Washington, D.C.: APA Books.

Patton, M. Q., (1990). *Qualitative evaluation and research methods.* (2nd Ed.). Newbury Park, CA: Sage.

Piper, W. E., & Ogrodniczuk, J. S. (1999). Therapy manuals and the dilemma of dynamically oriented therapists and researchers. *American Journal of Psychotherapy, 53,* 467–482.

Reed, G. M. (2006). Clinical expertise. In J. C. Norcross, L. E. Beutler, & R. F. Levant (Eds.), *Evidence-based practices in mental health: Debate and dialogue on the fundamental questions* (pp. 13–23). Washington, D.C.: APA Books.

Safran, J. D. (2001). When worlds collide: Psychoanalysts and the "empirically supported treatment" movement. *Psychoanalytic Dialogues, 11,* 659–681.

Seligman, M. E. P. (2002). *Authentic happiness/Using the new positive psychology to realize your potential for lasting fulfillment.* New York: Free Press.

Slife, B. D. (2005). Testing the limits of Henriques' proposal: Wittgensteinian lessons and hermeneutic dialogue. *Journal of Clinical Psychology, 61,* 1–14.

Slife, B. D., & Gantt, E. (1999). Methodological pluralism: A framework for psychotherapy research. *Journal of Clinical Psychology, 55*(12), 1–13.

Slife, B. D., Wiggins, B. J., & Graham, J. T. (2005). Avoiding an EST monopoly: Toward a pluralism of philosophies and methods. *Journal of Contemporary Psychotherapy, 35*(1), 83–97.

Slife, B. D., & Williams, R. N. (1995). *What's behind the research? Discovering hidden assumptions in the behavioral sciences*. Thousand Oaks, CA: Sage Publications.

Stirman, S. W., & DeRubeis, R. J. (2006). Research patients and clinical trials are frequently representative of clinical practice. In J. C. Norcross, L. E. Beutler, & R. F. Levant (Eds.), *Evidence-based practices in mental health: Debate and dialogue on the fundamental questions* (pp. 171–179). Washington, D.C.: APA Books.

Viney, W. (2004). Pluralism in the sciences is not easily dismissed. *Journal of Clinical Psychology, 60,* 1275–1278.

Westen, D. (2006). Patients and treatments in clinical trials are not adequately representative of clinical practice. In J. C. Norcross, L. E. Beutler, & R. F. Levant (Eds.), *Evidence-based practices in mental health: Debate and dialogue on the fundamental questions* (pp. 161–171). Washington, D.C.: APA Books.

Westen, D., & Bradley, R. (2005). Empirically supported complexity: Rethinking evidence-based practice in psychotherapy. *Current Directions in Psychological Science, 14,* 266–271.

# CHALLENGE QUESTIONS

## Are Traditional Empirical Methods Sufficient to Provide Evidence for Psychological Practice?

1. The label "objective" is typically used only in reference to empirical evidence. Why is this typical, and what would Slife and Wendt say about this practice?
2. The APA Task Force bases its definition of evidence-based practice on a conception formulated by the Institute of Medicine. Find out what this definition is and form your own informed opinion about its relevance or irrelevance to psychotherapy. Support your answer.
3. Many people think they would feel safer if their therapist used practices that have been validated by science. Explain what it is about science that leads people to feel this way.
4. William James is known as the father of American psychology. Why do you think the APA has largely neglected to take his pluralism into consideration?
5. Slife and Wendt believe that the methods of psychology (and any other science, for that matter) are based on and guided by philosophies, yet few psychology texts discuss these philosophies. Why do you feel that this is the case, and is the absence of this discussion justified?

# ISSUE 2

## Classic Dialogue: Was Stanley Milgram's Study of Obedience Unethical?

**YES: Diana Baumrind**, from "Some Thoughts on Ethics of Research: After Reading Milgram's 'Behavioral Study of Obedience,'" *American Psychologist* (vol. 19, 1964)

**NO: Stanley Milgram**, from "Issues in the Study of Obedience: A Reply to Baumrind," *American Psychologist* (vol. 19, 1964)

**ISSUE SUMMARY**

**YES:** Psychologist Diana Baumrind argues that Stanley Milgram's study of obedience did not meet ethical standards for research, because participants were subjected to a research design that caused undue psychological stress that was not resolved after the study.

**NO:** Social psychologist Stanley Milgram, in response to Baumrind's accusations, asserts that the study was well designed, the stress caused to participants could not have been anticipated, and the participants' anguish dissipated after a thorough debriefing.

Are there psychological experiments that should not be conducted? Is the psychological distress that participants experience in some studies too extreme to justify the experimental outcomes and knowledge gained? Or is it sometimes necessary to allow participants to experience some anguish so that a researcher can better understand important psychological phenomena? These questions lie at the heart of ethical considerations in psychological research. They have traditionally been answered by the researcher, who attempts to weigh the costs and benefits of conducting a given study.

The problem is that a researcher's ability to accurately anticipate the costs and benefits of a study is severely limited. Researchers are likely to have an investment in their studies, which may lead them to overestimate the benefits and underestimate the costs. For these and other reasons, in 1974 the U.S. Department of Health, Education, and Welfare established regulations for the protection of human subjects. These regulations include the creation of institutional review boards, which are responsible for reviewing research proposals and ensuring that researchers adequately protect research participants.

The establishment of these regulations can be traced to past ethical controversies, such as the one raised in the following selection by Diana Baumrind regarding Stanley Milgram's famous 1963 study of obedience. Baumrind's primary concern is that the psychological welfare of the study's participants was compromised not only through the course of the study but also through the course of their lives. She contends that participants were prone to obey the experimenter because of the atmosphere of the study and the participants' trust in the experimenter. As a result, participants behaved in ways that disturbed them considerably. Baumrind maintains that these disturbances could not be resolved through an after-study debriefing but rather remained with the participants.

In response to these accusations, Milgram argues that the atmosphere of a laboratory generalizes to other contexts in which obedience is prevalent and is thus appropriate to a study of obedience. Furthermore, he and a number of other professionals never anticipated the results of the study; they were genuinely surprised by its outcome. Milgram also asserts that the psychological distress experienced by some participants was temporary, not dangerous, and that it dissipated after the true nature of the study was revealed.

| POINT | COUNTERPOINT |
|---|---|
| • Milgram's indifference toward distressed participants reveals his lack of concern for their well-being. | • Milgram made special efforts to assure participants that their behavior was normal. |
| • A study of obedience should not be conducted in the laboratory because subjects are particularly prone to behave obediently and to put trust in the researcher. | • The laboratory setting is well suited to a study of obedience because it is similar to other contexts in which obedience is prevalent. |
| • The psychological distress experienced by participants exceeded appropriate limits. | • The psychological distress was brief and not injurious. |
| • Participants experienced long-term negative psychological consequences as a result of their participation in Milgram's experiment. | • Participants spoke positively about the experiment, indicating that it was psychologically beneficial. |
| • In planning and designing the study, Milgram ignored issues regarding the extreme psychological distress that was experienced by some participants. | • The extreme psychological tension experienced by some participants was unanticipated by Milgram and many other professionals. |

YES 

**Diana Baumrind**

# Some Thoughts on Ethics of Research

Certain problems in psychological research require the experimenter to balance his career and scientific interests against the interests of his prospective subjects. When such occasions arise the experimenter's stated objective frequently is to do the best possible job with the least possible harm to his subjects. The experimenter seldom perceives in more positive terms an indebtedness to the subject for his services, perhaps because the detachment which his functions require prevents appreciation of the subject as an individual.

Yet a debt does exist, even when the subject's reason for volunteering includes course credit or monetary gain. Often a subject participates unwillingly in order to satisfy a course requirement. These requirements are of questionable merit ethically, and do not alter the experimenter's responsibility to the subject.

Most experimental conditions do not cause the subjects pain or indignity, and are sufficiently interesting or challenging to present no problem of an ethical nature to the experimenter. But where the experimental conditions expose the subject to loss of dignity, or offer him nothing of value, then the experimenter is obliged to consider the reasons why the subject volunteered and to reward him accordingly.

The subject's public motives for volunteering include having an enjoyable or stimulating experience, acquiring knowledge, doing the experimenter a favor which may some day be reciprocated, and making a contribution to science. These motives can be taken into account rather easily by the experimenter who is willing to spend a few minutes with the subject afterwards to thank him for his participation, answer his questions, reassure him that he did well, and chat with him a bit. Most volunteers also have less manifest, but equally legitimate, motives. A subject may be seeking an opportunity to have contact with, be noticed by, and perhaps confide in a person with psychological training. The dependent attitude of most subjects toward the experimenter is an artifact of the experimental situation as well as an expression of some subjects' personal need systems at the time they volunteer.

The dependent, obedient attitude assumed by most subjects in the experimental setting is appropriate to that situation. The "game" is defined by the experimenter and he makes the rules. By volunteering, the subject agrees implicitly to assume a posture of trust and obedience. While the experimental

From *American Psychologist,* vol. 19, issue 6, June 1964, pp. 421–423. 

conditions leave him exposed, the subject has the right to assume that his security and self-esteem will be protected.

There are other professional situations in which one member—the patient or client—expects help and protection from the other—the physician or psychologist. But the interpersonal relationship between experimenter and subject additionally has unique features which are likely to provoke initial anxiety in the subject. The laboratory is unfamiliar as a setting and the rules of behavior ambiguous compared to a clinician's office. Because of the anxiety and passivity generated by the setting, the subject is more prone to behave in an obedient, suggestible manner in the laboratory than elsewhere. Therefore, the laboratory is not the place to study degree of obedience or suggestibility, as a function of a particular experimental condition, since the base line for these phenomena as found in the laboratory is probably much higher than in most other settings. Thus experiments in which the relationship to the experimenter as an authority is used as an independent condition are imperfectly designed for the same reason that they are prone to injure the subjects involved. They disregard the special quality of trust and obedience with which the subject appropriately regards the experimenter.

Other phenomena which present ethical decisions, unlike those mentioned above, *can* be reproduced successfully in the laboratory. Failure experience, conformity to peer judgment, and isolation are among such phenomena. In these cases we can expect the experimenter to take whatever measures are necessary to prevent the subject from leaving the laboratory more humiliated, insecure, alienated, or hostile than when he arrived. To guarantee that an especially sensitive subject leaves a stressful experimental experience in the proper state sometimes requires special clinical training. But usually an attitude of compassion, respect, gratitude, and common sense will suffice, and no amount of clinical training will substitute. The subject has the right to expect that the psychologist with whom he is interacting has some concern for his welfare, and the personal attributes and professional skill to express his good will effectively.

Unfortunately, the subject is not always treated with the respect he deserves. It has become more commonplace in sociopsychological laboratory studies to manipulate, embarrass, and discomfort subjects. At times the insult to the subject's sensibilities extends to the journal reader when the results are reported. Milgram's (1963) study is a case in point. The following is Milgram's abstract of his experiment:

> This article describes a procedure for the study of destructive obedience in the laboratory. It consists of ordering a naive S to administer increasingly more severe punishment to a victim in the context of a learning experiment. Punishment is administered by means of a shock generator with 30 graded switches ranging from Slight Shock to Danger: Severe Shock. The victim is a confederate of E. The primary dependent variable is the maximum shock the S is willing to administer before he refuses to continue further. 26 Ss obeyed the experimental commands fully, and administered the highest shock on the generator. 14 Ss broke off the experiment at some point after the victim protested and refused to

> provide further answers. The procedure created extreme levels of nervous tension in some Ss. Profuse sweating, trembling, and stuttering were typical expressions of this emotional disturbance. One unexpected sign of tension—yet to be explained—was the regular occurrence of nervous laughter, which in some Ss developed into uncontrollable seizures. The variety of interesting behavioral dynamics observed in the experiment, the reality of the situation for the S, and the possibility of parametric variation within the framework of the procedure, point to the fruitfulness of further study [p. 371].

The detached, objective manner in which Milgram reports the emotional disturbance suffered by his subject contrasts sharply with his graphic account of that disturbance. Following are two other quotes describing the effects on his subjects of the experimental conditions:

> I observed a mature and initially poised businessman enter the laboratory smiling and confident. Within 20 minutes he was reduced to a twitching, stuttering wreck, who was rapidly approaching a point of nervous collapse. He constantly pulled on his earlobe, and twisted his hands. At one point he pushed his fist into his forehead and muttered: "Oh, God, let's stop it." And yet he continued to respond to every word of the experimenter, and obeyed to the end [p. 377].
>
> In a large number of cases the degree of tension reached extremes that are rarely seen in sociopsychological laboratory studies. Subjects were observed to sweat, tremble, stutter, bite their lips, groan, and dig their fingernails into their flesh. These were characteristic rather than exceptional responses to the experiment.
>
> One sign of tension was the regular occurrence of nervous laughing fits. Fourteen of the 40 subjects showed definite signs of nervous laughter and smiling. The laughter seemed entirely out of place, even bizarre. Full-blown, uncontrollable seizures were observed for 3 subjects. On one occasion we observed a seizure so violently convulsive that it was necessary to call a halt to the experiment . . . [p. 375].

Milgram does state that,

> After the interview, procedures were undertaken to assure that the subject would leave the laboratory in a state of well being. A friendly reconciliation was arranged between the subject and the victim, and an effort was made to reduce any tensions that arose as a result of the experiment [p. 374].

It would be interesting to know what sort of procedures could dissipate the type of emotional disturbance just described. In view of the effects on subjects, traumatic to a degree which Milgram himself considers nearly unprecedented in sociopsychological experiments, his casual assurance that these tensions were dissipated before the subject left the laboratory is unconvincing.

What could be the rational basis for such a posture of indifference? Perhaps Milgram supplies the answer himself when he partially explains the subject's destructive obedience as follows, "Thus they assume that the discomfort caused the victim is momentary, while the scientific gains resulting from the experiment are enduring [p. 378]." Indeed such a rationale might suffice to justify the means used to achieve his end if that end were of inestimable value to humanity or were not itself transformed by the means by which it was attained.

The behavioral psychologist is not in as good a position to objectify his faith in the significance of his work as medical colleagues at points of breakthrough. His experimental situations are not sufficiently accurate models of real-life experience; his sampling techniques are seldom of a scope which would justify the meaning with which he would like to endow his results; and these results are hard to reproduce by colleagues with opposing theoretical views. . . . [T]he concrete benefit to humanity of his particular piece of work, no matter how competently handled, cannot justify the risk that real harm will be done to the subject. I am not speaking of physical discomfort, inconvenience, or experimental deception per se, but of permanent harm, however slight. I do regard the emotional disturbance described by Milgram as potentially harmful because it could easily effect an alteration in the subject's self-image or ability to trust adult authorities in the future. It is potentially harmful to a subject to commit, in the course of an experiment, acts which he himself considers unworthy, particularly when he has been entrapped into committing such acts by an individual he has reason to trust. The subject's personal responsibility for his actions is not erased because the experimenter reveals to him the means which he used to stimulate these actions. The subject realizes that he would have hurt the victim if the current were on. The realization that he also made a fool of himself by accepting the experimental set results in additional loss of self-esteem. Moreover, the subject finds it difficult to express his anger outwardly after the experimenter in a self-acceptant but friendly manner reveals the hoax.

A fairly intense corrective interpersonal experience is indicated wherein the subject admits and accepts his responsibility for his own actions, and at the same time gives vent to his hurt and anger at being fooled. Perhaps an experience as distressing as the one described by Milgram can be integrated by the subject, provided that careful thought is given to the matter. The propriety of such experimentation is still in question even if such a reparational experience were forthcoming. Without it I would expect a naive, sensitive subject to remain deeply hurt and anxious for some time, and a sophisticated, cynical subject to become even more alienated and distrustful.

In addition the experimental procedure used by Milgram does not appear suited to the objectives of the study because it does not take into account the special quality of the set which the subject has in the experimental situation. Milgram is concerned with a very important problem, namely, the social consequences of destructive obedience. He says,

> Gas chambers were built, death camps were guarded, daily quotas of corpses were produced with the same efficiency as a manufacture of appliances. These inhumane policies may have originated in the mind of a single person, but they could only be carried out on a massive scale if a very large number of persons obeyed orders [p. 371].

But the parallel between authority-subordinate relationships in Hitler's Germany and in Milgram's laboratory is unclear. In the former situation the SS man or member of the German Officer Corps, when obeying orders to slaughter, had no reason to think of his superior officer as benignly disposed towards himself or their victims. The victims were perceived as subhuman and not worthy of consideration. The subordinate officer was an agent in a great cause. He did not need to feel guilt or conflict because within his frame of reference he was acting rightly.

It is obvious from Milgram's own descriptions that most of his subjects were concerned about their victims and did trust the experimenter, and that their stressful conflict was generated in part by the consequences of these two disparate but appropriate attitudes. Their distress may have resulted from shock at what the experimenter was doing to them as well as from what they thought they were doing to their victims. In any case there is not a convincing parallel between the phenomena studied by Milgram and destructive obedience as that concept would apply to the subordinate-authority relationship demonstrated in Hitler Germany. If the experiments were conducted "outside of New Haven [Connecticut] and without any visible ties to [Yale University]," I would still question their validity on similar although not identical grounds. In addition, I would question the representativeness of a sample of subjects who would voluntarily participate within a noninstitutional setting.

In summary, the experimental objectives of the psychologist are seldom incompatible with the subject's ongoing state of well being, provided that the experimenter is willing to take the subject's motives and interests into consideration when planning his methods and correctives. Section 4b in *Ethical Standards of Psychologists* (APA, undated) reads in part:

> Only when a problem is significant and can be investigated in no other way, is the psychologist justified in exposing human subjects to emotional stress or other possible harm. In conducting such research, the psychologist must seriously consider the possibility of harmful aftereffects, and should be prepared to remove them as soon as permitted by the design of the experiment. Where the danger of serious aftereffects exists, research should be conducted only when the subjects or their responsible agents are fully informed of this possibility and volunteer nevertheless [p. 12].

From the subject's point of view procedures which involve loss of dignity, self-esteem, and trust in rational authority are probably most harmful in the long run and require the most thoughtfully planned reparations, if engaged in at all. The public image of psychology as a profession is highly related to our own actions, and some of these actions are changeworthy. It is important that as research psychologists we protect our ethical sensibilities rather than adapt our personal standards to include as appropriate the kind of indignities to which Milgram's subjects were exposed. I would not like to see experiments such as Milgram's proceed unless the subjects were fully informed of the dangers of serious aftereffects and his correctives were clearly shown to be effective in restoring their state of well being.

## References

American Psychological Association. *Ethical Standards of Psychologists: A summary of ethical principles*. Washington, D.C.: APA, undated.

Milgram, S. Behavioral study of obedience. *J. Abnorm. Soc. Psychol.*, 1963, 67, 371–378.

**Stanley Milgram**

# Issues in the Study of Obedience: A Reply to Baumrind

Obedience serves numerous productive functions in society. It may be ennobling and educative and entail acts of charity and kindness. Yet the problem of destructive obedience, because it is the most disturbing expression of obedience in our time, and because it is the most perplexing, merits intensive study.

In its most general terms, the problem of destructive obedience may be defined thus: If X tells Y to hurt Z, under what conditions will Y carry out the command of X, and under what conditions will he refuse? In the concrete setting of a laboratory, the question may assume this form: If an experimenter tells a subject to act against another person, under what conditions will the subject go along with the instruction, and under what conditions will he refuse to obey?

A simple procedure was devised for studying obedience (Milgram, 1963). A person comes to the laboratory, and in the context of a learning experiment, he is told to give increasingly severe electric shocks to another person. (The other person is an actor, who does not really receive any shocks.) The experimenter tells the subject to continue stepping up the shock level, even to the point of reaching the level marked "Danger: Severe Shock." The purpose of the experiment is to see how far the naive subject will proceed before he refuses to comply with the experimenter's instructions. Behavior prior to this rupture is considered "obedience" in that the subject does what the experimenter tells him to do. The point of rupture is the act of disobedience. Once the basic procedure is established, it becomes possible to vary conditions of the experiment, to learn under what circumstances obedience to authority is most probable, and under what conditions defiance is brought to the fore (Milgram, in press).

The results of the experiment (Milgram, 1963) showed, first, that it is more difficult for many people to defy the experimenter's authority than was generally supposed. A substantial number of subjects go through to the end of the shock board. The second finding is that the situation often places a person in considerable conflict. In the course of the experiment, subjects fidget, sweat, and sometimes break out into nervous fits of laughter. On the one hand, subjects want to aid the experimenter; and on the other hand, they do not want to shock the learner. The conflict is expressed in nervous reactions.

In a recent issue of *American Psychologist,* Diana Baumrind (1964) raised a number of questions concerning the obedience report. Baumrind expressed concern for the welfare of subjects who served in the experiment, and wondered whether adequate measures were taken to protect the participants. She also questioned the adequacy of the experimental design.

Patently, "Behavioral Study of Obedience" did not contain all the information needed for an assessment of the experiment. But . . . this was only one of a series of reports on the experimental program, and Baumrind's article was deficient in information that could have been obtained easily. . . .

At the outset, Baumrind confuses the unanticipated outcome of an experiment with its basic procedure. She writes, for example, as if the production of stress in our subjects was an intended and deliberate effect of the experimental manipulation. There are many laboratory procedures specifically designed to create stress (Lazarus, 1964), but the obedience paradigm was not one of them. The extreme tension induced in some subjects was unexpected. Before conducting the experiment, the procedures were discussed with many colleagues, and none anticipated the reactions that subsequently took place. Foreknowledge of results can never be the invariable accompaniment of an experimental probe. Understanding grows because we examine situations in which the end is unknown. An investigator unwilling to accept this degree of risk must give up the idea of scientific inquiry.

Moreover, there was every reason to expect, prior to actual experimentation, that subjects would refuse to follow the experimenter's instructions beyond the point where the victim protested; many colleagues and psychiatrists were questioned on this point, and they virtually all felt this would be the case. Indeed, to initiate an experiment in which the critical measure hangs on disobedience, one must start with a belief in certain spontaneous resources in men that enable them to overcome pressure from authority.

It is true that after a reasonable number of subjects had been exposed to the procedures, it became evident that some would go to the end of the shock board, and some would experience stress. That point, it seems to me, is the first legitimate juncture at which one could even start to wonder whether or not to abandon the study. But momentary excitement is not the same as harm. As the experiment progressed there was no indication of injurious effects in the subjects; and as the subjects themselves strongly endorsed the experiment, the judgment I made was to continue the investigation.

Is not Baumrind's criticism based as much on the unanticipated findings as on the method? The findings were that some subjects performed in what appeared to be a shockingly immoral way. If, instead, every one of the subjects had broken off at "slight shock," or at the first sign of the learner's discomfort, the results would have been pleasant, and reassuring, and who would protest?

## Procedures and Benefits

A most important aspect of the procedure occurred at the end of the experimental session. A careful post-experimental treatment was administered to all subjects. The exact content of the dehoax varied from condition to condition and with increasing experience on our part. At the very least all subjects were told that the victim had not received dangerous electric shocks. Each subject had a friendly reconciliation with the unharmed victim, and an extended discussion with the experimenter. The experiment was explained to the defiant subjects in a way that supported their decision to disobey the experimenter. Obedient subjects were assured of the fact that their behavior was entirely normal and that their feelings of conflict or tension were shared by other participants. Subjects were told that they would receive a comprehensive report at the conclusion of the experimental series. In some instances, additional detailed and lengthy discussions of the experiments were also carried out with individual subjects.

When the experimental series was complete, subjects received a written report which presented details of the experimental procedure and results. Again their own part in the experiments was treated in a dignified way and their behavior in the experiment respected. All subjects received a follow-up questionnaire regarding their participation in the research, which again allowed expression of thoughts and feelings about their behavior.

The replies to the questionnaire confirmed my impression that participants felt positively toward the experiment. In its quantitative aspect (see Table 1), 84% of the subjects stated they were glad to have been in the experiment; 15% indicated neutral feelings, and 1.3% indicated negative feelings. To be sure, such findings are to be interpreted cautiously, but they cannot be disregarded.

Further, four-fifths of the subjects felt that more experiments of this sort should be carried out, and 74% indicated that they had learned something of personal importance as a result of being in the study. . . .

The debriefing and assessment procedures were carried out as a matter of course, and were not stimulated by any observation of special risk in the experimental procedure. In my judgment, at no point were subjects exposed to danger and at no point did they run the risk of injurious effects resulting from participation. If it had been otherwise, the experiment would have been terminated at once.

*Table 1*

**Excerpt From Questionnaire Used in a Follow-up Study of the Obedience Research**

| Now that I have read the report and all things considered . . . | Defiant | Obedient | All |
|---|---|---|---|
| 1. I am very glad to have been in the experiment | 40.0% | 47.8% | 43.5% |
| 2. I am glad to have been in the experiment | 43.8% | 35.7% | 40.2% |
| 3. I am neither sorry nor glad to have been in the experiment | 15.3% | 14.8% | 15.1% |
| 4. I am sorry to have been in the experiment | 0.8% | 0.7% | 0.8% |
| 5. I am very sorry to have been in the experiment | 0.0% | 1.0% | 0.5% |

*Note:* Ninety-two percent of the subjects returned the questionnaire. The characteristics of the nonrespondents were checked against the respondents. They differed from the respondents only with regard to age; younger people were overrepresented in the nonresponding group.

Baumrind states that, after he has performed in the experiment, the subject cannot justify his behavior and must bear the full brunt of his actions. By and large it does not work this way. The same mechanisms that allow the subject to perform the act, to obey rather than to defy the experimenter, transcend the moment of performance and continue to justify his behavior for him. The same viewpoint the subject takes while performing the actions is the viewpoint from which he later sees his behavior, that is, the perspective of "carrying out the task assigned by the person in authority."

Because the idea of shocking the victim is repugnant, there is a tendency among those who hear of the design to say "people will not do it." When the results are made known, this attitude is expressed as "if they do it they will not be able to live with themselves afterward." These two forms of denying the experimental findings are equally inappropriate misreadings of the facts of human social behavior. Many subjects do, indeed, obey to the end, and there is no indication of injurious effects.

The absence of injury is a minimal condition of experimentation; there can be, however, an important positive side to participation. Baumrind suggests that subjects derived no benefit from being in the obedience study, but this is false. By their statements and actions, subjects indicated that they had learned a good deal, and many felt gratified to have taken part in scientific research they considered to be of significance. A year after his participation one subject wrote:

> This experiment has strengthened my belief that man should avoid harm to his fellow man even at the risk of violating authority.

Another stated

> To me, the experiment pointed up . . . the extent to which each individual should have or discover firm ground on which to base his decisions, no matter how trivial they appear to be. I think people should think more deeply about themselves and their relation to their world and to other people. If this experiment serves to jar people out of complacency, it will have served its end.

These statements are illustrative of a broad array of appreciative and insightful comments by those who participated.

The 5-page report sent to each subject on the completion of the experimental series was specifically designed to enhance the value of his experience. It laid out the broad conception of the experimental program as well as the logic of its design. It described the results of a dozen of the experiments, discussed the causes of tension, and attempted to indicate the possible significance of the experiment. Subjects responded enthusiastically; many indicated a desire to be in further experimental research. This report was sent to all subjects several years ago. The care with which it was prepared does not support Baumrind's assertion that the experimenter was indifferent to the value subjects derived from their participation.

Baumrind's fear is that participants will be alienated from psychological experiments because of the intensity of experience associated with laboratory procedures. My own observation is that subjects more commonly respond with distaste to the "empty" laboratory hour, in which cardboard procedures are employed, and the only possible feeling upon emerging from the laboratory is that one has wasted time in a patently trivial and useless exercise.

The subjects in the obedience experiment, on the whole, felt quite differently about their participation. They viewed the experience as an opportunity to learn something of importance about themselves, and more generally, about the conditions of human action.

A year after the experimental program was completed, I initiated an additional follow-up study. In this connection an impartial medical examiner, experienced in outpatient treatment, interviewed 40 experimental subjects. The examining psychiatrist focused on those subjects he felt would be most likely to have suffered consequences from participation. His aim was to identify possible injurious effects resulting from the experiment. He concluded that, although extreme stress had been experienced by several subjects,

> none was found by this interviewer to show signs of having been harmed by his experience. . . . Each subject seemed to handle his task [in the experiment] in a manner consistent with well established patterns of behavior. No evidence was found of any traumatic reactions.

Such evidence ought to be weighed before judging the experiment.

## Other Issues

Baumrind's discussion is not limited to the treatment of subjects, but diffuses to a generalized rejection of the work.

Baumrind feels that obedience cannot be meaningfully studied in a laboratory setting: The reason she offers is that "The dependent, obedient attitude assumed by most subjects in the experimental setting is appropriate to that situation [p. 421]." Here, Baumrind has cited the very best reason for examining obedience in this setting, namely that it possesses "ecological validity." Here is one social context in which compliance occurs regularly. Military and job situations are also particularly meaningful settings for the study of obedience precisely because obedience is natural and appropriate to these contexts. I reject Baumrind's argument that the observed obedience does not count because it occurred where it is appropriate. That is precisely why it does count. A soldier's obedience is no less meaningful because it occurs in a pertinent military context. A subject's obedience is no less problematical because it occurs within a social institution called the psychological experiment.

Baumrind writes: "The game is defined by the experimenter and he makes the rules [p. 421]." It is true that for disobedience to occur the framework of the experiment must be shattered. That, indeed, is the point of the design. That is why obedience and disobedience are genuine issues for the subject. *He must really assert himself as a person against a legitimate authority.*

Further, Baumrind wants us to believe that outside the laboratory we could not find a comparably high expression of obedience. Yet, the fact that ordinary citizens are recruited to military service and, on command, perform far harsher acts against people is beyond dispute. Few of them know or are concerned with the complex policy issues underlying martial action; fewer still become conscientious objectors. Good soldiers do as they are told, and on both sides of the battle line. However, a debate on whether a higher level of obedience is represented by (*a*) killing men in the service of one's country, or (*b*) merely shocking them in the service of Yale science, is largely unprofitable. The real question is: What are the forces underlying obedient action?

Another question raised by Baumrind concerns the degree of parallel between obedience in the laboratory and in Nazi Germany. Obviously, there are enormous differences: Consider the disparity in time scale. The laboratory experiment takes an hour; the Nazi calamity unfolded in the space of a decade. There is a great deal that needs to be said on this issue, and only a few points can be touched on here.

1. In arguing this matter, Baumrind mistakes the background metaphor for the precise subject matter of investigation. The German event was cited to point up a serious problem in the human situation: the potentially destructive effect of obedience. But the best way to tackle the problem of obedience, from a scientific standpoint, is in no way restricted by "what happened exactly" in Germany. What happened exactly can *never* be duplicated in the laboratory or anywhere else. The real task is to learn more about the general problem of destructive obedience using a workable approach. Hopefully, such inquiry will stimulate insights and yield general propositions that can be applied to a wide variety of situations.
2. One may ask in a general way: How does a man behave when he is told by a legitimate authority to act against a third individual? In trying to find an answer to this question, the laboratory situation is one useful starting point—and for the very reason stated by Baumrind—namely, the experimenter does constitute a genuine authority for the subject. The fact that trust and dependence on the experimenter are maintained, despite the extraordinary harshness he displays toward the victim, is itself a remarkable phenomenon.
3. In the laboratory, through a set of rather simple manipulations, ordinary persons no longer perceived themselves as a responsible part of the causal chain leading to action against a person. The means through which responsibility is cast off, and individuals become thoughtless agents of action, is of general import. Other processes were revealed that indicate that the experiments will help us to understand why men obey. That understanding will come, of course, by examining the full account of experimental work and not alone the brief report in which the procedure and demonstrational results were exposed.

At root, Baumrind senses that it is not proper to test obedience in this situation, because she construes it as one in which there is no reasonable alternative to obedience. In adopting this view, she has lost sight of this fact: A substantial proportion of subjects do disobey. By their example, disobedience is shown to be a genuine possibility, one that is in no sense ruled out by the general structure of the experimental situation.

Baumrind is uncomfortable with the high level of obedience obtained in the first experiment. In the condition she focused on, 65% of the subjects obeyed to the end. However, her sentiment does not take into account that within the general framework of the psychological experiment obedience varied enormously from one condition to the next. In some variations, 90% of the subjects *dis*obeyed. It seems to be *not* only the fact of an experiment, but the particular structure of elements within the experimental situation that accounts for rates of obedience and disobedience. And these elements were varied systematically in the program of research.

A concern with human dignity is based on a respect for a man's potential to act morally. Baumrind feels that the experimenter *made* the subject shock the victim. This conception is alien to my view. The experimenter tells the subject to do something. But between the command and the outcome there is a paramount force, the acting person who may obey or disobey. I started with the belief that every person who came to the laboratory was free to accept or to reject the dictates of authority. This view sustains a conception of human dignity insofar as it sees in each man a capacity for *choosing* his own behavior. And as it turned out, many subjects did, indeed, choose to reject the experimenter's commands, providing a powerful affirmation of human ideals.

Baumrind also criticizes the experiment on the grounds that "it could easily effect an alteration in the subject's . . . ability to trust adult authorities in the future [p. 422]." But I do not think she can have it both ways. On the one hand, she argues the experimental situation is so special that it has no generality; on the other hand, she states it has such generalizing potential that it will cause subjects to distrust all authority. But the experimenter is not just any authority: He is an authority who tells the subject to act harshly and inhumanely against another man. I would consider it of the highest value if participation in the experiment could, indeed, inculcate a skepticism of this kind of authority. Here, perhaps, a difference in philosophy emerges most clearly. Baumrind sees the subject as a passive creature, completely controlled by the experimenter. I started from a different viewpoint. A person who comes to the laboratory is an active, choosing adult, capable of accepting or rejecting the prescriptions for action addressed to him. Baumrind sees the effect of the experiment as undermining the subject's trust of authority. I see it as a potentially valuable experience insofar as it makes people aware of the problem of indiscriminate submission to authority.

## Conclusion

My feeling is that viewed in the total context of values served by the experiment, approximately the right course was followed. In review, the facts are these: (*a*) At the outset, there was the problem of studying obedience by means of a simple experimental procedure. The results could not be foreseen before the experiment was carried out. (*b*) Although the experiment generated momentary stress in some subjects, this stress dissipated quickly and was not injurious. (*c*) Dehoax and follow-up procedures were carried out to insure the subjects' well-being. (*d*) These procedures were assessed through questionnaire and psychiatric studies and were found to be effective. (*e*) Additional steps were taken to enhance the value of the laboratory experience for participants, for example, submitting to each subject a careful report on the experimental program. (*f*) The subjects themselves strongly endorse the experiment, and indicate satisfaction at having participated.

If there is a moral to be learned from the obedience study, it is that every man must be responsible for his own actions. This author accepts full responsibility for the design and execution of the study. Some people may feel it should not have been done. I disagree and accept the burden of their judgment.

Baumrind's judgment, someone has said, not only represents a personal conviction, but also reflects a cleavage in American psychology between those whose primary concern is with *helping* people and those who are interested mainly in *learning* about people. I see little value in perpetuating divisive forces in psychology when there is so much to learn from every side. A schism may exist, but it does not correspond to the true ideals of the discipline. The psychologist intent on healing knows that his power to help rests on knowledge; he is aware that a scientific grasp of all aspects of life is essential for his work, and is in itself a worthy human aspiration. At the same time, the laboratory psychologist senses his work will lead to human betterment, not only because enlightenment is more dignified than ignorance, but because new knowledge is pregnant with humane consequences.

## References

Baumrind, D. Some thoughts on ethics of research: After reading Milgram's "Behavioral study of obedience." *Amer. Psychologist,* 1964, **19,** 421–423.

Lazarus, R. A laboratory approach to the dynamics of psychological stress. *Amer. Psychologist,* 1964, **19,** 400–411.

Milgram, S. Behavioral study of obedience. *J. Abnorm. Soc. Psychol.,* 1963, **67,** 371–378.

Milgram, S. Some conditions of obedience and disobedience to authority. *Hum. Relat.,* in press.

# CHALLENGE QUESTIONS

## Classic Dialogue: Was Stanley Milgram's Study of Obedience Unethical?

1. Investigate the role that your college's institutional review board (see the introduction to this issue) plays in protecting subjects from undue harm.
2. Sometimes people make the wrong decisions and end up hurting other people. Apart from utilizing institutional review boards, what can researchers do to avoid making wrong decisions regarding potentially harmful studies?
3. Imagine that you have just participated in Milgram's study. How would you feel about the deception that occurred? Is it ever appropriate to deceive participants in research studies? If so, when? If not, why not?
4. Both Baumrind and Milgram might agree that there are cases in which some low-level tension for research participants is allowable. Under what conditions might it be acceptable to allow participants to experience some distress? Under what conditions is it inappropriate to subject participants to any distress?
5. Baumrind raises the issue of trust. Do you think the participants in the Milgram study lost trust in psychological researchers or authority figures in general? Why, or why not?
6. If you were on an ethics review board and the Milgram study was brought before you, would you allow Milgram to run the study? Support your answer.

# ISSUE 3

## Does the Research Support Evolutionary Accounts of Female Mating Preferences?

**YES: David M. Buss,** from *Evolutionary Psychology: The New Science of the Mind, 3rd Edition* (Allyn and Bacon, 2008)

**NO: David J. Buller,** from *Adapting Minds: Evolutionary Psychology and the Persistent Quest for Human Nature* (MIT Press, 2005)

### ISSUE SUMMARY

**YES:** Professor of Psychology David M. Buss contends that the research data indicate an evolved female preference for high-status, resource-possessing males.

**NO:** Philosopher of Science David J. Buller argues that the research data support several alternative explanations for Buss's findings.

Have you ever wondered why women choose the partners they do? The relatively new field of Evolutionary Psychology has made some fascinating claims in answer to this question. One highly publicized claim is that women have an evolved preference for older men. Beginning with our Pleistocene ancestors, females who preferred older males were better able to protect and provide for their children, and thus were more likely to pass this preference onto the next generation. Evidence that this evolved preference remains today, according to evolutionary psychologists, can be seen in the behavior of several Hollywood celebrities, such as actress Catherine Zeta Jones marrying actor Michael Douglas, 25 years her senior.

While the general public seems to be intrigued by such evolutionary claims, some scholars have been critical. They believe that evolutionary accounts of human behavior reduce important aspects of our emotional lives, such as romantic and parental love, to an impersonal desire for reproductive success. These critics might sarcastically ask, "Is there really nothing more in Catherine Zeta Jones's choice to marry Michael Douglas than a desire to pass genes onto the next generation?" Evolutionary psychologists appear to have paid little heed to these criticisms, however, partly because they have been largely political or ideological, with little examination of the research behind evolutionary claims. To the authors' credit in the following articles, the question debated is whether or not the *research* provides real evidence of the evolutionary accounts of female mating preferences.

According to the author of the first selection, David Buss, the answer is a resounding "yes." In fact, he points to the study of human mating strategies as "one of the first empirical success stories of evolutionary psychology." In these passages from Buss's college textbook, *Evolutionary Psychology,* he cites findings from several studies that support his claim that females have an evolved preference for high-status, resource-possessing males, including women's responses to personal ads and demographic statistics of whom women actually marry. Finally, Buss recognizes that alternative hypotheses have been offered for women's preferences, such as the structural powerlessness hypothesis, but he ultimately argues that "this hypothesis receives no support from the existing empirical data."

On the other hand, David Buller argues against evolutionary accounts of female mating preferences based on the methodological problems of the studies cited by Buss and others. He begins by attacking the theoretical underpinnings of evolutionary psychology, stating that "given our lack of knowledge of our ancestors' lifestyles, we simply do not know whether selection would have favored and made universal a female preference for high-status males, resource-holding males." After a thorough examination of the research findings, Buller claims the data better explain a female preference for males of similar status than a robust universal preference for males of high-status. The supposed discovery of a female preference for high status males is "largely an illusion." As people let go of this illusion, he claims, "we will not be so convinced by impoverished evidence that human females prefer high-status males." Instead, we will see more clearly the complexities that are involved in female mate preferences.

| **POINT** | **COUNTERPOINT** |
| --- | --- |
| • Women have an evolved universal preference for high-status, resource holding males. | • We do not know the history of our ancestors well enough to know whether such preferences have evolved. |
| • The data provide convincing evidence of a female preference for good financial prospects in males. | • The data better explain a preference for males of similar status. |
| • The findings about high-SES women's mating preferences contradict the structural powerlessness hypothesis. | • The findings of evolutionary psychology do not rule out alternative hypotheses such as the structural powerlessness hypothesis. |
| • Elder's findings provide evidence for a robust preference for men with status and resources. | • Elder's findings are better understood as a correlation between high status and high attractiveness among men. |
| • Buss's cross cultural studies provide evidence for a universal, evolved female preference for high-SES mates. | • Assortative mating by status cannot be ruled out as an alternative explanation of Buss's cross-cultural findings. |

**David M. Buss**

# Evolutionary Psychology: The New Science of the Mind

Nowhere do people have an equal desire for all members of the opposite sex. Everywhere some potential mates are preferred, others shunned. Imagine living as our ancestors did long ago—struggling to keep warm by the fire; hunting meat for our kin; gathering nuts, berries, and herbs; and avoiding dangerous animals and hostile humans. If we were to select a mate who failed to deliver the resources promised, who had affairs, who was lazy, who lacked hunting skills, or who heaped physical abuse on us, our survival would be tenuous, our reproduction at risk. In contrast, a mate who provided abundant resources, who protected us and our children, and who devoted time, energy, and effort to our family would be a great asset. As a result of the powerful survival and reproductive advantages that were reaped by those of our ancestors who chose mates wisely, many specific desires evolved. As descendants of those winners in the evolutionary lottery, modern humans have inherited a specific set of mate preferences. . . .

Choosing a mate is a complex task, and so we do not expect to find simple answers to what women want. Perhaps no other topic has received as much research attention in evolutionary psychology, however, and so we have some reasonably firm answers to this long-standing question.

## Preference for Economic Resources

The evolution of the female preference for males offering resources may be the most ancient and pervasive basis for female choice in the animal kingdom. Consider the gray shrike, a bird living in the Negev Desert of Israel (Yosef, 1991). Just before the start of the breeding season, male shrikes begin amassing caches of edible prey such as snails and useful objects such as feathers and pieces of cloth in numbers ranging from 90 to 120. They impale these items on thorns and other pointed projections within their territories. Females scan the available males and choose to mate with those with the largest caches. When Yosef arbitrarily removed portions of some males' stock and added edible objects to the supplies of others, females still preferred to mate with the males with the larger bounties. Females avoided entirely males without resources, consigning them to bachelorhood. Wherever females show a mating preference, the male's resources are often the key criterion.

Among humans the evolution of women's preference for a permanent mate with resources would have required two preconditions. First, resources would have to be accruable, defensible, and controllable by men during human evolutionary history. Second, men would have to differ from each other in their holdings and their willingness to invest those holdings in a woman and her children, because if all men possessed the same resources and showed an equal willingness to allocate them, there would be no need for women to develop such a preference for them.

These conditions are easily met in humans. Territory and tools, to name just two resources, are acquired, defended, monopolized, and controlled by men worldwide. Men vary tremendously in the quantity of resources they command—from the homeless to the jetsetters. Men also differ widely in how willing they are to invest their time and resources in long-term mateships. Some men prefer to mate with many women, investing little in each. Other men channel all their resources to one woman and her children (Belsky, Steinberg, & Draper, 1991).

Over the course of human evolutionary history women could often garner far more resources for their children through a single spouse than through several temporary sex partners. Men invest in their wives and children with provisions to an extent unprecedented among primates. In all other primates, females must rely solely on their own efforts to acquire food because males rarely share those resources with their mates (Smuts, 1995). Men, in contrast, provide food, find shelter, defend territory, and protect children. They tutor children in sports, hunting, fighting, hierarchy negotiation, friendship, and social influence. They transfer status, aiding offspring in forming reciprocal alliances later in life. These benefits are unlikely to be secured by a woman from a temporary sex partner.

So the stage was set for the evolution of women's preferences for men with resources. But women needed cues to signal a man's possession of those resources. These cues might be indirect, such as personality characteristics that signal a man's upward mobility. They might be physical, such as a man's athletic ability or health. They might include reputation, such as the esteem in which a man is held by his peers. The possession of economic resources, however, provides the most obvious cue.

## Preference for Good Financial Prospects

Currently held mate preferences provide a window for viewing our mating past, just as our fears of snakes and heights provide a window for viewing ancestral hazards. Evidence from dozens of studies documents that modern U.S. women indeed value economic resources in mates substantially more than men do. In a study conducted in 1939, for example, U.S. men and women rated eighteen characteristics for their relative desirability in a marriage partner, ranging from irrelevant to indispensable. Women did not view good financial prospects as absolutely indispensable, but they did rate them as important, whereas men rated them as merely desirable but not very important. Women in 1939 valued good financial prospects in a mate about twice as highly as men did, a finding that was replicated in 1956 and again in 1967 (Buss, Shackelford, Kirkpatrick, & Larson, 2001).

The sexual revolution of the late 1960s and early 1970s failed to change this sex difference. In an attempt to replicate the studies from earlier decades, in the mid-1980s 1,491 people in the United States were surveyed using the same questionnaire (Buss, 1989a). Women and men from Massachusetts, Michigan, Texas, and California rated eighteen personal characteristics for their value in a marriage partner. As in the previous decades, women still valued good financial prospects in a mate roughly twice as much as did men. In 1939, for example, women judged "good financial prospect" to be 1.80 in importance on a scale ranging from 0 (irrelevant) to 3 (indispensable); men in 1939 judged "good financial prospect" to be only 0.90 in importance. By 1985 women judged this quality to be 1.90 in importance, whereas men judged it to be 1.02 in importance—still roughly a twofold difference between the sexes (Buss, Shackelford, Kirkpatrick, & Larsen, 2001).

The premium that women place on economic resources has been revealed in a diversity of contexts. Douglas Kenrick and his colleagues devised a useful method for revealing how much people value different attributes in a marriage partner by having men and women indicate the "minimum percentiles" of each characteristic they would find acceptable (Kenrick et al., 1990). The percentile concept was explained with such examples as the following: "A person at the 50th percentile would be above 50% of the other people on earning capacity, and below 49% of the people on this dimension" (p. 103). U.S. college women indicate that their minimum acceptable percentile for a husband on earning capacity is the seventieth percentile, or above 70 percent of all other men, whereas men's minimum acceptable percentile for a wife's earning capacity is only the fortieth. Women also show higher standards for economic capacity in a dating partner, in a sexual relationship, and in a steady dating context.

Personal ads in newspapers and magazines confirm that women actually on the marriage market desire strong financial resources. A study of 1,111 personal ads found that female advertisers seek financial resources roughly eleven times as often as male advertisers do (Wiederman, 1993). In short, sex differences in preference for resources are not limited to college students and are not bound by the method of inquiry.

Nor are these female preferences restricted to America, to Western societies, or to capitalist countries. A large cross-cultural study was conducted of thirty-seven cultures on six continents and five islands using populations ranging from coast-dwelling Australians to urban Brazilians to shantytown South African Zulus (Buss, Abbott, Angleitner, Asherian, Biaggio, et al., 1990). Some participants came from nations that practice *polygyny* (the mating or marriage of a single man with several women), such as Nigeria and Zambia. Other participants came from nations that are more *monogamous* (the mating of one man with one woman), such as Spain and Canada. The countries included those in which living together is as common as marriage, such as Sweden and Finland, as well as countries in which living together without marriage is frowned on, such as Bulgaria and Greece. The study sampled a total of 10,047 individuals in thirty-seven cultures (Buss, 1989a).

Male and female participants in the study rated the importance of eighteen characteristics in a potential mate or marriage partner, on a scale from unimportant to indispensable. Women across all continents, all political systems (including socialism and communism), all racial groups, all religious groups, and all systems of mating (from intense polygyny to presumptive monogamy) placed more value than men on good financial prospects. Overall, women valued financial resources about 100 percent more than men, or roughly twice as much. There are some cultural variations. Women from Nigeria, Zambia, India, Indonesia, Iran, Japan, Taiwan, Colombia, and Venezuela valued good financial prospects a bit higher than women from South Africa (Zulus), the Netherlands, and Finland. In Japan, for example, women valued good financial prospect roughly 150 percent more than men, whereas women from the Netherlands deem it only 36 percent more important than their male counterparts, less than women from any other country. Nonetheless, the sex difference remained invariant: Women worldwide desired financial resources in a marriage partner more than men.

These findings provided the first extensive cross-cultural evidence supporting the evolutionary basis for the psychology of human mating. Since that study, findings from other cultures continue to support the hypothesis that women have evolved preferences for men with resources. A study of mate selection in the country of Jordan found that women more than men valued economic ability, as well as qualities linked to economic ability such as status, ambition, and education (Khallad, 2005). Using a different method—analysis of folktales in forty-eight cultural areas including bands, tribes, preindustrial states, Pacific islands, and all the major continents—Jonathan Gottschall and colleagues found the same sex difference (Gottschall, Berkey, Cawson, Drown, Fleischner, et al., 2003). Substantially more female than male characters in the folktales from each culture placed a primary emphasis on wealth or status in their expressed mate preferences. Gottschall found similar results in a historical analysis of European literature (Gottschall, Martin, Quish, & Rea, 2004). A study of 500 Muslims living in the United States found that women sought financially secure, emotionally sensitive, and sincere partners, the latter likely being a signal of willingness to commit to a long-term relationship (Badahdah & Tiemann, 2005). Finally, an in-depth study of the Hadza of Tanzania, a hunter-gatherer society, found that women place a great importance on a man's foraging abilities—primarily his ability to hunt (Marlow, 2004).

This fundamental sex difference also appears prominently in modern forms of mating, such as speed dating and mail-order brides. In a study of speed dating, in which individuals engage in four-minute conversations to determine whether they are interested in meeting the other person again, women chose men who indicated that they had grown up in affluent neighborhoods (Fisman et al., 2006). A study of the mate preferences of mail-order brides from Colombia, the Philippines, and Russia found that these women sought husbands who had status and ambition—two key correlates of resource acquisition (Minervini & McAndrew, 2005). As the authors conclude, "women willing to become MOBs [mail-order brides] do not appear to have a different agenda than other mate-seeking women; they simply have discovered a novel way to expand their pool of prospective husbands" (p. 17).

The enormous body of empirical evidence across different methods, time periods, and cultures supports the hypothesis that women have evolved a powerful preference for long-term mates with the ability to provide resources. Because ancestral women faced the tremendous burdens of internal fertilization, a nine-month gestation, and lactation, they would have benefited tremendously by selecting mates who possessed resources. Today's women are the descendants of a long line of women who had these mate preferences—preferences that helped their ancestors solve the adaptive problems of survival and reproduction.

## Preference for High Social Status

Traditional hunter-gatherer societies, which are our closest guide to what ancestral conditions were probably like, suggest that ancestral men had clearly defined status hierarchies, with resources flowing freely to those at the top and trickling slowly down to those at the bottom (Betzig, 1986; Brown & Chia-Yun, n.d.). Cross-culturally, groups such as the Melanesians, the early Egyptians, the Sumerians, the Japanese, and the Indonesians include people described as "head men" and "big men" who wield great power and enjoy the resource privileges of prestige. Among various South Asian languages, for example, the term "big man" is found in Sanskrit, Hindi, and several Dravidian languages. In Hindi, for example, *bara asami* means "great man, person of high position or rank" (Platts, 1960, pp. 151–152). In North America, north of Mexico, "big man" and similar terms are found among groups such as the Wappo, Dakota, Miwok, Natick, Choctaw, Kiowa, and Osage. In Mexico and South America "big man" and closely related terms are found among the Cayapa, Chatino, Mazahua, Mixe, Mixteco, Quiche, Terraba, Tzeltal, Totonaco, Tarahumara, Quechua, and Hahuatl. Linguistically, therefore, it seems that many cultures have found it important to invent words or phrases to describe men who are high in status. A man's social status, as indicated by these linguistic phrases, would provide a powerful cue to his possession of resources.

Women desire men who command a high position because social status is a universal cue to the control of resources. Along with status come better food, more abundant territory, and superior health care. Greater social status bestows on children social opportunities missed by the children of lower-ranking males. For male children worldwide, access to more and better quality mates typically accompanies families of higher social status. In one study of 186 societies ranging from the Mbuti Pygmies of Africa to the Aleut Eskimos, high-status men invariably had greater wealth and more wives and provided better nourishment for their children (Betzig, 1986).

One study examined short-term and long-term mating to discover which characteristics people especially valued in potential spouses, as contrasted with potential sex partners (Buss & Schmitt, 1993). Several hundred individuals evaluated sixty-seven characteristics for their desirability or undesirability in the short or long term, rating them on a scale ranging from −3 (extremely undesirable) to +3 (extremely desirable). Women judged the likelihood of success in a profession and the possession of a promising career to be highly desirable in a spouse, giving average ratings of +2.60 and +2.70, respectively. Significantly, these cues to future status are seen by women as more desirable in spouses than in casual sex partners, with the latter ratings reaching only +1.10 and +0.40, respectively. U.S. women also place great value on education and professional degrees in mates—characteristics that are strongly linked with social status.

The importance that women grant to social status in mates is not limited to the United States or even to capitalist countries. In the vast majority of the thirty-seven cultures considered in the international study on choosing a mate, women valued social status in a prospective mate more than men in both communist and socialist countries, among Africans and Asians, among Catholics and Jews, in the southern tropics and the northern climes (Buss, 1989a). In Taiwan, for example, women valued status 63 percent more than men, in Zambia women valued it 30 percent more, in West Germany women valued it 38 percent more, and in Brazil women valued it 40 percent more.

Hierarchies are universal features among human groups, and resources tend to accumulate to those who rise in the hierarchy. Women historically appear to have solved the adaptive problem of acquiring resources in part by preferring men who are high in status. . . .

## Effects of Women's Personal Resources on Mate Preferences

An alternative explanation to the evolutionary psychological theory has been offered for the preferences of women for men with resources—the structural powerlessness hypothesis (Buss & Barnes, 1986; Eagly & Wood, 1999). According to this view, because women are typically excluded from power and access to resources, which are largely controlled by men, women seek mates who have power, status, and earning capacity. Women try to marry upward in socioeconomic status because this provides their primary channel for gaining access to resources. Men do not value economic resources in a mate as much as women do because they already have control over these resources and because women have fewer resources anyway.

The society of Bakweri, from Cameroon in West Africa, casts doubt on this theory by illustrating what happens when women have real power (Ardener, Ardener, & Warmington, 1960). Bakweri women hold greater personal and economic power because they have more resources and are in scarcer supply than men. Women secure resources through their own labors on plantations but also from casual sex, which is a lucrative source of income. There are roughly 236 men for every hundred women, an imbalance that results from the continual influx of men from other areas of the country to work on the plantations. Because of the extreme imbalance in numbers of the sexes, women have considerable latitude to exercise their choice in a mate. Women thus have more money than men and more potential mates to choose from.

Yet Bakweri women persist in preferring mates with resources. Wives often complain about receiving insufficient support from their husbands. Indeed, lack of sufficient economic provisioning is the reason for divorce most frequently cited by women. Bakweri women change husbands if they find a man who can offer them more money and pay a larger bride-price. When women are in a position to fulfill their evolved preference for a man with resources, they do so. Having dominant control of economic resources apparently does not negate this mate preference.

Professionally and economically successful women in the United States also value resources in men. A study of married couples identified women who were financially successful, as measured by their salary and income, and contrasted their preferences in a mate with those of women with lower salaries and income (Buss, 1989a). The financially successful women were well educated, tended to hold professional degrees, and had high self-esteem. The study showed that successful women place an even greater value than less professionally successful women on mates who have professional degrees, high social status, and greater intelligence and who are tall, independent, and self-confident. Women's personal income was positively correlated with the income they wanted in an ideal mate (+.31), the desire for a mate who is a college graduate (+.29), and the desire for a mate with a professional degree (+.35). Contrary to the structural powerlessness hypothesis, these women expressed an even stronger preference for high-earning men than did women who are less financially successful.

In a separate study psychologists Michael Wiederman and Elizabeth Allgeier found that college women who expect to earn the most after college put more weight on the promising financial prospects of a potential husband than do women who expect to earn less. Professionally successful women, such as medical and law students, also place heavy importance on a mate's earning capacity (Wiederman & Allgeier, 1992).

Cross-cultural studies consistently find small but positive relationships between women's personal access to economic resources and preferences for mates with resources. A study of 1,670 Spanish women seeking mates through personal advertisements found that women who have more resources and status were more likely to seek men with resources and status (Gil-Burmann, Pelaez, & Sanchez, 2002). A study of 288 Jordanians found that both women and men with high socioeconomic status place more, not less, value on the mate characteristics of having a college graduate degree and being ambitious-industrious (Khallad, 2005). A study of 127 individuals from Serbia concluded that "The high status of women correlated positively with their concern with a potential mate's potential socio-economic status, contrary to the prediction of the socio-structural model" (Todosijevic, Ljubinkovic, & Arancic, 2003, p. 116). An Internet study of 1,851 women found that *attitudes* toward financial and career independence, including items such as "How important is having a career to you?" found that women who endorsed these attitudes valued physical attractiveness more than good financial prospects in a mate (Moore et al., 2006). However, in examining the effects of women's actual income, this study found that "wealthier women prefer good financial prospects over physical attractiveness" (Moore, Cassidy, Smith, & Perrett, 2006, p. 201). Taken together, these results not only fail to support the structural powerlessness hypothesis, they directly contradict it. . . .

## How Women's Mate Preferences Affect Actual Mating Behavior

For preferences to evolve, they must affect actual mating decisions because it is those decisions that have reproductive consequences. For a number of reasons, however, preferences should not show a *perfect* correspondence with actual mating behavior. People can't always get what they want for a variety of reasons. First, there is a limited number of highly desirable potential mates. Second, one's own mate value limits access to those who are highly desirable. In general only the most desirable women are in a position to attract the most desirable men, and vice versa. Third, parents and other kin sometimes influence one's mating decisions, regardless of personal preferences. Despite these factors, women's mate preferences must have affected their actual mating decisions some of the time over the course of human evolutionary history or they would not have evolved. Following are several sources of evidence that preferences do affect mating decisions.

## Women's Responses to Men's Personal Ads

One source of evidence comes from women's responses to personal ads posted by men in newspapers. If women's preferences affected their mating decisions, then they would be predicted to respond more often to men who indicate that they are financially well off. Baize and Schroeder (1995) tested this prediction using a sample of 120 personal ads placed in two different newspapers, one from the West Coast and the other from the Midwest. The authors mailed a questionnaire to those who posted the ads, asking for information about personal status, response rate, and personality characteristics.

Several variables significantly predicted the number of letters men received in response to their ads. First, *age* was a significant predictor, with women responding more often to older men than to younger men ($r = +.43$). Second, *income* and *education* were also significant predictors, with women responding more to men with ads indicating higher salaries ($r = +.30$) and more years of education ($r = +.37$). Baize and Schroeder ended their article on a humorous note by recalling the question posed by Tim Hardin in his famous folk song: "If I were a carpenter and you were a lady, would you marry me anyway, would you have my baby?" Given the cumulative research findings, the most likely answer is: No.

Similar results have now been found in Poland in a study of response rates to ads placed by 551 men (Pawlowski & Koziel, 2002). Men with higher levels of education, men who were somewhat older, men who were taller, and men who offered more resources all received a larger number of responses from women than did men who lacked these qualities.

## Women's Marriages to Men High in Occupational Status

A second source of findings pertains to women who are in a position to get what they want—women who have the qualities that men desire in a mate such as physical attractiveness (see Chapter 5). What are the mate choices of these women? In three separate sociological studies, researchers discovered that physically attractive women in fact marry men who are higher in social status and financial holdings than do women who are less attractive (Elder, 1969; Taylor & Glenn, 1976; Udry & Ekland, 1984). In one study, the physical attractiveness of women was correlated with the occupational prestige of their husbands (Taylor and Glenn, 1976). For different groups the correlations were all positive, ranging between +.23 and +.37.

A longitudinal study was conducted at the Institute of Human Development in Berkeley, California (Elder, 1969). Physical attractiveness ratings were made by staff members of then unmarried women when they were adolescents. This sample of women was then followed up in adulthood after they had married, and the occupational statuses of their husbands were assessed.

The results were examined separately for working-class and middle-class women. The correlations between a woman's attractiveness in adolescence and her husband's occupational status roughly a decade later was +.46 for women with working-class backgrounds and +.35 for women coming from middle-class backgrounds. For the sample as a whole, a woman's physical attractiveness correlated more strongly with her husband's status (+.43) than did other women's variables such as class of origin (+.27) or IQ (+.14). In sum, attractiveness in women appears to be an important path to upward mobility; women who are most in a position to get what they want appear to select men who have the qualities that most women desire—men with status and resources. . . .

## Summary

We now have the outlines of an answer to the mystery of women's long-term mate preferences. Modern women have inherited from their successful ancestors wisdom about the men they consent to mate with. Ancestral women who mated indiscriminately were likely to have been less reproductively successful than those who exercised choice. Long-term mates bring with them a treasure trove of assets. Selecting a long-term mate who has the relevant assets is clearly an extraordinarily complex endeavor. It involves a number of distinctive preferences, each corresponding to a resource that helps women solve critical adaptive problems.

That women seek resources in a marriage partner might seem obvious. Because resources cannot always be directly discerned, however, women's mating preferences are keyed to other qualities that signal the likely possession, or future acquisition, of resources. Indeed, women may be less influenced by money per se than by qualities that lead to resources, such as ambition, intelligence, and older age. Women scrutinize these personal qualities carefully because they reveal a man's potential. . . .

According to the structural powerlessness hypothesis, women who have a lot of personal access to resources are predicted not to value resources in a mate as much as women lacking resources. This hypothesis receives no support from the existing empirical data, however. Indeed, women with high incomes value a potential mate's income and education more, not less, than women with lower incomes. . . .

**David J. Buller**

**NO**

# Adapting Minds: Evolutionary Psychology and the Persistent Quest for Human Nature

## Women Seeking Men

"Choosing a mate is a complex task," David Buss says, "and so we do not expect to find simple answers to what women want. Perhaps no other topic has received as much research attention in evolutionary psychology, however, and so we have some reasonably firm answers to this longstanding question." Indeed, female mate preferences have been the focus of roughly twice as many studies in Evolutionary Psychology as male mate preferences. But, despite the efforts on this front, Evolutionary Psychology's answer to the question of what women want is not exactly firm.

As we have seen, Evolutionary Psychologists claim that women have an evolved preference for high-status men because, "in general, the higher a male is in status . . . the greater his ability to control resources across many situations" and to invest those resources in his mate and their offspring. This presupposes that, throughout our evolutionary history as hunter-gatherers, males have been the primary providers of food and other resources to their mates and their offspring and that, as a consequence, females evolved to prefer the males who excelled in this role.

. . . However, there is significant variation among hunter-gatherer populations with respect to male contributions to the diets of their young. In some hunter-gatherer populations female foraging provides a full 67 percent of the total daily caloric intake. And Kristen Hawkes found that a Hadza woman and her children receive more food from her mother than from her mate. As I argued, it's not clear which of the various hunter-gatherer populations we are to take as representative of our Pleistocene ancestors, or even whether Pleistocene hunter-gatherers led a uniform lifestyle.

This fact poses a problem for the claim that females have evolved a universal preference for males who show signs of being able providers. For, if ancestral hunter-gatherer populations were just as variable as contemporary hunter-gatherer populations with respect to the degree of male provisioning, then a preference for high-status males may have evolved in populations with high male provisioning, but not in populations where males provided relatively little in the way of essential resources. Given our lack of knowledge of our ancestors' lifestyles . . . we simply don't know whether selection would have favored and made universal a female preference for high-status, resource-holding males.

In keeping with this skepticism, a number of researchers—for example, Linnda Caporael, Alice Eagly, and Sarah Blaffer Hrdy—have challenged Evolutionary Psychology's account of female mate preferences. They argue that female preference for high-status males results from current economic inequality, not past selection. In this view, a preference for males with resources is a rational response to a social situation in which males control economic resources, since in such circumstances a female can gain access to economic resources only through her choice of mate.

Evolutionary Psychologists have dubbed this view the "structural (or economic) powerlessness hypothesis." They argue that this hypothesis entails the prediction that women in high-paying professions should place less emphasis on status in mate choice than unemployed women or women in low-paying jobs. Evolutionary Psychologists claim to have shown this prediction to be false. Thus, they claim, the evidence favors the evolutionary hypothesis over the structural powerlessness hypothesis.

What's at stake here is whether female preference for high-status males is an adaptation. Evolutionary Psychologists claim it is, and the structural powerlessness hypothesis claims it isn't. As I mentioned earlier, this debate is not my central concern. For, despite their disagreement with Evolutionary Psychology, advocates of the structural powerlessness hypothesis still accept that there is a robust female preference for high-status males. But, in what follows, I will argue that there is no good evidence of such a robust preference among women. . . .

The most fun studies purporting to demonstrate that females prefer high-SES males were conducted by the anthropologist John Marshall Townsend and the psychologist Gary Levy. The procedures and results of these studies were almost identical, so I will focus primarily on one of them, since it is representative of the others and discussion of it applies equally to the others.

In Townsend and Levy's study, 112 white female undergraduates from Syracuse University were shown photographs of two male models, who were selected for this purpose because an independent group had rated one as very handsome and the other as very homely. In the photographs, each male model was dressed in each of three different "costumes." One was the uniform of a Burger King employee, intended to depict low SES. Another was a plain off-white shirt, to depict medium SES. And the third was "a white dress shirt with a designer paisley tie, a navy blazer thrown over the left shoulder, and a Rolex wristwatch showing on the left wrist," to depict high SES.

The female subjects were asked to indicate their degree of willingness to enter six types of relationship, ranging from very casual to very serious, with "someone like" the models. The six types of relationship were described as "coffee and conversation," "date," "sex only," "serious involvement, marriage potential," "sexual and serious, marriage potential," and "marriage." Subjects were instructed

*Table 1*

**Average Female Willingness to Enter a Relationship as a Function of Male "Costume"**

*Handsome model*

| Level of involvement | Costume: High SES | Medium SES | Low SES |
|---|---|---|---|
| Date | 2.16 | 1.94 | 2.82 |
| Serious involvement | 2.58 | 2.74 | 3.87 |
| Marriage | 2.53 | 2.77 | 3.84 |

*Homely model*

| Level of involvement | Costume: High SES | Medium SES | Low SES |
|---|---|---|---|
| Date | 2.57 | 4.00 | 3.69 |
| Serious involvement | 3.20 | 4.35 | 4.13 |
| Marriage | 3.17 | 4.38 | 4.18 |

to indicate their degree of willingness on the following five-point scale: (1) very willing, (2) willing, (3) undecided, (4) unwilling, and (5) very unwilling.

To simplify discussion, I'll focus on three representative relationship types: "date," "serious involvement, marriage potential," and "marriage." The average ratings from the female subjects for these three relationship types are presented in table 1.

Townsend and Levy found two aspects of the results in table 1 to be significant. First, at each level of involvement (from date to marriage), each model got better ratings in the high-SES costume than in the other costumes. The sole exception was that the handsome model was a slightly more desirable date in the medium-SES costume than in the high-SES costume. As the level of involvement became more serious, however, even the handsome model scored better in the high-SES costume than in either of the other costumes. Second, high status appears to compensate for homeliness, since the high-SES costume raised the homely model's acceptability at every level of involvement over that of the handsome model in the low-SES costume. Townsend and Levy conclude that females prefer high-status mates. And the Evolutionary Psychologist Bruce Ellis interprets the experiment as showing that "status and economic achievement are highly relevant barometers of male attractiveness, more so than physical attributes."

But, if we look at the data in a different way, we see a different barometer. For, at every level of involvement and at every status level, the handsome male is preferred over the homely male. In fact, the handsome male in the medium-SES costume scored better than the homely male in the high-SES costume, despite the fact that the latter can presumably provide more resources than the former. So the results could equally well be interpreted as showing that physical attributes are "highly relevant barometers of male attractiveness," more so than male status.

In addition, although Townsend and Levy claim that status compensates for homeliness, since the homely model in the high-SES costume scored higher than the handsome model in the low-SES costume, the homely model scored 3.20 and 3.17 for serious involvement and marriage respectively. Both of these scores lie between "undecided" and "unwilling" in the scale used to indicate degree of willingness to enter a relationship with someone like the model. So high SES doesn't appear to make females *willing* to enter a serious relationship with someone they find homely. (Also, the homely model inexplicably scored better in the low-SES costume than in the medium-SES costume, despite the fact that medium-SES males can provide resources that low-SES males can't. There is no doubt some fashion advice lurking here about who should wear plain off-white shirts.)

While Evolutionary Psychologists typically deemphasize the role of male physical attractiveness in female mate preferences, both of these objections could easily be accommodated simply by claiming that women weigh both physical attractiveness and status in choosing a mate. The data, it could be claimed, demonstrate that both have significant effects on female mate preferences. Thus, the data don't have to be a perfect fit to the prediction that females prefer high-status males, they only need to show that status plays a role in female mate preferences. And the data do seem to demonstrate this.

But there is a problem with the data nonetheless, which is due to the fact that Townsend and Levy's subjects were all university students. As we have seen, homogamy is the most robust mating phenomenon, and status homogamy is second only to race homogamy in the strength of its effect on mate choice. There are two possible explanations for this. First, it may be that everyone competes for high-status mates, but only high-status individuals succeed in attracting high-status mates. This effect could trickle down to other status levels, with the result that everyone ends up with a mate of comparable status. Second, it may be that people actually prefer mates of comparable status, and status homogamy results from this preference. The sociological evidence actually favors the second explanation. People mate with those of comparable status primarily out of preference, rather than settling for a mate of comparable status because of an inability to get a mate of higher status.

But why would anyone prefer to mate with a fellow medium-status individual, say, rather than a high-status individual? The reason could well be the one that Kenrick and Keefe give for why age similarity is important in mate choice. Recall that Kenrick and Keefe argued that *all forms* of similarity between mates may facilitate long-term parental cooperation, since homogamously mated individuals have "similar expectations, values, activity levels, and habits." Consequently, they suggested, selection may have favored homogamous mating—a "birds of a feather mate together" principle—among our ancestors. If this is right, then we should expect people to prefer mates of comparable status in addition to mates of similar age. As a consequence, assortative mating by status would be fairly robust, which in fact it is.

Studies of status homogamy have considered four different dimensions of status: education level, cultural status of occupation, income level, and social-class origins. Of these, educational homogamy is the most robust. Overwhelmingly, people select mates who have achieved (or will achieve) a comparable level of education. Indeed, one of the boundaries that is very rarely crossed in mating relationships is the boundary between those who have some college education (like Townsend and Levy's female subjects) and those who have only a high-school education (presumably like Townsend and Levy's Burger King employee). Consequently, the fact that Townsend and Levy's subjects preferred medium- to high-SES males over low-SES males could simply be an artifact of assortative mating by status. The results could simply be due to the fact that the female subjects perceived the low-SES model as uneducated and tended to consider only males of probable comparable education level as prospective mates.

This explains why the models would score so low in the low-SES costumes, but why would they score higher in the high-SES costumes than in the medium-SES costumes? Is this also the effect of status homogamy, or does it reveal a genuine preference for high-SES males?

To know for sure, we would need status information about Townsend and Levy's female subjects, and Townsend and Levy don't report having gathered such information. But recall that status involves social-class origins and cultural status of occupation in addition to level of education. The relevant information about respondent status would thus include information about social-class origins. Respondents with higher class origins should be expected to favor the high-SES models. Relevant information would also include not simply education level achieved at the time of response (which was sufficient to already place a social barrier between the respondents and the low-SES models), but also *anticipated* achieved level of education. Similarly, it would include anticipated occupation. Status homogamy should lead us to expect that all of these factors would influence female preference. And, if more of Townsend and Levy's female respondents were themselves high SES than medium SES, and if all respondents gave the highest score to the models from their own SES, then the average ratings of the high-SES models would be higher than the medium-SES models, even if all medium-SES respondents rated the medium-SES models highest.

There is reason to think that Townsend and Levy's sample *was* composed predominantly of high-SES females (or at least females who were toward the upper end of the SES continuum). For all the female subjects were white female undergraduates at one of the nation's most expensive private universities, and at least half of them belonged to sororities (half were interviewed in sororities). So it is highly probable that females with upper-middle-class origins were overrepresented in the sample. Further, there should be a correlation between these class origins and higher levels of anticipated educational achievement and anticipated occupational status. And females who are high-SES along these dimensions would prefer the high-SES models on the basis of status homogamy alone. Since the sample was no doubt composed predominantly of high-SES females, then, it should be expected that the average ratings of the high-SES models would exceed those of the medium-SES models.

Interestingly, Townsend repeated this experiment with 82 female law students, this time supplementing the pictures with descriptions. The model in the Burger King uniform was described as training to be a waiter who would earn a starting salary of $15,000 a year, the model in the off-white shirt as training to be a teacher who would earn $22,000 a year, and the model in the Rolex as training to be a doctor who would earn $80,000 a year. Guess what. The female law students preferred the doctor. But this doesn't necessarily indicate a preference for high SES per se. For this preference is precisely what we should expect if female law students were choosing mates of comparable education level, comparable cultural status of occupation, and comparable projected income level.

Further, the female law students rated the high-SES models higher than the college students had. This is also precisely what we should expect from assortative mating by status, since the law students form a more homogeneously high-status sample than the undergraduates. Because the undergraduate sample was less status homogeneous, containing a higher ratio of medium-SES respondents, they gave a lower average score to the high-SES model. In short, the Townsend and Levy data fit the preference ratings that would result from status homogamy alone.

Thus, given the composition of the subject groups in these experiments, none of the experiments can distinguish whether female respondents were indicating a genuine preference for a mate with high SES or whether their ratings were a product of simple assortative mating by status. Given the independently documented robustness of status homogamy, we already know that, if you ask medium- and high-SES females what they want in a mate, they will show a preference bias against low-SES males. In order to distinguish a genuine preference for high status from assortative mating by status, we would need data on the preferences of low-SES females. We would also need a subgroup analysis by status of female preferences; that is, we would need to see female preference orderings broken down by SES of female respondent. Evolutionary Psychologists have provided no such data, but it would be needed to substantiate their claim that females desire high-SES males. For without this data, there is no evidence that medium-SES females don't prefer the medium-SES model over the ostentatious high-SES model, or that low-SES females don't find the handsome model in the Burger King uniform most desirable of all. Only if low-SES females systematically indicate a preference for high-status males can we infer a real preference for high status. However, the independent evidence of status homogamy suggests that the latter preference pattern would not be found.

Of course, it is entirely possible that women actually have an evolved preference for high-status men, but that the experiments conducted by Evolutionary Psychologists have simply failed to reveal that fact because their results are confounded by status homogamy. This could be the case, for example, if dominance and high SES, as those are articulated in the experimental instruments used by Evolutionary Psychologists, are poor measures of the kind of status that women have evolved to prefer. After all, this preference is supposed to have evolved long before people had education levels and incomes or had careers as doctors and lawyers. . . . So maybe Evolutionary Psychologists have simply used experimental procedures that are incapable of detecting female preference for high-status mates, though it is there waiting to be detected.

Although this is a possibility, I doubt it's true. As Evolutionary Psychologists standardly define the concept, status "refers to an individual's *relative position in a social group;* it is a measure of where one stands among one's peers and competitors." If selecting a high-status mate had, and continues to have, significant fitness consequences for women, as Evolutionary Psychologists claim, we should expect women to have evolved techniques of detecting *social relations* among males. They should have evolved to be sensitive to the structural features of male interactions, detecting how males form a hierarchy in their interactions with one another, regardless of which particular intrinsic male qualities are correlated with high or low status. And, if women have evolved to be sensitive in this way to where a male stands in relation to other males, and to prefer those who are in the upper strata of male hierarchies, the kinds of experiment we've discussed should detect that preference. So, the fact that the results of these experiments are confounded by status homogamy probably isn't due to the experiments' making use of cues that didn't indicate status in the Pleistocene.

At this point Evolutionary Psychologists could respond that assortative mating by status cannot explain the sex differences they consistently find. For studies of mate preferences consistently find that women place a greater emphasis on a potential mate's status than do men. If female preferences for high status are simply a by-product of the fact that the female experimental subjects are relatively high status themselves and are merely indicating a preference for males of comparable status, then we should expect male experimental subjects (who tend to be from the same social classes as female subjects) to place a comparable emphasis on a potential mate's status. For, if people prefer mates of similar status, that should be evident not only in female preferences, but in male preferences as well. But study after study finds that a potential mate's status doesn't matter to men in the way that it matters to women.

The studies showing a sex difference with respect to preferences for high-status mates have focused on the income dimension of status, finding that women care more about a potential mate's earning capacity than men do. In Buss one such study was conducted by Douglas Kenrick in collaboration with the psychologists Edward Sadalla, Gary Groth, and Melanie Trost. Kenrick and his collaborators provided 64 female and 29 male undergraduates with a list of characteristics and asked them how they would weigh those characteristics in choosing a partner for a date, for steady exclusive dating, and for marriage. "Participants were asked to give the minimum and maximum percentiles of each characteristic that they would find acceptable in a partner at each level of

*Table 2*

**Average Minimum Acceptable Earning Capacity of a Potential Partner**

| | Earning capacity (expressed as percentile) | |
|---|---|---|
| **Level of involvement** | **Female respondents** | **Male respondents** |
| Date | 44.58 | 23.79 |
| Steady dating | 61.08 | 36.86 |
| Marriage | 67.17 | 42.21 |

involvement. Several examples were given to clarify any questions about the percentile concept, e.g., 'A person at the 50th percentile would be above 50% of other people on [the characteristic] kind and understanding, and below 49% of the people on this dimension.' "

The primary evidence supporting the claim that females desire high-status mates came from responses regarding *minimum acceptable earning capacity*. With respect to this characteristic, average responses for each sex were as presented in table 2, and these results do appear to show that male earning capacity plays a strong role in female mate choice. Indeed, in accordance with Evolutionary Psychologists' expectations, as the level of involvement becomes more serious, and consequently a male's ability to provide resources becomes increasingly important, females appear to place increasing weight on earning capacity. And this result appears to confirm that women prefer high-SES males.

Again, however, the female subjects were all American undergraduates, hence, on average, of medium SES or higher. (Education level alone would make them of medium SES, but some may be higher because of higher social-class origins, anticipated high-status occupations, or anticipated high income levels after college.) Thus, again, it is not clear whether the results actually demonstrate a preference for high status per se, or whether they merely reflect status homogamy. For, again, if the subjects are predominantly from the upper half of the socioeconomic continuum, and if they express preferences for same-status males, their average preference rating will fall in the upper half of the socioeconomic continuum.

But what about the sex difference in the results? Males clearly placed much less emphasis than females on earning capacity, although males did, like females, place greater emphasis on earning capacity as the level of involvement increased. If the results are a product of assortative mating by status, we should expect males to express the same preferences as females: Medium- to high-SES males should indicate a preference for females whose earning capacities fall in the medium- to high-SES range. But, in fact, the average minimum acceptable earning percentiles preferred by males run a full 20 to 25 percentile points lower than female averages. Doesn't this show that the results are not an artifact of status homogamy and that females have a genuine preference for high status per se in a mate?

In short, no. Recall that status has four dimensions: education level, cultural prestige of occupation, social-class origins, and income level. In American society (from which the subjects in this experiment were drawn), earning capacity is a cue to, or a predictor of, other dimensions of a male's status in a way that it is not for a female. In American society, women hold only about one-quarter of the jobs in professions paying over $40,000 a year. And, in professions and trades where women hold a larger fraction of the jobs, women earn only about three-quarters as much as men performing the same job. Given this significant economic inequality between the sexes, a medium-SES male seeking a medium-SES female can expect his prospective mate to earn significantly less than he does, even if they are perfectly matched on other dimensions of status. Consequently, even if upper-SES subjects chose mates by employing the criterion of similar status alone, females should specify significantly higher minimum acceptable earning percentiles for prospective mates than males, since income is a better predictor of other dimensions of male status than it is of other dimensions of female status.

If people select mates of comparable status because people of comparable status have "similar expectations, values, activity levels, and habits," and these similarities facilitate parental cooperation (as per Kenrick and Keefe's argument), surely education level, occupation, and social-class origins are better indicators of one's values and so on than income level alone. Social-class origins and the education level one achieves play a role in shaping personality, expectations, and values, and chosen occupation is a reflection of one's values and expectations in life. One's income, in itself, is much less a reflection of one's values and character than the other dimensions of status. So, education level, occupation, and social-class origins should be more important factors in mate choice than income level. And the sociological evidence of status homogamy does show these factors to have a stronger effect on mate choice than income level. Since economic inequality between the sexes makes income level a better predictor among males than females of these other dimensions of status, if subjects are asked specifically to rate the importance of income level in mate choice, we should expect females to accord it greater weight than males. Thus, under conditions of economic inequality between the sexes, a sex difference in the importance attached to a potential mate's earning capacity is fully consistent with simple assortative mating by status.

In addition, if you reread the instructions given to participants in Kenrick's study, which I quoted above, you'll see that subjects were instructed to provide percentile rankings for each characteristic *relative to the whole population* ("50th percentile would be above 50% of other people"), not just relative to the sex of a potential mate. So males indicated a preference to marry a woman whose income is in the 42nd percentile of all Americans, not just in the 42nd percentile of American women. Similarly, females indicated a preference to marry a man whose income is in the 67th percentile of all Americans, which includes the lower-earning female half of the population. Thus, if the earning-capacity percentile rankings were adjusted to accommodate the economic inequality between the sexes, the sex difference in the rankings would virtually disappear.

My argument sounds suspiciously like the structural powerlessness hypothesis, but it's not exactly the same. According to the structural powerlessness hypothesis, women desire high-SES mates because, under conditions of economic inequality between the sexes, the only way a woman can gain access to economic resources is through her mate. The suggestion I'm making is that, in the results obtained by Kenrick and his collaborators (and in similar studies), women only *appear* to desire high-SES mates because only upper-SES women have been asked about their preferences, and the economic inequality between the sexes results in a sex difference in the percentiles assigned to the characteristic *minimum acceptable earning capacity.* The structural powerlessness hypothesis takes the reality of a female preference for high earning capacity for granted, and I'm suggesting that females merely appear to prefer high earning capacity, but that the data don't provide good evidence that they in fact do. Nonetheless, my suggestion is similar enough to the structural powerlessness hypothesis to warrant examining the evidence that Evolutionary Psychologists present against the latter.

Evolutionary Psychologists contend that the structural powerlessness hypothesis entails that female preference for high earning capacity should vary with a female's own economic power, so that women with a high earning capacity should place less emphasis on earning capacity in choosing a mate than do women with a low earning capacity. Evolutionary Psychologists claim that two studies have shown this to be false. First, from his large survey, Buss had data on personal income and class background for 100 of the female respondents from his United States sample. Among this group, he found that "women who make *more* money tend to value monetary and professional status of mates *more* than those who make less money." Second, the Evolutionary Psychologists Michael Wiederman and Elizabeth Allgeier asked 637 female undergraduates and 167 women in two Ohio communities to rate the importance of several characteristics in the selection of a husband, one of which was *good financial prospect.* They also asked them to indicate the annual income they expected to earn in the following year or in the years immediately after finishing college. They found that "the more personal income the women in the sample expected to earn, the more likely they were to value good financial prospects in a mate." Evolutionary Psychologists claim that both results directly contradict the prediction entailed by the structural powerlessness hypothesis and support their evolutionary hypothesis.

But there are a few problems with this claim. First, it's not clear that the structural powerlessness hypothesis in fact entails the prediction tested. The structural powerlessness hypothesis claims only that females will prefer high-income mates under conditions of economic inequality, in which women gain access to economic resources primarily through their mates. One way that a preference for high-income mates could become prevalent among women under such conditions is through "socialization" during formative childhood and teen years. Women could be encouraged by their family members, friends, or other advisors to select high-SES mates (doctors, lawyers, or the like). There is no reason why a preference formed through twenty or so years of such socialization should disappear simply because a woman finds herself earning a good salary. So, the structural powerlessness hypothesis doesn't actually entail that high-paid women will not share a preference for high-SES mates with other women.

Second, it's not at all clear how the data support Evolutionary Psychology's hypothesis. If women have an evolved preference for high-status males, which translates into a preference for high-income males in contemporary societies, they should prefer as high an income as they can get in a mate, regardless of their own income. Evolutionary Psychology's hypothesis doesn't entail that medium-SES women should have lower standards for income in a potential mate than high-SES women.

However, third, if women prefer males in their own socioeconomic group, then medium-SES women will, on average, exhibit a preference for medium-SES males, which will appear as a preference for a moderate ability to provide resources. High-SES women, on the other hand, will exhibit a preference for high-SES men, which will make them appear to desire an even greater ability to provide resources than is desired by medium-SES women. Such preference patterns are precisely those that assortative mating by status should lead us to expect. So, again, the data are unable to demonstrate a female preference for high status per se rather than simple assortative mating by status.

Of course, all the studies so far considered have involved only American female subjects. So perhaps the results of these studies are confounded by status homogamy simply because the studies made use of unrepresentative samples. If so, a much larger, cross-cultural study should be able to provide results that are not confounded by status homogamy.

This larger study would obviously be Buss's cross-cultural study, in which he had his male and female respondents rate the importance of eighteen characteristics in choosing a mate. Respondents used a four-point scale, ranging from 0 (irrelevant or unimportant) to 3 (indispensable). In thirty-six of Buss's thirty-seven samples, females valued the characteristic *good financial prospect* significantly more than did males. In the remaining sample (Spain), females valued it more than males, but the difference was not significant. In the entire study, the average female rating of *good financial prospect* was 1.76 and the average male rating was 1.51. This appears to show that female preference for high-SES mates is not an artifact of unrepresentative American samples, but is in fact a robust universal preference.

Despite the size of Buss's sample, however, and despite the number of cultures sampled, the sample is still not representative in the way that would be needed to distinguish a preference for high SES per se from simple assortative mating by status. As Buss himself admits: "The samples obtained cannot be viewed as representative of the populations in each country. In general, rural, less-educated, and lower levels of socioeconomic status are underrepresented." But these underrepresented groups are precisely those who might, on average, place much less emphasis on earning capacity because of status homogamy. In fact, the preference ratings of these groups could significantly lower the average rating of *good financial prospect* and thereby remove the appearance of a female preference for high-SES mates. For, as we have seen, in samples that are skewed toward the upper half of the socioeconomic continuum, assortative mating by status biases preference ratings in favor of males in the upper half, and against males in the lower half, of the socioeconomic continuum.

Further, the psychologists Alice Eagly and Wendy Wood reanalyzed Buss's data and compared it with transnational data on economic inequality between the sexes gathered by the United Nations. They found that the sex difference in ratings of *good financial prospect* by Buss's subjects was greater in societies with greater economic inequality between the sexes. Where there was less economic inequality between the sexes, the sex difference in ratings of *good financial prospect* was smaller.

If, as I have argued, income is a better predictor of other dimensions of status among males than among females under conditions of economic inequality between the sexes, this is precisely the result we should expect. For, under conditions of strict economic equality between the sexes, income will be as good a predictor of other dimensions of status for one sex as for the other, and the sex difference in emphasis on earning power will disappear. The fact that Eagly and Wood found a correlation between degree of economic inequality across societies and the strength of the sex difference in emphasis on *good financial prospect* is thus fully consistent with assortative mating by status. Therefore, since low-SES groups are strongly underrepresented in Buss's study, and since the sex difference in emphasis placed on *good financial prospect* diminishes as economic inequality between the sexes diminishes, even Buss's study fails to demonstrate a female preference for high-SES mates per se. . . .

Another study sometimes cited by Evolutionary Psychologists as indirect evidence of a female preference for high-status mates was conducted by the sociologist Glen Elder. Published in 1969, Elder's study was based on an "exchange theory" of human mating, according to which women offer what males desire in exchange for the male characteristics they desire. Elder took for granted that males desire youth and attractiveness in a mate and that females desire high status in a mate, so he expected to find very attractive women mated to higher-status men. Among 76 married women he studied, he found a correlation between female attractiveness and husband's status. Indeed, he concluded that very attractive lower-class women were often able to use their attractiveness to "marry up" and secure a high-status husband.

Commenting on this study, Buss says: "High-status men, such as the aging rock stars Rod Stewart and Mick Jagger and the movie stars Warren Beatty and Jack Nicholson, frequently select women two or three decades younger. . . . Men who are high in occupational status are able to marry women who are considerably more physically attractive than are men who are low in occupational status." Presumably, the attractive young women are in very high demand, so the greater ability of high-status men to marry them attests to the fact that women desire them more. Indeed, women with the attractiveness that men desire appear to use it to bag the high-status husbands that every woman wants.

There is, however, a problem with this argument. For Elder's study obtained attractiveness ratings for the female subjects, but not for their husbands. Indeed, the only measure of the husbands' desirability that Elder used was status level. This raises the possibility that Elder's findings were confounded by male physical attractiveness. To test this idea, the sociologists Gillian Stevens, Dawn Owens, and Eric Schaefer analyzed the wedding announcements of 129 couples that appeared in the major daily newspaper of a small city. Each wedding announcement contained information about the education levels and occupations of the bride and groom, plus a wedding photograph. The images of bride and groom in these photographs were separated, so that spouses didn't appear together, and a mixed-sex panel rated each bride and each groom for physical attractiveness. Since all couples were dressed in formal wedding attire in the photographs, differences in attractiveness judgments weren't affected by differences in the everyday attire of the brides and grooms. So there were no "Burger King uniform" effects in the attractiveness judgments.

Stevens and her colleagues found a strong correlation between the attractiveness ratings of spouses. Very attractive females married very attractive males, average-looking females married average-looking males, and unattractive females married unattractive males. Indeed, there was a much stronger correlation between the attractiveness of spouses than between female attractiveness and male social status. They concluded that "physical attractiveness plays a large and an approximately equal role in marriage choices for men and for women." In short, mating is strongly assortative by degree of attractiveness.

Further, a number of independent sociological studies have demonstrated a strong positive correlation between attractiveness and both income level and occupational achievement. Highly attractive people have better jobs and make more money, on average, than do average-looking people, who in turn have better jobs and make more money than people who are judged to be homely. Perhaps contrary to what you'd expect, this effect is even stronger among men than among women. Thus, Elder's finding that higher-status men tended to be married to more attractive women may simply be a by-product of a correlation between high status and high attractiveness among men. Attractive women marry attractive men, who incidentally tend to be more successful than less attractive men. Thus, Elder's study doesn't actually provide the support that Buss claims it does for the idea that women prefer high-status men.

Finally, there is significant evidence from a much larger sample that directly contradicts Evolutionary Psychologists' claim that high-status males enjoy greater mating success (as a result of female preference for high-status males). The sexologists Martin Weinberg and Colin Williams analyzed the data collected by Alfred Kinsey from 5,460 white males in the United States between 1938 and 1963, which remain the most comprehensive data ever collected on sexual behavior. Analyzing sexual behavior by social class of male respondents in the Kinsey data, Weinberg and Williams found a *negative correlation* between social status and mating success (that is, the higher one's social status, the lower one's mating success). They found that low-SES males had coitus at a significantly younger age than high-SES males and that they had more coital partners than high-SES males. The averages, broken down by three social classes, are presented in table 3. Weinberg and Williams subsequently conducted a study, in 1969–1970, of 284 white males, that replicated these findings. . . . These larger, more representative samples present a picture of the

*Table 3*

**Mating Success of Males by Class**

| | Social class | | |
|---|---|---|---|
| | **Low SES** | **Medium SES** | **High SES** |
| Age at first coitus | 17.3 | 17.8 | 20.5 |
| Number of partners | 18.9 | 10.5 | 9.6 |

relation between status and mating success that is directly at odds with Evolutionary Psychology's claim that females preferentially mate with high-status males. Indeed, this evidence seems to indicate that sexual activity is greater among low-status males than among high-status males. *Somebody* must like low-status males. . . .

Although we have long been held captive by a picture in which high-status primate males are the preferred mates of primate females, there are reasons for thinking that the picture has been largely an illusion. If we let go of that picture, we will also let go of the reflexive expectation that the link between male high status and female preference exists in us, too. And, if we let go of that reflexive expectation, we will not be so easily convinced by impoverished evidence that human females prefer high-status males. We will then be able to look at the evidence with eyes unclouded by an antecedent conviction regarding what we'll find. When we do, as I have argued, we will see that there is no convincing evidence of a robust female preference for high-status males. Just as male mate preferences will turn out to be more complex than Evolutionary Psychologists have claimed, female mate preferences will no doubt turn out to be more strongly tied to physical attributes of males (physical attractiveness, bodily symmetry, or chemical signaling of histocompatibility) than Evolutionary Psychologists have claimed. Indeed, evidence of this association is already beginning to accumulate. . . .

# CHALLENGE QUESTIONS

## Does the Research Support Evolutionary Accounts of Female Mating Preferences?

1. Both Buss and Buller are considered to be rigorous scholars who are pro-evolution, and yet each has a different interpretation of the same data. How can we account for this different interpretation, and what does this say about evolutionary psychology?
2. If Buss's research findings on female and male mate preferences are correct, what implications do they have for you and your relationships?
3. Buller argues that many of the findings for an evolved female mate preference could be accounted for by societal influences. How might society influence a person's mate selections?
4. What about lesbian sexual orientation? How might evolution account for same-sex orientation when it does not accommodate reproductive success?
5. Read the sections on the evolution of male mating preferences in Buss's and Buller's books. Do you feel there is an inherent double standard in evolutionary accounts of male and female mate preferences? Why or why not?
6. Evolutionary accounts of human mating assume that male and female mate preferences are determined by reproductive success. If this is true, how might this explain to whom you are attracted and whom you choose to date or marry?

# Internet References . . .

## The Seville Statement on Violence

The United Nations Educational, Scientific, and Cultural Organization (UNESCO) drafted a statement regarding violence in 1986 known as the Seville Statement on Violence. This link provides that statement.

**http://portal.unesco.org/education/en/ev.php-URL_ID=3247&URL_DO=DO_TOPIC&URL_SECTION=201.html**

## The Differences Between Men and Women

This site provides a statement prepared by the Relationship Institute regarding the differences between men and women.

**http://www.relationship-institute.com/freearticles_detail.cfm?article_ID=151**

## The National Center for Learning Disabilities

This site provides information, research, methods, and forums for parents and educators of children with learning disabilities.

**www.ncld.org**

# UNIT 2

# Biological Issues

*No behavioral or mental activity can occur without one's body. Many psychologists view our bodies and our biological processes as fundamental to all human activities including emotion, perception, communication, sexuality, and mental health. However, does this fundamental role of the body mean that it is the sole cause of our behaviors and our minds? Do biological differences determine behavioral differences, such as sex determining the differences in male and female communication styles? Does the development of our bodies influence our most important emotions and behaviors, such as love and attraction? Can all of our behaviors ultimately be explained by natural biological processes, such as evolution and natural selection? If so, what does this mean for our conceptions of human morality and agency? Many researchers believe that matter (biology) is all that matters, as evidenced by the growth in the field of neuroscience. Are there other factors, such as culture and spirituality, that also matter?*

# ISSUE 4

## Are Gender Differences in Communication Biologically Determined?

**YES: Louann Brizendine,** from *The Female Brain* (Morgan Road Books, 2006)

**NO: Brenda J. Allen,** from *Difference Matters: Communicating Social Identity* (Waveland Press, 2004)

### ISSUE SUMMARY

**YES:** Physician Louann Brizendine argues that gender differences in communication are the necessary result of "hard wired" differences in female and male brains.

**NO:** Professor of Communications Brenda J. Allen contends that communication differences between genders are the result of social and contextual influences and that changing these influences could change communication styles.

Scholars and social critics have long recognized that men and women generally tend to communicate differently. Women, for example, are generally recognized to be more verbal than men. Women seem to have more words at their disposal than men, and they often speak more quickly than men. Likewise, men tend to prioritize the "facts" in their communications, whereas women frequently evidence more awareness of their relationships in their communications with others. Why do men and women communicate so differently? What is the origin of these disparities?

These questions have generally taken researchers in two dissimilar directions—biological explanations and sociocultural explanations. The first approach argues that the physiological and neurological discrepancies of men and women lead to communication differences. This biological position is generally viewed as a type of "hard determinism," because men and women are thought to be determined (with no choice in the matter) to take on communication styles because of the "hard wiring" of their brains. Conversely, the second approach argues that gender disparities in communication are the result of social forces that shape the way males and females experience the world, including their linguistic experience of the world. This approach can be less deterministic than the biological approach, because it can include the possibility that people can choose to respond differently to these social forces, and perhaps even change them.

In the first article, physician Louann Brizendine argues for the biological explanation of gender dissimilarities in communication. Brizendine explains that recent neurological research has revealed that "the female brain is so deeply affected by hormones that their influence can be said to create a woman's reality." According to Brizendine, hormonal differences *in utero* lead to greater growth in the communication and emotional processing centers of women's brains and to greater growth in the sex and aggression centers of men's brains. These brain variations, Brizendine contends, lead women to be more acutely attuned to emotional and relational cues and to be more verbally expressive than men, while sex and aggression brain centers leave men at a linguistic disadvantage to their female counterparts.

In the second article, communications expert Brenda J. Allen argues that gender differences in communication are the result of social and contextual influences. She contends that communication styles are rooted in our "social identities"—"aspects of a person's self-image derived from the social categories to which an individual perceives herself/himself as belonging." According to Allen, "we learn communication styles and rules based upon our membership in certain groups, and we communicate with other people based upon how we have been socialized about ourselves and about them." Allen describes how the social identities of men and women are based on differing power dynamics and how this leads to differing patterns of communication. She warns against attributing these communication disparities to already determined physiological differences, arguing that such an attribution masks the real possibility of moving toward greater equality in communication styles across gender.

**POINT**

- Communication differences are due primarily to neurological differences.
- Women are "programmed" to seek out social harmony and thus use language that prioritizes such harmony.
- Neurological differences between men and women give women a verbal advantage over men.
- Women and men should accept and understand their differences so that they can accommodate one another's inborn communication styles.

**COUNTER POINT**

- Communication differences are due primarily to the way boys and girls are socialized to conform to cultural traditions.
- Women are socialized to be more nurturing and relational in their communication style, compared to the more competitive and instrumental style of men.
- Women communicate in ways that reflect their social disadvantage, whereas men's language reflects their own social advantage.
- We can and should change our communication styles and the power dynamics they imply, moving toward greater gender equality.

YES  **Louann Brizendine**

# The Female Brain

## What Makes Us Women

More than 99 percent of male and female genetic coding is exactly the same. Out of the thirty thousand genes in the human genome, the less than one percent variation between the sexes is small. But that percentage difference influences every single cell in our bodies—from the nerves that register pleasure and pain to the neurons that transmit perception, thoughts, feelings, and emotions.

To the observing eye, the brains of females and males are not the same. Male brains are larger by about 9 percent, even after correcting for body size. In the nineteenth century, scientists took this to mean that women had less mental capacity than men. Women and men, however, have the same number of brain cells. The cells are just packed more densely in women—cinched corsetlike into a smaller skull.

For much of the twentieth century, most scientists assumed that women were essentially small men, neurologically and in every other sense except for their reproductive functions. That assumption has been at the heart of enduring misunderstandings about female psychology and physiology. When you look a little deeper into the brain differences, they reveal what makes women women and men men.

Until the 1990s, researchers paid little attention to female physiology, neuroanatomy, or psychology separate from that of men. . . .

The little research that was available, however, suggested that the brain differences, though subtle, were profound. . . .

What we've found is that the female brain is so deeply affected by hormones that their influence can be said to create a woman's reality. They can shape a woman's values and desires, and tell her, day to day, what's important. Their presence is felt at every stage of life, right from birth. Each hormone state—girlhood, the adolescent years, the dating years, motherhood, and menopause—acts as fertilizer for different neurological connections that are responsible for new thoughts, emotions, and interests. Because of the fluctuations that begin as early as three months old and last until after menopause, a woman's neurological reality is not as constant as a man's. His is like a mountain that is worn away imperceptibly over the millennia by glaciers, weather, and the deep tectonic movements of the earth. Hers is more like the weather itself—constantly changing and hard to predict.

New brain science has rapidly transformed our view of basic neurological differences between men and women. . . .

As a result, scientists have documented an astonishing array of structural, chemical, genetic, hormonal, and functional brain differences between women and men. We've learned that men and women have different brain sensitivities to stress and conflict. They use different brain areas and circuits to solve problems, process language, experience and store the same strong emotion. Women may remember the smallest details of their first dates, and their biggest fights, while their husbands barely remember that these things happened. Brain structure and chemistry have everything to do with why this is so.

The female and male brains process stimuli, hear, see, "sense," and gauge what others are feeling in different ways. Our distinct female and male brain operating systems are mostly compatible and adept, but they perform and accomplish the same goals and tasks using different circuits. . . .

Until eight weeks old, every fetal brain looks female—female is nature's default gender setting. . . . A huge testosterone surge beginning in the eighth week will turn this unisex brain male by killing off some cells in the communication centers and growing more cells in the sex and aggression centers. If the testosterone surge doesn't happen, the female brain continues to grow unperturbed. The fetal girl's brain cells sprout more connections in the communication centers and areas that process emotion. How does this fetal fork in the road affect us? For one thing, because of her larger communication center, this girl will grow up to be more talkative than her brother. Men use about seven thousand words per day. Women use about twenty thousand. For another, it defines our innate biological destiny, coloring the lens through which each of us views and engages the world. . . .

Baby girls are born interested in emotional expression. They take meaning about themselves from a look, a touch, every reaction from the people they come into contact with. From these cues they discover whether they are worthy, lovable, or annoying. But take away the sign-posts that an expressive face provides and you've taken away the female brain's main touchstone for reality. . . .

## Don't Fight

So why is a girl born with such a highly tuned machine for reading faces, hearing emotional tones in voices, and responding to unspoken cues in others? Think about it. A machine like that is built for connection. That's the main job of the girl brain, and that's what it drives a female to do from birth. This is the result of millennia of genetic and evolutionary hardwiring that once had—and probably still has—real consequences for survival. If you can read faces and voices, you can tell what an infant needs. You can predict what a bigger, more aggressive male is going to do. And since you're smaller, you probably need to band with other females to fend off attacks from a ticked off caveman—or cavemen.

If you're a girl, you've been programmed to make sure you keep social harmony. This is a matter of life and death to the brain, even if it's not so important in the twenty-first century. . . .

Typical non-testosteronized, estrogen-ruled girls are very invested in preserving harmonious relationships. From their earliest days, they live most comfortably and happily in the realm of peaceful interpersonal connections. They prefer to avoid conflict because discord puts them at odds with their urge to stay connected, to gain approval and nurture. The twenty-four-month estrogen bath of girls' infantile puberty reinforces the impulse to make social bonds based on communication and compromise. . . .

It is the brain that sets up the speech differences—the genderlects—of small children, which Deborah Tannen has pointed out. She noted that in studies of the speech of two-to-five-year-olds, girls usually make collaborative proposals by starting their sentences with "let's"—as in "Let's play house." Girls, in fact, typically use language to get consensus, influencing others without telling them directly what to do. . . .

Boys know how to employ this affiliative speech style, too, but research shows they typically don't use it. Instead, they'll generally use language to command others, get things done, brag, threaten, ignore a partner's suggestion, and override each other's attempts to speak. . . .

The testosterone-formed boy brain simply doesn't look for social connection in the same way a girl brain does. In fact, disorders that inhibit people from picking up on social nuance—called autism spectrum disorders and Asperger's syndrome—are eight times more common in boys. Scientists now believe that the typical male brain, with only one dose of X chromosome (there are two X's in a girl), gets flooded with testosterone during development and somehow becomes more easily socially handicapped. Extra testosterone in people with these disorders may be killing off some of the brain's circuits for emotional and social sensitivity.

By age two and a half, infantile puberty ends and a girl enters the calmer pastures of the juvenile pause. The estrogen stream coming from the ovaries has been temporarily stopped; how, we don't yet know. But we do know that the levels of estrogen and testosterone become very low during the childhood years in both boys and girls—although girls still have six to eight times more estrogen than boys. When women talk about "the girl they left behind," this is the stage they are usually referring to. This is the quiet period before the full-volume rock 'n' roll of puberty. It's the time when a girl is devoted to her best friend, when she doesn't usually enjoy playing with boys. Research shows that this is true for girls between the ages of two and six in every culture that's been studied. . . .

Many women find biological comfort in one another's company, and language is the glue that connects one female to another. No surprise, then, that some verbal areas of the brain are larger in women than in men and that women, on average, talk and listen a lot more than men. The numbers vary, but on average girls speak two to three times more words per day than boys. We know that young girls speak earlier and by the age of twenty months have double or triple the number of words in their vocabularies than do boys. Boys eventually catch up in their vocabulary but not in speed. Girls speak faster on average—250 words per minute versus 125 for typical males. Men haven't always appreciated that verbal edge. In Colonial America, women were put in the town stocks with wooden clips on their tongues or tortured by the "dunking stool," held underwater and almost drowned—punishments that were never imposed on men—for the crime of "talking too much". . . .

And why do girls go to the bathroom to talk? Why do they spend so much time on the phone with the door closed? They're trading secrets and gossiping to create connection and intimacy with their female peers. They're developing close-knit cliques with secret rules. In these new groups, talking, telling secrets, and gossiping, in fact, often become girls' favorite activities—their tools to navigate and ease the ups and downs and stresses of life. . . .

There is a biological reason for this behavior. Connecting through talking activates the pleasure centers in a girl's brain. Sharing secrets that have romantic and sexual implications activates those centers even more. We're not talking about a small amount of pleasure. This is huge. It's a major dopamine and oxytocin rush, which is the biggest, fattest neurological reward you can get outside of an orgasm. Dopamine is a neurochemical that stimulates the motivation and pleasure circuits in the brain. Estrogen at puberty increases dopamine and oxytocin production in girls. Oxytocin is a neurohormone that triggers and is triggered by intimacy. When estrogen is on the rise, a teen girl's brain is pushed to make even more oxytocin—and to get even more reinforcement for social bonding. At midcycle, during peak estrogen production, the girl's dopamine and oxytocin level is likely at its highest, too. Not only her verbal output is at its maximum but her urge for intimacy is also peaking. Intimacy releases more oxytocin, which reinforces the desire to connect, and connecting then brings a sense of pleasure and well-being. . . .

## Why the Teen Girl Brain Freaks

Think about it. Your brain has been pretty stable. You've had a steady flow—or lack—of hormones for your entire life. One day you're having tea parties with Mommy, the next day you're calling her an asshole. And, as a teen girl, the last thing you want to do is create conflict. You used to feel like a nice girl, and now, out of nowhere, it's as though you can't rely on that personality anymore. Everything you thought you knew about yourself has suddenly come undone. It's a huge gash in a girl's self-esteem, but it's a pretty simple chemical reaction, even for an adult woman. It makes a difference if you know what's going on. . . .

Studies show that when a conflict or argument breaks out in a game, girls typically decide to stop playing to avoid any angry exchange, while boys generally continue to play intensely—jockeying for position, competing, and arguing hour after hour about who'll be the boss or who will get access to the coveted toy. If a woman is pushed over the edge by finding out that her husband is having an affair, or if her child is in danger, her anger will blast right through and she will go to the mat. Otherwise, she will avoid anger or confrontation the same way a man will avoid an emotion.

Girls and women may not always feel the initial intense blast of anger directly from the amygdale that men feel. . . . Women talk to others first when they are angry at a third person. But scientists speculate that though a woman is slower to act out of anger, once her faster verbal circuits get going, they can cause her to unleash a barrage of angry words that a man can't match. Typical men speak fewer words and have less verbal fluency than women, so they may be handicapped in angry exchanges with women. Men's brain circuits and bodies may readily revert to a physical expression of anger fueled by the frustration of not being able to match women's words.

Often when I see a couple who are not communicating well, the problem is that the man's brain circuits push him frequently and quickly to an angry, aggressive reaction, and the woman feels frightened and shuts down. Ancient wiring is telling her it's dangerous, but she anticipates that if she flees she'll be losing her provider and may have to fend for herself. If a couple remains locked in this Stone Age conflict, there is no chance for resolution. Helping my patients understand that the emotion circuits for anger and safety are differences in the male and female brains is often quite helpful.

**Brenda J. Allen**

# Difference Matters: Communicating Social Identity

## Communicating Social Identity

Our study of difference (and similarity!) centers on communication. I use the verb form, communicating, to represent the dynamic nature of processes that humans use to produce, interpret, and share meaning. Our study of communicating views these processes as constitutive of social reality. To see how communicating helps to create reality, we will explore various relationships between social identity and discourse. *Discourse* refers to "systems of texts and talk that range from public to private and from naturally occurring to mediated forms. . . ."

Scholars from disciplines such as sociology, psychology, communication, anthropology, and philosophy study identity as an individual and/or a collective aspect of being. As sociologists Judith Howard and Ramira Alamilla observe, identity is based not only on responses to the question "Who am I?" but also on responses to the question "Who am I in relation to others?" Our exploration of difference matters focuses on ***social identity,*** aspects of a person's self-image derived from the social categories to which an individual perceives herself/himself as belonging. Most human beings divide their social worlds into groups, and categorize themselves into some of those groups. In addition, we become aware of other social groups to which we do not belong, and we compare ourselves to them. We often define ourselves in opposition to others: "I know who I am because I am not you." Thus, social identity refers to "the ways in which individuals and collectivities are distinguished in their social relations with other individuals and collectivities."

Because social identity stems from perceptions of social group membership, social identity is somewhat distinct from personal identity, which encompasses the conception of the self in terms of variables such as personality traits. For instance, a person may be characterized as "shy" or "outgoing." However, "a person's self actually consists of a personal identity and multiple social identities, each of which is linked to different social groups."

An individual can "belong" to numerous social identity groups. I self-identify as: professor, black, woman, homeowner, U.S. citizen, baby boomer, middle-class, and volunteer. Although infinite possibilities exist for categories of social identity groups, I focus on six that are especially significant in contemporary society: gender, race, social class, ability, sexuality, and age. Nationality and religion also are important aspects of identity. . . .

Central are the interconnected ideas that all identity is relational, and that human beings develop their social identities primarily through communicating. This perspective represents the ***social constructionist*** school of thought, which contends that "self is socially constructed through various relational and linguistic processes." In other words, "our identity arises out of interactions with other people and is based on language." Let's look at how communication helps to construct social identity.

From the time we are born (and even prior to birth, due to tests that determine a baby's sex or congenital defects), socially constructed categories of identity influence how others interact with us (and vice versa), and how we perceive ourselves. When a child is born, what do people usually want to know? Generally, they ask if "it" is a boy or a girl. Why is the sex of the child so important? Sex matters because it cues people on how to treat the baby. If the newborn is a girl, relatives and friends may buy her pink, frilly clothes and toys designated for girls. Her parent(s) or guardian(s) may decorate her room (if she's fortunate enough to have her own room) or sleep area in "feminine" colors and artifacts, or she may share a room with other family members. These actions and others will help to "create a gendered world which the infant gradually encounters and takes for granted as her social consciousness dawns, and which structures the responses to her of others."

And that's just the beginning. As she develops, she will receive messages from multiple sources, including family members, teachers, peers, and the media about what girls are allowed and supposed to do (as contrasted with boys). This process is known as ***socialization***. . . .

The same scenario applies for a male child. He too will receive numerous messages, blatant and subtle, that will mold his self-perception. Simultaneously, both female and male children will learn about additional identity categories like race, class, and ability. What they learn may vary depending on their identity composites. For instance, a white Jewish boy in a middle-class family probably will be socialized differently than a Latino Catholic in a working-class family, even as they each may receive similar messages about being male. Meanwhile, as both males receive comparable lessons about masculinity, a nondisabled Asian-American boy will probably receive different messages than a white boy labeled as "developmentally challenged." These individuals also will learn communication styles particular to their groups, such as vocabulary, gestures, eye contact, and use of personal space.

As these children become indoctrinated into social identity groups, they will receive information about other groups, including contrasts between groups, and "rules" for interacting (or not) with members of other groups. They will be exposed to stereotypes about groups, and they may accept these stereotypes as facts. They also will learn about hierarchies of identity. They may learn that being young is more desirable than being elderly, or that being heterosexual is preferable to being gay. These and other "lessons" about distinctions between and within groups will recur throughout their lives.

Due to socialization, children will accept social identity categories as real and natural designations. Yet, they are not. Historically, persons in power have constructed categories and developed hierarchies based on characteristics of groups. For example, in 1795 a German scientist named Johann Blumenbach constructed a system of racial classification that arranged people according to geographical location and physical features. He also ranked the groups in hierarchical order, placing Caucasians in the most superior position.

Although scientists have since concluded that race is not related to capability, many societies in the world still adhere to various racial classification systems because the idea of race has become essentialized. ***Essentialism*** refers to assumptions that social differences stem from intrinsic, innate, human variations unrelated to social forces. For example, so-called racial groups are viewed as if they have an "ultimate essence that transcends historical and cultural boundaries.

Thus, while we accept social identity groups as real and natural, we also perceive them as fixed (essentialized) and unchanging. However, not only are such categories artificial, but they also are subject to change. In different times and different places, categories we take for granted either did/do not exist or they were/are quite unlike the ones that we reference in the United States in the twenty-first century. Currently, the same person identified as black in the United States may be considered white in the Dominican Republic; in the nineteenth century choices for racial designations in the United States included gradations of enslaved blacks (mulattos were one-half black, quadroons were one-quarter black, and octoroons were one-eighth black). . . .

The tendency to compartmentalize humans according to physical characteristics is logical because "labels can be helpful devices used to identify people." If we did not have labels to distinguish groups of items that are similar, we would have to create and remember a separate "name" for everything and everyone. What a pain that would be! Therefore, it makes sense that we use cues like skin color, facial features, body parts, and so forth to distinguish and group people.

However, problems can arise when people assign meaning to previously neutral descriptors. They may use categories not only to distinguish, but also to discriminate and dominate. Categorizing can lead to in-group/out-group distinctions that may negatively affect intergroup interactions. For instance, ***social identity theory*** (SIT) describes humans' tendency to label self and others based on individual and group identity. This theory contends that members of social identity groups constantly compare their group with others, and they tend "to seek positive distinctiveness for one's own group." When an individual perceives someone else to be a member of an out-group, that person will tend to react more to perceived *group* characteristics than to the other person *as an individual.* Stereotypes and prejudice occur more frequently in this scenario. In contrast, stereotypes and prejudice are less likely when a communicator views another person as an individual, especially when both persons belong to the same social identity group(s).

[I]ndividuals often use identity markers like skin color to develop hierarchies. Moreover, many people accept and reinforce such hierarchies as natural and normal. Organizational communication scholars explain: "As people *internalize* the values and assumptions of their societies they also internalize its class, race, gender, and ethnicity-based hierarchical relationships." One consequence of these perceptions is the social construction of inequality, which results in favoritism and privilege for some groups and disadvantage for others. . . .

Privilege is a key concept in understanding how difference matters. ***Privilege*** refers to advantaged status based upon social identity. Sociologist Peggy McIntosh coined this term to refer to men's advantages in society, based upon her experiences teaching women's studies. McIntosh noticed that while men in her classes were willing to concede women's disadvantages, they were unaware of advantages they enjoyed simply because they were men. She later extended her analysis to encompass race, and she developed the concept of white privilege. . . .

Privilege tends to "make life easier; it is easier to get around, to get what one wants, and to be treated in an acceptable manner." On the Public Broadcasting System's video *People Like Us,* which explores social class in the United States, a white male plumber describes how sales clerks tend to treat men in suits better than they respond to him when he wears his work clothes. Similarly, a working-class college student reported that he would change out of his work clothes before going to campus because he felt that faculty and staff treated him less favorably when he wore them. . . .

Opposing standpoints of privileged and nonprivileged persons can negatively impact interactions. A person who is not privileged (or who does not feel privileged) may seem hypersensitive to an individual who is privileged. In contrast, the person who is privileged (or whom the other person perceives to be privileged) may seem totally insensitive. Privileged individuals sometimes diminish, dismiss, or discount experiences of others who are not advantaged. If a privileged person witnesses an incident in which a less privileged person is demeaned or humiliated, she or he may characterize it as exceptional rather than routine and may assess the less-privileged person's complaints about this type of treatment as an overreaction or misinterpretation of the situation. . . .

Most individuals simultaneously occupy privileged and nonprivileged social identity groups. Although I may experience discrimination based upon my race and/or gender, I also reap benefits associated with being heterosexual, nondisabled, and middle-class. We will consider the concept of privilege and its complexities as we study gender, race, class, ability, sexuality, and age.

In addition to constructing inequality, another consequence of internalizing dominant values and assumptions about social identity groups is that members of nondominant groups often help to perpetuate hierarchies because they believe that their group is inferior and that the dominant group is superior. Accepting these ideas and believing negative stereotypes about one's group is known as ***internalized oppression***. . . .

To summarize, social identities are created in context; they emerge mainly from social interactions. We learn communication styles and rules based upon our membership in certain groups, and we communicate with other people based upon how we have been socialized about ourselves and about them. We learn who we are and who we might become through interaction with others, within a variety of social contexts, from a variety of sources. These sources also give us information about other groups. To every interaction, we bring preconceptions and expectations about social identities that can affect what, how, when, why, and whether or not we communicate. Most of these interactions occur "within prevailing normative and structural circumstances. . . ."

## Power Dynamics and Gender

Although scholars have studied gender and communication for over fifty years, academic and popular writing on the topic has surged in the past two decades. Two recurring topics that reveal power dynamics are sexist language and gender differences in styles of communicating.

### Language

As communication scholars Diana Ivy and Phil Backlund observe, "English is a patriarchal language." However, as they also note, we did not invent this male-dominated language; we inherited it. Therefore, referring to English as patriarchal and sexist is not an indictment against those of us (men and women) who use it: "It's nobody's fault (nobody alive anyway) that we have a language that favors one sex over the other, but it's also not something that we 'just have to live with.'" As I share examples of the sexist nature of English, I hope you will reflect on how you might avoid them.

Language reflects patriarchy and sexism in numerous ways. Some of these are subtle; others are blatant. A prevalent example is the use of generic masculine pronouns. Although proponents of "he," "him," or "his" contend that these terms are neutral and inclusive of women and men, research indicates that exclusive masculine pronoun usage helps to maintain sex-biased perceptions and shape attitudes about appropriateness of careers for women or men. Such usage also helps to perpetuate a gender hierarchy. One compelling example is the volume of derogatory words in English for women with a smaller number of such terms for men. Among negative synonyms for women/girls and for men/boys, many have sexual denotations or connotations. Moreover, pejorative terms for men/boys often are feminine.

A gender hierarchy also is implied in gendered pairs of words such as "old maid" and "bachelor." Additional examples include gendered titles such as Mrs., Ms., Miss, and Mr., which differentiate women according to marital status, but not men. Man-linked terminology such as "mankind," "foreman," "man-hours" and feminine suffixes (-ette, -ess, -enne) are other examples. These uses of language help to inculcate the idea that men are more valuable than women.

Linguistic practices also reveal patriarchy. For instance, in everyday talk and writing, communicators usually place masculine words prior to feminine words. Consider the following phrases: "boys and girls," "he or she," "his and hers," "husband and wife," and "masculine and feminine." While writing this book, I found myself routinely enacting that norm. To resist this tendency, I conscientiously placed the feminine in the first position. Exceptions to this rule include "ladies and gentlemen," "bride and groom," and "mom and dad." Why do you think these are exceptions? They may reflect patriarchal expectations about gender roles. For example, in writing or speaking contexts, placing "mom" before "dad" may emphasize the female's parental role. Although these and similar uses of language may seem trivial, they reflect deep structures of power that most people do not even realize exist.

## Communication Styles

Another stream of research investigates differences in women's and men's communication styles. Rarely do such studies assess similarities between women's and men's communication. This body of research studies sex/gender differences in: (1) communication styles, and (2) perceptions about the function of communication.

A recurring depiction of women's speech as tentative encompasses several patterns. Women sometimes use tag questions such as "isn't that right?" or "don't you think?" Or, they employ question intonation in declarative contexts; that is, they say a statement as if it were a question and as if seeking approval. Other examples of speech styles frequently used by women include hesitation forms such as "um" or "like"; overuse of polite forms; and the frequent use of qualifiers and intensifiers like "sort of," "rather," "very," and "really." Some communicators overuse these ways of speaking to the extent that listeners may not take them seriously.

Rather than view these deferential differences in speech styles as gender-based, some scholars refer to them as "powerless" speech styles that anyone can employ. Although women tend to use powerless language more frequently than men, other users include poorly educated or lower status individuals. Thus, some linguists argue that this speech style is related more to women's relatively powerless position in society rather than to essentialist characteristics of females. Experimental courtroom research found that jurors and judges were less likely to view powerless speakers, regardless of gender, as credible.

Results of research on functions of communication tend to correspond with the femininity/masculinity clusters (nurturing-expressive/instrumental-active). For example, Ivy and Backlund offer a "relational/content" differentiation: "We believe that men approach conversation more with the intent of imparting information (the content aspect) than to convey cues about the relationship (the relational aspect)."

Sociolinguist Deborah Tannen offers similar perspectives on gender differences in her influential book entitled *You Just Don't Understand.* Tannen labels female communication style "rapport," meaning that women establish connections and negotiate relationships. In contrast, she terms the male style of communication "report," to indicate men's need to preserve independence and to impart information.

Communication differences between women and men may be due to socialization processes, including the proliferation of literature that asserts such differences. Men tend to be socialized to use language that is valued, while the opposite usually occurs for women. Several research conclusions support this claim: men tend to talk about their accomplishments using comparative and competitive terms, while women may understate their contributions and acknowledge others' assistance. Women often are more relational and dialogic; men tend to be more competitive and monologic. Women tend to provide support work in interaction. They offer verbal and nonverbal encouragement, such as nodding or smiling, ask questions returning to points made by earlier speakers, and attempt to bring others into the conversation.

Communication scholars Daniel Canary and Kimberley Hause criticize research on sex differences in communication for relying on and perpetuating sex stereotypes, using invalid measures of gender, a dearth of theory, and a tendency to polarize the sexes. In a meta-analysis of communication studies, they conclude, "given this research, we should *not* expect to find substantial sex differences in communication" (emphasis added). Indeed, they did not. Communication scholars Daena Goldsmith and Patricia Fulfs draw a similar conclusion in a refutation of Tannen's claims about gender differences. From their analysis of Tannen's evidence, they report that communication differences between women and men are typically minimal and are contingent upon situational factors. They conclude that differences tend to be nonverbal rather than verbal. Basically, they assert that women's and men's communication behaviors are more similar than different.

Some scholars critique researchers' propensity to denote females and males as a dualism with each embodying clear-cut, uniform characteristics. Rather than assuming a "two worlds" approach to gender interaction, they advocate research that explores different forms of femininity and masculinity. For instance, Deborah Cameron problematizes the tendency to homogenize women's and men's communication behaviors. She asserts a need in gender studies of language to consider contextual factors such as setting, purpose of communication, and relationship between communicators, as well as complex facets of communicators themselves.

Researchers have attended to both context and complexity of gendered communication. Some studies found that women and men behave differently according to context. These projects indicate differences among women or among men, instead of concentrating on differences between women and men. Men in all-male groups such as sports teams or in combat situations may exhibit caring characteristics that usually are attributed to women. Women in positions of authority often are more assertive than those who are in powerless jobs. Finally, the significance of context and complexity is evident in a volume of research projects about black women across a variety of contexts, including contemporary university students, nineteenth-century "club women" who worked for the social uplift of black people, and female hip-hop artists. The diverse perspectives shown in this collection underscore the need to consider intersections of social identity, rather than focusing only on one. . . .

## Social Identities Are Social Constructions

Humans create schemes to classify groups of people based on characteristics such as skin color and perceived ability. These classifications designate social identity categories that we may assume to be natural and permanent.

However, social identity categories are artificial and subject to change. Meanings and classifications of gender, race, class, ability, sexuality, and age have varied throughout history. Classifications of these groups always are products of their times, as humans engage in social processes to manufacture differences, conclude that some differences are more important than others, and assign particular meanings to those differences.

We do not have to accept traditional notions that social identity groups are natural and unchangeable. We can change our beliefs and behaviors regarding social identity groups. For example, we can imagine and enact alternative meanings of our own social identities. We can affirm our "humanity as free agents with a capacity to create, to construct, to wonder, and to venture. . . ."

It seems ironic that although the United States is defined as an individualist culture, people rarely seem to behave as individuals. Even though we are relatively free to choose how we enact identity, we usually are predictable. We tend to choose occupations, clothing, food, music, recreational activities, and so forth, based on the social identity groups to which we "belong." We often seem to make decisions based on group identity rather than considering our options.

I encourage you to make conscientious choices rather than be a puppet or a parrot. Snip the invisible strings that control your behaviors. Rewrite the scripts that tell you what to say in certain situations. Resist the pressure to conform to societal expectations about the social identity groups you belong to. Remember that your attitudes and actions help to create who you are.

## Power Matters

Across history, humans have enacted power relations to construct social identity classifications. Authoritative sources such as those from science, politics, medicine, religion, the media, and so forth use dominant belief systems to create and disseminate hierarchies of human differences. Most people take for granted these hierarchies and the ideologies that undergird them. Persons in positions of privilege tend to reap the benefits of these hierarchies and their consequences, while people categorized in lower levels of classification systems are more likely to be disadvantaged.

However, throughout the history of the United States, some members of nondominant and dominant groups have challenged ideological systems that discriminate against certain groups and favor others. Advocates for change have initiated social movements, campaigned for laws, developed social and economic programs, and engaged in other actions to challenge the status quo. Countless individuals have endeavored to achieve freedom and equality for everyone in the United States.

Once you realize that dominant ideologies underlie beliefs and behaviors related to difference, that you and others have been socialized to believe many ideas about matters of difference, and recognize the power of socialization and the persistence of dominant ideologies, you can make a conscious decision to contest forces that compel humans to comply with unjust dominant belief systems.

## Communication Rules!

Humans use communication to construct social identities. Communication comprises discourse and discursive practices that produce, interpret, and share meaning about social identity groups. Through communication, we develop and disseminate classifications and hierarchies of gender, race, class, sexuality, ability, and age. We create labels, ascribe meaning to them, and use them to refer to one another. And, we use communication to co-create and re-create our identities as we interact with one another. A significant proportion of these interactions occurs in the various organizations that pervade our lives.

Socialization practices, which are primarily communicative, teach us about in-groups and out-groups. We inherit meanings about social identity groups from our families, peers, the media, teachers, and other sources, and we accept those meanings as our own. We use communication to create and consume media reports about social identity groups and media portrayals (factual and fictitious) of social identity groups. Many, if not most, of these reports and portrayals reinforce dominant ideologies and stereotypes.

Even as communication can reinforce dominant meanings of difference, communication can facilitate social change. For instance, the media sometimes offer alternative narratives, depictions, and information that challenge mainstream conceptions of social identity groups. In addition, advocacy groups use communication to develop and distribute information, engage in marches and rallies, and construct symbols to represent and advance their causes. Groups that oppose social change also employ these communication processes. Thus, communication can impede or facilitate progress toward equal opportunity for life, liberty, and the pursuit of happiness for everyone in the United States. Therefore, communication is central to applying what you have learned.

To summarize how to apply what you learned: appreciate and value difference, contest and re-imagine conceptions of social identities, assume agency, and acknowledge the power of communication.

# CHALLENGE QUESTIONS

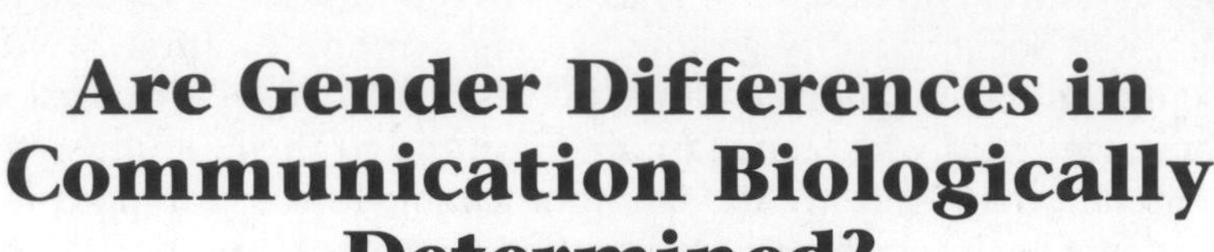

## Are Gender Differences in Communication Biologically Determined?

1. Brizendine suggests that gender differences in communication are "hard wired" in the brain, implying that these differences are inevitably determined by biology. Conversely, Allen argues that these gender differences are the result of social processes that are subject to human agency—i.e., we can choose other communication patterns. Based on the evidence that each chapter provides, do you believe that such gender differences are necessarily determined by our biology or do you believe that these differences are subject to human agency?
2. Both authors discuss advantages and disadvantages that each gender enjoys because of its respective communication style. Do you find any of these advantages or disadvantages problematic? Why or why not? If so, what might we do to correct these problems?
3. Are Brizendine's claims of biological determinism incompatible with Allen's claims of social and self determinism? In other words, can we be hard wired to behave in a certain way and at the same time have agency that affords us the ability to do otherwise from what we do? If the two approaches are compatible, how so? If not, in what ways might they be adjusted to account for both the biological and the social/agentic?
4. These authors tend to favor either nature (biological explanations) or nurture (sociocultural explanations). How might an "interaction" between nature and nurture explain these communications differences, where natural and nurtural factors are both involved as necessary conditions to the differences?

# ISSUE 5

## Is Homosexuality Biologically Based?

**YES: Qazi Rahman**, from "The Neurodevelopment of Human Sexual Orientation." *Neuroscience & Biobehavioral Reviews* (October 2005)

**NO: Stanton L. Jones and Alex W. Kwee**, from "Scientific Research, Homosexuality, and the Church's Moral Debate: An Update," *Journal of Psychology and Christianity* (Winter 2005)

### ISSUE SUMMARY

**YES:** Professor of Psychobiology Qazi Rahman claims that the current research on the biology of homosexuality supports prenatal biological determination and refutes learning models of sexual orientation

**NO:** Professor of Psychology Stanton L. Jones and Clinical Psychologist Alex W. Kwee claim the current research on the biology of homosexuality provides no firm evidence for biological causation and leaves room for learning models of sexual orientation.

Many of the so-called "culture wars" in the United States have been fought over the issue of homosexuality. On one side of this "war" are those who claim that homosexuality is a moral issue, perhaps even a "sin." Yet, for this to be a moral issue, homosexuals would have to have some measure of control over or even a choice of their sexual orientation. Do they have such control? If this orientation is biologically determined, whether at birth or later, the control or choice necessary for sexual preference to be a "moral issue" would seem to be unavailable. If, on the other hand, homosexuals have made choices that lead them learn to "prefer" (chose) a certain type of sexual orientation, then a moral understanding of homosexuality could be justified.

Only relatively recently have psychologists and neuroscientists begun to conduct scientific research to address these issues. One of the earliest of these researchers, neuroscientist Simon LeVay, a self-declared gay person, found dramatic brain differences between gay and straight men. This investigation led many to speculate that sexual orientation was completely biological. Indeed, other scientific findings have been reported, especially as sensationalized by the media, that would seem to have confirmed this speculation. Do we now have enough evidence to conclude that homosexuality is completely biologically based? Can we omit the role of learning factors in homosexuality all together?

One of the foremost researchers in this area, Dr. Qazi Rahman, answers these questions in the first article by reviewing research on the neurodevelopment of human sexual orientation. He claims the research supports the proposal that homosexuality is biologically determined, even before birth. In support of his claim he cites evidence from twin-studies, genetic scanning, brain structure studies, and the fraternal birth order effect. He even refutes the idea that learning plays a role in the development of homosexuality by arguing that the theories which attempt to explain sexual orientation through cultural socialization, either by authority figures or peers, are simply "not supported."

In the second selection, on the other hand, noted psychologists Stanton Jones and Alex Kwee review much of the same research on the biology of homosexuality but come to very different conclusions. In discussing relevant twin studies, for example, they point to methodological weaknesses and side with one of the original studies' researchers that there is "no statistically significant indication of genetic influence on sexual orientation." While they agree that the research points to a correlation between biology and homosexuality, they contend that there is still no evidence of the cause of this correlation, whether learning from the environment or "hard-wiring" of the brain. They argue that there is still plenty of room for a learning model in the development of homosexuality by citing a recent study about the influence of parental socialization on homosexuality.

| **POINT** | **COUNTERPOINT** |
| --- | --- |
| • Evidence from twin-studies points to a genetically heritable homosexuality. | • Twin-studies suffer from methodological weaknesses that call into question the genetic influence on sexual orientation. |
| • Genetic scanning shows that homosexuality is correlated with several genes. | • Findings based on genetic scanning are ambiguous. |
| • The maternal immune theory is well established because it relies on the very reliable fraternal birth order effect. | • The maternal immune theory relies on disputed findings regarding the fraternal birth order effect. |
| • The fraternal birth order effect is accounted for in the prenatal environment. | • The fraternal birth order effect can be accounted for in the postnatal social environment. |
| • Brain structures differ between homosexual and heterosexual men. | • Brain structure difference could be the effect rather than the cause of homosexuality. |
| • Research shows that learning plays no appreciable role in the development of sexual orientation. | • Research shows that learning plays a role in the development of sexual orientation. |

# YES 

**Qazi Rahman**

# The Neurodevelopment of Human Sexual Orientation

## 1. Introduction

Sexual orientation refers to a dispositional sexual attraction towards persons of the opposite sex or same sex. Sexual orientation appears 'dispositional' in that it comprises a target selection and preference mechanism sensitive to gender, motivational approach behaviours towards the preferred target, and internal cognitive processes biased towards the preferred target (such as sexual fantasies). In contrast, sexual orientation does not appear to be a matter of conscious self-labelling or past sexual activity because these are subject to contingent social pressures, such as the presence of linguistic descriptors and visible sexual minorities within an individual's culture, and the availability of preferred sexual partners. Therefore, in human investigations, sexual orientation is often assessed using self-report measures of 'sexual feelings' (i.e. sexual attraction and sexual fantasies) rather than self-labelling or past hetero- or homosexual activity.

Sexual orientation appears to be a dichotomous trait in males, with very few individuals demonstrating an intermediate (i.e. 'bisexual') preference. This is borne out by fine-grained analyses of self-reported heterosexual and homosexual orientation prevalence rates (using measures of sexual feelings) in population-level samples, and work on physiological genital arousal patterns (e.g. using penile plethysmography) in response to viewing preferred and non-preferred sexual imagery. Both lines of evidence consistently demonstrate a bimodal sexual orientation among men—heterosexual or homosexual, but rarely 'bisexual'. This is less so in the case among women. For example, Chivers et al. demonstrated a 'bisexual' genital arousal pattern among both heterosexual and lesbian women, suggesting a decoupling of self-reported sexual feelings (which appears broadly bimodal) from peripheral sexual arousal in women.

If sexual orientation among humans is a mostly bimodal trait, this implicates a canalization of development along a sex-typical route (heterosexual) or a sex-atypical (homosexual) route. Statistical taxometric procedures have confirmed this by demonstrating that latent taxa (i.e. non-arbitrary natural classes) underlie an opposite-sex, or same-sex, orientation in both men and

From *Neuroscience & Biobehavioral Reviews,* Vol. 29, Issue 7, October 2005, pp. 1057–1058, 1060, 1062, 1063 (excerpts). 

women. Less well established are the factors that may be responsible for this 'shunting' of sexual orientation along two routes (the edges of which are fuzzier in women). These factors are the subject of the remaining discussion and it is suggested that they probably operate neurodevelopmentally before birth.

## 2. Behavioural and Molecular Genetics

A natural starting point for the neurodevelopment of physiological and behavioural traits must begin with the genetic level of investigation. Several family and twin studies provide clear evidence for a genetic component to both male and female sexual orientation. Family studies, using a range of ascertainment strategies, show increased rate of homosexuality among relatives of homosexual probands. There is also evidence for elevated maternal line transmission of male homosexuality, suggestive of X linkage, but other studies have not found such elevation relative to paternal transmission. Among females, transmission is complex, comprising autosomal and sex-linked routes. Twin studies in both community and population-level samples report moderate heritability estimates, the remaining variance being mopped up by non-shared environmental factors. Early attempts to map specific genetic loci responsible for sexual orientation using family pedigree linkage methods led to the discovery of markers on the Xq28 chromosomal region, with one subsequent replication limiting the effect to males only. However, there is at least one independent study which produced null findings, while a recent genome wide scan revealed no Xq28 linkage in a new sample of families but identified putative additional chromosomal sites (on 7q36, 8pl2 and 10q26) which now require denser mapping investigations. These studies are limited by factors such as the unclear maternal versus paternal line transmission effects, possible autosomal transmission and measurement issues. Two candidate gene studies which explored the putative hormonal pathways in the neurodevelopment of sexual orientation (see Section 3): one on the androgen receptor gene and another on aromatase (CYP19A1) both produced null findings. . . .

## 3. The Fraternal Birth Order Effect and Maternal Immunity

The maternal immunity hypothesis is certainly the most revolutionary neurodevelopmental model of human sexual orientation. Empirically, it rests on one very reliable finding—the fraternal birth order effect (FBO): that is, homosexual men have a greater number of older brothers than heterosexual men do (and relative to any other category of sibling), in diverse community and population-level samples, and as early as they can be reliably surveyed. The estimated odds of being homosexual increase by around 33% with each older brother, and statistical modelling using epidemiological procedures suggest that approximately 1 in 7 homosexual men may owe their sexual orientation to the FBO effect. It has been suggested that the remaining proportions of homosexual men may owe their sexual orientation to other causes, such as differential prenatal androgen levels. Homosexual and heterosexual women do not differ in sibling sex composition or their birth order, thus any neurodevelopmental explanation for the FBO effect is limited to males. Importantly, recent work has demonstrated that homosexual males with older brothers have significantly lower birth weights compared to heterosexual males with older brothers. As birth weight is undeniably prenatally determined, some common developmental factor operating before birth must underlie FBO and sexual orientation among human males.

Specifically, investigators have proposed a role for the progressive immunization of some mothers to male-linked antigens produced by carrying each succeeding male foetus. That is, the maternal immune system 'sees' male-specific antigens as 'non-self' and begins producing antibodies against them. One possible group of antigens are the Y-linked minor histocompatibility antigens, specifically *H–Y.* The accumulating H–Y antibodies may divert male-typical sexual differentiation of the foetal brain, leading the individual to be sexually attracted to males. For example, male-specific antibodies may bind to, and inactivate, male-differentiating receptors located on the surface of foetal neurons thus preventing the morphogenesis of masculinized sexual preferences.

The maternal immunity theory is consistent with a number of observations: the number of older sisters is irrelevant to sexual orientation in later born males; the H–Y antigen is expressed by male foetuses only and thus the maternal immune system 'remembers' the number of males carried previously and may modulate its response; and H–Y antigens are strongly represented in neural tissue. Nonetheless, there is no data specifying a role for these particular antigens in sexual preferences among humans. There are several alternative candidate antigens to H–Y, including the distinct Y-linked protein families' *protocadherin* and *neuroligin,* both which have been found in humans. These cell adhesion proteins are thought to influence cell–cell communication during early male-specific brain morphogenesis and may have male-typical behavioural consequences. Consistent with these studies is neurogenetic evidence for the direct transcription of Y-linked sex determination genes *SRY* and *ZFY* in the male human brain (including hypothalamus). The maternal immunity model may also explain the link between birth weight and sexual preferences: mouse models show that maternal immunization to male-derived antigens can affect foetal weight. Furthermore, male mice whose mothers are immunized to H–Y prior to pregnancy show reduced male-typical consummatory sexual behaviour towards receptive females.

The maternal immunity model implicitly relies on a non-hormonal immunologic neurodevelopmental explanation and thus cannot immediately explain the hyper-male features (e.g. 2D:4D and AEPs) associated with male homosexuality. It is possible that male-specific antibodies may interact with sexual differentiation processes controlled by sex hormones or be completely independent of them—this is unknown as yet. . . .

## 4. Neural Circuitry

Neurodevelopmental mechanisms must wire neural circuits differently in those with same-sex attractions from those with opposite-sex attractions, but we still know very little about this circuitry. The first indication for neural correlates of sexual partner preference came from Simon LeVay autopsy study of the third interstitial nucleus of the anterior hypothalamus (INAH-3) which he found to be smaller in homosexual men than in presumed heterosexual men, and indistinguishable from presumed heterosexual women. Another study found a non-significant trend for a female-typical INAH-3 among homosexual men (and confirmed the heterosexual sex difference), but this was not evidenced the main sexually dimorphic parameter reported by this study (the total number of neurons). This preceding finding is noteworthy as a prediction from the prenatal androgen theory would be that a parameter which shows significant sexual dimorphism should also demonstrate within-sex variation attributable to sexual orientation. A conservative conclusion regarding these data is that while INAH-3 is larger in heterosexual men than in heterosexual women, and possibly smaller in homosexual men, structurally speaking this within-sex difference may not be very large at all.

One recent positron emission tomography study has demonstrated stronger hypothalamic response to serotonergic challenge in heterosexual than in homosexual men, and neuroimaging studies comparing heterosexual men and women while viewing preferred sexual imagery show significantly greater hypothalamic activation in heterosexual men. These findings, coupled with the anatomical findings described earlier, could be taken to suggest that there is a functionally distinct anterior hypothalamic substrate to sexual attraction towards women. This supposition is further supported by mammalian lesion models of the preoptic area (POA) of the anterior hypothalamus showing reduced appetitive responses towards female by male animals. Nevertheless, investigations comparing heterosexual and homosexual women are needed to support a role for this region in sexual preference towards females among humans.

While animal models point to a role for prenatal androgens in producing sexual variation in hypothalamic regions, a similar relationship in humans is unclear. One study found no sexual-orientation-related differences in the distribution of androgen receptors in sexually dimorphic hypothalamic regions. However, one animal model often overlooked by scientists may provide some guidance. Some males of certain species of sheep show an exclusive same-sex preference, and also show reduced aromatase activity and smaller ovine sexually dimorphic nuclei (a possible homolog to the human INAH-3) compared to female-oriented sheep. A role for aromatized metabolites of testosterone in underscoring possible hypothalamic variation related to human sexual orientation requires further study in light of these findings. Moreover, putative sexual orientation differences in aromatase activity in human males may go some way to explaining the 'mosaic' profile of hypo- and hyper-masculinized traits described earlier. For example, a reduction in aromatase activity in homosexual compared to heterosexual men (predicted from the

Roselli findings) may lead to reduced availability of aromatized testosterone (i.e. estradiol) which typically masculinizes the male mammalian brain. This may lead to hypo-masculinized hypothalamic circuitry and yet leave excess non-aromatized testosterone to hyper-masculinize additional androgen sensitive traits (e.g. 2D:4D) through other metabolic pathways, such as 5-alpha reductase. Note, one mitigating piece of evidence with respect to these suggestions is the null finding of DuPree et al. regarding sexual-orientation-related variation in the aromatase gene. . . .

## 5. Is There a Role for Learning in the Development of Human Sexual Orientation?

The role of learning in the development of human sexual orientation has been the subject of much debate and controversy, most likely because it is erroneously believed to result in particular socio-political consequences associated with homosexuality. While data are a little thin on the ground, several lines of evidence mitigate the involvement of learning mechanisms. In animal models, there are documented effects of conditioning on sexual arousal, approach behaviour, sexual performance and strength of sexual preference towards opposite-sex targets, but no robust demonstrations of learning in the organization of same-sex preferences among males. Interestingly, one study in female rats demonstrated that the volume of the sexually dimorphic nucleus of the preoptic region was increased (male-typical) by testosterone administration coupled with same-sex sexual experience. This suggests that sexual experience may interact with steroid exposure to shape sexual partner preferences in females.

In humans, the extent of childhood or adolescent homosexual versus heterosexual activity does not appear to relate to eventual adult sexual orientation. Documented evidence regarding the situational or cultural 'initiation' of juvenile males into extensive same-sex experience (for example, in single-sex public schools in Britain or the obligatory homosexual activity required of young males in the Sambia tribe of New Guinea) does not result in elevated homosexuality in adulthood.

An alternative explanation for the FBO effect is that sexual interaction with older brothers during critical windows of sexual development predisposes towards a homosexual orientation. Studies in national probability samples show that sibling sex-play does not underscore the link between FBO and male sexual orientation, and that the sexual attraction component of sexual orientation, but not sexual activity, are best predicted by frequency of older brothers. In further support, same-sex play between pairs of gay brothers is also unrelated to adult homosexual attraction.

Perhaps parent–child interactions influence the sexual orientation of children? An informative test here is to examine the sexuality of children of homosexual parents because this type of familial dynamic could promote same-sex preferences through observational learning mechanisms. However, evidence from retrospective and prospective studies provides no support for this supposition. Nonetheless, one must bear in mind that if parental behaviour does determine offspring sexual orientation, it could be equally common in homosexual and heterosexual parents.

While a role for learning factors can never be entirely omitted, it is perplexing that several of the key routes by which these could have their effect, such as through sexual experience during childhood or adolescence, or through parental socialization, are not supported. Almost certainly the expression of homosexual *behaviour* has varied over time and across cultures, but there is little reason to think that dispositional homosexuality varies greatly cross-culturally or even historically. . . .

**Stanton L. Jones and Alex W. Kwee**

# NO

# Scientific Research, Homosexuality, and the Church's Moral Debate: An Update

## Etiological Research

Significant new research on etiology has emerged in six areas: 1) behavioral genetics; 2) genetic scanning, 3) human brain structure studies, 4) studies of "gay sheep" and "gay fruit flies," 5) fraternal birth order research, and 6) familial structure impact.

### Behavioral Genetics

Bailey's behavioral genetics studies of sexual orientation in twins and other siblings seemed to provide solid evidence of a substantial degree of genetic influence on formation of homosexual orientation. Jones and Yarhouse criticized these studies severely, most importantly on the grounds that both studies were making population estimates of the degree of genetic influence on sexual orientation on *potentially biased samples,* samples recruited from advertisements in gay publications and hence potentially biased by differential volunteerism by subjects inclined to favor a genetic hypothesis for the causation of their orientation. Later research by Bailey and other associates with a truly representative sample of twins drawn from the Australian Twin Registry in fact refuted the earlier findings by failing to find a significant genetic effect in the causation of homosexual orientation.

Not included in our review was a major behavioral genetics study paralleling the work of Bailey: Kendler, Thornton, Gilman, and Kessler. This study is remarkable in two ways. First, it replicates almost exactly the findings of the earlier Bailey studies in reporting relatively strong probandwise concordances for homosexual monozygotic twins. Kendler et al. report their findings as pairwise concordances, but when the simple conversions to probandwise concordances are done, Kendler et al.'s 48% probandwise concordance for males and females together (reported as a 31.6% pairwise concordance) is remarkably similar to Bailey's reports of probandwise concordances of 52% for men and 48% for women.

From *Journal of Psychology and Christianity (JPC),* Vol. 24, Issue 4, Winter 2005, pp. 304–307, 308–312 (excerpts). 

Second, the Kendler et al. study is also remarkably similar to the earlier Bailey studies in its methodological weaknesses. Trumpeted as a study correcting the "unrepresentative and potentially biased samples" of the Bailey studies by using a "more representative sample," specifically a "U. S. national probability sample" (p. 1843), this study appears actually to suffer all of the original problems of volunteer sample bias of the 1991 and 1993 Bailey studies. Further, the methodological problems give every sign of compounding one upon the next. The description of the methodology is confusing: Kendler et al. state that their sample comes from a MacArthur Foundation study of 3,032 representatively chosen respondents, but then they note that since this sample produced too few twins and almost no homosexual twins (as would be expected), they turned to a different sample of 50,000 households that searched for twins, and here the clear sampling problems begin: 14.8% of the households reported a twin among the siblings, but only 60% gave permission to contact the twin. There was further erosion of the sample as only 20.6% of the twins agreed to participate if the initial contact was with another family member, compared to 60.4% if the initial contact was a twin him- or herself (and given the lower likelihood of an initial contact being with a twin, this suggests a low response rate for twins overall). Yet further erosion may have occurred at the next step of seeking contact information of all siblings in the family; the write-up is confusing on this point. With all these potential sampling problems, it is then quite striking that the absolute number of identical/monozygotic twin pairs concordant for homosexuality were only 6 (out of a total of 19 pairs where at least one twin was "non-heterosexual"). With such a small absolute number of monozygotic twin pairs concordant for homosexuality, the smallest bias in the assembly of the sample would introduce problems in data interpretation; loss of just two concordant twin pairs would have wiped out the findings. It is remarkable that Kendler et al. give no explicit attention to these problems. Thus, we must regard this new study, promoted by some as a replication of Bailey's original 1991 and 1993 studies, as having the same fatal flaws as those earlier studies and as rightly superseded by Bailey's report in 2000 that there is no statistically significant indication of genetic influence on sexual orientation.

## Genetic Scanning

Mustanski et al. reported on a "full genome scan of sexual orientation in men" (p. 272). This is the third study of genetics and homosexuality to emerge from the laboratory of the associates of Dean Hamer, and this study utilized 146 families; 73 families previously studied by either Hamer, Hu, Magnuson, Hu, and Pattatucci or Hu et al., and 73 new families not previously studied. The same sample limitations are present in these studies as were discussed in Jones and Yarhouse (pp. 79–83). If these studies were attempting to establish population estimates, these would constitute biased samples, but because they explicitly state that they are looking for genetic factors in a subpopulation of homosexual men predetermined to be more likely to manifest genetic factors, these are limitations and not methodological weaknesses. They obtained their sample through "advertisements in local and national homophile publications" and the "sole inclusion criterion was the presence of at least two self-acknowledged gay male siblings" (p. 273), a rare occurrence indeed.

Two findings are worth noting. First, the Mustanski et al. study continued the pattern of failing to replicate the original 1993 Hamer finding of an Xq28 region of the X chromosome being linked to male homosexuality, this despite somewhat heroic statistical focus in this study. This is yet another blow to the credibility of their original findings.

Second, while media outlets headlined the Mustanski et al. study as having found genes linked to homosexuality on chromosomes 7, 8, and 10, this is precisely what they did *not* find, but rather "we found one region of near significance and two regions close to the criteria for suggestive linkage" (p. 273). None of their findings, in other words, achieved statistical significance. It is hard to tell whether these findings represent a cluster of near false positives that will fail future replication, or clues that will lead to more fine-grained and statistically significant findings. If the latter, these genetic segments may be neither necessary nor sufficient to cause homosexual orientation, and may either contribute to the causation of the orientation directly or indirectly. This is an intriguing but ambiguous report.

## Human Brain Structure Studies

New brain research allows us to expand the reported findings on the relationship of brain structure to sexual orientation, and to correct one element of our prior presentation of the data in this complex field. We duplicate [here] . . . (Table 1) part of the table summarizing brain findings from pages 68–69 of Jones and Yarhouse.

***Table 1***

**Summary of Brain Differences by Biological Sex and Sexual Orientation**

| | Brain Region | | | |
|---|---|---|---|---|
| **Study** | **INAH1** | **INAH2** | **INAH3** | **INAH4** |
| Swaab & Fliers (1985) | HetM > HetF | | | |
| Swaab & Hoffman (1988) | HetM = HomM; (HetM & HomM) > HetF | | | |
| Allen et al. (1989) | HetM = HetF | HetM > HetF | HetM > HetF | HetM = HetF |
| LeVay (1991) | HetM = HetF | HetM = HetF | HetM > (HetF & HomM) | HetM = HetF |
| Byne et al. (2000) | HetM = HetF | HetM = HetF | HetM > HetF | HetM = HetF |
| Byne et al. (2001) | HetM = HetF | HetM = HetF | HetM > HetF | HetM = HetF |
| | | | HetM = HomM in number of neurons | |

HetM = heterosexual males; HetF = heterosexual females; HomM = homosexual males.

Our correction is to recategorize in Table 1 the findings of Swaab and Hoffman from our listing, following the original report, as from the SDNH or sexually differentiated nucleus of the hypothalamus to a finding reporting on the INAH1 or interstitial nucleus of the hypothalamus, area 1. The review of Byne et al. pointed out that the SDNH *is* the INAH1; Swaab's 1988 report was an extension of his earlier work and not an exploration of a new area. The new work of Byne et al. continued the pattern of refuting Swaab's reported findings.

The new findings reporting on brain structure and sexual orientation (summarized in Table 1) come from the respected laboratory of William Byne and his colleagues. We cited Byne heavily in our critique of the famous Simon LeVay studies of brain differences in the INAH3 region. Byne et al. replicated the previous findings of sexual dimorphism (male-female differences) in INAH3, and thus it is now safe to say that this is a stable finding. Further, Byne and his team have refined the analysis to be able to say, based on their 2000 study, that the INAH3 size difference by sex "was attributable to a sex difference in neuronal number and not in neuronal size or density." Simply put, the INAH3 area in women is, on average, smaller than it is in men, and this is because women have fewer neurons in this area, and *not* because their neurons are smaller or less dense.

This makes the findings of Byne et al. on sexual orientation yet more curious; they found the size (specifically, volume) of the INAH3s of homosexual males to be intermediate (to a statistically nonsignificant degree) between heterosexual males and heterosexual females. In other words, the volume of the INAH3s was, on average, between the average volumes of heterosexual males and heterosexual females such that the differences did not achieve statistical significance in comparison to either heterosexual males or females. Hence, "Sexual orientation cannot be reliably predicted on the basis of INAH3 volume alone." Further, and to complicate things more, they found that the nonsignificant difference noted between homosexual and heterosexual males was *not* attributable (as it was for the male-female difference) to numbers of neurons, as homosexual and heterosexual males were found to have comparable neuronal counts. So, there may be a difference between homosexual and heterosexual males, but if there is, it is not the same type of difference as that between males and females.

To complicate the analysis even further, Byne et al. point out that these differences, if they exist, are not proof of prenatal, biological determination of sexual orientation. While it is possible that differences in INHA3 may be strongly influenced by prenatal hormones, "In addition, sex related differences may also emerge later in development as the neurons that survive become part of functional circuits" (p. 91). Specifically, the difference in volume could be attributed to "a reduction in neuropil within the INAH3 in the homosexual group" (p. 91) as a result of "postnatal experience." In other words, if there are brain structure differences between homosexuals and heterosexuals, they could as well be the result rather than the cause of sexual behavior and sexual preference. (The same conclusion about directionality of causation can be drawn about the new study showing activation of sexual brain centers in response to female pheromones by male heterosexuals, and to male pheromones by female heterosexuals *and* male homosexuals. The authors themselves point out that these brain activations could be the result of learning as well as evidence of the "hard-wiring" of the brain.) . . .

Second, and in a rare admission for those advancing biological explanations of sexual orientation, Roselli et al. admit that the direction of causation is at this time completely unclear, in the process echoing the possible causal role of postnatal experience mentioned by Byne et al. above:

> However, the existing data do not reveal which is established first—oSDN size or mate preference. One might assume that the neural structure is determined first and that this, in turn, guides the development of sexual partner preference. However, it is equally possible that some other factors(s), including social influences or learned associations, might shape sexual partner preference first. Then, once a sexual partner preference is established, the continued experiences and/or behaviors associated with a given preference might affect the size of the oSDN. (p. 241)

A new study released in June, 2005 has ignited the latest frenzy about biological causation of sexual orientation. In response to this study, the president of the Human Rights Campaign ("the largest national lesbian, gay, bisexual and transgender political organization") stated that "Science is closing the door on right-wing distortions. . . . The growing body of scientific evidence continues to refute the opponents of equality who maintain that sexual orientation is a 'choice.'" Chairman of the Case Western Reserve University Department of Biochemistry Michael Weiss expressed for the *New York Times* his hope that this study "will take the discussion about sexual preferences out of the realm of morality and put it into the realm of science." Both quotes epitomize the over-interpretation and illogic of those anxious to press findings from science to moral conclusions.

The new study appears to be a strong piece of scientific research that will have important implications for our understanding of the biological bases of sexual behavior. The researchers generated a gene fragment (the *"fruitless (fru)"* allele) that was "constitutively spliced in either the male or the female mode" in the chromosomes of the opposite sex (i.e., male fruit flies had the allele inserted in a female mode and female fruit flies had the allele inserted in a male mode) with dramatic effects: "Forcing female splicing in the male results in a loss of male courtship behavior and orientation, confirming that male-specific splicing of *fru* is indeed essential for male behavior. More dramatically, females in which *fru* is spliced in the male mode behave as if they were males: they court other females" (p. 786). The results reported were indeed powerful; the behavioral distinctions in the modified fruit flies were almost unequivocal.

The authors of this study were reasonably circumspect in their report of the implications of their findings, though others were not as noted before. Three issues deserve attention. First, as in our discussion of "gay sheep," the differences between human and animal (or insect) mating patterns are enormous, and those differences limit application to the human situation. Demir and Dickson noted that male courtship of the female fruit fly is highly scripted, "largely a fixed-action pattern" (p. 785). The finding that the normal, almost robotic mating patterns of this creature are hard-wired is hardly surprising; in contrast, the enormous complexity of human sexual and romantic response indicates that such a finding will be challenging to apply to the human condition. Further, the interpretation that this study establishes a genetic base for "sexual orientation" in fruit flies is careless; the study rather finds genetic determination (to some degree) of an entire pattern of mating/reproductive behavior. The genetic control of mating behavior in this study is of something both more and less than sexual orientation as experienced by humans.

Second, we have plenty of existing data to indicate that no such encompassing genetic determination of sexual behavior exists in humans. The behavior genetics evidence of sexual orientation (see the earlier discussion of the Kendler et al. study) provides strong evidence that genetic factors provide (at most) incomplete determination of sexual orientation, even if genetic factors are part of a multivariant causal array.

Third, we must question the following claim of the authors:

> Thus, male-specific splicing of *fru* is both necessary and *sufficient* [emphasis added] to specify male courtship behavior and sexual orientation. A complex innate behavior is thus specified by the action of a single gene, demonstrating that behavioral switch genes do indeed exist and identifying *fru* as one such gene.

Strictly understood, the authors appear to be claiming that the presence of *fru* elicits, *necessarily and sufficiently,* stereotypical male courtship by males of female fruit flies, but a famous study from a decade before falsifies the sufficiency of *fru* causation. Zhang and Odenwald reported on genetic alterations in male fruit flies which produced "homosexual behavior" in the altered fruit flies. This study too resulted in many tabloid headlines heralding the creation of a "homosexual gene." Media reports failed to cite the other curious finding of the study: when genetically normal or "straight" fruit flies were introduced into the habitat of the "gay" flies without females present, the normal (genetically unaltered) male flies began engaging in the same type of "homosexual" behavior as the genetically altered flies. In other words, genetically normal ("straight") flies began to act like homosexual flies because of their *social environment.* Thus, in a most biological experiment, evidence of environmental ("psychological") influence emerged once again. So if the authors of the 2005 study are claiming that the presence of *fru* elicits (is sufficient to produce) stereotypical male courtship, that claim was falsified a decade before by the finding that normal male fruit flies (presumably with intact *fru* alleles), when exposed to certain social contexts ("gay" flies), engage in behavior that violates the stereotypical male courtship of females; other conditions—specifically, *social* conditions—are also sufficient to elicit homosexual behavior in fruit flies.

Together, these three issues suggest that, as powerful as the recent findings about fruit flies are, interpretive caution in application to humans is indicated.

## Fraternal Birth Order Research

The fraternal birth order studies by Ray Blanchard, Anthony Bogaert, and various other researchers purport to show that sexual orientation in men correlates with an individual's number of older brothers. Specifically, it is claimed that male homosexuals tend to be born later in their sibships than male heterosexuals, and that male homosexuality is statistically (and causally) related to the number of older biological brothers (but not sisters) in the family. This purported relationship within the fraternal birth order is such that each additional older brother, it is claimed, increases the odds of homosexuality by 33%, and for gay men with approximately 2.5 older brothers, older brothers equal all the other causes of homosexuality combined.

Blanchard, Bogaert, and others advance the so-called maternal immune hypothesis to explain the fraternal birth order effect. According to this hypothesis, some mothers progressively produce, in response to each succeeding male fetus, antibodies to a substance called the H-Y antigen, which is produced by male fetuses and foreign to female bodies. The maternally produced anti-H-Y antibodies are thought to be passed on to the male fetus, preventing the fetal brain from developing in a male typical pattern, thereby causing the affected sons to develop homosexual orientations in later life. So much hyperbole surrounds the maternal immune causal hypothesis that it appears the assumption is simply being made that the fraternal birth order effect itself is indisputable when, in fact, it is not. We will direct the bulk of our critical attention to the birth order phenomenon. The maternal immune theory underlying the phenomenon can be quite readily dispatched at this point by stating that no direct evidence has ever been found for it, and so it remains purely speculative.

The major flaw of the fraternal birth order research is that the main studies were conducted on nonrepresentative samples. For example, one of the "landmark" studies that demonstrated the birth order effect recruited its sample from the 1994 Toronto Gay Pride Parade and several LGBT community organizations. Nonrepresentative samples are known to be vulnerable to a variety of selection biases. For instance, perhaps later-born gay men were overrepresented in this sample because they were more apt to be "out and proud," participate in Gay Pride events, and affiliate with overtly LGBT groups. If later born siblings tend to be less conventional and more rebellious as some research shows, later-born gay men, accordingly, may be less gender conforming and more likely to flaunt their sexual orientation. This may have resulted in an overrepresentation of later-born gay men and an underrepresentation of earlier-born gay men at Gay Pride events and within LGBT groups, which naturally exaggerated the fraternal birth order effect in this sample. This is just one of several possible selection biases which may have flawed Blanchard and Bogaert's sample.

To his credit, Bogaert attempted to correct for the methodological flaw of selection bias by examining national probability samples in the United States and Britain respectively. His study yielded a finding of fraternal birth order effects in both samples. While this may appear to replicate initial research results, we must question the size of the effects given the large samples involved—over 1,700 subjects in each of the samples. Bogaert did not clearly report the effect sizes he found. It is well known that using large enough samples, even small differences can be found to be statistically significant. Since statistical significance is a function of both sample size and effect size, and we really care about the effect size (and not merely that it is non-zero), Bogaert's findings are quite unhelpful.

In an even more recent study, Bogaert and Cairney attempted to answer the question of whether there is a fraternal birth order and parental age interaction effect in the prediction of sexual orientation. The researchers examined two samples—a U.S. national probability sample, and the flawed Canadian sample which we discussed above. The study based on the U.S. sample found an interaction, but the data was so flawed—and acknowledged to be so by the authors themselves—that we cannot possibly take its conclusion seriously. Specifically, the preexisting U.S. data allowed for only an examination of absolute (not fraternal) birth order, surmised sexual orientation from behavior alone, and did not separate biological from non-biological siblings. The conclusion was counterintuitive in that while a positive association between (absolute) birth order and the likelihood of homosexuality was found, this association was weakened and in fact *reversed* with increasing maternal age. We believe that this conclusion highlights the problem of bias when researchers attempt to find putative phenomena in data to support a cherished theory. If one is trying to establish a link between maternal age and homosexuality, it seems counterintuitive that the likelihood of homosexuality weakens or is reversed with increasing maternal age. Of course, if there is no relationship between sexual orientation and maternal age (which we suspect), a finding of *any* relationship is probably spurious and a methodological artifact. The researchers acknowledge the counterintuitiveness of their result by stating that they "know of no evidence of a stronger maternal reaction [to the H-Y antigen] in younger (versus older) mothers" (p. 32), betraying their bias towards a theory for which no direct evidence has ever been established, and then calling for new research.

Turning to the Canadian sample, Bogaert and Cairney found a Parental Age x Birth Order interaction. Their weighted analysis (giving larger families a greater impact on the results) revealed that this interaction was carried by a Mother's Age x Older Sisters effect. This finding actually *undermines* the fraternal birth order theory because it provides some evidence that homosexuality is independent of the fraternal birth order effect. The authors acknowledge but downplay this, calling instead for the gathering of new data.

Other studies have falsified the fraternal birth order effect or showed no support for the maternal immune hypothesis. Using an enormous and nationally representative sample of adolescents that we discuss fully below, Bearman and Brückner found "no evidence for a speculative evolutionary model of homosexual preference" (i.e., the older-brother findings; p. 1199).

Despite various methodological problems with the fraternal birth order research, we concede that the evidence as a whole points to some sort of relationship between the number of older brothers and homosexuality. As responsible scientists, we should approach this body of research critically but not ignore the fact that it consistently shows some link between sexual orientation and fraternal but not sororal birth order. Research may well identify some pathway by which some men develop a stable same-sex attraction that is linked to their placement in the birth order. However, those who argue that the maternal immunosensitivity theory explains the fraternal birth order effect run into the problem of having to show that the same hypothesis does not underlie pedophilia, sexual violence, and other forms of sexual deviancy. While Blanchard, Bogaert, and other researchers deny any link between fraternal birth order and pedophilia, or they believe that any such link exists only for pedophiles who are homosexual, other studies have demonstrated a link between fraternal birth order and general (pedophilic and non-pedophilic) sexual offending, raising the possibility that homosexuality shares a common pathway with some forms of sexual deviance.

Research has not clearly established what this pathway is. One of the most natural but politically divisive speculations, which cautiously raises its head in the literature now and then, is that childhood sexualization and abuse has some causative relationship to homosexuality and pedophilia. This speculation is logical in relation to the fraternal birth order effect because younger brothers with higher fraternal birth order indices may have a higher probability of being victimized sexually by older brothers or otherwise experiencing same-sex sexualization. Preadolescent sexualization and abuse underlie the post-natal learning theory of homosexuality and pedophilia, which most recently has been supported by James in his review of several major studies. However plausible this theory appears, it is based on inferences from other studies and the direct empirical evidence for it is extremely weak.

## Familial Structure Impact

A particularly powerful study challenging all of the major paradigms asserting biological determination of sexual orientation, and of the claim that there is no meaningful evidence of psychological/experiential causation of orientation, was recently published. Bearman and Brückner reported on analyses of an enormous database of almost 30,000 sexuality interviews with adolescents, with fascinating findings on the determinants of same-sex attraction for males (they found no evidence of significant determinants for females). Their summary of their findings merits citation in full:

> The findings presented here confirm some findings from previous research and stand in marked contrast to most previous research in a number of respects. First, we find no evidence for intrauterine transfer of hormone effects on social behavior. Second, we find no support for genetic influences on same-sex preference net of social structural

*Table 2*

**Core Findings of Bearman & Brückner**

| Relationship (Subject is a . . .) | % Reporting Same-Sex Attraction | *N* (all males) |
|---|---|---|
| Opposite Sex Dizygotic Twin | 16.8% | 185 |
| Same Sex Dizygotic Twin | 9.8% | 276 |
| Same Sex Monozygotic Twin | 9.9% | 262 |
| Opposite Sex Full Sibling | 7.3% | 427 |
| Same Sex Full Sibling | 7.9% | 596 |
| Other (adopted non-related; half-sibling) | 10.6% | 832 |

constraints. Third, we find no evidence for a speculative evolutionary model of homosexual preference. Finally, we find substantial indirect evidence in support of a socialization model at the individual level. (p. 1199)

Their second conclusion is a direct reference to the types of genetic influence posited by Bailey and others; the third conclusion a direct reference to the "older-brother" findings of Blanchard, Bogaert and others. But not only do their findings contradict other research, a new finding of socialization effects on same-sex attraction emerge from their data (see Table 2).

Bearman and Brückner found a single family constellation arrangement that significantly increased the likelihood that an adolescent male would report same-sex attraction, and that was when the adolescent male was a dizygotic (fraternal) twin whose co-twin is a sister (what they call "male opposite-sex twins"); in this arrangement, occurrence of same-sex attraction more than doubled over the base-rate of 7% to 8%: "we show that adolescent male opposite-sex twins are *twice as likely* as expected to report same-sex attraction, and that the pattern of concordance (similarity across pairs) of same-sex preference for sibling pairs does not suggest genetic influence independent of the social context" (p. 1181). They advance a socialization hypothesis to explain this finding, specifically proposing that sexual attraction is an outgrowth of gender socialization, and that no arrangement presents as much a challenge to parents to gender socialization than for a boy to be born simultaneous with a girl co-twin. In other words, they suggest that the parental task of accomplishing effective solidification of male sexual identity is challenged by parents having to handle a mixed-sex twin pair. The result of the diminished effectiveness of sexual identity formation in boys on average is the increased probability of same-sex attraction in the group of boys with twin sisters.

Bearman and Brückner go on to explore in their data the possibility that there could be a hormonal explanation for this finding: "Our data falsify the hormonal transfer hypothesis [i.e., the hypothesis posited to explain the fraternal birth order phenomenon], by isolating a single condition that eliminates the OS effect we observe—the presence of an older same-sex sibling" (p. 1181). Put simply, they found their effect disappeared when the boy with the twin sister was born into a family where there was already an older brother, an effect they attributed to the family already having grown accustomed to the process of establishing the sexual identity of a boy child; parents appear to be able to better handle the special challenges of a mixed-sex twin pair when they have already had some practice with an older brother. They firmly suggest that their "results support the hypothesis that less gendered socialization in early childhood and preadolescence shapes subsequent same-sex romantic preferences" (p. 1181). At a moment in time when it is common for many to deny that any firm evidence exists for the influence of non-biological causes on sexual orientation, these are remarkable findings (perhaps especially when the presence of an older brother decreases rather than increases the likelihood of homosexual orientation). . . .

# CHALLENGE QUESTIONS

## Is Homosexuality Biologically Based?

1. Is homosexuality a product of biology or learning? Support your claims with research evidence.
2. Many argue that if it were proven that homosexuality is biologically based, discrimination against homosexuals would decrease. Support this argument with research on discrimination and prejudice.
3. In Rahman's review of the research, he believes the evidence clearly points to a biological, prenatal based homosexuality. On the other hand, Jones and Kwee find the same research to be ambiguous and flawed. In fact, they interpret much of the same findings as evidence of a postnatal, learned homosexuality. What would convince you to take one side or the other? Provide reasons for your position.
4. Read the section from Rahman's Controversial book *Born Gay* (co-authored with Glenn Wilson) about treating homosexuality. Also, find the full Jones and Kwee article and read the section entitled "Treatment Outcome Research." Each argues opposing viewpoints on the malleability of sexual orientation. Do you believe sexual orientation can be changed? Should we pursue such a research question?
5. Stanton Jones, the first author of the second article, has recently co-authored a book entitled, "Ex-Gays?" In this book, he reports a complex research study that he argues is an indicator that homosexuals can change their sexual orientation. If this is true, what would this finding mean for the possibility of biological determination of sexual orientation?

# ISSUE 6

## Is Evolution a Good Explanation for Psychological Concepts?

**YES: Glenn Geher**, from "Evolutionary Psychology Is Not Evil! (. . . And Here's Why . . .)" *Psychological Topics* (December 2006)

**NO: Edwin E. Gantt and Brent S. Melling**, from "Evolutionary Psychology Isn't Evil, It's Just Not Any Good," An Original Essay Written for This Volume

### ISSUE SUMMARY

**YES:** Evolutionary psychologist Glenn Geher maintains that evolution provides the best meta-theory for explaining and understanding human psychology.

**NO:** Theoretical psychologists Edwin Gantt and Brent Melling argue that an evolutionary account of psychology omits many important and good things about humans.

Given the wide-spread success of evolutionary explanations in biology, many psychologists have suggested that these explanations can adequately and powerfully explain psychological and social behavior. Evolutionary Psychology (EP) has become an increasingly recognized field, with numerous programs and institutes dedicated to researching its explanations. However, EP is not without its critics. Going beyond methodological issues (see issue 4 of this *Taking Sides* volume), those who are uncomfortable with EP argue that its philosophical assumptions ultimately deny important aspects of humanity, such as morality and personal responsibility. In response, evolutionary psychologists often observe that "evolution is not evil . . ."

There's little argument that evolutionary explanations have been useful, and not "evil," in the biological sciences. Still, there is considerable debate about whether such an explanation can account for all facets of human experience and behavior. Can it explain, for example, the human sense of morality? Some scholars have held that morality itself is evolutionarily derived, with our own innate sense of rightness and goodness evolved from what is evolutionarily effective and efficient. On the other hand, critics argue that such a stance confuses morality with biology and that morality involves much more than can be explained by biological mechanisms.

The author of the first article, Glenn Geher, disagrees. As the Director of the Evolutionary Studies Program at the State University of New York at New Paltz, he argues that the best way to understand all psychological phenomena is to borrow evolutionary explanations from the biological sciences. EP makes the "modest" claim, according to Geher, that "minds are on the same footing as bodies where . . . natural selection is concerned." He maintains that evolutionary explanations do no harm, because they do not deny important human meanings or morality. Critics who see EP as "sexist, racist, [or] eugenicist" are misinformed about the point of EP. Evolutionary psychology merely tries to explain human behavior, not prescribe what humans *should* do.

Psychological researchers Edwin Gantt and Brent Melling argue that evolutionary psychology is not as innocent as it seems and, in fact, has major negative implications for the study of human behavior. They suggest that EP has a number of implicit biases that distort the world of human meaning but are rarely discussed in the EP literature. Despite claims to the contrary, for example, Gantt and Melling argue that EP presumes humans have no real choices about their behaviors, and thus no personal responsibility for them. For this reason and others, Gantt and Melling prompt caution in whole-heartedly accepting the latest scientific "facts" of EP. They note, instead, that scientific history is littered with "obvious facts that are later found to be not only questionable but on occasion outright false and misleading" (e.g., phlogiston, phrenology). Gantt and Melling conclude that such misleading facts and assumptions ultimately undermine the efforts of evolutionary psychologists to promote neutrality and morality.

**POINT**

- Critics have unreasonable or outmoded biases against Evolutionary Psychology (EP).
- EP research is objective and shows the world as it is.
- Evolutionary psychology is not evil.
- EP is a powerful tool for understanding all aspects of psychology.

**COUNTERPOINT**

- Rational, thoughtful individuals can have serious issues with Evolutionary Psychology (EP).
- EP has implicit biases that skew how researchers understand their data.
- EP denies the possibility of good or evil.
- EP cannot account for many important aspects of human psychology.

YES 

Glenn Geher

# Evolutionary Psychology Is Not Evil! (. . . and Here's Why . . .)

**Abstract**

Evolutionary psychology has faced 'implacable hostility' (Dawkins, 2005) from a number of intellectual fronts. Critics of evolutionary psychology have tried to paint this perspective variously as reductionist and overly deterministic, at best, and as sexist, racist, and downright evil at worst. The current paper argues that all psychological frameworks which assume that human beings are the result of the organic evolutionary forces of natural and sexual selection are, essentially, evolutionary in nature (regardless of whether they traditionally fall under the label of evolutionary psychology). In other words, the perspective presented here argues that all psychology is evolutionary psychology. Two specific mis-characterizations of evolutionary psychology ((a) that it is eugenicist in nature and (b) that it is a fully non-situationist, immutable perspective on behavior) are addressed here with an eye toward elaborating on how these distorted conceptions of evolutionary psychology are non-constructive and non-progressive. A final section focuses on how the social sciences in general could benefit from being evolutionized.

"Evolutionary psychology (is) . . . subject to a level of implacable hostility which seems far out of proportion to anything even sober reason or common politeness might sanction."

If you are a modern scholar of human behavior who uses evolutionary theory to help guide your research and, accordingly, label yourself an evolutionary psychologist (as I do), you may find Dawkins' aforementioned quote as capturing the essence of how evolutionary psychology (EP) is perceived in many modern academic circles. In fact, based on my experiences, this quote captures the current state of affairs regarding EP in the broader landscape of academia in general so well that it is actually a bit unsettling.

Worded another way, this implacable hostility seems to result from scholars across disparate disciplines who conceptualize EP as downright evil. EP is often framed as evil by all sorts of people for all sorts of reasons. In terms of purely academic critiques, EP is often framed as overly deterministic and

From *Psychological Topics,* vol. 15, no. 2, December 2006, pp. 181–189, 194–197 (excerpts).

reductionistic while social critics of EP with more applied concerns paint EP as a sexist, racist, and even eugenicist doctrine designed with a hidden political agenda that should serve the status quo by, presumably, justifying such amoral acts as sexual harassment, murder, and war.

An unfortunate outcome regarding the current state of affairs pertains to the fact that EP is attacked from people holding political perspectives that span the spectrum of ideologies. Fundamentalist Christians, who necessarily reject ideas that are premised on evolution as an accepted theory of speciation, reject EP simply due to its reliance on evolutionary theory. This ideological hurdle is by no means small: A recent survey found that 87% of United States citizens do not believe that evolutionary forces in general (and natural selection, in particular), unaided by a supernatural deity, are responsible for human origins. Such individuals, whose numbers are, simply, daunting, are likely to reject EP as a sustainable perspective on any aspect of human functioning.

However, in addition to the resistance to EP presented by fundamentalist religious individuals, there is, in effect, a new kind of creationist, so to speak, rooted in secular intellectualism. These so-called new creationists are, in fact, very different from fundamentalist Christians in their ideological foundation. The new creationists may be conceptualized as academics and scholars who study varied aspects of human affairs from the perspective of the Standard Social Science Model, a model for understanding human behavior which is largely premised on the notion of the blank slate. The SSSM essentially conceives of human psychology as qualitatively different from the psychology of all other species. The SSSM presumes that there is no basic human nature—that the mind (and its corresponding physiological substrates) are fully malleable based on environmental stimuli and that all behavioral and psychological aspects of people are the result of experiences with environmental stimuli across ontogenetic time.

This denial of human nature, which is prevalent in many of the social sciences, has come to serve as the only politically acceptable paradigm in much of academia. Champions of this perspective are often more critical of EP than are adherents of fundamentalist Christianity. From the perspective of the SSSM, EP is problematic largely because its basic premises focus on understanding the nature of human nature.

For instance, consider David Buss' work which revolves around understanding sex-differentiated mating strategies in humans from an evolutionary perspective. Research by Buss and his colleagues has documented many basic sex differences in the psychology of human mating. Several different studies, using varied methods, have replicated Buss' basic finding that men desire more lifetime sexual partners than do women. Buss' evolution-based explanation of these findings is rooted in Trivers' parental investment theory which suggests that males and females should differ in their mating tactics as a result of fundamentally different costs faced by each sex associated with bearing and raising children across the evolution of our species. From this perspective, women in our ancestral past who were driven to pursue short-term sexual strategies would have, on average, had less reproductive success compared with males pursuing similarly promiscuous strategies. A result of this sex-specific differential reproduction associated with variability in promiscuity over deep time would have led to sex-specific mating strategies (favoring promiscuity in males over females).

Critics of EP who may be thought to represent new creationism have tried hard to argue that findings which demonstrate such sex differences in mating strategies are based on flawed research. Further, such critics argue that even if such phenomena as sex differences in number of sex partners desired have been documented via sound research, these findings are best understood as resulting completely from environmental conditions during ontogenetic time. In other words, the SSSM perspective argues that all differences between the sexes in number of sexual partners desired results from males and females learning different messages about sexuality across their lifetimes. In short, this perspective argues that this phenomenon does not reflect basic and natural differences between male and female mating psychology—it only reflects differences in socialization between the sexes (differences that exist, in varying degrees, across human cultures).

Adherents of the SSSM perspective argue that appealing to evolutionarily shaped differences between the psychologies of men and women to explain something such as universal sex differences in desire for multiple sex partners is an inherently sexist approach. In short, these new creationists believe that any appeals to an evolutionarily shaped human nature to explain psychological phenomena (regardless of how well the said phenomena are documented) imply that human behavior is highly constrained by our nature, is genetically determined, and is, in effect, immutable. As such, adherents of the SSSM feel something of an obligation to fight EP, as they believe they are fighting an intellectual doctrine which sees human behavior as largely immutable and which ultimately provides a scholarly rationale for the status quo (which inherently treats people unfairly).

From the SSSM perspective, EP paints a picture of humans as fully under the control of genes. Further, the SSSM perspective sees EP as a doctrine that endorses all aspects of the status quo related to sexism. As seen through the lens of the SSSM, all phenomena documented by evolutionary psychologists and, subsequently, framed as resulting from evolutionary forces, are implicitly endorsed by evolutionary psychologists. As such, phenomena such as male promiscuity, filicide, rape, murder, and war are seen, from the SSSM perspective, as phenomena that are, essentially, supported, condoned, and, perhaps, encouraged by evolutionary psychologists as they are phenomena that evolutionary psychologists have studied from an evolutionary perspective and have tried to explain in terms of the nature of human nature.

Let me go on the record saying that I am very uncomfortable (on both moral and intellectual grounds) with any perspective that sees humans as fully incapable of choosing their own behaviors. Further, I am ardently opposed to sexism—ardently opposed to the idea that men and women (and boys and girls) should be treated differently by rules created by a society and should be given different opportunities within a society. I am, further, from a personal standpoint, not someone who encourages males to engage in promiscuous behavior and not someone who supports men who fly into violent jealous rages with females as targets of their anger and aggression. Additionally, I am strongly opposed to war, murder, rape, and filicide. I would feel a moral obligation to reject outright any doctrine which is inconsistent with these fundamental aspects of my belief system. In sum, I would see such a doctrine as downright evil.

So herein lies the problem, a problem which, as I see it, is largely one of perspective. If EP were the kind of intellectual doctrine that I describe in the prior paragraph, then it would be a morally disturbing framework. However, as several scholars have argued before me, EP is simply not such a doctrine. In the remainder of this paper, I argue that EP is the following:

A. A basic intellectual framework for understanding all psychological phenomena
B. A set of principles which, at its core, simply asserts that the human nervous system and resultant behavior are ultimately products of organic evolutionary processes
C. One of the most situationist/contextualist perspectives that exists within psychology writ large
D. A perspective that has the potential to serve as an underlying metatheory to guide all the behavioral sciences in the future.

## Evolutionary Psychology Is Not Evil

In engaging in the thought exercise of trying to empathize with academics who characterize EP as downright evil, I have concluded that the problem seems to lie largely in the naturalistic fallacy. Often, when people hear that some phenomenon is being framed as part of our nature, shaped by evolutionary forces across thousands of generations, they infer that the scientists who are documenting said evolutionarily shaped quality see this quality as something about us that should be the case. In other words, for instance, if one hears Daly, Wilson, and Weghorst argue that male sexual jealousy, and violence that has been directed toward countless women as a result of such jealousy, may be part of our evolutionary heritage, one may infer that these authors are arguing that men should show marked, intense, and emotional jealousy when faced with cheating partners and, further, that they should use violence against women as a solution to such problems.

Of course, Daly et al. believe nothing of the kind. Documenting that something is part of our nature is not synonymous with arguing that it should be condoned by society. Similarly, when David Buss argues that natural selection has shaped patterns of homicide and murder in a non-random way, such that our ancestors were most likely to murder when murder was likely to have increased the possibility of passing on genes of the murderer (i.e., under conditions in which murder had fitness benefits), he is not arguing that murder is good and/or that society should support murder. He is, rather, using evolutionary theory, the most powerful intellectual framework that exists in the life sciences, to help understand behaviors that are of high relevance to the functioning of society.

In sum, the naturalistic fallacy corresponds to conflating phenomena that naturally are with phenomena that should be. As evolutionary psychologists are charged with the task of understanding the nature of human psychological processes, they are at particular risk of having their work mis-characterized by others who are employing the reasoning that typifies the naturalistic fallacy. Further, for someone who is conflating some findings and ideas from EP with statements by evolutionary psychologists regarding how things should be, EP is likely to come across as appearing morally deficient and, yes, perhaps even evil!

## What Evolutionary Psychology Is

While there are different brands of EP, with some variability in basic assertions, EP is, in its most basic form, simply an understanding of behavior that is guided by evolutionary theory. In the words of Richard Dawkins: "The central claim . . . (that evolutionary psychologists) . . . are making is not an extraordinary one. It amounts to the exceedingly modest assertion that minds are on the same footing as bodies where Darwinian natural selection is concerned."

As such, EP is an explanatory framework that has implications for understanding all psychological phenomena. It essentially conceptualizes humans as products of natural selection—thereby not conceiving of our species as somehow immune from the laws that govern the natural world. It is a humbling perspective in some respects.

In any case, this perspective is monistic at its core; it conceives of human behavior as resulting from the nervous system—including the brain—which was, according to this perspective (and to most modern scientists who study psychological phenomena), shaped by evolutionary processes such as natural selection.

If the nervous system were shaped by natural selection, then individual humans with certain neuronal qualities in our ancestral past (e.g., those with features of the autonomic nervous system) were more likely to survive and reproduce compared with conspecifics (other humans) with nervous systems that were less likely to ultimately lead to reproduction.

Ancestral humans with features of the autonomic nervous system were more likely to respond optimally to immediate threatening stimuli in requisite situations (e.g., running from a predator). Thus, they were more likely to survive than others with less advanced autonomic nervous systems. A simple logical truth is that being more likely to survive necessarily increases the likelihood of reproduction (corpses are not very good at successfully mating). As such, this (partly) genetically shaped feature of human anatomy (with integral implications for human behavior), the autonomic nervous system, was 'naturally selected' and has thereby come to typify our species.

This same reasoning applies to all domains of psychology. Human behavioral patterns are part of the natural world—and human beings are living organisms that have come about by evolutionary processes. As such, attempts

*Table 1*

**Web-Based Resources that Provide Basic Information about Evolutionary Psychology**

1. Syllabus from Glenn Geher's section of Evolutionary Psychology taught at SUNY New Paltz: http://www.newpaltz.edu/~geherg/classes/fall08/syl307r.doc
2. The website for the international Evolutionary Studies (EvoS) Consortium: http://www.evostudies.org
3. Information on the Evolutionary Studies Program at the State University of New York at New Paltz http://www.newpaltz.edu/EvoS
4. Information on the Evolutionary Studies Program at Binghamton University http://evolution.binghamton.edu/evos/ directed by David Sloan Wilson (http://evolution.binghamton.edu/dswilson/)
5. Ed Hagen's Chapter on Controversies Surrounding Evolutionary Psychology (published in David Buss' Handbook of Evolutionary Psychology) http://itb.biologie.hu-berlin.de/%7Ehagen/papers/Controversies.pdf
6. Leda Cosmides and John Tooby's Introduction to the Field of Evolutionary Psychology http://www.psych.ucsb.edu/research/cep/primer.html
7. Ed Hagen's "Frequently Asked Questions about Evolutionary Psychology (e.g., "Is Evolutionary Psychology Sexist?")" http://www.anth.ucsb.edu/projects/human/evpsychfaq.html
8. Russil Durant and Bruce Ellis's Introduction to Evolutionary Psychology http://media.wiley.com/product_data/excerpt/38/04713840/0471384038.pdf
9. Human Behavior and Evolution Society page introducing the field: http://www.hbes.com/intro_to_field.htm
10. Personal Accounts about Applying for Academic Jobs While Branded as an Evolutionary Psychologist http://human-nature.com/ep/articles/ep02160173.html

at understanding such basic aspects of the human experience—mind and behavior—without understanding the broad evolutionary factors that have given rise to our species and, ultimately, to our psychology, is, from the perspective of EP, simply misguided. We can do better in understanding human psychology by understanding the nuances of evolutionary principles.

From my perspective, these are the basic ideas of EP. Note that I provide a list of resources (mostly developed by others; see Table 1) to introduce the reader to this field from various angles that fall under the general umbrella of EP. In sum, EP is simply a framework for understanding human behavior that has the capacity to unite all areas of psychology more so than any other paradigm that has existed in the history of psychology as a discipline. It is not driven by ideology; it is driven by the basic scientific motive of increasing understanding of the natural world.

## Evolutionary Psychology Mischaracterized as an Immutable, Hyper-Dispositionist, Non-Situationist Perspective

One of the beliefs that many people tend to hold about EP is that it is a non-situationist doctrine, suggesting that organisms have just a few immutable, invariant ways of responding which are under the direct control of genes.

This portrait of EP is simply inaccurate. EP posits that species-typical psychological design features with some heritable component have been shaped by natural and sexual selection. Often, many (but not all) evolutionary psychologists will conceive of such design features as adaptations. In any case, such adaptations are rarely understood by evolutionary psychologists as being context-independent.

Evolutionary psychologists and biologists make an important distinction between non-conditional and conditional strategies that describe the phenotypes of different organisms. A classic example of a non-conditional, folly genetically determined (and immutable) strategy is found in male sunfish, which come in two varieties. The first variety includes large males who have the ability to acquire sufficient territories in intra-sexual competition. The second variety includes smaller, sneakier males, who are nearly indiscernible from females and who do not elicit aggressive responses from territory-holding males. While territory-holding males reproduce by honestly attracting females, sneaker males use a somewhat dishonest strategy: they blast their gametes after a female has released her eggs in a large male's territory, thereby using deception as a tool for reproduction. It turns out that the differences between these kinds of males is attributable to genetic differences. As such, the strategies employed are non-conditional.

The notion of conditional strategies, on the other hand, corresponds to situations in which an organism modifies its strategy *vis a vis* variability in situational factors. For instance, male tree frogs use strategies similar to the male sunfish when it comes to mating. Sometimes, a male will carve out a territory and croak loudly. At other times, a male will hide near a territory-holding male and try to mate with females that are attracted to the croaking, territory-holding male. Importantly, in this species, males have been documented to show strategic pluralism; they modify their choice of strategy depending on the nature of such situational factors as the number of male territory-holders at a given time.

The use of a variety of strategies by male wood frogs does not suggest that their repertoire of mating behaviors is somehow outside the bounds of natural law or that these strategies are not designed with for 'purpose' of reproduction. Clearly, these mating strategies are related to optimal reproduction, a fact that speaks to their selection by evolutionary processes. As such, evolutionary geneticists and evolutionary psychologists have come to apply evolutionary reasoning to our understanding of mixed behavioral strategies that are highly context-sensitive.

In fact, modern-day EP is an extraordinarily situationist perspective. Consider, for instance, evolutionary informed research on homicide and familial violence. All of the most highly cited work in this area focuses on situational factors that underlie family violence. For instance, Daly and Wilson's often-cited work on violence toward children is all about contextual factors that covary with this atrocious act. Simply, the presence of a step-parent in a household has been shown to be the primary contextual factor that predicts fatal violence toward children. Another contextual factor that Daly and Wilson document as having a significant relationship with such violence has to do with the age of a given child (another contextual factor). In fact, their research, which is, in this regard, very prototypical of much work in EP overall, is all about contextual factors that underlie behaviors.

Consider, as another example, research on factors that predict promiscuous behavior on the part of women. Evolutionary psychologists have uncovered such important contextual factors as localized sex ratios, ovulation cycles, a woman's age, and the presence of children from prior mateships—each such contextual factor serving as an important statistical predictor of female promiscuity. In short, EP is, in fact, a highly situationist perspective, generally conceiving of human behavioral strategies as being extremely flexible and as falling within the realm of this general idea of strategic pluralism.

EP does not conceptualize humans as genetically guided automatons whose conscious decision-making processes are irrelevant or non-existent. Rather, this perspective sees humans as capable of extraordinary conscious decision-making. Further, with its roots in strategic pluralism, EP is situationist at its core. Importantly, EP has lessons to provide regarding the nature of situationism as an epistemological doctrine. While situationism in the social sciences is often framed as conceiving of human behavior as highly under the influence of situational influences (both small and large), this generic brand of situationism has generally been framed in a manner that is devoid of any insights into how important psychological design features have been ultimately shaped by evolutionary forces for the purpose of reproduction.

The kind of situationism that characterizes modern-day EP may be thought of as a sort of evolutionary situationism. This particular brand of situationism suggests that while human behavior is largely under the control of situational influences, the particular situational factors that should matter most in affecting behavior are ones that bear directly on factors associated with survival and reproductive success. As such, Daly and Wilson did not document just any factors that underlie familial violence—they specifically uncovered the role of step-parenting, a situational factor with clear and theoretically predictable relevance to issues tied to genetic fitness (from a strictly genetic-fitness perspective, a step-child shares no genes with a step-parent, and is, thus, costly).

Given the tremendous potential for EP to inform the search for contextual factors that underlie human psychological outcomes, this idea of evolutionary situationism has the potential to create extraordinary bridges between traditional social psychology and EP. . . .

## The Future of Evolutionary Psychology

Evolutionary psychology has proven extremely powerful in (a) providing coherent explanations for many basic human behavioral patterns, (b) generating new research questions that simply would not be on the radar screen without EP as a guiding framework, and (c) generating novel findings about what it means to be human.

In terms of providing coherent explanations for basic psychological processes, consider Ekman and Friesen's landmark work demonstrating the universal nature of emotional expression. The evolutionary reasoning that these authors draw upon, arguing, essentially, that emotional-expression abilities must have been positively selected for across the evolution of our species due to the fitness-related benefits of such abilities, provides an extremely useful and coherent framework for understanding human emotion in general. I am fully confident that it is very much in the interest of all the behavioral sciences to ultimately support efforts designed to understand human behavioral patterns in light of our evolutionary history.

In generating novel research questions, consider Haselton and Miller's research demonstrating that women are particularly attracted to indices of creativity in potential mates during peaks in their ovulatory cycles. This research is excessively rooted in evolutionary ideas. First, the general idea that female mating psychology should vary as a function of variability in fertility across the ovulatory cycle is an idea that only makes sense when we think of psychological processes as being designed for the purposes of successfully reproducing. Additionally, the fact that this research focuses on attraction to indices of creative intelligence is rooted in Miller's theory of higher-order human cognitive abilities (such as creative intelligence) as having resulted from sexual selection pressures across evolutionary time and as serving the function of affording individuals benefits in the domain of intrasexual competition. Again, without guidance from EP, which suggests that basic psychological processes likely serve a reproductive function, the questions addressed in this research simply never would have made it onto the radar screen.

Just as EP allows novel questions to be asked, it allows such questions to be answered, thereby providing the world with all kinds of discoveries regarding our nature. While research in the domain of adaptations to ovulation strongly demonstrates several novel findings regarding human mating behavior, such research only provides the tip of the iceberg when it comes to novel findings obtained by evolutionary psychologists. In fact, evolutionary psychologists are responsible for uncovering novel findings across the entire range of psychological phenomena such as the inter-play between mating and homicide, the neuropsychological substrates underlying the detection of individuals who cheat in social-exchange situations the phenomenology of stranger anxiety experienced by babies, and the nature of altruistic tendencies across species.

(For a reader interested in reading more about the scientific utility of EP across the modern landscape of the behavioral sciences, I strongly recommend Ketelaar and Ellis' paper which conceives of EP as a meta-theory that guides research in a coherent manner and a paper by Schmitt and Pilcher which provides a model regarding the thorough methodology employed by evolutionary psychologists when they are at their best in trying to uncover human nature.)

In light of the powerful nature of EP in generating new questions and findings, I believe, strongly, that psychology writ large can only reach its potential by incorporating an evolutionary perspective across all its areas. Further, I believe that there is reason for optimism regarding the future of EP and the future of an evolutionarily informed psychology in general. Consider, for example, a recent analysis of articles published in a leading journal in the behavioral sciences, Behavioral and Brain Sciences, which revealed that more than 30% of articles published in the last decade include evolution in the title or as a keyword. These findings suggest that evolution is, in fact, making its way into the behavioral sciences.

However, with that said, an analysis regarding the education of the authors of these evolutionarily informed articles tells a different story. When authors of these articles were interviewed about their education, they generally reported being self-taught with regard to evolutionary principles. Such an effect is consistent with the portrait of academic institutions as less than fully embracing of the incorporation of evolution into the realm of human behavior.

Taken together, the different ideas presented in this section paint a variegated picture with regard to the inclusion of evolution into the behavioral sciences. On the one hand, a great deal of research on the evolutionary origins of human behavior and psychological processes is being conducted. This research is leading to novel findings regarding topics that cut across all areas within psychology. On the other hand, EP is a target of hostility from adherents of multiple political and ideological perspectives. Such implacable hostility emanates from characterizations of EP as overly deterministic, reductionistic, sexist, racist, and, simply, evil.

Importantly, there are several critiques of EP that are reasonable and that should be addressed. For instance, Panksepp and Panksepp, argue that evolutionary psychologists could improve their work by taking a less modularistic approach, working more closely on neurological substrates of behavior, and paying more attention to research regarding the neuroplasticity which seems to characterize much of the human brain. To be fair to these critics (and to others), I strongly believe that EP is not perfect and this approach to psychology has room for improvement. However, I see no reason to throw the baby out with the bath water. As Dawkins writes regarding recent critiques of EP: "Some individual evolutionary psychologists need to clean up their methodological act. Maybe many do. But that is true of scientists in all fields."

In short, EP has proven itself as having extraordinary abilities to (a) yield novel ways of thinking about who we are and to (b) generate new findings that shed light on the depths of our minds. While this approach may not be perfect, and while certain studies conducted under the general banner of EP may need improvement, the overall approach to understanding human behavior—focusing on understanding how basic psychological processes ultimately bear on issues tied to reproductive success—has an enormous capacity to improve our understanding of ourselves. I urge psychological researchers and students to go down the path of evolutionary enlightenment so as to allow psychology to realize its full potential—ultimately allowing our discipline to best help people deal with the many problems associated with what it means to be human.

## Conclusion

My intellectual passions permeate my teaching and my research. After learning about applications of evolutionary theory to issues regarding behavior in Benjamin Sachs' Animal Behavior course in 1990 at the University of Connecticut, I came to see the evolutionary informed approach to psychology as the most coherent and powerful framework for understanding behavior across species (including *Homo Sapiens*). This intellectual approach to understanding psychology has permeated my teaching and my research since that time.

As stated prior, I do not believe that all EP is perfect. In the future, evolutionary approaches to psychology will surely benefit from better understanding the interrelationship between cultural and genetic forces that underlie behavior, studying the nature of neuroplasticity from an evolutionary perspective, teasing apart psychological qualities that were shaped for survival versus reproductive purposes, and addressing the interplay between behaviors that emerge in an ontogenetic timescale versus behaviors that are the result of thousands of generations of selection across our phylogenetic history. Further, I am certain that other improvements to an evolutionary approach to psychology are out there!

However—my student Warren Greig tells me that I need to be less apologetic when it comes to my passion for EP. And, as usual, he is right. As such, I end by making some simple points. First, EP is not an inherently evil approach to understanding human behavior. It is not overly immutable in its portrait of humans. It is, alternatively, one of the most situationistic/contextualistic doctrines that exists regarding human behavior. EP is not the new eugenics. In fact, EP and eugenics have virtually no commonalities whatsoever.

Evolutionary psychology is an extraordinarily coherent framework for understanding virtually all of human psychology. Its basic assumptions, suggesting (a) that fundamental human psychological processes were shaped by evolutionary forces and that (b) such psychological processes and behavioral patterns can be best understood in light of such evolutionary forces, are as solid and reasonable as the theory of evolution itself. Acknowledging this point is sure to benefit all work conducted in the realm of psychology.

**Edwin E. Gantt and**
**Brent S. Melling**

# NO

# Evolutionary Psychology Isn't Evil, It's Just Not Any Good

". . . If there is a sure road to intellectual atrophy, it is paved with the complacent certainty that one's critics are deluded."

It is hard not to be amused when one hears advocates of evolutionary psychology (EP), such as Richard Dawkins, Daniel Dennett, and Glenn Geher, grumble that so many people take issue with their ideas. After all, couldn't one reasonably suspect that such firm believers in the universal truth of evolution would welcome the opportunity to see how their theories fare in the cutthroat competitive marketplace of ideas? Academics, red in tooth and claw, and all that? Certainly, if the theories of EP are true, they are strong enough to take on all comers and prove their hardiness by adapting to the challenges of lesser ideas. In the end, isn't that what evolutionary theory is all about anyway?

Oddly, most evolutionary psychologists seem to prefer to short-circuit critique instead of welcoming it, declaring critical examination to be off-limits at the outset. When not casting aspersions on critics by claiming they can only be motivated by unscientific or religious impulses, they treat objections to EP as though they were wholesale rejections of well-established Darwinian principles in biology. While this may be a clever debating move, and might win you a few points with the high school debating club, it is nonetheless pure sophistry and unworthy of the serious intellectual examination that science demands. Still, since Geher begins his defense of EP by chiding the motives of any who might venture a critique, it is important to be very clear at the outset here about what our response is NOT. What we have to say here is NOT some fundamentalist Christian rejection of evolutionary biology or Darwin's theories of natural selection. Neither is this article motivated by some desire to defend Creationism, Young Earth Theology, or Intelligent Design Theory. Although some of the controversies presently surrounding Darwinism in biology and its Intelligent Design rivals are thought-provoking, those issues are not our issues. The fact is that it is possible to be a strident and thoughtful critic of EP and have no commitment whatsoever to a religious worldview, fundamentalist or otherwise.

Additionally, this paper is in no way a defense of what evolutionary psychologists (EPs) like to call the "Standard Social Science Model (SSSM)" or "Secular Creationism." Indeed, despite all of the bluster to the contrary by folks like Geher, Steven Pinker, and others, it is hard to imagine that there is anyone in contemporary psychology who would defend what these people claim that advocates of the SSSM believe, especially given that "no serious figure embraces that view since, perhaps, John Watson in the early twentieth century." This "rhetoric of exclusion," whereby "whomever is not for the program is against Darwin," clearly owes more to hidebound dogmatism than it does to open-minded, scientific thinking.

What, then, is our purpose here? It is simply this: We seek to engage in a critical scientific and philosophical reflection about fundamental concepts in the social sciences, as well as consider of some of the implications of taking EP seriously. In short, what we propose to do here is a brief bit of critical thinking about some of the assumptions, implications, and claims of EP. We aim to show that EP is not nearly as coherent, obvious, or harmless as its defenders suggest.

## Rhetoric, Values, and Ideology

In addition to the rhetoric of exclusion, EPs often employ the rhetoric of objectivism. Although there are various ways in which the term "objectivism" is defined, we will use it to refer to the assumption that one's methods are value-neutral and unbiased and, thus, that one's reporting of research findings is the reporting of objective facts about the world rather than particular interpretations of it. As is often the case in scientific research, the findings of EP researchers are usually presented as being objective in nature, the products of a value-neutral and unbiased mode of inquiry. For example, Geher offers up the research findings of many of his colleagues in order to support his contention about the significant contributions that EP is making to the study of human nature. While citing supporting research is necessary, it is important to note the language that Geher employs in so doing. Like other evolutionary psychologists, he frequently states that EP research has "documented" or is "demonstrating" some fact about human nature and the evolution of behavior. This rhetorical strategy helps paint a mental picture in which psychologists like Geher are engaged in simply observing the world of human behavior and documenting the facts of such behavior—facts that would be obvious to any rational being using the scientific method and not blinded by personal ambition, cultural shortsightedness, or religious bigotry. Likewise, when Geher maintains that EP is not "driven by ideology; it is driven by the basic scientific motive of increasing understanding of the natural world," he is invoking the authority of objectivism to persuade us that we can have confidence both in both his own claims and that of his EP colleagues because such claims are free of the self-serving and biasing influences of values and ideologies.

Unfortunately, Geher's confident assurances to the contrary, EP is inescapably undergird with a variety of biases, values, and ideological commitments that serve not only to direct and shape EP's study of human behavior, but also provide the conceptual framework from within which data is interpreted. There are at least three such biases that often go unexamined or unacknowledged by EP theorists and researchers: objectivism, materialism, and instrumentalism. The first of these—objectivism—has already been discussed above in terms of its role in the rhetoric employed by advocates of EP. Objectivism is not just a rhetorical strategy, but is also a particular value—though rarely admitted as such. Objectivism is a bias not only in holding that the results of scientific research are value-neutral and free of the taint of human bias, but also in suggesting that the results of scientific investigation *ought to be* free of such flaws. Ironically, this claim that science "ought" to be objective to be good science is itself a subjective preference (or value) regarding how researchers should go about conducting their science and is not the only valid or possible perspective.

Likewise, materialism is a commonly taken-for-granted assumption in the natural and social sciences, particularly among EPs. Materialism is the notion that matter is the only reality and that everything, including thought, feeling, mind, and will, can be exhaustively explained in terms of matter and physical phenomena. This stance is not an incontrovertible fact of the universe conclusively demonstrated by scientific investigation but an assumption about the nature of reality that itself cannot be proven or disproven, especially by a materialist science that begins by assuming that materialism is true. In other words, materialism is a sort of faith, or set of beliefs and ideas that one assumes to be true but for which there is not—nor ever can be—conclusive proof. It is, in this way, clearly an ideology and not a demonstrated fact of the universe. Thus, EPs prefer materialist accounts of human behavior, not because such accounts have been *proven* in any way to be the best, the truest, or the most rational ones available, but rather because materialism is the ideology they have come to endorse for philosophical, theological, and/or cultural reasons.

Finally, EP accounts of human behavior assume instrumentalism, or the idea that all behavior is governed by some manner of calculative means-ends rationale, whereby any given behavior is best understood as just a means to attaining some other goal. In the case of EP, the ultimate goal or end toward which all behavior is striving is, of course, reproductive success. In fact, as Richard Dawkins has argued, from the EP perspective we are really just "survival machines" designed by our genes over eons of evolutionary history to ensure that these genes are able to continue on into future generations. "Their preservation," says Dawkins, "is the ultimate rationale for our existence." Thus, Geher speaks of "mating tactics" and "sexual strategies" and asserts that caring for step-children is "costly" because such children share no genes with the step-parent. Similarly, Robert Wright, another ardent advocate of EP, argues that "beneath the thoughts and feelings and temperamental differences marriage counselors spend their time sensitively assessing are the stratagems of the genes—cold hard equations composed of simple variables: social status, age of spouse, number of children, their ages, outside romantic opportunities, and so on." Nonetheless, even though EPs are strident and vocal in their assertion that all human behavior can be explained in terms of means-ends calculation, such claims are not based on any indisputable or documented fact but on certain philosophical assumptions about human nature and what constitutes the ultimate good in life. Even though instrumentalist assumptions may be so widely held in modern Western culture as to seem obvious, it is still the case that instrumental reasoning reflects a particular set of values arising from a particular ideology.

## What the Data Says

Although their commitment to objectivism leads EPs to present their research findings as though the data is obvious and can only be explained from an evolutionary perspective, it is simply not the case that data ever speaks for itself. Data must always be interpreted in some way. Scientists must always provide some meaningful context within which particular findings can be understood and rendered sensible. Indeed, some authors have shown that not only does one's data require interpretation to be meaningful, but one's chosen method of investigation itself reflects an interpretation of the world that directs researchers to particular ways of making sense of one's data. Thus, no one is surprised when a feminist interprets an event as evidence of gender inequality, or by a Marxist who interprets the same event as the result of class-struggle. So we shouldn't be surprised when an evolutionary psychologist interprets the same event as a product of natural selection. None of these theorists use their particular explanatory framework because there is inherently more factual evidence for them—it is the framework itself that determines what counts as evidence and how it is to be interpreted. Thus, a feminist theorist will tend to see all situations as providing evidence of feminist assumptions, a Marxist will tend to see confirmation of Marxist assumptions, and an EP will tend to see evidence of evolutionary processes at work.

While most contemporary philosophers of science recognize that the interpretation of data requires an assumed framework, many EPs seem to think that their interpretive framework—or "meta-theory"—is inherently better because it is more parsimonious, more rational, or can explain all of the empirical data. What they seem to fail to realize is that all other reasonably sophisticated meta-theories can do the same. The ability to explain psychological phenomena by means of concepts borrowed from evolutionary biology is not testament to the fact that such explanations are true, only that evolution is a sophisticated and encompassing worldview—but, then again, so are many others.

Thus, while Geher cites the work of David Buss on mate-age selection as empirical proof that females select older men due the imperatives of natural selection, what is actually being offered is a particular way of interpreting the data at hand. Other interpretations are not only possible but viable. For example, rather than evidence of natural selection's instrumental operation for reproductive advantage, it could be that the age differential in mate-selection might reflect that women typically mature earlier than men and are more socially and verbally inclined. Thus, the observed age differences might simply reflect women's efforts to assure themselves of more socially skilled, verbally expressive, and interesting companions. Likewise, Geher offers up Daly and Wilson's research on domestic violence to demonstrate what has come to be known as the Cinderella Effect. Namely that children living with step-parents are about 100 times more likely to be fatally abused because natural selection shaped humans to take better care of our biological offspring than children with whom we do not share genes. Here too, alternative explanations are available that account for the data and are rationally defensible. A child is only going to be living with a stepparent if there has been some significant emotional, economic, and/or social disturbance of the family in the first place. Therefore, the social and relational problems that have contributed to the break-up of the original family are likely to continue with parents and children into subsequent family arrangements. It should be apparent that one need not invoke some powerful underlying genetic recognition and selection process to make adequate sense of this particular situation (for additional examples of alternative interpretations of EP research findings).

These examples of data reinterpretation aren't just interesting and clever intellectual exercises. Rather, we feel that they are important illustrations of critically reflecting on scientific knowledge claims, especially in terms of how data is interpreted and reported, for the history of science is replete with examples of researchers discovering and reporting presumably obvious facts that are later found to be not only questionable but on occasion outright false and misleading (e.g., phlogiston, phrenology, the geocentric theory of the universe, the Meckel-Serres Law, and classical Newtonian physics). The proper conduct of science requires, we believe, humility and continual critical self-reflection, not the dogmatic and repetitious assertion that one has found once and for all the indisputable truth of life, the universe, and everything.

## Reductionism and Determinism

Another guiding ideology of EP is monism—the idea that all of reality is of the same kind, subject to the same rules and laws. The advantage to this position is that it avoids some of the tricky issues inherent in "the mind-body problem" (e.g., how do minds and bodies interact, how can mind be observed or measured, etc.). By starting from the assumption that "minds are on the same footing as bodies where Darwinian natural selection is concerned," EPs hope to sidestep the problem of how something seemingly immaterial, such as a thought or an emotion can have an effect on the material world. The way evolutionary psychologists achieve this monism, however, is by reducing one side of our experience (i.e., the immaterial side of minds, thoughts, and emotions) to another side of our experience (i.e., the material side of genes, brains, and bodies). As Geher states, the evolutionary perspective fundamentally "conceives of human behavior as resulting from the nervous system." In such a scheme, what we experience as immaterial (like feelings of love) is seen to be really nothing more than an expression of complicated physical realities (e.g., elevated hormones, particular neuronal firings, genetic tendencies and environmental conditions). Instead of integrating the immaterial and material into a meaningful whole, however, one facet of human experience is simply explained away by reducing it down to another. The end result of this sort of approach is not monism, but rather a "one-sided dualism" in which important but less easily or accurately measured features of the mind (i.e., thoughts, intentions, emotions, etc.) are ignored or discounted so that attention can be solely focused on the precisely measurable features of the brain such as synaptic activity and neurotransmitter levels. Unfortunately for EP, however, simply ignoring or discounting the essential nature of mental phenomena does little to actually explain how such things might arise out of one's genes or nervous system in the first place. After all, while a well-functioning nervous system may certainly be something that is necessary for having thoughts, making choices, and experiencing emotions, this does not mean that the nervous system is the only thing that one has to attend to when trying to make sense of where our thoughts, choices, and feelings come from or what they mean.

Unfortunately, this reductionism perpetuates the problems that evolutionary psychologists typically seek to avoid—a loss of meaning, morality, and choice. All of these things—though intangible in nature—are nonetheless real phenomena common to human experience that cannot be easily dismissed. By reducing mind to brain, however, EPs ultimately reduce the rich meanings of our lives and relationships into the merely mechanical happenings of our bodies. Instead of being human persons capable of making genuine choices, we become, as the novelist Terry Bisson once famously wrote, "Thinking meat! Conscious meat! Loving meat! Dreaming meat! The meat is the whole deal!" If we take EP seriously, our values and ethics are ultimately really nothing more than the chance result of a complicated interaction of genetic survival mechanisms and environmental happenstance. What is morally good in life, what is worthy and right is simply whatever increases our likelihood to survive, or at least pass on our genetic material to subsequent generations.

Evolutionary psychologists often protest these sorts of criticisms, arguing that they do not reduce all human activity to biology because other factors—such as culture and personal disposition—play a significant role in how our genetic predispositions are realized. However, when accounting for the origins of culture and its variations, EP ultimately falls back on biological reductionism. As Geher states, genetic shaping by natural selection (determinism) "applies to all domains of psychology" and any account that does not see how "the broad evolutionary factors that have given rise to our species and, ultimately, to our psychology, is . . . simply misguided." According to EP, culture is itself a product of natural selection and exists primarily to provide particular mating rituals that will help to ensure genetic fitness in our offspring. So, if complex social and cultural behaviors are part of the natural world and not immune from the laws that govern it, then it is hard to believe defenders of EP when they say that human beings are not determined by their biology. Granted, it is not a direct genetic determinism where "behavior is controlled exclusively by genes, with little or no role for environmental influence." But, such assurances provide little comfort in the face of EP's contention that our behavior is controlled *mutually* by our genes AND the cultural forces that genetic selection has produced. So, if Geher and other EPs are, in fact, "uncomfortable (on both moral and intellectual grounds) with any perspective that sees humans as fully incapable of choosing their own behaviors," then perhaps it is time for them to be a little more uncomfortable with evolutionary psychology's conception of human nature.

## The Problem of Nihilism

Possibly the most troubling problem inherent to an EP approach is that it is fundamentally nihilistic. Nihilism is the notion that life is, at its root, without ultimate meaning or purpose, and that the genuine moral distinctions between good and bad, right and wrong, cannot be rationally defended. If all human behavior is just the causal outcome of the unthinking, undirected, mechanical processes of natural selection, then human actions are no longer meaningful in any real sense. In other words, if our behavior is something that is determined for us by something beyond of our control or active participation, then what we do or think or feel does not possess any intrinsic meaning.

For example, consider the day-long motion of blades of grass as they slowly bend and change position relative to the location of the sun. As a fundamentally biological and determined event, this phenomenon is simply what it is, and has no intrinsic meaning. Granted, a golfer might attribute meaning to the "lean of the grass" while preparing to make a putt, but this attribution of meaning is merely subjective and, as such, does not reflect any real meaning in the events of the natural world taking place there on the green. Of course, if the golfer's subjective meaning is itself just the causal product of something going on in her brain, then that too would lack any genuine meaning and be basically the same as what is taking place with the grass. Only if there is the genuine possibility that a given event could be otherwise than it is does it make any sense to consider it to be genuinely meaningful (as opposed to merely subjectively meaningful).

Thus, if to be human is to be nothing more than a "gigantic lumbering robot" whose sole purpose for existing is the preservation of our genes, the meaning of our lives, our loves, our friends and families seems quite hollow. Sure, we may experience ourselves as being deeply in love with our spouse but such feelings are simply "illusions" caused by particularly complex biochemistry striving to get our body motivated enough to find a suitable mate for replicating our genes. All this romantic fuss is just so much clever claptrap meant to manipulate suitable others into sticking around long enough for successful reproduction. If EP is correct on this point, and matter is all that matters, then in the end nothing else about us *really* matters at all.

Given their commitment to objectivity, EP is typically presented as nothing more than an account of the "is" of human behavior. Advocates of EP, such as Geher, passionately reject any suggestion that their theories of human nature have anything whatsoever to say about how human behavior "ought" to be, claiming that such criticism simply reflects the naturalistic fallacy. However, if one of the most basic claims of EP is true (i.e., human nature is the causal product of material events and natural laws), and culture is itself just a byproduct of evolutionary forces acting on material events (i.e., brain function and genetic selection), then it makes little sense to say that there are any legitimate "oughts" in the world at all. If culture "originates in, is transmitted by, and is propagated through mental mechanisms that evolved through natural selection," and evolution through natural selection is fundamentally a purposeless, random process reliant on the chance interplay of natural events, then the "oughts" we experience and which constitute our cultural moral norms are really just accidental developments in the long march of human evolutionary history. If our fundamental sensibilities of right and wrong, good and evil are such accidents, then it makes no more sense to argue that murder or rape or theft is morally wrong than it does to claim that elephants should have smaller trunks or longer tusks. Unless morality is ultimately grounded in something a bit more solid and trustworthy than contingent evolutionary history, it is impossible to maintain that any particular way of life is really better or more meaningful than any other.

In closing, after all that has been said so far, one cannot help but wonder whether EP is ultimately not only an enemy of meaning and morality, but also of science and reason. A basic claim of EP—and one with which we have taken repeated issue in this brief essay—is materialism, or the notion that at the root of all of our thoughts and ideas there are really just the happenstance events of the brain and the genes. This truly startling claim has become so commonplace in our modern world that it's deeply disturbing implications for not only how we understand ourselves but also how we understand science typically go entirely unnoticed. We have tried to explore a few of those implications throughout this piece. There is, however, one last implication of this line of thinking that we would like mention before concluding.

Because of its fundamental commitment to materialism and determinism, EP claims that all of our thoughts, feelings, and behaviors are rooted in unthinking, non-rational, non-caring processes and causes aimed solely at ensuring successful reproduction. Therefore, because the driving purpose behind evolution is reproduction, not rationality, we cannot assume that the fruits of evolution, including human thought and culture, reflect the rise of anything inherently rational. Natural selection's fundamental aim, after all, is not to shape a human mind capable of producing true beliefs but to produce a mind whose beliefs motivate us toward reproductively advantageous behaviors, whether those beliefs are true or not. As Churchland, a prominent advocate of EP, has stated:

> "Looked at from an evolutionary point of view, the principle function of nervous systems is to enable the organism to move appropriately. Boiled down to essentials, a nervous system enables the organism to succeed in the four F's: feeding, fleeing, fighting, and reproducing. The principle chore of nervous systems is to get the body parts where they should be in order that the organism may survive. . . . Truth, whatever that is, definitely takes the hindmost."

There is more than a little irony in such a confident pronouncement, especially when the one making it is doing so in the name of scientific progress and truth. For, if our thoughts are simply the results of our biochemistry moving us toward reproduction, then the thought "evolutionary psychology is the best way to understand people" is itself not a rationally defensible or inherently true thought. Rather, it is simply something our brains make us think and say so that we might impress other reproductively viable members of our species in order to get them to mate with us.

The irony doesn't end here, though, for whether you accept the notion that evolutionary psychological theories of human behavior are true or reject them as pseudoscientific fables depends entirely on which genes are influencing your current neurological interactions with the environment AND NOT on whether you have been or could ever be persuaded by reasoned argument and the convincing power of truth. To put it another way, if EP is true, then the only reason anyone would advocate it is because (anyone, they) must do so given their evolutionary history and the particular mental mechanisms that their genes have provided them. Likewise, critics of the theory are only critics because they don't happen to possess the appropriate "evolutionary psychology is true" thought generating brain functions or genes. So much for reason, so much for science, so much for truth!

Ultimately, then, if EP is the "basic intellectual framework for understanding all psychological phenomena," as Geher argues, then natural selection is also the undergirding explanation for all of the activities and ideas of scientific researchers. The theories and conclusions of these scientists, including the evolutionary psychologist, are nothing more than the results of complex interactions between meaningless arrangements of matter and, as such, provide no assurance that they accurately reflect the truth of things. Indeed, if what Geher asserts is true, then his own scientific article is to be explained as really just an elaborate manipulation of his readers by his genes to maximize their chances of reproductive success. If EP is taken to its logical conclusion, then, there is nothing left of truth, meaning or morality in *any* human phenomenon, let alone the phenomenon of generating a scientific theory like EP and writing an article about it. In the end, we can't help but conclude that Geher is correct when he states that EP isn't evil—because from the EP perspective there is ultimately no such thing as good or evil, right or wrong, meaning or reason or truth. So, while its own perspective guarantees that EP cannot be evil, it also makes a pretty strong case that it isn't any good.

# CHALLENGE QUESTIONS

## Is Evolution a Good Explanation for Psychological Concepts?

1. A major contention between these two positions is the objectivity of EP. Are evolutionary accounts of human behavior unbiased in their explanations? Should they be?
2. The authors of both articles agree that evolution is not evil, but for different reasons. What are these reasons? Do the articles differ about the "goodness" of EP? Why or why not?
3. Geher claims that EP works well for all aspects of psychology. How well does it account for the claims of humanistic or existential psychologists? If EP has trouble accounting for these claims, then what might this suggest about these schools of psychology? What does it suggest for EP?
4. What results have we gained from EP research? What would Gantt and Melling say about these results?
5. Geher suggests that EP is monism because the mind is governed by the same natural processes as the body. However, Gantt and Melling accuse this position of being a type of dualism. Which do you feel is correct on this issue, and why?
6. Geher suggests that EP is not overly deterministic because it takes account of environment and circumstance. Does this avoid the charge of determinism (i.e., all so-called human choices are determined by other factors and thus the person really has no true options)?

# Internet References . . .

## Developmental Psychology

This website provides academic resources and links related to developmental psychology.

**http://www.psy.pdx.edu/PsiCafe/Areas/Developmental/**

## Divorcerate.org

This site gives up-to-date information on the divorce rates of the United States, Great Britain, Canada, and other countries. It also provides information on whether or not divorced couples have children, have been previously married, and what age those couples were when they decided to get married.

**http://www.divorcerate.org/**

## Children of Divorce: All Kinds of Problems

This Americans for Divorce Reform page offers links to studies of problems experienced by children of divorce.

**http://www.divorcereform.org/all.html**

## Family Research Institute

The Family Research Institute is a nonprofit organization that conducts research on issues pertaining to families. This site has links to many publications of studies and papers on different topics, including divorce and homosexuality.

**http://www.familyresearchinst.org/index.html**

## Research on Social Network Sites

Provides numerous links to research articles on social networking sites from communications, information science, anthropology, sociology, economics, political science, cultural studies, computer science, and psychology. Regularly updates with new research on sites such as MySpace, Facebook, LiveJournal and many others.

**http://www.danah.org/SNSResearch.html**

## A Portrait of "Generation Next"

Looks at the perspective of "Generation Next" (youth born after 1981) including opinions on life, the future, and politics. Also shows comparisons between Generation Next, Generation X, The Baby Boomers, and Seniors.

**http://people-press.org/report/300/a-portrait-of-generation-next**

# UNIT 3

## Human Development

*The objective of most developmental psychologists is to document the course of our physical, social, and cognitive changes over the entire span of our lives. Childhood and adolescence have probably received the most attention because they are often thought to set the stage for the rest of human development. But what has the greatest influence on human development during these early years? Some suggest that parental influences have profound effects on children's later lives. How does the divorce of parents affect the children involved? If the divorce is preceded by bitter fighting and relationship tensions, could divorce have benefits? If adolescents turn from parent to peers for developmental cues, what effect does this have? With the prevalence of internet communication, online relationships are increasingly taking the place of traditional face-to-face communication? Is this good? The promotion of electronic communications has also allowed young people to dedicate websites and pages to themselves, such as Facebook and MySpace. Is such a practice helpful in establishing positive self-esteem? If today's youth are more self-centered then earlier generations, is this a bad thing?*

# ISSUE 7

## Does Divorce Have Positive Long-Term Effects for the Children Involved?

**YES: Constance Ahrons,** from *We're Still Family: What Grown Children Have to Say About Their Parents' Divorce* (HarperCollins, 2004)

**NO: Elizabeth Marquardt,** from "The Bad Divorce," *First Things* (February 2005)

**ISSUE SUMMARY**

**YES:** The founding co-chair of the Council on Contemporary Families, Constance Ahrons, argues not only that the commonly assumed negative effects on children of divorced families are myths but also that these children actually emerge stronger, wiser, and with closer family connections.

**NO:** Director of the Center for Marriage and Families at the Institute for American Values, Elizabeth Marquardt, addresses perceived flaws in Ahrons' study and claims from her own work and experience that divorce negatively affects children for the rest of their lives.

One of the unfortunate facts of modern life is that first marriages are likely to fail 50 percent of the time. The failure rate for second marriages is even worse, with an approximately 67 percent rate of failure. Because these percentages have been fairly constant for almost two generations, some researchers have estimated that almost a quarter of all the people living today between the ages of 18 and 44 have parents who are divorced. What effect, if any, does the divorce of parents have on their children? Does divorce have a lasting negative influence, or is it potentially beneficial, with lessons learned and relationships corrected?

Answering these questions is one of the many interests of two subdisciplines of psychology—clinical and developmental. Clinical psychologists are concerned with influences that would hinder a person from living a fulfilling life. They might wonder if divorce contributes to the problems that prevent such a life and lead to the need for psychotherapy and counseling. Developmental psychologists have similar interests. Their emphasis, however, is on how the events of childhood or adolescence, such as parental divorce, influence successful aging and development. With all these practical implications in the balance, one might think that researchers had long ago decided the effects of divorce. Perhaps surprisingly, the issue is still hotly contested, with leading researchers coming to dramatically different conclusions in the following articles.

In the first article, Constance Ahrons argues that adult children of divorce are no more troubled or disoriented about relationships than those of intact families. She contends that a "cultural lag" is the reason society is so reluctant to see divorce as a positive change in children's lives. She addresses what she views as the cultural misconceptions about divorce. For example, the popular stereotype is that divorce is the defining factor in a child's overall happiness, when, in fact, adult children view their parent's divorce as merely a part of their history. Ahrons admits that divorce can be a stressful event, but she believes that it can actually enhance a person's life when handled correctly.

Elizabeth Marquardt directly counters Ahrons' article. Her main point is that divorce can be traumatic for the children involved, which leads ultimately to lasting effects. She concurs with Ahrons that society can stigmatize the children of divorce. However, she argues that these stigmas can hinder the ability to cope positively with the divorce itself. Indeed, to minimize the negative effects of divorce is problematic. As she puts it, "Treating a sad, unfortunate experience . . . as something neutral or even positive is merely one example of what can happen when a person attempts to conform to a culture that insists that divorce is no big deal." Marquardt also criticizes Ahrons' sample selection and methods, and ultimately concludes that Ahron's results are unreliable.

**POINT**

- Good divorces are invisible due to a "cultural lag" that insists divorce is bad and harmful.
- There are seven misconceptions that lead society to believe that divorce is bad.
- Family ideals are changing, but this doesn't mean they cannot meet the needs of children.
- Many children emerge from their parent's divorce wiser, stronger, and with healthier relationships.

**COUNTERPOINT**

- Our culture insists that divorce is no big deal, thus keeping children from healing.
- Ahron's misconceptions are formed from skewed and biased data.
- Merely changing terms and definitions does not avoid the real anguish of divorce.
- The trauma of divorce is unlikely to leave anyone, especially vulnerable children, unscathed.

YES  **Constance Ahrons**

# No Easy Answers: Why the Popular View of Divorce Is Wrong

It was a sunny, unseasonably warm Sunday morning in October. In a quaint country inn in New Jersey, surrounded by a glorious autumn garden, my young grandchildren and I waited patiently for their Aunt Jennifer's wedding to begin. The white carpet was unrolled, the guests were assembled, and the harpist was playing Pachelbel's Canon.

A hush came over the guests. The first member of the bridal party appeared. Poised at the entry, she took a deep breath as she began her slow-paced walk down the white wedding path. Pauline, my grandchildren's stepgreat-grandmother, made her way down the aisle, pausing occasionally to greet family and friends. A round of applause spontaneously erupted. She had traveled fifteen hundred miles to be at her granddaughter's wedding, when only days before, a threatening illness made her presence doubtful.

Next in the grand parade came the best man, one of the groom's three brothers. Proudly, he made his way down the aisle and took his position, ready to be at his brother's side. Then the two maids of honor, looking lovely in their flowing black chiffon gowns, made their appearance. My grandchildren started to wiggle and whisper: "It's Aunt Amy [my younger daughter]! And Christine [the longtime girlfriend who cohabits with Uncle Craig, my daughters' half-brother]!" As they walked down the aisle and moved slowly past us, special smiles were exchanged with my grandchildren—their nieces and nephew.

Seconds later, my youngest granddaughter pointed excitedly, exclaiming, "Here comes Mommy!" They waved excitedly as the next member of the bridal party, the matron of honor—*their mother, my daughter*—made her way down the path. She paused briefly at our row to exchange a fleeting greeting with her children.

Next, the groom, soon officially to be their "Uncle Andrew," with his mother's arm linked on his left, and his father on his right. The happy threesome joined the processional. Divorced from each other when Andrew was a child, his parents beamed in anticipation of the marriage of their eldest son.

Silence. All heads now turned to catch their first glimpse of the bride. Greeted with oohs and aahs, Aunt Jennifer was radiant as she walked arm in arm with her proud and elegant mother, their stepgrandmother, Grandma

Susan. Sadly missed at that moment was the father of the bride, my former husband, who had passed away a few years earlier.

When I told friends in California I was flying to the East Coast for a family wedding, I stumbled over how to explain my relationship to the bride. To some I explained: "She's my exhusband's daughter by his second wife." To others, perhaps to be provocative and draw attention to the lack of kinship terms, I said, "She's my daughters' sister." Of course, technically she's my daughters' halfsister, but many years ago my daughters told me firmly that that term "half-sister" was utterly ridiculous. Jennifer wasn't a half anything, she was their *real* sister. Some of my friends thought it strange that I would be invited; others thought it even stranger that I would travel cross-country to attend.

The wedding reception brought an awkward moment or two, when some of the groom's guests asked a common question, "How was I related to the bride?" With some guilt at violating my daughters' dictum, but not knowing how else to identify our kinship, I answered, "She is my daughters' halfsister." A puzzled look. It was not that they didn't understand the relationship, but it seemed strange to them that I was a wedding guest. As we talked, a few guests noted how nice it was that I was there, and then with great elaboration told me stories about their own complex families. Some told me sad stories of families torn apart by divorce and remarriage, and others related happy stories of how their complex families of divorce had come together at family celebrations.

At several points during this celebratory day, I happened to be standing next to the bride's mother when someone from the groom's side asked us how we were related. She or I pleasantly answered, "We used to be married to the same man." This response turned out to be a showstopper. The question asker was at a loss to respond. First and second wives aren't supposed to be amicable or even respectful toward one another. And certainly, first wives are not supposed to be included in their exhusband's new families. And last of all, first and second wives shouldn't be willing to comfortably share the information of having a husband in common.

Although it may appear strange, my exhusband's untimely death brought his second and first families closer together. I had mourned at his funeral and spent time with his family and friends for several days afterward. A different level of kinship formed, as we–his first and second families–shared our loss and sadness. Since then, we have chosen to join together at several family celebrations, which has added a deeper dimension to our feelings of family.

You may be thinking, "This is all so rational. There's no way my family could pull this off." Or perhaps, like the many people who have shared their stories with me over the years, you are nodding your head knowingly, remembering similar occasions in your own family. The truth is we are like many extended families rearranged by divorce. My ties to my exhusband's family are not close but we care about one another. We seldom have contact outside of family occasions, but we know we're family. We hear stories of each other's comings and goings, transmitted to us through our mutual ties to my daughters, and now, through grandchildren. But if many families, like my own, continue to have relationships years after divorce, why don't we hear more about them?

Quite simply, it's because this is not the way it's supposed to be. My family and the many others like mine, don't fit the ideal images we have about families. They appear strange because they're not tidy. There are "extra" people and relationships that don't exist in nuclear families and are awkward to describe because we don't have familiar and socially defined kinship terms to do so. Although families rearranged and expanded by divorce are rapidly growing and increasingly common, our resistance to accepting them as normal makes them appear deviant.

Societal change is painfully slow, which results in the situation wherein the current realities of family life come into conflict with our valued images. Sociologists call this difference "cultural lag," the difference between what is real and what we hold as ideal. This lag occurs because of our powerful resistance to acknowledging changes that challenge our basic beliefs about what's good and what's bad in our society.

## Why Good Divorces Are Invisible

Good divorces are those in which the divorce does not destroy meaningful family relationships. Parents maintain a sufficiently cooperative and supportive relationship that allows them to focus on the needs of their children. In good divorces children continue to have ties to both their mothers and their fathers, and each of their extended families, including those acquired when either parent remarries.

Good divorces have been well-kept secrets because to acknowledge them in mainstream life threatens our nostalgic images of family. If the secret got out that indeed many families that don't fit our "mom and pop" household ideal are healthy, we would have to question the basic societal premise that marriage and family are synonymous. And that reality upsets a lot of people, who then respond with familiar outcries that divorce is eroding our basic values and destroying society.

Although we view ourselves as a society in which nuclear families and lifelong monogamous marriages predominate, the reality is that 43 percent of first marriages will end in divorce. Over half of new marriages are actually remarriages for at least one of the partners. Not only have either the bride or groom (or both) been divorced but increasingly one of them also has parents who are divorced.

Families are the way we organize to raise children. Although we hold the ideal image that marriage is a precursor to establishing a family, modern parents are increasingly challenging this traditional ideal. Families today arrange—and rearrange—themselves in many responsible ways that meet the needs of children for nurturance, guidance and economic support. Family historian Stephanie Coontz, in her book *The Way We Never Were,* shows how the "tremendous variety of workable childrearing patterns in history suggests that, with little effort, we should be able to forge new institutions and values."

One way we resist these needed societal changes is by denying that divorce is no longer deviant. We demean divorced families by clinging to the belief that families can't exist outside of marriage. It follows then that stories of healthy families that don't fit the tidy nuclear family package are rare and stories that show how divorce destroys families and harms children are common. In this way, bad divorces appear to represent the American way of divorce and good divorces become invisible.

## Messages That Hinder Good Divorces

When the evils of divorce are all that families hear about, it makes coping with the normal transitions and changes that inevitably accompany divorce all the more difficult. Negative messages make children feel different and lesser, leading to feelings of shame and guilt. Parents who feel marginalized in this way are less likely to think about creative solutions to their problems. That all of this unnecessary anxiety is fueled by sensationalized reports of weak findings, half-truths and myths of devastation is deplorable. Only by sorting out the truths about divorce from the fiction can we be empowered to make better decisions, find healthy ways to maintain family relationships, and develop important family rituals after divorce. Let's take a close look at the most common misconceptions about divorce.

### Misconception 1: Parents Should Stay Married for the Sake of the Kids

This is a message that pervades our culture, and it rests on a false duality: Marriage is good for kids, divorce is bad. Underlying this premise is the belief that parents who divorce are immature and selfish because they put their personal needs ahead of the needs of their children, that because divorce is too easy to get, spouses give up on their marriages too easily and that if you're thinking about divorcing your spouse, you should "stick it out till the kids are grown." A popular joke takes this message to its extreme. A couple in their nineties, married for seventy years, appears before a judge in their petition for a divorce. The judge looks at them quizzically and asks, "Why now, why after all these years?" The couple responds: "We waited until the children were dead."

The research findings are now very clear that reality is nowhere near as simple and tidy. Unresolved, open interparental conflict between married spouses that pervades day-to-day family life has been shown again and again to have negative effects on children. Most experts agree that when this is the case it is better for the children if parents divorce rather than stay married. Ironically, prior to the initiation of no-fault legislation over twenty years ago, in most states this kind of open conflict in the home was considered "cruel and inhumane" treatment and it was one of the few grounds on which a divorce would be granted—if it could be proved.

But the majority of unsatisfying marriages are not such clearcut cases. When most parents ask themselves if they should stay married for the sake of their children, they have clearly reached the point where they are miserable in their marriages but wouldn't necessarily categorize them as "high-conflict." And here is where, in spite of the societal message, there is no agreement in the research findings or among clinical experts. That's because it's extremely complex and each individual situation is too different to allow for a "one-size-fits-all" answer.

A huge list of factors comes into play when assessing whether staying married would be better for your kids. For example,

- Is the unhappiness in your marriage making you so depressed or angry that your children's needs go unmet because you can't parent effectively?
- Do you and your spouse have a cold and distant relationship that makes the atmosphere at home unhealthy for your children?
- Do you and your spouse lack mutual respect, caring or interests, setting a poor model for your children?
- Would the financial hardships be so dire that your children will experience a severely reduced standard of living?

Add to this your child's temperament, resources and degree of resilience, and then the personal and family changes that take place in the years after the divorce, and you can see how the complexities mount.

It is a rare parent who divorces *too easily.* Most parents are responsible adults who spend years struggling with the extremely difficult and complex decision of whether to divorce or stay married "for the sake of the children." The bottom line is that divorce is an adult decision, usually made by one spouse, entered into in the face of many unknowns. Without a crystal ball, no one knows whether their decision will be better for their children. As you read further in this book, however, you may gain some perspective on what will be most helpful in your situation, with your children, by listening carefully to the reactions and feelings of various children of divorce *as they have changed over twenty years.*

## Misconception 2: "Adult Children of Divorce" Are Doomed to Have Lifelong Problems

If your parents divorced when you were a child, you are often categorized as an ACOD, an "adult child of divorce," and we all know there's nothing good to be said about that. I dislike this label because it is stigmatizing. It casts dark shadows over divorcing parents and their children, results in feelings of shame and guilt, and is another way of pathologizing divorce.

Years ago I coined a term, "divorcism," to call attention to the stereotypes and stigma attached to divorce. To put children with divorced parents in a special category is divorcism in action. It stereotypes them as a group with problems, and like all stereotypes it ignores individual differences.

If your parents didn't divorce, are you then called an "adult child of marriage"? No, you're just "normal." Normal kids must have two parents of different genders who live in the same household; anything else is abnormal, and if you're abnormal then you must be dysfunctional. That's the way the American family story goes.

Perhaps the worst outcome of this labeling is that it makes parents and children feel that this one event has doomed them and they don't have the power to change anything. This pinpointing of divorce as the source of personal problems is pervasive. Parents worry that whatever problems their kids have, even when they are normal developmental issues, were caused by the divorce. Children are encouraged to blame the divorce for whatever unhappiness they may feel, which makes them feel helpless about improving their lives. Teachers are often too quick to identify divorce as the reason for a child's school behavior problem. The greater society points a finger at divorce as the reason for a wide range of greater social problems.

The truth is that, for the great majority of children who experience a parental divorce, the divorce becomes part of their history but it is not a defining factor. Like the rest of us, most of them reach adulthood to lead reasonably happy successful lives. Although children who grew up with divorced parents certainly share an important common experience, their ability to form healthy relationships, be good parents, build careers, and so on, are far more determined by their individual temperaments, their sibling relationships, the dynamics within their parents' *marriages* and the climate of their *postdivorce* family lives.

## Misconception 3: Divorce Means You Are no Longer a Family

There's this myth that as long as you stay married your family is good but as soon as you announce you're separating, your family is thrown into the bad zone. Your family goes from being "intact" to being "dissolved," form two-parent to single parent, from functional to dysfunctional. Even though we all know that people don't jump from happy marriages right into divorce, there is an assumption that the decision to separate is the critical marker. It doesn't seem to matter whether your marital relationship was terrible, whether you were miserable and your children troubled. Just as long as you are married and living together in one household, the sign over the front door clearly states to the world, "We're a normal family."

The inaccurate and misleading message that divorce destroys families is harmful to both parents and children because it hides and denies all the positive ways that families can be rearranged after divorce. It sends the destructive message to children that divorce means they only get to keep one parent and they will no longer be part of a family. Although two-parent first-married households now represent less than 25 percent of all households, and an increasing number of children each year are raised by unmarried adults, many people cling to the belief that healthy families can only be two-parent married families and social change is always bad and threatening to our very foundations.

---

When Julie, one of the participants in my study, married recently, she walked down the aisle with a father on either side. On her left was her biological father, on her right was her stepfather of eighteen years. Her mother was her matron of honor, who joined her former and present husbands, all standing together to witness the marriage. Two best men, the groom's eleven-year-old twin sons from his first marriage, stood next to him. Helen, the groom's former wife, sat close by, accompanied by Tony, her live-in partner.

While this wedding ceremony doesn't fit the traditional pattern, Don and Julie have joined the three-quarters of American households who have living arrangements other than that of the "traditional" family.

My older daughter thanked me for coming to Jennifer's wedding. She told me that my being there made it possible for her to share this happy occasion with *all* her family, instead of feeling the disconnections that some children feel in divorced families. This bonding spreads to the third generation so that my grandchildren know us all as family.

The truth is that although some divorces result in family breakdown, the vast majority do not. While divorce changes the form of the family from one household to two, from a nuclear family to a binuclear one, it does not need to change the way children think and feel about the significant relationships within their families. This does not mean that divorce is not painful or difficult, but over the years, as postdivorce families change and even expand, most remain capable of meeting children's needs for family.

## Misconception 4: Divorce Leaves Children without Fathers

This message is linked closely with the preceding one because when we say that divorce destroys families we really mean that fathers disappear from the family. The myths that accompany this message are that fathers are "deadbeat dads" who abandon their kids and leave their families impoverished. The message strongly implies that fathers don't care and are unwilling or unable to make continuing commitments to their children. While this reflects the reality for a minority of divorced fathers, the majority of fathers continue to have loving relationships with their children and contribute financially to their upbringing.

The truth is that many fathers do spend less time their children after divorce, but to stereotype them as parents who abandon their children only creates more difficulty for both fathers and their children. It establishes a myth that men are irresponsible parents who don't care about their children, when in reality most feel great pain that they are not able to see their children more frequently. In the vast majority of divorces, over 85 percent, mothers are awarded sole custody, or in the case of joint custody, primary residence. This means that most fathers become nonresidential parents after divorce. Being a nonresidential father is a difficult role with no preparation or guidelines.

Most of the research on dads after divorce focuses on absentee fathers, while involved fathers are frequently overlooked. Many fathers continue to be excellent parents after divorce and in fact some fathers and children report that their relationships actually improve after the divorce. In much the same way that good divorces are invisible in the public debate, so are involved fathers.

## Misconception 5: Exspouses Are Incapable of Getting Along

When I first started to study divorce in the early 1970s, it was assumed in the literature that any continuing relationship between exspouses was a sign of serious pathology, an inability to adjust to the divorce, to let go and to move on with their lives.

In the late 1970s, when joint custody was first introduced, it was met with loud cries of skepticism from the opposition. How could two parents who couldn't get along well enough to stay married possibly get along well enough to continue to share parenting? Two decades ago I confronted the skeptics by writing several articles arguing that we needed to accept the reality of our divorce rates and needed to transform our values about parenting after divorce. The issue was no longer *whether* divorced parents should share parenting to meet their children's needs but *how.*

Although there have been many legal changes over the years, and some form of joint custody legislation exists now in all states, questions about its viability still prevail. These accusations, citing joint custody as a failed "social experiment," are not based on research findings, which are still very limited and inconclusive, but instead on the ill-founded stereotype that all divorcing spouses are bitter enemies, too lost in waging their own wars to consider their children. Certainly this is true for some divorcing spouses, the ones that make headlines in bitter custody disputes, but it is not true for the majority.

Although we have come to realize that parents who divorce still need to have some relationship with one another, the belief that it's not really possible still lingers. In fact, when exspouses remain friends they are viewed as a little strange and their relationship is suspect. Yet, the truth is that many divorced parents *are* cooperative and effective coparents. Like good divorces and involved fathers, they are mostly invisible in the media.

Despite much resistance, joint custody has become increasingly common, and new words, such as "coparents," have emerged in response to this reality. The newest edition of *Webster's College Dictionary* (2000) recognizes the term, defining it as separated or divorced parents who share custody and child rearing equally. While I don't agree that coparenting is limited only to those parents who share child rearing equally, or even that those who coparent need to share equally in time or responsibility, the inclusion of the word in the dictionary sanctions important new kinship language for divorced families, thereby advancing our ability to acknowledge complex family arrangements.

## Misconception 6: Divorce Turns Everyone into Exfamily; In-Laws Become Outlaws

When it comes to the semantics of divorce-speak, all of the kinship ties that got established by marriage dissolve abruptly. On the day of the legal divorce, my husband and all of his relatives suddenly became exes. But even though the kinship is *legally* terminated, meaningful relationships often continue. My friend Jan, during her fifteen-year marriage, formed a very close relationship with her mother-in-law. Now, twenty years later, she still calls her eighty-two-year-old exmother-in-law "Mom," talks with her several times a week and has dinner with her weekly. Exmother-in-law is certainly not an adequate description of this ongoing relationship.

As a culture we continue to resist accepting divorce as a normal end-point to marriage even though it is an option chosen by almost half of those who marry. It is this cultural lag, this denial of current realities that causes the inaccurate language, not only for the family ties that continue but also for the family we inherit when we, our former spouses, our parents or our children remarry. Kinship language is important because it provides a shorthand way for us to identity relationships without wading through tedious explanations.

We have terms like "cousin," "great-aunt" or uncle, and "sister-in-law" that help us quickly identify lineage in families. Even these kinship terms are sometimes inadequate and confusing. For example, "sister-in-law" can mean my brother's wife, or my husband's sister, or my husband's brother's wife. And even though you don't know exactly *how* she is related to me, you do at least know that she belongs in the family picture. The in-law suffix quickly tells you that we are not blood relatives but we are related through marriage lines.

Our failure to provide kinship language that recognizes some kind of viable relationship between parents who are no longer married to each other, as well as language that incorporates old and new family as kin, makes children feel that their identity is shattered by divorce. It is no wonder that we remain in the dark ages when it comes to normalizing complex families after divorce and remarriage.

Our language and models for divorce and remarriage are inadequate at best, and pejorative at worst. Relegating the relationship between divorced spouses who are parents to the term "exspouse" hurls children and their parents into the dark territory of "exfamily." The common terms of "broken home," "dissolved family," and "single-parent family" all imply that children are left with either no family or only one parent.

This lack of positive language is one more way that the invisibility of good divorces impacts postdivorce families.

## Misconception 7: Stepparents Aren't Real Parents

One of the implications of the high divorce rate is that the shape and composition of families have changed dramatically in the last twenty years. All over the world, weddings no longer fit the traditional model: there are stepparents, half siblings, stepsiblings, stepchildren, intimate partners of parents, stepgrandparents and even, on rate occasions, exspouses of the bride or groom.

To complicate the wedding picture even more, one or both of the bride and groom's parents may have been divorced. And given that well over half of those who divorce eventually remarry, we are likely to find that the majority of those who have divorced parents also have stepparents. Add the dramatic increase in cohabitation to that equation and it is not unusual for an "unmarried intimate partner" of one of the parents to be present as well. These complex families require photographers to quickly switch to their wide-angle lens and totally revamp their traditional formats for wedding photos.

Over half the children today have adults in their lives for whom they can't attach socially accepted kinship terms. They lack social rules that would help them know how they are supposed to relate and how to present these adults to the social world around them. I am reminded here of a *Herman* cartoon, showing a boy holding his report card and asking his teacher: "Which parent do you want to sign it: my natural father, my stepfather, my mother's third husband, my real mother or my natural father's fourth wife who lives with us?"

As the cartoon clearly suggests, there are real and natural parents, and then there are stepparents. Stepmothers are stereotyped in children's literature as mean, nasty and even abusive. The only time we hear about stepfathers is when the media highlights the sensationalized case of sexual abuse. Added to these negative images is the reality that stepparents have no legal rights to their stepchildren. The research on stepparents is still very limited and positive role models are lacking.

Children and their new stepparents start off their relationships with two strikes against them. They have to fight an uphill battle to overcome negative expectations, and they have to do so without much help from society. Since almost 85 percent of the children with divorced parents will have a stepparent at some time in their lives, it is shocking that we know so little about how these relationships work. Clearly, societal resistance to recognizing the broad spectrum of postdivorce families has hindered the development of good role models for stepchildren and their stepparents.

### Painting a False Picture

Taken together, these negative messages paint a false picture of divorce, one that assumes family ties are irretrievably broken so that postdivorce family relationships appear to be nonexistent. Despite these destructive messages, many divorced parents meet the needs of their children by creating strong families after divorce. Without a doubt, divorce is painful and creates stress for families, but it is important to remember that most recover, maintaining some of their kinship relationships and adding new ones over time.

By making good divorces invisible we have accepted bad divorces as the norm. In so doing, children and their divorced parents are being given inaccurate messages that conflict with the realities they live and make them feel deviant and stigmatized. It is time we challenge these outdated, ill-founded messages and replace them with new ones that acknowledge and accurately reflect current realities.

## The Distortions of Oversimplifying

Just a little over a decade ago, in January 1989, the *New York Tunes* Magazine ran a cover story called "Children after Divorce," which created a wave of panic in divorced parents and their children. Judith Wallerstein and her coauthor,

Sandra Blakeslee, a staff writer for the *New York Times,* noted their newest unexpected finding. Calling it the "sleeper effect," they concluded that only ten years after divorce did it become apparent that girls experience "serious effects of divorce at the time they are entering young adulthood."

When one of the most prestigious newspapers in the world highlights the findings of a study, most readers take it seriously. "That 66 percent of young women in our study between the ages of nineteen and twenty-three will suffer debilitating effects of their parents' divorce years later" immediately became generalized to the millions of female children with divorced parents. The message—just when you think everything may be okay, the doom of divorce will rear its ugly head—is based on a *mere eighteen out of the grand total of twenty-seven women* interviewed in this age group. This detail wasn't mentioned in the fine print of the article but is buried in the appendix of the book that was scheduled for publication a month after the *New York Times* story appeared. And it is on this slim data that the seeds of a myth are planted. We are still living with the fallout.

In sharp contrast to Wallerstein's view that parental divorce has a powerful devastating impact on children well into adulthood, another psychologist made headlines with a completely opposite thesis. In her book, *The Nurture Assumption: Why Children Turn Out the Way They Do,* Judith Rich Harris proposes that what parents do makes little difference in how their children's lives turn out. Half of the variation in children's behavior and personality is due to genes, claims Harris, and the other half to environmental factors, mainly their peer relationships. For this reason, Harris asserts parental divorce is not responsible for all the ills it is blamed for.

These extreme positions—of divorce as disaster and divorce as inconsequential—oversimplify the realities of our complex lives. Genes and contemporary relationships notwithstanding, we have strong evidence that parents still make a significant difference in their children's development. Genetic inheritance and peer relationships are part of the story but certainly not the whole story.

## Sorting Out the Research Findings

Drawing conclusions across the large body of research on divorce is difficult. Studies with different paradigms ask different questions that lead to different answers. A classic wisdom story shows the problem. Three blind men bumped into an elephant as they walked through the woods. They didn't know what it was, but each prided himself on his skill at "seeing." So one blind man reached out and carefully explored the elephant's leg. He described in great detail the rough, scratchy surface that was huge and round. "Aha, this is an ancient mighty tree. We're in a new forest." "No, no," said the blind man who had taken hold of the elephant's trunk. "We're in great danger—this is a writhing snake, bigger than any in our hometown. Run!" The third man laughed at them both. He'd been touching the elephant's tusk, noticing the smooth hard surface, the gentle curve, the rounded end. "Nonsense! We have discovered an exquisitely carved horn for announcing the emperor's arrival."

The blind men described what they "saw" accurately. Their mistake was to claim that what they saw was the whole. Much like the three blind men, researchers see different parts of the divorce elephant, which then frames their investigations.

It should come, then, as no surprise that reports of the findings about divorce are often contradictory and confusing. It is impossible for any study to take account of all the complexities of real life, or of the individual differences that allow one family to thrive in a situation that would create enormous stress, and frayed relationships, in another. But it is in these variations that we can begin to make sense of how divorce impacts the lives of individuals and families.

## Facing Reality

Hallmark Cards recently launched a line of greeting cards called "Ties That Bind" aimed at various nontraditional unions—from stepfamilies to adopted child households to unmarried partnerships. "Our cards reflect the times," says Marita Wesely-Clough, trend group manager at Hallmark. "Relationships today are so nebulous that they are hard to pin down, but in creating products, we have to be aware that they are there. Companies need to respect and be sensitive to how people are truly living their lives now, and not how they might wish or hope for them to live."

Advertising agencies and marketing services make it their business to assess social realities. To sell their products, they have to evaluate the needs and desires of their potential consumers. They do not share the popular cultural anxiety about the changes in families. Instead they study them and alter their products to suit. Policy makers would do well to take some lessons from them and alter their preconceived notions about families to reflect current realities.

While the political focus today is on saving marriages and preserving traditional family values, Americans in large numbers are dancing to their own drummers. They're cohabiting in increasingly large numbers, having more children "out of wedlock" and engaging in serial marriages. While the rates of divorce have come down from their 1981 highs, they have leveled off at a high rate that is predicted to remain stable. To meet the needs of children and parents, we need to burst the balloon about idealized families and support families as they really live their lives. And that means we have to face the true complexities of *our* families and not search for simple answers.

As you read this book, keep in mind that we can all look back on our childhoods and note something about our mothers or fathers or sisters or brothers that has had lasting effects on our personalities. If you are looking to answer the question of whether a parental divorce results in children having more or less problems than children who grew up in other living situations, you will be disappointed. Nor will you find answers to whether the stresses of divorce are worse for children than other stresses in life. However, you will find answers here to questions about how and why individual children respond in different ways to the variations in their divorced families.

Divorce is a stressful life event that requires increased focus on parenting. The effort and care that parents put into establishing their postdivorce families are crucial and will pay off over the years in their many benefits to the children. But remember, families are complex, and if you find easy answers, they are likely to be wrong.

**Elizabeth Marquardt**

# NO

# The Bad Divorce

It is often said that those who are concerned about the social and personal effects of divorce are nostalgic for the 1950s, yearning for a mythical time when men worked, women happily stayed home baking cookies for the kids, and marriages never dissolved. Yet often the same people who make the charge of mythology are caught in a bit of nostalgia of their own, pining for the sexual liberationism of the 1970s, when many experts began to embrace unfettered divorce, confident that children, no less than adults, would thrive once "unhappy" marriages were brought to a speedy end.

Constance Ahrons, who coined the term "the good divorce" in the title of an influential 1992 book that examined ninety-eight divorcing couples, is very much a member of the latter camp. In her new book, *We're Still Family: What Grown Children Have to Say About Their Parents' Divorce,* Ahrons returns to those ninety-eight couples to survey their now-grown children. The result is a study based on telephone interviews with 173 young adults from eighty-nine families that tries to advance the idea it is not divorce itself that burdens children but rather the way in which parents divorce. As in her earlier book, Ahrons argues that the vocabulary we use to discuss divorce and remarriage is negative; she would prefer that we regard divorced families as "changed" or "rearranged" rather than broken, damaged, or destroyed. She claims that upbeat language will, above all, help children feel less stigmatized by divorce. Both of her books offer many new terms, such as "binuclear" and "tribe," to describe divorced families. The specific novelty of the new book is Ahrons' claim that her interviewees view their parents' divorces in a positive light.

It is with delight, then, that Ahrons shares surprising new findings from her on-going study. According to Ahrons, over three quarters of the young people from divorced families who she interviewed do not wish their parents were still together. A similar proportion feel their parents' decision to divorce was a good one, that their parents are better off today and that they themselves are either better off or not affected by the divorce. To general readers who have been following the debates about children of divorce in recent years, such findings might sound like big news. But there are problems.

According to Ahrons, over three-quarters of the young people whom she interviewed do not wish that their parents were still together. A similar proportion feel that their parents' decision to divorce was a good one, that their parents are better off today, and that they themselves are either better off because of the divorce or have not been affected by it. Statistically, that sounds overwhelmingly convincing. But an answer to a survey question tells us very little unless we have a context for interpreting it and some grasp of the actual experiences that gave rise to it.

Like those whom Ahrons interviewed, I grew up in a divorced family, my parents having split when I was two years old. Like Ahrons, I am a researcher in the field, having led, with Norval Glenn, a study of young adults from both divorced and intact families that included a nationally representative telephone survey of some 1,500 people. As someone who studies children of divorce and who is herself a grown child of divorce, I have noticed that the kinds of questions that get asked in such studies and the way the answers are interpreted often depend on whether the questioner views divorce from the standpoint of the child or the parent.

Take, for example, Ahrons' finding that the majority of people raised in divorced families do not wish that their parents were together. Ahrons did not ask whether as children these young people had hoped their parents would reunite. Instead, she asked if they wish today their parents were still together. She presents their negative answers as gratifying evidence that divorce is affirmed by children. But is that really the right conclusion to draw?

Imagine the following scenario. One day when you are a child your parents come to you and tell you they are splitting up. Your life suddenly changes in lots of ways. Dad leaves, or maybe Mom does. You may move or change schools or lose friendships, or all of the above. Money is suddenly very tight and stays that way for a long time. You may not see one set of grandparents, aunts, uncles, and cousins nearly as much as you used to. Then, Mom starts dating, or maybe Dad does. A boyfriend or girlfriend moves in, perhaps bringing along his or her own kids. You may see one or both of your parents marry again; you may see one or both of them get divorced a second time. You deal with the losses. You adjust as best you can. You grow up and try to figure out this "relationship" thing for yourself. Then, some interviewer on the telephone asks if you wish your parents were still together today. A lifetime of pain and anger and adjustment flashes before your eyes. Any memory of your parents together as a couple—if you can remember them together at all—is buried deep under all those feelings. Your divorced parents have always seemed like polar opposites to you. No one could be more different from your mother than your father, and vice versa. "No," you reply to the interviewer, "I don't wish my parents were still together." Of course, one cannot automatically attribute such a train of thought to all of Ahrons' interview subjects. Still, it is plausible, and it might explain at least some of the responses. But Ahrons does not even consider it.

Ahrons tells us that the vast majority of young people in her study feel that they are either better off or not affected by their parents' divorce. For a child of divorce there could hardly be a more loaded question than this one. The generation that Ahrons is interviewing grew up in a time of massive changes in family life, with experts assuring parents that if they became happier after divorce, their children would as well. There wasn't a lot of patience for people who felt otherwise—especially when those people were children, with their aggravating preference for conventional married life over the adventures of divorce, and their tendency to look askance at their parents' new love interests.

However, a child soon learns the natural lesson that complaining about a parent's choices is a surefire way to be ignored or worse, and that what parents want above all is praise for those choices. Few things inspire as much admiration among divorced parents and their friends as the words of a child reassuring them that the divorce was no big deal—or even better, that it gave the child something beneficial, like early independence, or a new brother or sister. Parents are proud of a resilient child. They are embarrassed and frustrated by a child who claims to be a victim. And who among us wants to be a victim? Who would not rather be a hero, or at least a well-adjusted and agreeable person? When the interviewer calls on the telephone, what will the young adult be more likely to say? Something like "I'm damaged goods"? Or "Yes, it was tough at times but I survived it, and I'm stronger for it today." It is the second reply that children of divorce have all their lives been encouraged to give; and the fact that they are willing to give it yet again is hardly, as Ahrons would have it, news.

Thus, Ahrons' statistics on their own hardly constitute three cheers for divorce. Far more meaningful and revealing are the extended quotations from interview subjects with which the book is liberally studded. She writes, for instance, that Andy, now thirty-two, sees "value" in his parents' divorce. Why? Because:

> "I learned a lot. I grew up a lot more quickly than a lot of my friends. Not that that's a good thing or a bad thing. People were always thinking I was older than I was because of the way I carried myself."

Treating a sad, unfortunate experience (like being forced to grow up more quickly than one's peers) as something neutral or even positive is merely one example of what can happen when a person attempts to conform to a culture that insists that divorce is no big deal. To take such an ambivalent response as clear evidence that divorce does no damage, as Ahrons does is inexcusable.

Ahrons cheerfully reports other "good" results of divorce. Here for example is Brian, whose parents split when he was five:

> "In general, I think [the divorce] has had very positive effects. I see what happens in divorces, and I have promised myself that I would do anything to not get a divorce. I don't want my kids to go through what I went through."

Tracy, whose parents divorced when she was twelve, sees a similar upside to divorce:

> "I saw some of the things my parents did and know not to do that in my marriage and see the way they treated each other and know not to do that to my spouse and my children. I know [the divorce] has made me more committed to my husband and my children."

These are ringing endorsements of divorce as a positive life event? Like the testimony of a child who's learned a painful but useful lesson about the dangers of playing with fire, such accounts indicate that the primary benefit of divorce is to encourage young people to avoid it in their own lives if at all possible.

Then there are the significant problems with the structure of Ahrons' study itself. While the original families were recruited using a randomized method, the study lacks any control group. In other words, Ahrons interviewed plenty of young people from divorced families but spoke to no one of similar ages from intact families. So she really can't tell us anything at all about how these young people might differ from their peers.

Rather than acknowledging that her lack of a control group is a serious limitation, Ahrons sidesteps the issue. In several places she compares her subjects to generalized "social trends" or "their contemporaries" and decides, not surprisingly, that they are not all that different. Thus, Ahrons notes that many of the young people from divorced families told her they frequently struggled with issues of "commitment, trust, and dealing with conflict," but on this finding she comments, "These issues are precisely the ones that most adults in this stage of their development grapple with, whether they grow up in a nuclear family or not." Never mind that she has not interviewed any of those other young people, or cited any studies to back up her contention, or acknowledged the possibility that, while all young people do have to deal with these kinds of interpersonal issues, some have a much harder time doing it than others. Ahrons instead wholly dismisses the pain expressed by the children of divorce and assures us that they are simply passing through a normal development phase.

When it comes to her conclusions, Ahrons claims that "if you had a devitalized or high-conflict marriage, you can take heart that the decision to divorce may have been the very best thing you could have done for your children." While research does show that children, on average, do better after a high-conflict marriage ends (the same research, by Paul Amato and Alan Booth, also shows that only one-third of divorces end high-conflict marriages), no one—Ahrons included—has shown that children do better when an adult ends a marriage he or she perceives as "devitalized." Children don't much care whether their parents have a "vital" marriage. They care whether their mother and father live with them, take care of them, and don't fight a lot. . . .

Ahrons' also remains preoccupied with the concept of stigma. She writes, for instance, that we are seeing "progress" because a high divorce rate has the effect of reducing the stigma experienced by children of divorce. That's all well and good, but one wonders why Ahrons gives stigma so much attention while saying nothing about a far more damaging social problem for children of divorce—namely, silence. Consider my own experience. The type of family in which I grew up was radically different from the intact family model. Yet no one around me, not even therapists, ever once acknowledged that fact. Never mind that my beloved father lived hours away, or that the mother I adored was often stressed as she tried to earn a living while also acting as a single parent. I was left to assume, like many children of divorce, that whatever problems I struggled with were no one's fault but my own. The demand that children of divorce keep quiet and get with the program puts them in the position of protecting adults from guilt and further stress—effectively reversing the natural order of family life in which the adults are the protectors of children.

Ahrons is remarkably unsympathetic to the children on whom this burden is laid. What do children of divorce long for? According to Ahrons, they nurture unrealistic hopes for "tidy," "perfect" families. She uses these words so frequently—the first term appears at least six times in the book and the second at least four times—that she sometimes appears to be portraying children of divorce as weird obsessives. Speaking directly to children of divorce, Ahrons offers the following advice: "You may not have the idyllic family you dreamed of . . . [but] often the only thing within our control is how we perceive or interpret an event." "For example, you can choose to see your family as rearranged, or you can choose to see it as broken." Indeed, the curative powers of social constructivism are nothing short of miraculous. Encouraging readers to stop using the descriptive term "adult child of divorce," she asserts that "it's a stigmatizing label that presumes you are deficient or traumatized. . . . If you have fallen prey to using it to explain something about yourself, ask yourself if it is keeping you from making changes that might bring you more satisfaction in your life." Apparently, coming to grips with one's family history and the deepest sources of one's sadness and loneliness is the worst thing a child can do. . . .

Ahrons surely knows more about the tragedies of divorce than her thesis allows her to admit. She has studied divorced families for years. She has worked with them as a clinician. She has been through divorce herself. Yet she inevitably follows up heartbreaking observations of interviewees with the confident assertion that everyone involved would be so much happier if only they talked themselves out of—and even walked away from—their anguish. As she writes in one (unintentionally haunting) passage, "Over the years I have listened to many divorcing parents in my clinical practice talk about how much they look forward to the day when their children will be grown and they won't have to have anything more to do with their exes." Is it possible to image a sadder or more desperate desire than this one—the longing for one's children to grow up faster so that relations with one's ex-spouse can be more effectively severed? In such passages it becomes obvious that all of Ahrons' efforts to explain away the tragedy of divorce and its legacy are in vain. In the end, the theory collapses before reality.

Ahrons' poorly structured study and far too tendentious thesis are of no help to us in thinking through our approach to divorce and its consequences. Children of divorce are real, complex people who are deeply shaped by a new kind of fractured family life—one whose current prevalence is unprecedented in human history. These children are not nostalgic for "tidy," "perfect," "idyllic" families. They grieve the real losses that follow from their parents' divorce. They don't need new words to describe what they've been through. Ordinary words will serve quite well—provided that people are willing to listen to them.

# CHALLENGE QUESTIONS

## Does Divorce Have Positive Long-Term Effects for the Children Involved?

1. How is it that two top researchers, the authors of these articles, can differ so much in their conclusions about this vital area of developmental and mental health? Does this necessarily mean that one of their conclusions is wrong?
2. Interview a student whose parents are divorced. Make sense of his or her experiences in the light of one of the author's perspectives.
3. What political policies might be enacted if those in governmental power were to become aware of only one of these authors' conclusions?
4. If you and your (present or future) spouse were faced with the likelihood of divorce, what would you do with the information obtained from one or both of these articles?
5. What impact, if any, would the information contained in both articles make on a couple considering marriage?

# ISSUE 8

## Do Online Friendships Hurt Adolescent Development?

**YES: Lauren Donchi and Susan Moore**, from "It's a Boy Thing: The Role of the Internet in Young People's Psychological Wellbeing," *Behavior Change* (vol. 21, no. 2, 2004)

**NO: Patti M. Valkenburg and Jochen Peter**, from "Online Communication and Adolescent Well-Being: Testing the Stimulation Versus the Displacement Hypothesis," *Journal of Computer-Mediated Communication* (vol. 12, issue 4, 2007)

### ISSUE SUMMARY

**YES:** Psychologists Lauren Donchi and Susan Moore report that adolescent males who rate online friendships higher than face-to-face friendships are more likely to be lonely and experience low self-esteem.

**NO:** Professors of communication Patti M. Valkenburg and Jochen Peter maintain that online relationships actually *enhance* an adolescent's face-to-face peer relations and psychological wellbeing.

Although virtually non-existent a generation ago, the internet has rapidly become a staple of modern life. The internet is used to shop, watch television, conduct investigations, hold business meetings, and even perform remote surgeries. Perhaps one of the most common uses of the internet is personal communication (e-mails, text messages, blogs, etc). Social networking sites, in which users can share content and communicate with friends, have experienced an exponential rise in popularity, with sites such as Facebook.com (which only opened to the public in September 2006) boasting over 200 million active users.

A significant factor in this networking boom has been the increasing online presence of adolescent users. A 2005 Pew Report found that over 87% of American teenagers had regular access to the internet. Along with this increase in access, some lawmakers and parents have expressed concern with the possible detrimental effects of excessive online activity. While highly publicized cases have focused on internet-related suicides and sex crimes, there is a broader concern over the social development of teenagers who seem to spend more and more time in the virtual world and less time in the "real" world.

In their article, Donchi and Moore review a number of research reports detailing the negative psychological effects of adolescent internet use. They specifically examine studies of loneliness, the number of online and offline friends, and the quality of friendships; they conclude that "all well-being measures were negatively related to Internet focus." They also note a "gender effect," meaning that these negative effects appear to be more pronounced for males than for females. Consequently, they argue that online relationships cannot adequately substitute for offline face-to-face friendships in promoting social-emotional development in teenage boys.

Valkenburg and Peter, in the second article, make the distinction between online activities that *stimulate* offline relationships and those that *displace* them. The latter activities mean that time spent online is time spent away from developing meaningful human connections (displacing them). On the other hand, the authors suggest that there are many online activities—such as instant messaging (IM), e-mail, and chat rooms—that enhance an adolescent's offline relationships. They report a study that examines several hypotheses related to these two ways of interacting online. They conclude that online activity benefits offline peer development, at least for direct communication, such as IM,. As they put it, "Internet communication is positively related to [an adolescent's] well being."

**POINT**

- Internet use can psychologically impair adolescent development.
- Time spent with online friends displaces offline relationships.
- Gender is an important variable influencing the effect of the internet.
- Time online negatively affects both social and emotional measures (e.g., loneliness).

**COUNTERPOINT**

- Online friends do not damage psychological wellbeing.
- Online friendships enhance offline relationships.
- Type of online activity is an important variable influencing the effect of the internet.
- Internet involvement increases intimate self-disclosure, helping teens foster trust and caring.

YES 

**Lauren Donchi and Susan Moore**

# It's a Boy Thing: The Role of the Internet in Young People's Psychological Wellbeing

. . . In Australia, 37% of all households currently have Internet access and this percentage is continuing to rise (Australian Bureau of Statistics, 2001). However, while the majority of Australians (61%) have some access to the Internet, the largest single grouping of users is teenage children. Males, particularly younger males, are more frequent users than females, although Odell, Korgen, Schumacher and Delucchi (2000) argue that the gender gap is closing quickly. Given these statistics, it would not be surprising to hear that the Internet has a marked effect on social life. . . .

One way to assess the relationships between social wellbeing and Internet use among young people is to examine the role that online and offline (face-to-face) friendships play in the alleviation of loneliness and the maintenance or development of self-esteem. . . . While it is well known that friendship is important to wellbeing, is this importance specific to face-to-face friends? . . .

Another variable of importance in examining wellbeing in Internet-use relationships is the actual time spent online. Longer amounts of time could be interpreted as relatively antisocial, and may reduce possibilities for social learning and social reinforcement in 'real-life' situations. On the other hand, if the time is spent engaged in Internet relationships, social learning and social rewards may still be available. Thus, in this study, we investigated the associations between time spent on the Internet (in different pursuits including personal communication, entertainment and information-seeking), number and importance of online and offline friendships, and social wellbeing.

This study focuses on Internet use and social relationships of young people in the 15 to 21 years age group, . . . a time in which friendship and peer-group belongingness is particularly salient to psychosocial development. . . . Peer interactions present opportunities for adolescents to develop the social competencies and social skills required for participation in adult society. Research affirms that peer friendships are important for maintaining psychological health and that peer-relationship difficulties are likely to be a source of stress to young people that leads to feelings of loneliness (Demir & Tarhan, 2001; Parkhurst & Asher, 1992). . . .

While adolescent social relations typically take place in face-to-face settings the introduction of communication applications on the Internet (e.g., email, chatrooms, Usenet newsgroups), . . . has led to the suggestion that Internet networks may also function as important social networks for users. Some support for this view is provided by Parks and Floyd (1996), who . . . found that nearly two-thirds of respondents had formed personal relationships with people they had met via an Internet newsgroup. . . . Further, a study by the Pew Internet and American Life Project (2001) . . . found that Internet communication was an essential feature of young people's social lives and had partially replaced face-to-face interactions. So while the Internet enables people to form online social networks, whether these online friendships can provide a substitute for face-to-face friendships in assisting development towards social maturity and psychological wellbeing is an open question. . . .

Disturbing signs that the Internet fosters loneliness in users first emerged in a longitudinal study conducted by Kraut and colleagues (Kraut et al., 1998; Kraut & Mukopadhyay, 1999) . . . [who] found that after controlling for initial-outcome variables, greater use of the Internet was associated with increased loneliness. They also found that teenagers used the Internet for more hours than adults and increases in Internet use were associated with larger increases in loneliness for teenagers than for adults. These findings were somewhat controversial, and the study was criticized for methodological reasons (small sample; no control group without access to the Internet). . . .

Since the publication of Kraut et al.'s (1998) . . . study that claimed 'using the Internet adversely affects psychological wellbeing' (p. 1028), social scientists have shown . . . interest in the Internet. However, much of the available research . . . has produced mixed results.

Some research has substantiated claims that Internet use is associated with reduced psychological wellbeing. For example, Armstrong, Phillips and Saling (2000) examined Internet use and self-esteem levels . . . [and found] that more time spent on the Internet was associated with lower self-esteem.

[On the other hand, a] recent longitudinal study conducted by Shaw and Gant (2002) [investigating] Internet use, loneliness and self-esteem . . . found that over the course of the study, during which subjects chatted anonymously on the Internet, participants' loneliness decreased and self-esteem increased.

Other research has [also] shed doubt on the association between Internet use and psychological wellbeing. Gross, Juvonen and Gable (2002) found that time online was not associated with loneliness. They surveyed 130 adolescents between the ages of 11 and 13 years. . . . Kraut and colleagues (2002) [in] . . . a second longitudinal study . . . found no overall relationship between Internet use and loneliness or self-esteem. However, they [did report] that Internet use was associated with better outcomes for extroverts (i.e., decreased loneliness and increased self-esteem) and worse outcomes for introverts (i.e., increased loneliness and decreased self-esteem). Hence in [their] study, individual characteristics served as important moderating variables between internet use and psychological wellbeing. . . . In sum, while much research has studied the relationship between Internet use and psychological wellbeing, the available data is equivocal.

One reason for the mixed findings regarding Internet use and loneliness may be that while evidence points to the importance of employing a multidimensional concept of loneliness, there is little available research which links more complex conceptions of loneliness to Internet use. Most studies have employed the UCLA Loneliness Scale, which has come to be viewed as the standard scale to assess loneliness, measuring it as a global construct. One exception was Weiss (1973), who distinguished between emotional loneliness and social loneliness. Emotional loneliness is characterised by a feeling of abandonment, emptiness and apprehension due to the absence of a close, intimate attachment. Social loneliness refers to the feeling of boredom and marginality due to the lack of belonging to a social network or community. Weiss argues that relief from emotional loneliness requires the formation of an attachment relationship that promotes a sense of emotional security, whereas remediation from social loneliness requires being accepted as a member of a friendship network that provides a sense of social integration.

The association between Internet use and Weiss's (1973) bimodal theory of loneliness was examined by Moody (2001), who compared 166 university students' self-reported Internet use to their social and emotional loneliness and to their friendship networks both on the Internet and on a face-to-face basis. Moody developed the Social Network Scale to assess the latter. His findings revealed that while students who spent more time on the Internet communicating with friends were likely to have higher rates of emotional loneliness, they were less like to experience social loneliness than those who spent less time on the Internet communicating with friends. Moody concluded that the psychological effects of Internet use are more complex than previous studies have indicated. His findings suggest that by limiting the face-to-face component of social interaction, emotional loneliness might occur despite high Internet use, providing some individuals with a sense of social integration and thus lowered social loneliness.

Following Moody's (2001) lead, the present study employed Weiss's (1973) distinction between emotional and social loneliness in studying the associations between Internet use, social networks and psychological wellbeing. Furthermore, in keeping with previous research, global loneliness (as measured by the UCLA scale) and self-esteem were also used as measures of psychological wellbeing. The study distinguished between time spent on different activities on the Internet, and used measures of social networks which included, but were not limited to, number of friends. . . . In short, this study examined the relationships between wellbeing, time spent on the Internet, and social networks, including online and offline (face-to-face) networks. Patterns of relationships were examined separately for the sexes because of previous research suggesting differences in the ways young men and young women use the Internet, even though differences in the amount of time spent on the Internet by males and females are closing (Odell et al., 2000).

# Method

## Participants

There were 336 participants, aged 15 to 21 years in the sample (114 males and 222 females). This included 110 [secondary school students (mean age 16.16) and] 226 university-based [students (mean age 18.55)]. . . .

## Materials

The questionnaire consisted of sections designed to measure demographic variables (gender, age, education level), Internet use, social networks, loneliness and self-esteem.

**Measuring Internet use** In order to assess the amount of time young people spend on the Internet on an average day, respondents were presented with a list of internet activities. Thirteen of the activities related to three categories of Internet use: interpersonal communication (4 items; e.g., 'visiting chat rooms'), entertainment (5 items; e.g., 'searching for things of personal interest') and information (4 items; e.g., 'finding articles and references'). For each Internet activity, participants were asked to indicate in minutes the time spent on each activity 'on an average day'. . . .

**Measuring social networks** Respondents use of the Internet and face-to face relations for communicating with friends was measured using the 12-item Social Network Scale (Moody, 2001). . . . Respondents were asked to indicate how well each item described them on a 5-point Likert scale. . . .

In order to assess the number of friends young people regularly communicate with on the Internet and on a face-to-face basis, participants were asked to answer two questions: 'How many friends do you talk to regularly on the Internet?' and 'How many friends do you talk to regularly on a face-to-face basis?'

**Measuring loneliness** The UCLA Loneliness Scale was used to measure loneliness conceptualized as a global, unidimensional construct. . . . The 20-item scale has 10 descriptive feelings of loneliness and 10 descriptive feelings of satisfaction with social relationships. . . .

[The] . . . 10-item Emotional and Social Loneliness Scale . . . was used to measure loneliness conceptualized as a multidimensional construct. The scale comprises two 5-item subscales that distinguish between emotional loneliness (e.g., 'I don't have a special love relationship') and social loneliness (e.g., 'Mostly, everyone around me seems like a stranger'). . . .

**Measuring self-esteem** The measure used to obtain an assessment of self-esteem was Form A of the 16-item Texas Social Behaviour Inventory. . . .

# Results

## Gender Differences in Internet Use

. . . Males and females spent similar lengths of time on the Internet on an average day engaged in personal communication: female mean—65.4 minutes, male mean—68.7 minutes; and information-seeking: female mean—56.5 minutes, male mean—59.1 minutes. However, males spent significantly longer using the Internet for entertainment on an average day, in fact, about twice as much time as females: female mean—63.9 minutes, male mean—121.6 minutes. . . . In addition, males said they had more regular Internet friends than females. . . . For face-to-face regular friendships the trend was reversed, with females indicating more friendships. . . . The sexes did not differ on the importance they attached to either Internet or face-to-face friendships.

## Relationships between Online and Face-to-Face Friendships

. . . The numbers of friends on- and offline were positively associated for both sexes; the more friends in one domain, the more in the other (they may indeed be an overlapping set). An interesting gender difference occurred for the scales measuring perceived importance of the two domains; for females these two scales were unrelated, suggesting that online and offline networks were not developed at the expense of one another. For males, these two scales were negatively associated, suggesting that the young men in this study tended to emphasise one domain over the other.

## Network Group Differences on Wellbeing

The number of regular face-to-face friends (face-to-face friends) and number of regularly-communicated-with online friends (online friends) were divided at their respective medians into high and low face-to-face and high and low online friendship groups. A four-way multivariate analysis of variance was conducted with gender (male, female), education level (school university), face-to-face friendship group (high, low) and online friendship group (high, low) as the independent variables. The dependent variables were the four measures of wellbeing: general loneliness (UCLA loneliness score), social loneliness, emotional loneliness and self-esteem.

The main effects of gender . . . and face-to-face friendship group . . . were significant; other main effects did not show significant group differences. . . .

Males were significantly more socially lonely than females, . . . and males were also significantly more emotionally lonely than females. . . . The trends for the males in the sample to have lower self-esteem and score higher on the UCLA loneliness scale than females were not statistically significant.

Not surprisingly, face-to-face friendship group was also related to the wellbeing measures. Specifically, those with more face-to-face friends had higher self-esteem than those in the low face-to-face friendship group. . . . The high friendship group was also less socially lonely, . . . and less generally lonely on the UCLA scale than the low face-to-face friendship group. . . .

There were gender-by-friendship group interactions for both online and face-to-face friendship groups. . . . [Females] with more online friends were higher on self-esteem and lower on loneliness than females with fewer online friends, but . . . the opposite was true for males. Higher numbers of online regular friendships seemed to militate against self-esteem and be related to greater loneliness for males. . . .

For face-to-face friendships, the effects on wellbeing were in the same direction for males and females, but they were stronger for males. [Those] with more face-to-face friendships were higher on self-esteem and less lonely, with males showing greater extremes of loneliness and low self-esteem than females, and wellbeing as more strongly associated with face-to-face friendships for males than for females.

## Predicting Wellbeing from Number of Friends (On- and Offline), Social Network Importance (On- and Offline) and Time Spent on the Internet

Regressions were conducted (separately for males and females) to assess whether the set of variables including number of online and face-to-face friends, perceived importance of online and face-to-face networks and time spent on the Internet predicted wellbeing (self-esteem and 3 measures of loneliness). None of the potential predictor variables were correlated at greater than. 6. . . . Correlations . . . showed a pattern for girls of significant positive correlations between wellbeing and face-to-face friendship indicators, and weak or nonsignificant correlations between wellbeing and online friendship indicators. There were no significant correlations between time spent on the Internet and wellbeing for girls. For boys, the correlations between wellbeing and face-to-face friendship indicators were significant and positive and between wellbeing and both time spent on the Internet and online friendship indicators were significant and negative. . . .

The regressions show a similar pattern of findings to the MANOVA, in the sense that the results for males suggest a greater implication of Internet use in loneliness and lower self-esteem. While the importance associated with face-to-face friendships and, to some extent, the number of face-to-face friends were the strongest predictors of loneliness and self-esteem, online relationship activity was also consistently associated with well being for males, but in a negative direction. In other words, young men who rated their online friendship networks as very important were more likely to have lower self-esteem and to be lonely. None of the measures of the time spent online (for communication, entertainment or information-related activities) were significant predictors of wellbeing.

# Discussion

The present study supported previous research suggesting that young males would spend more time on the Internet on an average day than young females (Kraut & Mukopadhyay, 1999; Odell et al., 2000). Both sexes indicated that they spent large amounts of time with this medium, three hours per day for girls and four for boys. While these times may have been overestimated due to the form of measurement used (assessing minutes per average day across several categories of activity), they do suggest some cause for concern. The gender gap had closed for the Internet activities of personal communication and information-seeking, but was still very much in evidence for Internet entertainment, an activity on which boys spent about two hours per day—twice as long as the girls. In addition, boys had more Internet friends and fewer face-to-face friends than girls, although the total friendship numbers were equal. Boys who ascribed high importance to their Internet friends tended to estimate their face-to-face networks as less important, while girls rated the importance of their Internet and face-to-face friendships similarly. The picture that emerges is of young people spending long hours at the computer, with boys in particular limiting their time for face-to-face interactions and, to some extent, discounting these. Time available for offline activities is thus reduced, particularly for boys. How do these findings relate to wellbeing?

Young people reported that the number of face-to-face friendships were clearly related to wellbeing, with more friends associated with higher self-esteem and lower social and general loneliness. These effects were stronger for boys, indicating that offline friends were particularly important as markers of wellbeing for them. In addition, while online friendships were associated with better wellbeing for girls, the opposite was true for boys. Higher numbers of regular online friendships amongst boys were related to lower self-esteem and greater loneliness. In the regressions, offline friendship number and perceived importance positively predicted wellbeing for both sexes, while online friendship number and importance negatively predicted wellbeing for boys only. These effects of friendship patterns swamped any relationships between wellbeing and time spent online.

Thus, the answer to the question of whether online social interactions can substitute for (or enhance) offline face-to-face friendships for young people during adolescence and early adulthood appears to be a definite 'no' for boys. There is a great deal of evidence that peer relations play an important role in promoting adolescent and youth social–emotional development, act as a buffer against loneliness and enhance self-esteem (e.g., Demir & Tarhan, 2001; Parkhurst & Asher, 1992). This study suggests a need for young men to experience a significant proportion of these peer relationships in the real-world domain. Those young men who strongly emphasise the importance of their online relationships may be cutting off options for psychosocial development through the give and take of face-to-face friendships. This may be a result of lack of social confidence and poor social skills leading to avoidance of real-world friendships with all their difficulties. Or it may be that the nature of Internet relationships (e.g., possibilities for anonymity and role-playing, reduced need to 'work at' friendships) can undermine skills needed in face-to-face relationships. Or, more simply, online friendships may reduce time available for offline friendships which appear to have a greater potential to relate positively to wellbeing. Kraut and colleagues (1998) speculated that negative effects of Internet use could result from both the displacement of social activities and of strong ties. According to this view, the time an individual spends online might interrupt or replace time they had previously spent engaged in real-life social activities. Furthermore, by using the Internet, an individual may be substituting their better real-life relationships or 'strong ties', which are thought to lead to better psychological outcomes, for artificial online relationships or 'weak ties'.

Girls, on the other hand, seem to have developed mechanisms by which their online activity does not interfere with offline friendships, and may even enhance it. For girls, more friendships either on- or offline related to positive indicators of wellbeing. This may relate in part to the fact that girls spend less time on the Internet altogether. In addition, when they do access the Internet, around one-third of this time is devoted to personal communication activities, some of which may involve relating to friends who are substantially of the face-to-face type. Boys, on the other hand, spend only about one-quarter of their time in such activities, preferring to engage in Internet entertainment, games and so on, which have a greater potential to be socially isolating.

It has been suggested that the lack of clarity in the literature to date regarding the association between wellbeing and Internet use may relate to issues surrounding the measurement of wellbeing (Moody, 2001). We used 4 measures and, in particular, were able to test out Moody's (2001) idea that time spent on the Internet communicating with friends would be related to higher emotional, but not higher social, loneliness. This was not the case. In fact, all wellbeing measures were negatively related to Internet focus (time spent on the Internet, Internet friendships, and their perceived importance) for boys. For girls, the relationships between Internet activity and measures of loneliness were weakly negative or nonexistent. Thus boys appear to be disadvantaged both socially and emotionally by their reliance on Internet friendships, while social and emotional advantage is associated with online and offline friendships for girls, and offline friendships for both sexes. . . .

## References


Armstrong, L., Phillips, J.G., & Saling, L.L. (2000). Potential determinants of heavier Internet usage. *International Journal of Human-Computer Studies, 53,* 537–550.

Australian Bureau of Statistics. (2001). *Use of the Internet by householders, Australia: Catalogue No. 8147.0,* Canberra: Author.

Demir, A., & Tarhan, N. (2001). Loneliness and social dissatisfaction in Turkish adolescents. *Journal of Psychology, 135,* 113–124.

Gross, E.F., Juvonen, J., & Gable, S.L. (2002). Internet use and wellbeing in adolescence. *Journal of Social Issues, 58,* 75–91.

Kraut, R., Kiesler, S., Boneva, B., Cummings, J., Helgeson, V., & Crawford, A. (2002). Internet paradox revisited. *Journal of Social Issues, 58,* 49–74.

Kraut, R., & Mukopadhyay, T. (1999). Information and communication: Alternative uses of the Internet in households. *Information Systems Research, 10,* 287–304.

Kraut, R., Patterson, M., Lundmark, V., Kiesler, S., Mukopadhyay, T., & Scherlis, W. (1998). Internet paradox: A social technology that reduces social involvement and psychological well-being? *American Psychologist, 53,* 1017–1031.

Moody, E.J. (2001). Internet use and its relationship to loneliness. *CyberPsychology & Behaviour, 4,* 393–401.

Odell, P., Korgen, K., Schumacher, P., & Delucchi, M. (2000). Internet use among female and male college students. *CyberPsychology & Behaviour 3,* 855–862.

Parkhurst, J.T., & Asher, S.R. (1992). Peer rejection in middle school: Subgroup differences in behaviour, loneliness, and interpersonal concerns. *Developmental Psychology, 28,* 231–241.

Parks, M.R., & Floyd, K. (1996). Making friends in cyberspace. *Journal of Communication, 46. . . .*

Pew Internet & American Life Project. (2001). *Teenage life online: The rise of the instant-message generation and the Internet's impact on friendships and family relationships. . . .*

Shaw, L.H., & Gant, L.M. (2002). In defense of the Internet: The relationship between Internet communication and depression, loneliness, self-esteem, and perceived social support. *CyberPsychology & Behavior, 5,* 157–171.

Weiss, R.S. (1973). *Loneliness: The experience of emotional and social isolation.* Boston, MA: The MIT Press.

**Patti M. Valkenburg**
**and Jochen Peter**

# Online Communication and Adolescent Well-Being: Testing the Stimulation Versus the Displacement Hypothesis

## Introduction

Opportunities for adolescents to form and maintain relationships on the Internet have multiplied in the past few years. Not only has the use of Instant Messaging (IM) increased tremendously, but Internet-based chatrooms and social networking sites are also rapidly gaining prominence as venues for the formation and maintenance of personal relationships. In recent years, the function of the Internet has changed considerably for adolescents. Whereas in the 1990s they used the Internet primarily for entertainment, at present they predominantly use it for interpersonal communication (Gross, 2004).

The rapid emergence of the Internet as a communication venue for adolescents has been accompanied by diametrically opposed views about its social consequences. Some authors believe that online communication hinders adolescents' well-being because it displaces valuable time that could be spent with existing friends. . . . Adherents of this displacement hypothesis assume that the Internet motivates adolescents to form online contacts with strangers rather than to maintain friendships with their offline peers. Because online contacts are seen as superficial weak-tie relationships that lack feelings of affection and commitment, the Internet is believed to reduce the quality of adolescents' existing friendships and, thereby, their well-being.

Conversely, other authors suggest that online communication may enhance the quality of adolescents' existing friendships and, thus, their well-being. Adherents of this stimulation hypothesis argue that more recent online communication technologies, such as IM, encourage communication with existing friends (Bryant, Sanders-Jackson, & Smallwood, 2006). Much of the time adolescents spend alone with computers is actually used to keep up existing friendships (Gross, 2004; Valkenburg & Peter, 2007). If adolescents use the Internet primarily to maintain contacts with their existing friends, the prerequisite for a displacement effect is not fulfilled. . . .

From *Journal of Computer-Mediated Communication,* vol. 12, issue 4, 2007, pp. 1169–1182 (excerpts). 

Several studies have investigated the effect of Internet use on the quality of existing relationships and well-being. Some of these studies used depression or loneliness measures as indicators of well-being; others employed measures of life-satisfaction or positive/negative affect. The studies have provided mixed results: Some have yielded results in agreement with the displacement hypothesis. Others have produced results in support of the stimulation hypothesis. . . .

At least one omission in earlier research may contribute to the inconsistent findings regarding the Internet-well-being relationship. Most research to date has been descriptive or exploratory in nature. The studies investigate direct linear relationships between Internet use and one or more dependent variables, such as social involvement, depression, or loneliness. Hardly any research has been based on a-priori explanatory hypotheses regarding *how* Internet use is related to well-being. More importantly, there is no research that contrasts opposing explanatory hypotheses in the same study. . . .

The main aim of this study is to fill the gap in earlier research and pit the predictions of the displacement hypothesis against those of the stimulation hypothesis. By empirically studying the validity of the processes proposed by the two hypotheses, we hope to improve theory formation and contribute to a more profound understanding of the social consequences of the Internet. In fact, the two hypotheses are based on the same two mediators. Both hypotheses state that online communication affects adolescents' well-being through its influence on (1) their time spent with existing friends and (2) the quality of these friendships. However, the displacement hypothesis assumes a negative effect from online communication on time spent with existing friends, whereas the stimulation hypothesis predicts a positive relationship between these two variables. The two opposing hypotheses are stated below.

**H1a:** Online communication will reduce time spent with existing friends.
**H1b:** Online communication will enhance time spent with existing friends.

. . . Neither hypothesis predicts a direct relationship between online communication and well-being. Rather, both suggest that the influence of online communication on well-being will be mediated by the quality of friendships. There is general agreement that the quality of friendships is an important predictor of well-being. Quality friendships can form a powerful buffer against potential stressors in adolescence (Hartup, 2000), and adolescents with high-quality friendships are often more socially competent and happier than adolescents without such friendships. Based on these considerations, we hypothesize that if online communication influences well-being, it will be through its influence on the quality of existing friendships. Our second hypothesis, . . . therefore states:

**H2:** Adolescents' quality of friendships will positively predict their well-being and act as a mediator between online communication and well-being.

However, the relationship between online communication and the quality of friendships may also not be direct. Both the displacement and stimulation hypotheses assume that time spent with existing friends acts as a mediator between online communication and the quality of friendships. Based on these assumptions, we hypothesize an indirect relationship between online communication and the quality of friendships, via the time spent with existing friends:

> **H3:** Adolescents' time spent with friends will predict the quality of their friendships and act as a mediator between online communication and the quality of friendships.

### Type of Online Communication: IM Versus Chat

In earlier Internet effects studies, the independent variable Internet use has often been treated as a one-dimensional concept. This may be another important reason why the findings of these studies are so mixed. Many studies only employed a measure of daily or weekly time spent on the internet and did not distinguish between different types of Internet use, such as surfing or online communication. . . .

It is quite possible that daily time spent on the Internet does not affect one's well-being, whereas certain types of Internet use do have such an effect. In this study, we focus on the type of Internet use that is theoretically most likely to influence well-being and the quality of existing friendships: online communication. We believe that if the Internet influences well-being, it will be through its potential to alter the nature of social interaction through the use of online communication technologies. In this study, well-being is defined as happiness or a positive evaluation of one's life in general (Diener, Suh, Lucas, & Smith, 1999).

Online communication in itself is a multidimensional concept. We focus on two types of communication that are often used by adolescents. IM and chat in public chatrooms. Both types of online communication are synchronous and often used for private communication. However, they differ in several respects. First, whereas chat in a public chatroom is often based on anonymous communication between unacquainted partners, IM mostly involves non-anonymous communication between acquainted partners (Valkenburg & Peter, 2007). Second, whereas chat is more often used to *form* relationships, IM is typically used to *maintain* relationships (Grinter & Palen, 2004). Although there is no previous research on the social consequences of IM versus chat, it is entirely possible that these two types of online communication differ in their potential to influence the quality of existing friendships and well-being. . . . The second aim of our study is to investigate the differential effects of IM versus chat on well-being and the two mediating variables. Because previous research does not allow us to formulate a hypothesis regarding these differential effects of different types of online communication, our research question asks:

> **RQ1:** How do the causal predictions of the displacement and stimulation hypothesis differ for IM and chat in a public chatroom?

# Method

## Sample

In December 2005, an online survey was conducted among 1,210 Dutch adolescents between 10 and 17 years of age (53% girls, 47% boys). Sampling and fieldwork were done by Qrius, a market research company in Amsterdam, the Netherlands. . . . The sample was representative of Dutch children and adolescents who use the Internet in terms of age, gender, and education. . . . Adolescents were notified that the study would be about Internet and well-being and that they could stop participation at any time they wished. . . . Completing the questionnaire took about 15–20 minutes.

We preferred an online interviewing mode to more traditional modes of interviewing, such as face-to-face or telephone interviews. There is consistent research evidence that both adolescents and adults report sensitive behaviors more easily in computer-mediated interviewing modes than in non-computer-mediated modes. . . . Therefore, the response patterns in our study may have benefited from our choice of a computer-mediated interviewing mode as far as more intimate issues, such as the quality of friendships and well-being, are concerned.

# Measures

### *IM Use*

We measured adolescents' IM use with four questions: (a) "On *weekdays* (Monday to and including Friday), how many days do you usually use IM?" (b) "On the *weekdays* (Monday to and including Friday) that you use IM, how long do you then usually use it?" (c) "During *weekends* (Saturday and Sunday), how many days do you usually use IM?" The response options were: (1) *Only on Saturday;* (2) *Only on Sunday;* (3) *On both days;* and (4) *I do not use IM on the weekends.* If respondents selected response options 1 to 3 in the question on IM weekend use, they were asked the following question for Saturday and/or Sunday: (d) "On a Saturday (a Sunday), how long do you usually use IM?" Respondents' IM use per week was calculated by multiplying the number of days per week that they used IM (range 0 through 7) by the number of minutes they used it on each day. . . . The mean time spent with IM per week was 15 hours and 15 minutes (*SD* = 21 hours and 10 minutes).

### *Chat Use*

We measured respondents' chat use in the same way as their IM use. Using the same four questions, we asked the respondents to evaluate how much time per week they used chat in public chatrooms. The mean time spent with chat per week was 1 hour and 23 minutes (*SD* = 7 hours and 30 minutes).

### *Time Spent with Friends*

Time spent with existing friends was measured with three items that were adopted from the companionship subscale of Buhrmester's (1990) Network of Relationship Inventory. We first asked respondents to think of the friends they know from their offline environment, such as from school and the neighborhood. Then we asked them three questions: (a) "How often do you meet with one or more of these friends?," (b) "How often do you and these friends go to places and do things together?," and (c) "How often do you go out and have fun with one or more of these friends?" Response options ranged from 1 (*never*) to 9 (*several times a day*). The three items loaded on one factor, which explained 69% of the variance (Cronbach's alpha = .76, $M$ = 5.78; $SD$ =1.65).

### *Quality of Friendships*

The quality of existing friendships was measured with the relationship satisfaction (three items), approval (three items), and support (three items) subscales of Buhrmester's (1990) Network of Relationship Inventory. We asked respondents to think of the friends they know from their offline environment, such as from school and the neighborhood. Example items were: (1) "How often are you happy with your relationship with these friends?" (satisfaction), "How often do these friends praise you for the kind of person you are?" (approval), and (3) "How often do you turn to these friends for support with personal problems?" Response options ranged from 1 (*never*) to 5 (*always*). The nine items were averaged to form a quality of friendship scale (Cronbach's alpha = .93; $M$ = 3.44; $SD$ = 0.72).

### *Well-Being*

We used the five-item satisfaction with life scale developed by Diener, Emmons, Larsen, and Griffin (1985). Examples of items of this scale are "I am satisfied with my life" and "In most ways my life is close to my ideal." Response categories ranged from 1 (*agree entirely*) to 5 (*disagree entirely*) and were reversely coded. Cronbach's alpha for the scale was .88, which is comparable to the alpha of .87 reported by Diener et al. (1985).

# Results

## Time Spent with IM and Chat

Respondents spent significantly more time per day on IM than on chat. Specifically, they spent on average two hours and 11 minutes per day on IM and on average 12 minutes per day on chat. This greater amount of time spent on IM suggests that if any effect of the Internet is to be expected, it will occur through the use of IM. However, to verify this claim, we test the separate effects of IM and chat in the subsequent analyses.

### Online Communication with Existing Friends

We also investigated the assumption in this and earlier studies that IM is most often used to communicate with existing friends, whereas chat in a public chatroom is more often used to communicate with strangers. This assumption was supported. Ninety-one percent of the respondents indicated that they "often" to "always" used IM to communicate with existing friends. Thirty-seven percent of the respondents indicated that they "often" to "always" used chat to communicate with existing friends.

### Pitting the Displacement Hypothesis against the Stimulation Hypothesis

Following the displacement and stimulation hypothesis, we did not assume a direct relationship between online communication and well-being. Rather, we expected that the direct relationship between online communication would be mediated by the time spent with existing friends and the quality of these friendships. . . . In line with our expectations, neither IM nor chat use was directly related to well-being. However, the results do suggest a mediated positive effect of IM use and, to a lesser extent, a positive mediated effect of chat use on well-being through the time spent with friends and the quality of friendships.

We used a formal mediation analysis to test our hypotheses. In recent years, several approaches to examining indirect or mediated effects have been discussed. The most widely used approach is the causal steps approach developed by Judd and Kenny (1981). . . . The causal steps approach has recently been criticized, first because it does not provide a statistical test of the size of the indirect effects, and second because the requirement that there must be a significant direct association between the independent and dependent variable is considered too restrictive.

The problems inherent in the causal steps approach are solved in the intervening variable approach proposed by MacKinnon and his colleagues (MacKinnon, Lockwood et al., 2002), which was used in the present study. The first step in this approach is to run a regression analysis with the independent variable predicting the mediator. The second step is to estimate the effect of the mediator on the dependent variable, after controlling for the independent variable. However, because we hypothesized that two (rather than one) intervening variables would mediate the effect of online communication on well-being, we used a four-step procedure to test for mediation.

In the first step, the independent variable (online communication) predicted the first intervening variable (time spent with friends). In the second step, the first intervening variable (time spent with friends) predicted the second intervening variable (quality of friendships), while controlling for the independent variable (online communication). In the third step, the first intervening variable (time spent with friends) predicted the second intervening variable (quality of friendships), and in the fourth and final step, the second intervening variable (quality of friendships) predicted well-being, while controlling for the first intervening variable (time spent with friends). . . .

. . . The first mediation analysis shows that time spent with IM was positively related ($\beta = .15$, $p < .001$) to the time spent with existing friends, a result which supports the stimulation hypothesis and our H1b. The opposite displacement hypothesis expressed in H1a, which predicted a negative path between these two variables, was not supported. The regression analysis showed that time spent with chat was not significantly related to time spent with friends ($\beta = .02$, n.s.). This implies that the first condition for mediation was not met in the case of time spent with chat. In other words, the causal predictions of the two hypotheses (H1a and H1b) only applied to IM, but not to chat. Therefore, the subsequent mediation analyses were only conducted for time spent with IM.

Our second hypothesis stated that the quality of friendships would positively predict well-being and act as mediator between time spent with friends and well-being. This hypothesis was supported. . . . The second mediation analysis shows that the quality of friendships significantly predicted well-being ($\beta = .16$, $p < .001$), even when the first mediating variable (time spent with friends) was controlled. The fact that time spent with friends remained a significant predictor ($\beta = .13$, $p < .001$) of well-being when the quality of friendship was controlled indicates that the mediation of quality of friendship was only partial. Finally, in support of our third hypothesis time spent with friends acted as a full mediator between time spent with IM and the quality of friendships. . . .

We tested the significance of the indirect effects by means of a formula developed by Sobel (1982). If the Sobel test leads to the critical z-value of 1.96, the mediator carries the influence of the independent variable to the dependent variable. . . . The z-value for the first mediation analysis was 5.03, $p = .001$; the z-value for the second mediation analysis was 4.98, $p = .001$. These significant z-values indicate that both the time spent with friends and the quality of friendships are valid underlying mechanisms through which the effect of IM on well-being can be explained.

## Discussion

The aim of this study was to test the validity of two opposing explanatory hypotheses on the effect of online communication on well-being: the displacement hypothesis and the stimulation hypothesis. Both hypotheses assume that online communication affects adolescents' well-being through its influence on their time spent with existing friends and the quality of those friendships. However, the displacement hypothesis assumes a negative effect from online communication to time spent with existing friends, whereas the stimulation hypothesis predicts a positive relationship between these variables.

We used formal mediation analyses to test the validity of the two mediating variables. Our results were more in line with the stimulation hypothesis than with the displacement hypothesis. We found that time spent with IM was positively related to the time spent with existing friends. In addition, the quality of friendships positively predicted well-being and acted as a first mediator between time spent with IM and well-being. Finally, we found that time spent with friends mediated the effect of time spent with IM on the quality of friendships.

However, the positive effects of our study held only for the time spent with IM and not for time spent with chat in a public chatroom. IM and chat seem to have very different functions for adolescents. In line with earlier studies, we found that the majority of adolescents use IM to talk with their existing friends. Chat in a public chatroom is less often used by adolescents. However, when utilized, adolescents primarily seem to chat with strangers. It is important for future research to differentiate between the uses of online communication technologies. . . .

Overall, our study suggests that Internet communication is positively related to the time spent with friends and the quality of existing adolescent friendships, and, via this route, to their well-being. These positive effects may be attributed to two important structural characteristics of online communication: its controllability and its reduced cues. . . . Studies have shown that these characteristics of online communication may encourage intimate self-disclosure (e.g., Valkenburg & Peter, 2007), especially when adolescents perceive these characteristics of Internet communication as important (Valkenburg & Peter, 2007). Because intimate self-disclosure is an important predictor of reciprocal liking, caring, and trust, Internet-enhanced intimate self-disclosure may be responsible for a potential increase in the quality of adolescents' friendships. . . .

## References

Bryant, J. A., Sanders-Jackson, A., & Smallwood, A. M. K. (2006). IMing, text messaging, and adolescent social networks. *Journal of Computer-Mediated Communication, 11*(2), article 11. . . .

Buhrmester, D. (1990). Intimacy of friendship, interpersonal competence, and adjustment during preadolescence and adolescence. *Child Development, 61*(4), 1101–1111.

Diener, E., Emmons, R. A., Larsen, R. J., & Griffin, S. (1985). The satisfaction with life scale. *Journal of Personality Assessment, 49*, 71–75.

Diener, E., Suh, E. M., Lucas, R. E., & Smith, H. L. (1999). Subjective well-being: Three decades of progress. *Psychological Bulletin, 125*(2), 276–302.

Grinter, R. E., & Palen, L. (2004). Instant messaging in teen life. *Proceedings of the 2002 ACM Conference on Computer Supported Cooperative Work (CSCW '02)*. . . .

Gross, E. F. (2004). Adolescent Internet use: What we expect, what teens report. *Journal of Applied Developmental Psychology, 25*(6), 633–649.

Hartup, W. W. (2000). The company they keep: Friendships and their developmental significance. In W. Craig (Ed.), *Childhood Social Development: The Essential Readings* (pp. 61–84). Malden, MA: Blackwell.

Judd, C. M., & Kenny, D. A. (1981). Process analysis: Estimating mediation in treatment evaluations. *Evaluation Review, 5*(5), 602–619.

MacKinnon, D. P., Lockwood, C. M., Hoffman, J. M., West, S. G., & Sheets, V. (2002). A comparison of methods to test mediation and other intervening variable effects. *Psychological Methods, 7*(1), 83–104.

Sobel M. E (1982). Asymptotic intervals for indirect effects in structural equations models. In S. Leinhart (Ed.), *Sociological Methodology* (pp. 290–312). San Francisco: Jossey-Bass.

Valkenburg, P. M., & Peter, J. (2007). Preadolescents' and adolescents' online communication and their closeness to friends. *Developmental Psychology, 43*(2).

# CHALLENGE QUESTIONS

## Do Online Friendships Hurt Adolescent Development?

1. Both articles focus on general wellbeing and developmental issues related to online activity. How might their findings be related to the more sensationalized instances of online activity gone bad (e.g., teen suicide over MySpace.com messages, "sexting," and predatory activity)?
2. Why might Donchi and Moore have found a gender effect? What other "gender factors" may be involved in the differences between male and female approaches to friendship?
3. If Donchi and Moore are right about the negative effects of online usage of teens, what should be done to avoid these effects? If Valkenburg and Peter are correct, how can positive internet usage be promoted? Is there a way to do both?
4. What developmental differences do the "internet" youth of today face that their parents and grandparents did not face?
5. What in your view are the advantages and disadvantages of social networking sites (i.e. MySpace, Facebook, and YouTube)? Should there be restrictions placed on teen activity on such sites, or should they be entitled to the same access as adults? What are the pros and cons of your position?

# ISSUE 9

## Are Today's Youth More Self-Centered Than Previous Generations?

**YES: Jean M. Twenge, Sara Konrath, Joshua D. Foster, W. Keith Campbell, and Brad J. Bushman,** from "Egos Inflating Over Time: A Cross-Temporal Meta-Analysis of the Narcissistic Personality Inventory," *Journal of Personality* (August 2008)

**NO: Kali H. Trzesniewski, M. Brent Donnellan, and Richard W. Robins,** from "Do Today's Young People Really Think They Are So Extraordinary? An Examination of Secular Trends in Narcissism and Self-Enhancement" *Psychological Science* (February 2008)

### ISSUE SUMMARY


**YES:** Psychologist Jean Twenge and colleagues argue that the evidence suggests that young people are more egocentric than the previous generation.

**NO:** Professor Kali Trzesniewski and colleagues maintain that the evidence shows there is no change in the over-all level of narcissism since the previous generation.


It is not uncommon to hear complaints about the current generation of young people. Recent accusations suggest modern youth are increasingly materialistic and even selfish. For example, a Pew Research Center report from 2007 labeled today's college population as the "Look at Me" generation. Many observers suggest that the positive self-esteem movement has gone too far in encouraging children to have their own sense of worth. However, other commentators disagree, noting that there is a healthy amount of self-focus and that older generations have always complained about their younger counterparts.

Psychological investigators are attempting to provide some answers to this controversy. A common tool in this research is the Narcissistic Personality Inventory (NPI), which attempts to measure various non-clinical levels of narcissistic tendencies such as superiority, vanity, and entitlement. It accomplishes this through a number of forced-choice items (e.g., "I am going to be a great person" or "I hope I am going to be successful" answered yes or no). Because the NPI has been around for several decades, it has been used to measure the narcissism of several populations across relatively long periods of time.

In the first article, Dr. Jean Twenge and her colleagues use such measurements to argue that there has been a dramatic increase in the level of college-aged narcissism in the last 20 years. With a meta-analysis of 85 studies, they evaluated data from over 16,000 American college students who took the NPI between 1979–2006. They found NPI scores increasing by a third of a standard deviation, with two-thirds of recent college students scoring significantly higher than earlier students. They conclude that their results are consistent with beliefs that modern America is increasing in individualism and related traits, such as self-esteem and narcissism. They call for further research into the causes of this increased narcissism. Yet, they suggest that grade inflation, the self-esteem movement, and the proliferation of personal technological devices have all contributed.

Kali Trzesniewksi M. Brent Donnellan, and Richard Robins disagree. They acknowledge several valid criticisms of the self-esteem movement but argue that broadly labeling the current generation as more narcissistic is premature, at best. They conducted their own study of modern college students and found no evidence of an increase in levels of narcissism or self-enhancement since 1988. They maintain that their conclusions are more accurate than previous studies because they avoided several important method problems that have plagued previous research. Furthermore, the authors make use of the NPI's subscales to suggest that socially toxic aspects of narcissism, such as superiority, are decreasing, while benign traits, such as self-sufficiency, are increasing.

**POINT**

- Narcissism has increased in the past three decades
- Americans are increasingly individualistic
- An increase in narcissism is a bad thing
- An education that tries to promote self-esteem might have a negative impact

**COUNTER-POINT**

- Narcissism has not increased in the last generation
- Americans have increased some types of individualism but not others
- An increase in narcissism has some positive features
- Even if narcissism has increased, there is not sufficient evidence to blame the self-esteem movement

**Jean M. Twenge et al.**

# Egos Inflating Over Time: A Cross-Temporal Meta-Analysis of the Narcissistic Personality Inventory

It is common for older people to complain about "kids these days," describing the younger generation as self-centered, entitled, arrogant, and/or disrespectful. As a bromide set in a particular time, it is difficult to tell whether these perceptions are a function of age (maybe younger people are more self-centered than older people simply because they are young) or of generation (maybe the younger generation actually is more self-centered than the older generation was at the same age). It is also possible that older people will complain about the younger generation even if young people are actually less self-centered than they were when they were young themselves.

To study generational change scientifically, it is necessary to separate the effects of generation from age and to measure traits using psychometrically sound questionnaires. This is best accomplished through the time-lag method, which analyzes samples of people of the same age at different points in time. For example, college students from the 1980s can be compared with college students from the 1990s and 2000s. All samples are of the same age, but are from different generations (otherwise known as *birth cohorts*). Birth cohort is a useful proxy for the sociocultural environment of different time periods. For example, children growing up in the 1970s were exposed to a fundamentally different culture than children growing up in the 1990s. The logic underlying this approach is similar to that used to assess the self-conceptions and personality traits of individuals across different world regions, except that individual differences between birth cohorts (instead of cultural groups) are assessed. In support of this idea, several previous studies have found strong birth cohort differences in characteristics such as anxiety, self-esteem, locus of control, and sexual behavior. These studies used meta-analysis to locate samples of college students and children who completed the same psychological questionnaires at different points in historical time. The correlation between mean scores and the year the data were collected were then analyzed, using a method known as cross-temporal meta-analysis.

The present study uses cross-temporal meta-analysis to examine changes in scores on the Narcissistic Personality Inventory, or NPI. The NPI is the

From *Journal of Personality*, vol. 76, no. 4, August 2008, pp. 875–884, 889–894 (excerpts).

most widely used measure of narcissistic personality in the general population. The NPI is not designed as a clinical instrument for measuring narcissistic personality disorder (NPD), and there is no cut-off score for clinically high narcissism. Narcissism is characterized first and foremost by a positive and inflated view of the self, especially on agentic traits (e.g., power, importance, physical attractiveness). Second, narcissism is associated with social extraversion, although people high in narcissism have relatively little interest in forming warm, emotionally intimate bonds with others. Third, narcissism involves a wide range of self-regulation efforts aimed at enhancing the self. These efforts can range from attention seeking and taking credit from others to seeking high-status romantic partners and opportunities to achieve public glory. Those high in narcissism also lash out with aggression when they are rejected or insulted. Many of these behaviors can potentially be explained by the link between narcissism and impulsivity. In a sense, narcissism can be conceptualized as a self-regulating system, where self-esteem and enhancement are sought through a variety of social means but with little regard for the consequences borne by others.

The NPI is ideal for a cross-temporal meta-analysis assessing changes in narcissism. First, it is reliable, well validated, and widely used. Second, the NPI is somewhat protected from social desirability influences through its use of forced-choice dyads, and, perhaps as a result, is not correlated with measures of social desirability. For each of the 40 forced-choice dyads on the NPI, participants choose either the narcissistic response (e.g., "I can live my life anyway I want to") or the non-narcissistic response (e.g., "People can't always live their lives in terms of what they want"). The 40 items are summed together. Higher scores indicate higher levels of narcissism.

## Previous Literature

Most previous studies suggest that narcissistic traits should increase with the generations. Several authors have argued that American culture has increasingly emphasized individualism. Perhaps as a result, previous cross-temporal meta-analyses demonstrate a clear rise in individualistic traits. Between the 1970s and the 1990s, both college men and women scored higher on the agentic traits measured by the Bem Sex Role Inventory M scale, such as "independent," "individualistic, particular to me," and "leadership ability." College women and—on some scales—college men scored higher on assertiveness measures between the 1970s and the 1990s, and both sexes increased in extraversion. College students scored higher on the Rosenberg Self-Esteem Scale between the 1960s and the 1990s, and children scored higher on the Coopersmith Self-Esteem Inventory between the 1980s and the 1990s. Agentic traits, assertiveness, extraversion, and self-esteem are all positively correlated with narcissism. A study of changes in personality with age development shows that younger cohorts increase with age more than older cohorts in social dominance but also in agreeableness and conscientiousness over the young adulthood years between 18 and 40. . . .

Although most evidence points to increases in narcissism over the generations, an alternative model suggests a decrease in narcissism. Generational theorists Howe and Strauss describe Baby Boomers (in college early 1960s to early 1980s) as inner fixated and self-absorbed; they specifically use the word "narcissistic" in their description. In contrast, they portray Generation X (in college mid-1980s to late-1990s), as "lacking ego strength" and having "low self-esteem". Finally, they describe the "Millennials" (in college early 2000s to late 2010s, sometimes called "GenY") as outer-fixated, group-oriented, and civically responsible. "Are they self-absorbed? No. They're cooperative team players," say Howe and Strauss. They continue, "Individualism and the search for inner fulfillment are all the rage for many Boomer adults, but less so for their kids, [who are] not as eager to grow up putting self ahead of community the way their parents did." However, these descriptions are not based on empirical data collection. Although Strauss and Howe's portrayal of generations includes many traits that are not related to narcissism, the descriptions above suggest that Baby Boomers should be the highest in narcissism, GenXers the lowest, and "Millennials" either just as low or even lower (as Strauss and Howe specifically say that they are *not* self-absorbed). Thus, their characterization of generations suggests that narcissism decreased among college students between the 1980s and the 2000s, or, at the very least, stayed steady after the Baby Boomers left college in the mid-1980s.

### Overview

This article presents a cross-temporal meta-analysis of American college students' responses to the 40-item, forced-choice version of the NPI. This analysis will examine the correlation between NPI mean scores and the year the data were collected, showing how narcissism levels have changed over the generations. . . .

## Method

### Literature Search

Studies were primarily located using the Web of Knowledge citation index. The Web of Knowledge is an extensive database, including virtually all journals in the social sciences, biological and physical sciences, and medicine. We searched the citation index for articles that cited one of the original sources of the NPI. We also gathered unpublished means by posting a message to the Society for Personality and Social Psychology Listserv (spsp-discuss@stolaf.edu) asking for NPI means that fit the criteria outlined below, and we included unpublished means from our labs.

### Inclusion Rules

Possible data points for the analysis were included or excluded on the basis of specific inclusion rules. To be included in the analysis, a study had to meet the following criteria: (a) participants were undergraduates at conventional 4-year institutions (e.g., not 2-year colleges, not military academies); (b) participants were attending college in the United States; (c) means were reported for unselected groups of students, not those chosen for scoring high or low on the NPI or another measure or singled out for being maladjusted, clients at a counseling center, and so on; (d) samples were not more than 79% female or 79% male; and (e) the study used the 40-item forced-choice version of the NPI. The 40-item forced-choice version is by far the most common version of the NPI used by researchers, so it yielded the most data. Other versions of the NPI include different items and produce different means; one of the requirements of cross-temporal meta-analysis is that the means are from the same measure so they can be directly compared across time. In addition, the 40-item NPI is more internally reliable than other versions; when Raskin and Terry created the 40-item scale, they eliminated the 14 items from the original 54-item scale that did not correlate with the scale's primary factors. . . .

## Data Analytic Strategy

We analyzed how NPI scores have changed over time, primarily by examining correlations between mean scores and year of data collection. As in previous cross-temporal meta-analyses, means were weighted by the sample size of each study to provide better estimates of the population mean. We performed our analyses using SPSS, and the βs reported are standardized to allow for easier interpretation.

To calculate the magnitude of change in NPI scores, we used the regression equations and the averaged standard deviation (*SD*) of the individual samples. To compute the mean scores for specific years (e.g., 1982 or 2006), we used the regression equation from the statistical output (used to draw the regression line). The regression equation follows the algebraic formula y = Bx+C, where B = the unstandardized regression coefficient, x = the year, C = the constant or intercept, and y = the predicted mean NPI score. This formula yielded the position of the regression line (the mean NPI score, on the Y axis) for particular years. We obtained the average standard deviation (*SD*) by averaging the within-sample *SD*s reported in the data sources; thus this reflects the average variance of the measure in a sample of individuals. It is important to note that this method avoids the ecological fallacy, also known as *alerting correlations*. The ecological fallacy occurs when the magnitude of change is calculated using the variation in mean scores rather than the variation within a population of individuals. This exaggerates the magnitude of the effect, because mean scores do not differ as much as individual scores. The method used here, in contrast, uses the standard deviation of the individual studies to capture the variance of the scale among a population of individuals.

# Results

American college students score progressively higher on narcissism between the early 1980s and 2006. There is a significant and positive correlation between NPI scores and year of data collection when weighted by sample size ($\beta = .53$, $p < .001$, $k = 85$). Thus, more recent generations report more narcissistic traits. The regression equation (NPI mean = 0.09293 × year – 169.128) yields a score of 15.06 for 1982 and 17.29 for 2006. The average *SD* reported for the individual samples (from the articles we collected) is 6.86. Thus NPI scores increased 0.33 standard deviation from the early 1980s to 2006. This is a small-to-medium effect size (between .20 and .50) by Cohen's guidelines.

Converting the *SD* change to percentile scores is also informative. If the average student in the early 1980s scored at the 50th percentile of the distribution, the average student in 2006 scored at the 65th percentile (assuming a normal curve). In other words, almost two-thirds of recent college students are above the mean 1979–1985 narcissism score, a 30% increase (65 out of 100 in 2006, compared to 50 out of 100 in 1979–1985).

If we assume that the NPI still has a normal distribution, this shift in the mean score means that there are now more college students at the top end of the original distribution. For example, 24% of 2006 college students score 1 *SD* above the 1979–1985 narcissism mean, compared to 15% during that original data collection. (One *SD* above the 1979–1985 is a score of 22, representing someone who answers the clear majority of items—22 out of 40—in a narcissistic direction.) It is also interesting to note how recent means compare to data collected on a sample of celebrities such as movie stars, reality TV winners, and famous musicians. This celebrity sample had a mean NPI score of 17.84, not much higher than the 2006 regression equation mean of 17.29. Thus, recent college students approach celebrities in their levels of narcissism. . . .

## Discussion

A meta-analysis of 85 samples of American college students shows a systematic increase in scores on the Narcissistic Personality Inventory. The shift in scores means that the average college student now endorses about two more narcissism items than his or her predecessors did in the early 1980s. Although the effect size for the shift is statistically moderate rather than large (one-third of a standard deviation), it is larger than the effect of violent video games on aggression and most racial differences in self-esteem. The generational shift over 25 years is also twice as large as the current sex difference in narcissism; thus generation is a better predictor of narcissism scores than gender.

These data are consistent with theories positing an increase in individualism in American society and with previous studies finding generational increases in other individualistic traits such as self-esteem and agency. The most recent college students score about the same on the NPI as a sample of celebrities. The change is linear and steady, with the correlation significant when the analysis is limited to certain years only. It also appears that women are driving the increase in narcissism, consistent with the finding that the generational increase in agentic traits and assertiveness was stronger for women.

We were unable to analyze changes in specific subscales of the NPI, as very few researchers reported NPI means broken down by subscale. Thus, we do not know if only certain facets of narcissism are increasing among American college students, or if the change is evenly distributed across them. In addition, we do not know how the increase in narcissism is related to the previously documented rise in self-esteem. The rise in narcissism could be directly related to increases in self-esteem, or there could have been an increase in narcissistic traits independent of self-esteem.

## Correlates of Narcissism

Is this rise in narcissism a bad thing? As measured by the NPI, narcissism is linked to a range of positive emotional outcomes, including self-esteem, positive affect, extraversion, and life satisfaction. Narcissism is associated with other benefits to the self as well, such as short-term (but not long-term) likeability, enhanced performance on public evaluation tasks including being selected for reality television, short-term victories in competitive tasks, and emergent (though not successful) leadership. Narcissism also has many costs to the self, such as distorted judgments of one's abilities, risky decision making, potential addictive disorders including alcohol abuse, compulsive shopping, and pathological gambling. Many of the costs of narcissism are borne by other people. These include troubled romantic relationships, aggression, assault, white collar crime, and rapidly depleting common resources. In sum, narcissism is associated with benefits to the individual that are primarily affective and most evident in the short term, but the costs of narcissism are paid by others and, eventually, by the individual as well (for a more detailed discussion of the trade-offs of narcissism). Thus the implications of the rise in narcissism may be positive in the short term for individuals, but negative for other people, for society, and for the individual in the long term.

Many of the correlates of narcissism are also on the upswing, although we cannot be certain if they are directly tied to the rise in narcissism. Several positive personality traits correlated with narcissism have increased over the same time period, including self-esteem, agentic traits, extraversion and assertiveness. Behaviors and attitudes have also shifted in a direction consistent with a arise in narcissism. There is a trend among college students toward "hooking up" rather than having sex within committed relationships. Materialism has increased: 74% of college freshmen in 2004 cited "being very well-off financially" as an important life goal, compared to only 45% in 1967. In a 2006 survey, 81% of 18- to 25-year-olds said that getting rich was among their generation's most important goals; 64% named it as the most important goal of all. In addition, 51% said that becoming famous was among their generation's important goals. In contrast, only 30% chose helping others who need help, and only 10% named becoming more spiritual. . . .

## Future Research: The Uncertain Causes of Narcissism

The relationship between personality and culture is likely reciprocal, with societal changes driving increases in narcissism and vice versa. What societal trends may have led to the increased narcissism we found? We can speculate on several of these, although a great deal of future work needs to be done on the causes of narcissism. Schools and media activities may have promoted an increase in narcissism. Children in some preschools sing a song with the lyrics, "I am special/I am special/Look at me . . . ," and many television shows for children emphasize positive self-feelings and specialness. Future research should examine whether school and media programs intended to raise self-esteem also raise narcissism. Grade inflation may also play a role: In 1980, only 27% of college freshmen reported earning an A average in high school, but by 2004 almost half (48%) reported a high school A average. However, the amount of studying has actually declined (33% of American college freshmen in 2003 reported studying 6 or more hours a week during their last year of high school, compared to 47% in 1987), as has performance on tests like the SAT. Future research should determine whether grade inflation builds narcissism.

Finally, future research should examine whether current technology is related to narcissistic traits. Devices such as iPods and Tivo allow people to listen to music and watch television in their own individual ways, and websites such as MySpace and YouTube (whose slogan is "Broadcast yourself) permit self-promotion far beyond that allowed by traditional media. These trends motivated *Time* magazine to declare that the 2006 Person of the Year was "You," complete with a mirror on the cover. Most of the increase in narcissism occurred before the wide use of such technology, so these shifts—even if they do play a role—did not cause the initial upswing in narcissism scores. Instead, the rise in narcissism may have influenced the ways people use technology.

## Limitations

The present study provides the most comprehensive examination to date of generational change in narcissistic personality traits. Even so, it is not without its limitations. Any analysis of self-report data is potentially limited by socially desirable responding. However, the NPI is not significantly correlated with social desirability. In addition, there have not been concomitant changes in socially desirable responding, which did not change during this time period. This makes it very unlikely that changes in socially desirable responding account for the present results.

This study also limits its conclusions to American society and generations, partially because there is not much data available over time from other countries. Americans score higher on narcissism than people from other world regions. Future analyses might determine if narcissism is also increasing in other cultures or if this cultural trend is limited to the United States. . . .

This study also cannot determine whether the change in narcissism is a purely generational effect or a time-period effect. As with any time-lag study including people of only one age group, we cannot know if those in other age groups also changed. It is possible that both younger and older Americans became more narcissistic from the 1980s to the 2000s. It is also possible that older Americans did not change at all or even became less narcissistic. Given the relative stability of social dominance after young adulthood, as well as cross-sectional research showing lower narcissism scores in older adults, it seems likely that much of the shift is a generational rather than a time-period effect.

**Kali H. Trzesniewski, M. Brent Donnellan, and Richard W. Robins**

# NO

# Do Today's Young People Really Think They Are So Extraordinary?

## An Examination of Secular Trends in Narcissism and Self-Enhancement

Several decades ago, California State Congressman John Vasconcellos, who referred to himself as the "Johnny Appleseed of self-esteem," spearheaded a movement to create school programs designed to improve self-esteem. This movement came under attack almost immediately and continues to be attacked today. Although well-designed self-esteem interventions can have positive effects on children's outcomes, the Vasconcellos-inspired school programs often lacked precise implementation and grounding in research. Many of these programs seemed to emphasize feeling good over achieving, giving awards and good grades to all students even in the absence of real achievements. Similarly, American culture is stereotyped as being overly focused on seeking high self-esteem at all costs. As a result, there is widespread concern that the American "feel good culture" and the self-esteem programs it spawned have inadvertently produced a generation of young narcissists.

Most notably, Twenge has characterized Americans born in the 1970s, 1980s, and 1990s as "Generation Me," a label selected to capture their purported tendency to be more egotistical, entitled, and overconfident than previous generations, presumably because they grew up in this "culture of self-worth." Media reports based on Twenge, Konrath, Foster, Campbell, and Bushman's forthcoming analysis of generational changes in average scores on the Narcissistic Personality Inventory have further disseminated the idea that America's youth are increasingly narcissistic. Coverage of this work has been widespread, appearing in high-profile media outlets such as the *Atlantic Monthly, CBS News,* and *National Public Radio* as well as in major newspapers such as the *Boston Globe,* the *Los Angeles Times,* and the *Washington Post.*

The purpose of this report is to examine the evidence for the claim that today's young people are more self-centered and self-aggrandizing than young people of previous generations. We analyzed secular changes in narcissism using large samples of undergraduate students from northern California, the geographic epicenter of the self-esteem movement. In addition, we

From *Psychological Science,* vol. 19, no. 2, February 2008, pp. 181–187. 

examined secular changes in one prominent manifestation of narcissism, self-enhancement (i.e., the tendency to hold unrealistically positive beliefs about the self), using data from the college-student samples and from the Monitoring the Future project, a large national probability study of high school seniors conducted annually since 1976.

Why might narcissism and self-enhancement be increasing in recent generations? A number of social commentators have noted a shift in American culture from communitarian values and strong social ties toward an emphasis on individualism and the pursuit of one's own needs. These social values are thought to shape individual personality characteristics. As noted by Lasch, "Every society reproduces its culture—its norms, its underlying assumptions, its modes of organizing experience—in the individual, in the form of personality" (p. 76). It is difficult to devise models that explain the processes through which broad societal trends affect personality. However, identifying changes in personality associated with birth cohort is an important first step.

Unfortunately, identifying cohort effects is empirically challenging. One approach, pioneered by Twenge and her colleagues, is to conduct a cross-temporal meta-analysis in which changes in average personality scores are examined as a function of date of data collection. Using this methodology, Twenge et al. found that the average NPI score has increased steadily in college students since the scale was first administered in 1982. Although this is an important application of meta-analytic techniques, the results are nonetheless constrained by limitations in the sampling procedures used in the original studies. The college-student samples included in the meta-analysis were mostly small and perhaps subject to selection biases; thus, we believe that it is informative to examine secular trends in narcissism and self-enhancement in large samples of prescreening data and in a nationally representative sample.

In the present study, we tested the hypothesis that narcissism levels are increasing by comparing mean scores on the NPI using data collected on college students in the 1980s, 1990s, and 2000s. The NPI was designed to assess personality characteristics associated with the clinical definition of narcissistic personality disorder in the third edition of the *Diagnostic and Statistical Manual of Mental Disorders*. These attributes include a grandiose sense of importance, a preoccupation with power and success, exhibitionism, arrogance, exploitativeness, and a sense of entitlement. The NPI is the most widely used and well-validated measure of subclinical levels of narcissism and has been shown to predict psychologists' ratings of narcissism. Thus, the NPI provides one of the best ways to measure whether or not today's college students exhibit more narcissistic tendencies than previous generations. To complement our analysis of secular trends in the NPI, we also examined trends in self-enhancement, a construct that is associated with narcissism. We operationalized self-enhancement as the discrepancy between participants' ratings of their intelligence and more objective indicators of their intellectual ability (SAT scores and grade point average, or GPA). If young people have been getting more narcissistic over the past three decades, then the degree to which they overestimate their ability should have been increasing as well.

# Method

## Narcissism

We used data drawn from mass testing sessions of introductory psychology students conducted at the University of California, Davis and Berkeley campuses, in 1996 and annually from 2002 to 2007. We restricted the analyses to the 25,849 students between 18 and 24 years of age (*Mdn* = 19, *SD* = 1.40) who completed the 40-item forced-choice version of the NPI (alpha reliability ranged from .84 to .85 across years). We selected students who were of traditional college age to provide a cleaner test of the cohort-effect hypothesis. The sample was 66.3% female; 39.7% were Asian American, 30.9% were Caucasian, 2.2% were African American, 9.4% were Hispanic, and 17.8% were of mixed or other races or did not state their ethnic background. To extend our test of secular trends, we compared means from the 1990s and 2000s with means first published by Raskin and Terry; these means were based on 1,018 participants (52.5% female) who completed the NPI between 1979 and 1985.

## Self-Enhancement

To track secular trends in self-enhancement, we used data from two sources. First, in the mass testing sessions conducted at the University of California between 2003 and 2007 (self-enhancement data were not available in the 1996 and 2002 assessments), students were asked to "rate your intelligence compared to the general population," using a scale ranging from 1 (*bottom 5%*) to 10 (*top 5%*). To gauge self-enhancement, we computed the degree to which self-perceived intelligence was higher than objective indicators of academic ability (SAT scores and college GPA). Specifically, we conducted multiple regression analyses (using data from all assessment years, i.e., from 2003 through 2007) in which each indicator of ability was regressed on the self-ratings of intelligence and the unstandardized residuals were retained. Because the two resulting self-enhancement indices—one based on SAT scores and the other based on GPA—were almost perfectly correlated ($r = .90$), we computed a single combined index by entering both academic criteria simultaneously into a multiple regression predicting self-rated intelligence and then saving the unstandardized residuals. Positive values indicate self-enhancement (i.e., overestimation by the self), and negative values indicate self-diminishment (i.e., underestimation by the self). Residual scores have been widely used to assess self-enhancement. In this sample, self-enhancement correlated .27 with NPI score, a finding consistent with previous research.

Second, we examined long-term trends in self-enhancement using data from the Monitoring the Future project, a very large national probability study of high school seniors conducted annually since 1976 (total *N* across the 30 years used in these analyses = 410,527; 50.7% female . . .). Every year from 1976 to 2006, high school seniors were asked, "How intelligent do you think you are compared to others your own age?" This item was rated from 1 (*far below average*) to 7 (*far above average*). To assess self-enhancement bias, we used an unstandardized residual score (computed via regression using data from all years) reflecting the discrepancy between self-perceived intelligence and high school grades; standardized-test scores were not available in the Monitoring the Future data, but given the .90 correlation between self-enhancement based on grades and self-enhancement based on SAT scores in the University of California data, it is unlikely that the secular trends would have been different if test scores had been used as a criterion instead of grades. Because of privacy issues associated with publicly available data, ethnicity was coded as White or non-White (83.4% White).

# Results

## Secular Trends in Narcissism

Table 1 shows the means and standard deviations by year of data collection for the full-scale NPI. Given the large sample sizes, we focus on effect sizes rather than significance levels. We discuss all effects that meet or surpass Cohen's guideline of a small effect (i.e., an $r$ of .10 or a $d$ of 0.20).

Year of data collection (from 1996 to 2007) was uncorrelated with full-scale NPI score ($r$ = .01). Given the lack of time trend in these data, we computed the average score on the NPI for all participants from 1996 through 2007 and compared this aggregate score to that reported by Raskin and Terry. This comparison provides a direct test of the cohort hypothesis because it compares Generation Me (i.e., members of our sample were all born after 1971) with previous generations (i.e., participants in Raskin and Terry's study were all born before 1969). As Table 1 shows, there was a very small difference ($d$ = –0.06) between NPI means computed in our data (Generation Me) and in Raskin and Terry's original data. To further illustrate the effects, we standardized all NPI scores from 1996 through 2007 to Raskin and Terry's mean and standard deviation. . . . [All] of the means from 1996 through 2007 were slightly below Raskin and Terry's average (e.g., the largest standardized difference was –0.10, for scores in 2002, $N$ = 3,117). Thus, we found no evidence for a secular increase in NPI scores among college students from the 1980s to the 2000s, and if anything, we found weak support for a secular decline.

Gender, ethnicity, and age did not moderate the time trend (none of the interaction terms accounted for more than 0.1% of the variance), although we did find some main effects. Men ($M$ = 0.41) had higher narcissism scores than women ($M$ = 0.37; $d$ = 0.24), and Caucasians ($M$ = 0.39) had higher narcissism scores than Asian Americans ($M$ = 0.34; $d$ = 0.29). Age was uncorrelated with NPI scores in this age-restricted sample ($r$ = .01).

It is possible that specific aspects of narcissism have increased over time while others have decreased, producing no aggregate change at the full-scale level. However, an examination of time trends from 1996 to 2007 for NPI subscales created by Emmons and by Raskin and Terry (1988) provided no evidence for changes in specific aspects of narcissism ($r$ = –.01–.02 for correlations between subscale scores and year of data collection). Nonetheless, we found a few differences when comparing the subscale means for 1996 through

*Table1*

**Mean Full-Scale and Subscale Scores on the Narcissistic Personality Inventory (NPI) by Year of Data Collection**

| | | | Subscale | | | | | | |
|---|---|---|---|---|---|---|---|---|---|
| Year | *N* | Full NPI | Authority | Exhibitionism | Superiority | Entitlement | Exploitiveness | Self-Sufficiency | Vanity |
| 1982[a] | 1,018 | 0.39(0.17) | 0.52(0.27) | 0.32(0.25) | 0.51(0.27) | 0.28(0.23) | 0.29(0.34) | 0.35(0.25) | 0.46(0.36) |
| 1996 | 670 | 0.38(0.17) | 0.51(0.29) | 0.27(0.27) | 0.44(0.28) | 0.32(0.25) | 0.33(0.27) | 0.41(0.25) | 0.39(0.35) |
| 2002 | 3,117 | 0.37(0.17) | 0.49(0.28) | 0.27(0.25) | 0.41(0.28) | 0.30(0.24) | 0.31(0.26) | 0.41(0.25) | 0.37(0.35) |
| 2003 | 4,820 | 0.38(0.17) | 0.50(0.29) | 0.28(0.25) | 0.41(0.28) | 0.31(0.24) | 0.32(0.27) | 0.41(0.24) | 0.38(0.35) |
| 2004 | 4,770 | 0.38(0.17) | 0.50(0.28) | 0.28(0.25) | 0.40(0.28) | 0.32(0.24) | 0.32(0.27) | 0.41(0.25) | 0.39(0.36) |
| 2005 | 4,434 | 0.38(0.17) | 0.51(0.29) | 0.28(0.25) | 0.41(0.28) | 0.32(0.24) | 0.33(0.27) | 0.41(0.24) | 0.39(0.35) |
| 2006 | 4,974 | 0.38(0.17) | 0.50(0.28) | 0.28(0.25) | 0.42(0.28) | 0.32(0.25) | 0.32(0.27) | 0.41(0.24) | 0.39(0.35) |
| 2007 | 3,064 | 0.39(0.18) | 0.51(0.28) | 0.29(0.26) | 0.43(0.28) | 0.32(0.24) | 0.33(0.27) | 0.42(0.24) | 0.39(0.35) |
| $\alpha$ | — | .84 | .75 | .65 | .54 | .48 | .53 | .42 | .62 |
| $d^b$ | — | –0.06 | –0.07 | –0.16 | –0.36 | 0.17 | 0.10 | 0.24 | –0.20 |
| | | (–0.15 to 0.04) | (–0.17 to 0.02) | (–0.25 to –0.07) | (–0.45 to –0.26) | (0.07 to 0.26) | (0.02 to 0.20) | (0.16 to 0.34) | (–0.29 to –0.11) |

*Note.* For each year, standard deviations are given in parentheses.
[a]The data in this row were obtained from Raskin and Terry (1988); means and standard deviations were converted from sums to scale means. The data were collected from 1979 to 1985, so 1982 is the average year of data collection. [b]This row presents the standardized difference between the mean score in 1996 through 2007 and Raskin and Terry's (1998) mean score for 1979 through 1985. A positive value indicates that the mean was higher in 1996 through 2007. The numbers in parentheses are 95% confidence intervals.

2007 with subscale means from 1979 through 1985 reported by Raskin and Terry. As Table 1 shows, scores on four subscales decreased (Authority, Exhibitionism, Superiority, and Vanity), and scores on three increased (Entitlement, Exploitiveness, and Self-Sufficiency), although the largest effect size was a decline of only a third of a standard deviation in Superiority.

### Secular Trends in Self-Enhancement

We found no evidence that self-enhancement changed over time in either sample; the correlation (*r*) between self-enhancement and year of data collection was −.02 and −.03, respectively, for the University of California sample (2003–2007) and the Monitoring the Future sample (1976–2006). Moreover, neither gender nor ethnic group moderated the time trend (neither of the interaction terms accounted for more than 0.1% of the variance in either sample). Results were similar to those for narcissism in that men self-enhanced more than women in both the college sample (*M*s = 0.27 vs. −0.14, *d* = 0.39) and the high school sample (*M*s = 0.19 vs. −0.18, *d* = 0.36) and that Caucasian college students (*M* = 0.22) reported higher levels of self-enhancement than Asian college students (*M* = −0.24; *d* = 0.46). However, in the high school sample, non-Caucasians (*M* = 0.12) and Caucasians (*M* = 0.00) did not differ in self-enhancement (*d* = 0.12).

## Discussion

The goal of this study was to investigate secular changes in narcissism and self-enhancement using large samples of northern Californian college students and a nationally representative sample of high school students from the Monitoring the Future study. California is regarded as the home of the self-esteem movement, so data from universities in this state are particularly useful given recent claims about the negative impact of the culture of self-worth. Contrary to previous research and media reports, this study yielded no evidence that levels of narcissism have increased since Raskin and Terry first published their 40-item forced-choice version of the NPI. Likewise, we found no evidence that self-enhancement, defined as inflated perceptions of intelligence, has increased over the past 30 years. Thus, today's youth seem to be no more narcissistic and self-aggrandizing than previous generations.

Indeed, the means for the NPI from our sample closely resemble the means from a large Internet sample. In the latter sample, the average NPI score for Americans ages 20 to 24 was 15.58 (*N* = 775; J. Foster, personal communication, April 5, 2007) and in our sample, the mean NPI score for students ages 20 to 24 was 15.23 (*N* = 10,491). In addition, the mean reported by Foster et al. is very close to the average of 15.55 reported by Raskin and Terry. Thus, both our data and the Internet data collected by Foster et al. fail to show a robust secular trend toward increases in narcissism in young people over the past few decades.

Why do our findings differ from those of Twenge et al.? First, our NPI results are based on large prescreening samples, and our self-enhancement findings are based on a nationally representative sample, whereas the findings of Twenge et al. are meta-analytic results based on aggregated data from comparatively small samples of college students (median $N = 126$, range = 24–1,182). Aggregating means from small convenience studies of college students might not be the best strategy for making inferences about birth cohorts because students choose to participate in studies on the basis of titles and descriptions that might appeal to their individual characteristics, including narcissism. In contrast, we used data from large mass testing sessions, which makes our NPI samples considerably larger than those of most individual studies of college students (our average annual sample size was 3,692) and makes the possibility of selection effects less of a concern. Moreover, the Monitoring the Future results are based on a representative sampling of high school students, a sampling procedure that is particularly well suited for evaluating claims about secular increases in self-enhancement.

Indeed, we believe that issues of sampling are paramount when making generalizations about entire birth cohorts. Researchers who are interested in making point estimates of particular attitudes often pay careful attention to sampling procedures. Most college-student samples are generated using non-probability sampling techniques. As noted by Pedhazur and Schmelkin, "the incontrovertible fact is that, in non-probability sampling, it is not possible to estimate sampling errors. Therefore, validity of inferences to a population cannot be ascertained" (p. 321). To be sure, pooling together convenience samples of college students will never lead to estimates that can be defended as representative of an entire population of college students, let alone members of an entire birth cohort. That is, no amount of aggregation will circumvent the limitations of convenience sampling.

A second reason why our results differ from those of Twenge et al. is that cross-temporal meta-analyses yield ecological coefficients, which are calculated using summary statistics (e.g., sample means) rather than individual data points. As Rosenthal, Rosnow, and Rubin noted, "correlations based on aggregated data (e.g., group means) can be dramatically larger or smaller (even in the opposite direction) than correlations based on individual scores" (p. 2). We examined this issue by comparing the correlation between year of data collection and self-enhancement based on the full Monitoring the Future sample with the alerting correlation based on the mean self-enhancement score for each year (i.e., the data in Table 2). As reported in the Results section, the correlation based on the full sample was –.03; in contrast, the alerting correlation was –.57. Similarly, using the college-student data from 1996 to 2007, we compared the individual-level correlation between year of data collection and NPI score with the altering correlation for the mean scores reported in Table 1. The individual-level correlation was .01, whereas the alerting correlation was .40; likewise, the individual-level correlations ranged from .00 to .01 across Raskin and Terry's NPI subscales, whereas the alerting correlations ranged from –.41 (Superiority) to .82 (Exhibitionism). These often dramatic differences are consistent with the methodological literature, which indicates that alerting correlations overestimate individual effects in most behavioral research.

*Table 2*

**Mean Self-Enhancement by Year of Data Collection**

| Year | *N* | Mean (*SD*) |
|---|---|---|
| 1976 | 14,277 | –0.06 (0.95) |
| 1977 | 15,638 | –0.03 (0.97) |
| 1978 | 15,877 | 0.00 (0.96) |
| 1979 | 14,141 | –0.01 (0.96) |
| 1980 | 14,056 | 0.07 (0.99) |
| 1981 | 15,611 | 0.06 (0.99) |
| 1982 | 15,704 | 0.04 (0.99) |
| 1983 | 14,514 | 0.03 (0.99) |
| 1984 | 14,026 | 0.03 (1.00) |
| 1985 | 14,096 | 0.03 (1.00) |
| 1986 | 13,631 | 0.03 (1.01) |
| 1987 | 14,390 | 0.07 (1.01) |
| 1988 | 14,571 | 0.06 (1.03) |
| 1989 | 14,785 | 0.03 (1.04) |
| 1990 | 11,285 | 0.03 (1.03) |
| 1991 | 13,462 | 0.04 (1.04) |
| 1992 | 13,845 | 0.01 (1.06) |
| 1993 | 13,913 | –0.01 (1.06) |
| 1994 | 13,096 | –0.02 (1.08) |
| 1995 | 10,647 | 0.02 (1.06) |
| 1996 | 11,917 | 0.05 (1.07) |
| 1997 | 12,728 | 0.00 (1.09) |
| 1998 | 12,627 | 0.01 (1.09) |
| 1999 | 11,347 | –0.01 (1.09) |
| 2000 | 10,218 | –0.02 (1.10) |
| 2001 | 10,390 | –0.06 (1.09) |
| 2002 | 10,258 | –0.08 (1.09) |
| 2003 | 11,718 | –0.10 (1.08) |
| 2004 | 11,957 | –0.11 (1.07) |
| 2005 | 11,966 | –0.08 (1.09) |
| 2006 | 13,836 | –0.08 (1.08) |
| *d*[a] | — | –0.06 (–0.08 to –0.04) |

[a]This row presents the standardized difference between the mean for 2004 through 2006 and the mean for 1976 through 1978. The negative value indicates that the latter mean was higher. The numbers in parentheses are the 95% confidence interval.

Thus, the cross-temporal meta-analytic approach may amplify effects that are trivial from a psychological perspective.

A third issue to consider is that the NPI measures multiple facets of narcissism, and temporal changes at the facet level may not always map onto temporal changes in the full-scale score. Emmons showed that subscales of the NPI can have distinct external correlates, some of which might be considered psychologically adaptive. Similarly, Konrath, Bushman, and Campbell reported that the NPI Entitlement subscale is a better predictor of laboratory-based measures of aggression than the full scale is, which suggests that not all of the narcissistic tendencies assessed by the NPI are equally destructive. The most important concern, however, is that because the NPI assesses a number of constructs, it is unclear how to precisely interpret any changes in the summary score. A secular change in the NPI might signal changes in socially toxic traits (e.g., entitlement), socially noxious traits (e.g., vanity), or simply relatively benign traits (e.g., leadership). Our results illustrate this point: The largest increase was found for the seemingly benign trait of self-sufficiency, and the largest decrease was found for the seemingly socially toxic trait of superiority.

This study has several limitations. First, although we used large samples of college students to evaluate secular changes in narcissism, our large samples are not likely representative of the entire U.S. population of 18- to 24-year-olds. Indeed, students at 4-year colleges represent only 24% of the population ages 18 to 24. Moreover, it is unknown how students in psychology courses differ in psychological characteristics from other college students. Nonetheless, these two concerns are mitigated to some extent by the fact that we also failed to find a secular trend in self-enhancement in a representative sample of high school students. Thus, we failed to find evidence of a secular trend in self-enhancement using both representative and convenience samples. Second, we did not have an ideal proxy measure for intelligence to assess self-enhancement in the high school sample. However, this concern is ameliorated by the fact that the results were similar to those based on SAT scores in the college-student sample, which is not surprising because in the latter sample, the correlation between self-enhancement based on grades and self-enhancement based on test scores was .90. Thus, the strengths and limitations of our data sets are quite complementary, and the results converge in showing few indications of secular change in self-enhancement.

Finally, some of the findings we report are based on null results. However, null results can be critical in science when they counter a predicted effect and when they are based on large samples, which rules out concerns of a lack of power to detect predicted effects. The lack of a clear trend toward increasing narcissism directly addresses recent claims of secular increases in narcissism that have received a great deal of attention in the media, as shown by Jimmy Carter's response in *Rolling Stone* magazine. The degree of empirical support for claims of increasing narcissism among this generation of young American adults has important implications for how this generation is viewed by others and how young adults view themselves.

We believe that great care needs to be exercised when making broad generalizations about cohort-related increases in narcissism. We were unable to find evidence that either narcissism or the closely related construct of self-enhancement has increased over the past three decades. Moreover, even if we had found evidence for a secular increase in narcissism, placing the blame on the self-esteem movement would seem to go well beyond the data, especially when there is evidence that well-designed and well-implemented self-esteem programs are effective interventions for youth with certain problems. Our view is that the research findings concerning generational differences should be based on well-established results and presented to the public with a good degree of caution given the inherent complexities involved in studying cohort effects.

*Acknowledgments*—The first and second authors contributed equally to this article; the ordering of authorship was arbitrary. We thank Rob Ackerman, Kim Assad, Portia Dyrenforth, Richard Lucas, and Ed Witt for helpful comments on an earlier draft of this article.

# CHALLENGE QUESTIONS

1. The researchers on both sides of this issue used the same measurement tool (the NPI) but came to very different conclusions. Why might this be?
2. If today's youth really are more narcissistic, is this a bad thing? What might be the consequences of such a shift, and what, if anything, should be done to alter it?
3. What are the implications of these two positions for the self-esteem movement? Given the disagreement on the issue, what should we do about teaching self-esteem?
4. How does your own perceptions of your self affect your views of this issue? Would your position be different if you were not included in the population accused of being more narcissistic? Does caring about this issue suggest you are narcissistic?
5. Do you consider some internet sites, for example, MySpace, Facebook, and YouTube as self-centering sites? What are the implications of their proliferation?

# Internet References . . .

## The Dilemma of Determinism

This is a link to the classic paper written by William James, one of psychology's founding fathers, in which he discusses the doctrine of determinism versus the idea of human agency.

**http://www.rci.rutgers.edu/~stich/104_Master_File/104_Readings/James/James_DILEMMA_OF_DETERMINISM.pdf**

## Informal Education

This website is dedicated to expanding knowledge in many areas. The following link provides a brief history of Howard Gardner and his theory of multiple intelligences, as well as links to other helpful sites.

**http://www.infed.org/thinkers/gardner.htm**

# UNIT 4

## Cognitive Processes

*Psychology is often defined as the study of behavior and cognition. Consequently, cognitive processes are a pivotal arena for psychological research. How do our minds work? For example, are individual differences in cognition explained by a theory of multiple intelligences? Traditional intelligence tests typically provide one overall score, as if it is valid to speak of intelligence as one entity, cutting across all activities and skills. Does this have some validity? Recent research has seemed to question this overall intelligence notion. Is it better to think of many different intelligences corresponding to different aspects of thought and behavior? How much is knowledge and intelligence related to capacity for memory? Is it possible for memories to be false? Can you forget a major life event, such as sexual abuse, only to remember it latter through therapy? How much should we rely on such "recovered" memories to inform us about our actual past and present?*

# ISSUE 10

## Is the Theory of Multiple Intelligences Valid?

**YES: Howard Gardner,** from *Multiple Intelligences: New Horizons* (Basic Books, 2006)

**NO: John White,** from "Howard Gardner: The Myth of Multiple Intelligences," Lecture at Institute of Education, University of London (November 17, 2004)

### ISSUE SUMMARY

**YES:** Psychologist Howard Gardner argues for the validity of his theory of multiple intelligences because it both reflects the data collected about intelligent human behavior and explains why people excel in some areas but fail in others.

**NO:** Educational philosopher John White believes that Gardner cannot prove the existence of multiple types of intelligence and argues that people who are generally able to adapt well will excel in whatever field they choose.

People who saw Michael Jordan play professional basketball were amazed by his grace and poise. Even when ill, he could outscore most other players. What was the source of his abilities? Did his proficiency at playing basketball necessarily imply that he was good at other activities? After all, Jordan was also generally acknowledged as being bright, articulate, and socially skilled. On the other hand, his attempt to play major league baseball was less than successful. Can people only be really good at one thing and not any others, or is some general ability—some general intelligence—involved?

The traditional view of intelligence is that there is a single factor, often called *g*, that underlies most other abilities. The other abilities may require some unique pieces of information to perform successfully, such as playing a musical instrument, but those persons with a high *g* are thought to be quicker in acquiring this information or more easily adaptable to these new circumstances. Most tests of intelligence assume and reinforce this more traditional view of intelligence because they seem to imply that a person's intelligence can be represented as a single, measurable quantity or score.

Howard Gardner, however, has recently challenged this popular tradition. In the first article of this issue, this renowned psychologist has argued that intelligence is best understood not as a single general capacity, but as a number of distinct and relatively independent abilities. Michael Jordan may have bodily-kinesthetic intelligence, but that does not mean he has musical intelligence. Gardner argues that the single-factor theory of intelligence is outdated and should be replaced by a theory of multiple intelligences. He believes that individuals have profiles reflecting both strengths and weaknesses in different areas of intelligence. According to Gardner a good test-taker—the usual recipient of a high "IQ" score—is not necessarily any "smarter" than a good presenter; they both happen to be more intelligent in different areas.

In the second selection, John White examines Gardner's position in some detail, calling it the "myth of multiple intelligences." White begins his critique of Gardner's theory by describing Gardner's original attempt (1983) to define intelligence. According to White, Gardner's original definition was itself too narrow. Instead of defining different types of intelligence as Gardner does, White believes that intelligence has a lot to do with the general flexibility or adaptability of a person in achieving their goals. The more intelligent a person is, the more capable that person is of achieving his or her goals, no matter how divergent these goals may be. In this sense, then, White's proposal is a recent update of the more traditional general approach to intelligence that Gardner is attempting to replace.

| POINT | COUNTERPOINT |
| --- | --- |
| • Humans are best understood as having a number of relatively independent intellectual faculties. | • The existence of multiple types of intellectual faculties has not been proven. |
| • Multiple intelligence theory gives a framework for why people succeed in some areas but fail in others. | • People who are generally "intelligent" will be able to succeed because they understand how to adapt to the differing performance areas. |
| • Evidence from brain research, human development, evolution, and cross-cultural comparisons support the theory of multiple intelligences. | • The research cited by Gardner could just as well be used to support general intelligence theory. |
| • Multiple intelligence theory has important educational implications. | • The acceptance of multiple intelligence theory in educational settings could give students a false picture of themselves. |

**Howard Gardner**

# In a Nutshell

The original scene: Paris, 1900—La Belle Epoque. The city fathers approached a talented psychologist named Alfred Binet with an unusual request. Families were flocking to the capital city from the provinces, and a good many of their children were having trouble with their schoolwork. Could Binet devise some kind of a measure that would predict which youngsters would succeed and which would fail in the primary grades of Paris schools?

As almost everybody knows, Binet succeeded. In short order, his discovery came to be called the "intelligence test"; his measure, the IQ, for "intelligence quotient" (mental age divided by chronological age and multiplied by 100). Like other Parisian fashions, the IQ soon made its way to the United States, where it enjoyed a modest success until World War I, when it was used to test over one million American military recruits. With its use by the U.S. armed forces, and with America's victory in the conflict, Binet's invention had truly arrived. Ever since, the IQ test has looked like psychology's biggest success—a genuinely useful scientific tool.

What is the vision that led to the excitement about IQ? At least in the West, people had always relied on intuitive assessments of how smart other people were. Now intelligence seemed to be quantifiable. Just as you could measure someone's actual or potential height, now, it seemed, you could measure someone's actual or potential intelligence. We had one dimension of mental ability along which we could array everyone.

The search for the perfect measure of intelligence has proceeded apace. Here, for example, are some quotations from an advertisement for one such test:

> Need an individual test which quickly provides a stable and reliable estimate of intelligence in four or five minutes per form? Has three forms? Does not depend on verbal production or subjective scoring? Can be used with the severely physically handicapped (even paralyzed) if they can signal yes or no? Handles two-year-olds and superior adults with the same short series of items and the same format? Only $16.00 complete.

Now, a single test that can do all that is quite a claim. American psychologist Arthur Jensen suggests that we could look at reaction time to assess intelligence: a set of lights go on; how quickly can the subject react? British psychologist Hans Eysenck recommends that investigators of intelligence look directly at brain waves. And with the advent of the gene chip, many look forward to the day when we can glance at the proper gene locus on the proper chromosome, read off someone's IQ, and confidently predict his or her life chances. . . .

I would like to present an alternative vision—one based on a radically different view of the mind, and one that yields a very different view of school. It is a pluralistic view of mind, recognizing many different and discrete facets of cognition, acknowledging that people have different cognitive strengths and contrasting cognitive styles. I introduce the concept of an individual-centered school that takes this multifaceted view of intelligence seriously. This model for a school is based in part on findings from sciences that did not even exist in Binet's time: cognitive science (the study of the mind) and neuroscience (the study of the brain). One such approach I have called the theory of multiple intelligences. Let me tell you something about its sources and claims to lay the groundwork for the discussions on education in the chapters that follow.

I introduce this new point of view by asking you to suspend for a moment the usual judgment of what constitutes intelligence, and let your thoughts run freely over the capabilities of human beings—perhaps those that would be picked out by the proverbial visitor from Mars. Your mind may turn to the brilliant chess player, the world-class violinist, and the champion athlete; certainly, such outstanding performers deserve special consideration. Are the chess player, violinist, and athlete "intelligent" in these pursuits? If they are, then why do our tests of "intelligence" fail to identify them? If they are not intelligent, what allows them to achieve such astounding feats? In general, why does the contemporary construct of intelligence fail to take into account large areas of human endeavor?

To approach these questions I introduced the theory of multiple intelligences (MI) in the early 1980s. As the name indicates, I believe that human cognitive competence is better described in terms of a set of abilities, talents, or mental skills, which I call *intelligences*. All normal individuals possess each of these skills to some extent; individuals differ in the degree of skill and in the nature of their combination. I believe this theory of intelligence may be more humane and more veridical than alternative views of intelligence and that it more adequately reflects the data of human "intelligent" behavior. Such a theory has important educational implications.

## What Constitutes an Intelligence?

The question of the optimal definition of intelligence looms large in my inquiry. And it is here that the theory of multiple intelligences begins to diverge from traditional points of view. In the classic psychometric view, intelligence is defined operationally as the ability to answer items on tests of intelligence. The inference from the test scores to some underlying ability is supported by statistical techniques. These techniques compare responses of subjects at different ages; the apparent correlation of these test scores across ages and across different tests corroborates the notion that the general faculty of intelligence, called *g* in short, does not change much with age, training, or experience. It is an inborn attribute or faculty of the individual.

Multiple intelligences theory, on the other hand, pluralizes the traditional concept. An intelligence is a computational capacity—a capacity to process a certain kind of information—that originates in human biology and human psychology. Humans have certain kinds of intelligences, whereas rats, birds, and computers foreground other kinds of computational capacities. An intelligence entails the ability to solve problems or fashion products that are of consequence in a particular cultural setting or community. The problem-solving skill allows one to approach a situation in which a goal is to be obtained and to locate the appropriate route to that goal. The creation of a cultural product allows one to capture and transmit knowledge or to express one's conclusions, beliefs, or feelings. The problems to be solved range from creating an end for a story to anticipating a mating move in chess to repairing a quilt. Products range from scientific theories to musical compositions to successful political campaigns.

MI theory is framed in light of the biological origins of each problem-solving skill. Only those skills that are universal to the human species are considered (again, we differ from rats, birds, or computers). Even so, the biological proclivity to participate in a particular form of problem solving must also be coupled with the cultural nurturing of that domain. For example, language, a universal skill, may manifest itself particularly as writing in one culture, as oratory in another culture, and as the secret language composed of anagrams or tongue twisters in a third.

Given the desideratum of selecting intelligences that are rooted in biology and that are valued in one or more cultural settings, how does one actually identify an intelligence? In coming up with the list, I reviewed evidence from various sources: knowledge about normal development and development in gifted individuals; information about the breakdown of cognitive skills under conditions of brain damage; studies of exceptional populations, including prodigies, savants, and autistic children; data about the evolution of cognition over the millennia; cross-cultural accounts of cognition; psychometric studies, including examinations of correlations among tests; and psychological training studies, particularly measures of transfer and generalization across tasks. Only those candidate intelligences that satisfied all or a healthy majority of the criteria were selected as bona fide intelligences. A more complete discussion of each of these criteria and of the intelligences that were initially identified may be found in *Frames of Mind*, especially chapter 4. In that foundational book I also consider how the theory might be disproved and compare it with competing theories of intelligence. An update of some of these discussions is presented in *Intelligence Reframed*, and in the chapters that follow.

In addition to satisfying the aforementioned criteria, each intelligence must have an identifiable core operation or set of operations. As a neurally based computational system, each intelligence is activated or triggered by certain kinds of internal or external information. For example, one core of musical intelligence is the sensitivity to pitch relations, and one core of linguistic intelligence is the sensitivity to the phonological features of a language.

An intelligence must also be susceptible to encoding in a symbol system—a culturally contrived system of meaning that captures and conveys important forms of information. Language, picturing, and mathematics are but three nearly worldwide symbol systems that are necessary for human survival and productivity. The relationship of an intelligence to a human symbol system is no accident. In fact, the existence of a core computational capacity anticipates the actual or potential creation of a symbol system that exploits that capacity. While it may be possible for an intelligence to develop without an accompanying symbol system, a primary characteristic of human intelligence may well be its gravitation toward such an embodiment.

## The Original Set of Intelligences

Having sketched the characteristics and criteria for an intelligence, I turn now to a brief consideration of each of the intelligences that were proposed in the early 1980s. I begin each sketch with a thumbnail biography of a person who demonstrates an unusual facility with that intelligence. (These biographies were developed chiefly by my longtime colleague Joseph Walters.) The biographies illustrate some of the abilities that are central to the fluent operation of a given intelligence. Although each biography illustrates a particular intelligence, I do not wish to imply that in adulthood intelligences operate in isolation. Indeed, except in abnormal individuals, intelligences always work in concert, and any sophisticated adult role will involve a melding of several of them. Following each biography is a survey of the various sources of data that support each candidate as an intelligence.

### Musical Intelligence

When Yehudi Menuhin was three years old, his parents smuggled him into San Francisco Orchestra concerts. The sound of Louis Persinger's violin so entranced the young child that he insisted on a violin for his birthday and Louis Persinger as his teacher. He got both. By the time he was ten years old, Menuhin was an international performer.

Violinist Yehudi Menuhin's musical intelligence manifested itself even before he had touched a violin or received any musical training. His powerful reaction to that particular sound and his rapid progress on the instrument suggest that he was biologically prepared in some way for a life in music. Menuhin is one example of evidence from child prodigies that support the claim that there is a biological link to a particular intelligence. Other special populations, such as autistic children who can play a musical instrument beautifully but who cannot otherwise communicate, underscore the independence of musical intelligence.

A brief consideration of the evidence suggests that musical skill passes the other tests for an intelligence. For example, certain parts of the brain play important roles in the perception and production of music. These areas are characteristically located in the right hemisphere, although musical skill is not as clearly localized in the brain as natural language. Although the particular susceptibility of musical ability to brain damage depends on the degree of training and other individual characteristics, there is clear evidence that amusia, or a selective loss of musical ability, occurs. . . .

## Bodily-Kinesthetic Intelligence

Fifteen-year-old Babe Ruth was playing catcher one game when his team was taking a "terrific beating." Ruth "burst out laughing" and criticized the pitcher loudly. Brother Mathias, the coach, called out, "All right, George, YOU pitch!" Ruth was stunned and nervous: "I never pitched in my life . . . I can't pitch." The moment was transformative, as Ruth recalls in his autobiography: "Yet, as I took the position, I felt a strange relationship between myself and that pitcher's mound. I felt, somehow, as if I had been born out there and that this was a kind of home for me." As sports history shows, he went on to become a great major league pitcher (and, of course, attained legendary status as a hitter).

Like Menuhin, Babe Ruth was a prodigy who recognized his "instrument" immediately on his first exposure to it, before receiving any formal training.

Control of bodily movement is localized in the motor cortex, with each hemisphere dominant or controlling bodily movements on the contralateral side. In right-handers, the dominance for bodily movement is ordinarily found in the left hemisphere. The ability to perform movements when directed to do so can be impaired even in individuals who can perform the same movements reflexively or on a nonvoluntary basis. The existence of apraxia constitutes one line of evidence for a bodily-kinesthetic intelligence.

The evolution of specialized body movements is of obvious advantage to the species, and in human beings this adaptation is extended through the use of tools. Body movement undergoes a clearly defined developmental schedule in children; there is little question of its universality across cultures. Thus, it appears that bodily-kinesthetic "knowledge" satisfies many of the criteria for an intelligence.

The consideration of bodily-kinesthetic knowledge as "problem solving" may be less intuitive. Certainly carrying out a mime sequence or hitting a tennis ball is not solving a mathematical equation. And yet, the ability to use one's body to express an emotion (as in a dance), to play a game (as in a sport), or to create a new product (as in devising an invention) is evidence of the cognitive features of body usage. . . .

## Logical-Mathematical Intelligence

Along with the companion skill of language, logical-mathematical reasoning provides the principal basis for IQ tests. This form of intelligence has been thoroughly investigated by traditional psychologists, and it is the archetype of "raw intelligence" or the problem-solving faculty that purportedly cuts across domains. It is perhaps ironic, then, that the actual mechanism by which one arrives at a solution to a logical-mathematical problem is not as yet completely understood—and the processes involved in leaps like those described by McClintock remain mysterious.

Logical-mathematical intelligence is supported as well by empirical criteria. Certain areas of the brain are more prominent in mathematical calculation than others; indeed, recent evidence suggests that the linguistic areas in the frontotemporal lobes are more important for logical deduction, and the visuospatial areas in the parietofrontal lobes for numerical calculation. There are savants who perform great feats of calculation even though they are tragically deficient in most other areas. Child prodigies in mathematics abound. The development of this intelligence in children has been carefully documented by Jean Piaget and other psychologists.

## Linguistic Intelligence

. . . As with the logical intelligence, calling linguistic skill an intelligence is consistent with the stance of traditional psychology. Linguistic intelligence also passes our empirical tests. For instance, a specific area of the brain, called Broca's area, is responsible for the production of grammatical sentences. A person with damage to this area can understand words and sentences quite well but has difficulty putting words together in anything other than the simplest of sentences. Other thought processes may be entirely unaffected.

The gift of language is universal, and its rapid and unproblematic development in most children is strikingly constant across cultures. Even in deaf populations where a manual sign language is not explicitly taught, children will often invent their own manual language and use it surreptitiously. We thus see how an intelligence may operate independently of a specific input modality or output channel.

## Spatial Intelligence

Navigation around the Caroline Islands in the South Seas is accomplished by native sailors without instruments. The position of the stars, as viewed from various islands, the weather patterns, and water color are the principal signposts. Each journey is broken into a series of segments, and the navigator learns the position of the stars within each of these segments. During the actual trip the navigator must mentally picture a reference island as it passes under a particular star. From that envisioning exercise, he computes the number of segments completed, the proportion of the trip remaining, and any corrections in heading that are required. The navigator cannot see the islands as he sails along; instead he maps their locations in his mental picture of the journey.

Spatial problem solving is required for navigation and for the use of the notational system of maps. Other kinds of spatial problem solving are brought to bear in visualizing an object from different angles and in playing chess. The visual arts also employ this intelligence in the use of space.

Evidence from brain research is clear and persuasive. Just as the middle regions of the left cerebral cortex have, over the course of evolution, been selected as the site of linguistic processing in right-handed persons, the posterior regions of the right cerebral cortex prove most crucial for spatial processing. Damage to these regions causes impairment of the ability to find one's way around a site, to recognize faces or scenes, or to notice fine details. . . .

## Interpersonal Intelligence

. . . Interpersonal intelligence builds on a core capacity to notice distinctions among others—in particular, contrasts in their moods, temperaments, motivations, and intentions. In more advanced forms, this intelligence permits a skilled adult to read the intentions and desires of others, even when they have been hidden. This skill appears in a highly sophisticated form in religious or political leaders, salespersons, marketers, teachers, therapists, and parents. . . . All indices in brain research suggest that the frontal lobes play a prominent role in interpersonal knowledge. Damage in this area can cause profound personality changes while leaving other forms of problem solving unharmed—after such an injury, a person is often not the "same person". . . .

Biological evidence for interpersonal intelligence encompasses two additional factors often cited as unique to humans. One factor is the prolonged childhood of primates, including the close attachment to the mother. In cases where the mother (or a substitute figure) is not available and engaged, normal interpersonal development is in serious jeopardy. The second factor is the relative importance in humans of social interaction. Skills such as hunting, tracking, and killing in prehistoric societies required the participation and cooperation of large numbers of people. The need for group cohesion, leadership, organization, and solidarity follows naturally from this.

## Intrapersonal Intelligence

In an essay called "A Sketch of the Past," written almost as a diary entry, Virginia Woolf discusses the "cotton wool of existence"—the various mundane events of life. She contrasts this cotton wool with three specific and poignant memories from her childhood: a fight with her brother, seeing a particular flower in the garden, and hearing of the suicide of a past visitor:

> These are three instances of exceptional moments. I often tell them over, or rather they come to the surface unexpectedly. But now for the first time I have written them down, and I realize something that I have never realized before. Two of these moments ended in a state of despair. The other ended, on the contrary, in a state of satisfaction. . . . The sense of horror [in hearing of the suicide] held me powerless. But in the case of the flower, I found a reason; and was thus able to deal with the sensation. I was not powerless. . . . Though I still have the peculiarity that I receive these sudden shocks, they are now always welcome; after the first surprise, I always feel instantly that they are particularly valuable. And so I go on to suppose that the shock-receiving capacity is what makes me a writer. I hazard the explanation that a shock is at once in my case followed by the desire to explain it. I feel that I have had a blow; but it is not, as I thought as a child, simply a blow from an enemy hidden behind the cotton wool of daily life; it is or will become a revelation of some order; it is a token of some real thing behind appearances; and I make it real by putting it into words.

This quotation vividly illustrates the intrapersonal intelligence—knowledge of the internal aspects of a person: access to one's own feeling life, one's range of emotions, the capacity to make discriminations among these emotions and eventually to label them and to draw on them as a means of understanding and guiding one's own behavior. A person with good intrapersonal intelligence has a viable and effective model of him- or herself—one consistent with a description constructed by careful observers who know that person intimately. Since this intelligence is the most private, evidence from language, music, or some other more expressive form of intelligence is required if the observer is to detect it at work. In the above quotation, for example, linguistic intelligence serves as a medium in which to observe intrapersonal knowledge in operation.

We see the familiar criteria at work in the intrapersonal intelligence. As with the interpersonal intelligence, the frontal lobes play a central role in personality change. Injury to the lower area of the frontal lobes is likely to produce irritability or euphoria, whereas injury to the higher regions is more likely to produce indifference, listlessness, slowness, and apathy—a kind of depressive personality. In persons with frontal lobe injury, the other cognitive functions often remain preserved. In contrast, among aphasics who have recovered sufficiently to describe their experiences, we find consistent testimony: while there may have been a diminution of general alertness and considerable depression about the condition, the individual in no way felt himself to be a different person. He recognized his own needs, wants, and desires and tried as best he could to achieve them.

The autistic child is a prototypical example of an individual with impaired intrapersonal intelligence; indeed, the child may not even be able to refer to himself. At the same time, such children may exhibit remarkable abilities in the musical, computational, spatial, mechanical, and other non-personal realms. . . .

## The Unique Contributions of the Theory

As human beings, we all have a repertoire of skills for solving different kinds of problems. My investigation began, therefore, with a consideration of these problems, the contexts in which they are found, and the culturally significant products that are the outcome. I did not approach "intelligence" as a reified human faculty that is brought to bear in literally any problem setting; rather, I began with the problems that human beings solve and the products that they cherish. In a sense I then worked back to the intelligences that must be responsible.

Evidence from brain research, human development, evolution, and cross-cultural comparisons was brought to bear in the search for the relevant human intelligences: a candidate was included only if reasonable evidence to support its membership was found across these diverse fields. Again, this tack differs from the traditional one: since no candidate faculty is necessarily an intelligence, I could make an up-or-down decision on a motivated basis. In the traditional approach to intelligence, there is no opportunity for this type of empirical decision.

My belief is that these multiple human faculties, the intelligences, are to a significant extent independent of one another. Research with brain-damaged adults repeatedly demonstrates that particular faculties can be lost while others are spared. This independence of intelligences implies that a particularly high level of ability in one intelligence, say mathematics, does not require a similarly high level in another, like language or music. This independence of intelligences contrasts sharply with traditional measures of IQ that find high correlations among test scores. I speculate that the usual correlations among subtests of IQ tests come about because all of these tasks in fact measure the ability to respond rapidly to items of a logical-mathematical or linguistic sort; these correlations might be substantially reduced if one were to survey in a contextually appropriate way—what I call "intelligence-fair assessment"—the full range of human problem-solving skills.

Until now, my discussion may appear to suggest that adult roles depend largely on the flowering of a single intelligence. In fact, however, nearly every cultural role of any degree of sophistication requires a combination of intelligences. Thus, even an apparently straightforward role, like playing the violin, transcends a reliance on musical intelligence. To become a successful violinist requires bodily-kinesthetic dexterity and the interpersonal skills of relating to an audience and, in a different way, of choosing a manager; quite possibly it involves an intrapersonal intelligence as well. Dance requires skills in bodily-kinesthetic, musical, interpersonal, and spatial intelligences in varying degrees. Politics requires an interpersonal skill, a linguistic facility, and perhaps some logical aptitude.

Inasmuch as nearly every cultural role requires several intelligences, it becomes important to consider individuals as a collection of aptitudes rather than as having a singular problem-solving faculty that can be measured directly through pencil-and-paper tests. Even given a relatively small number of such intelligences, the diversity of human ability is created through the differences in these profiles. In fact, it may well be that the total is greater than the sum of the parts. An individual may not be particularly gifted in any intelligence, and yet, because of a particular combination or blend of skills, he or she may be able to fill some niche uniquely well. Thus, it is of paramount importance to assess the particular combination of skills that may earmark an individual for a certain vocational or avocational niche.

In brief MI theory leads to three conclusions:

1. All of us have the full range of intelligences; that is what makes us human beings, cognitively speaking.
2. No two individuals—not even identical twins—have exactly the same intellectual profile because, even when the genetic material is identical, individuals have different experiences (and identical twins are often highly motivated to distinguish themselves from one another).
3. Having a strong intelligence does not mean that one necessarily acts intelligently. A person with high mathematical intelligence might use her abilities to carry out important experiments in physics or create powerful new geometric proofs; but she might waste these abilities in playing the lottery all day or multiplying ten-digit numbers in her head.

All of these statements are about the psychology of human intelligence—to which MI theory seeks to make a contribution. But of course they raise powerful educational, political, and cultural questions. Those questions will engage us in later parts of the book.

## Conclusion

I believe that in our society we suffer from three biases, which I have nicknamed "Westist," "Testist," and "Bestist." "Westist" involves putting certain Western cultural values, which date back to Socrates, on a pedestal. Logical thinking, for example, is important; rationality is important; but they are not the only virtues. "Testist" suggests a bias towards focusing on those human abilities or approaches that are readily testable. If it can't be tested, it sometimes seems, it is not worth paying attention to. My feeling is that assessment can be much broader, much more humane than it is now and that psychologists should spend less time ranking people and more time trying to help them.

"Bestist" is a thinly veiled reference to David Halberstam's 1972 book *The Best and the Brightest.* Halberstam's title referred ironically to the figures, among them Harvard faculty members, who were brought to Washington to help President John F. Kennedy and in the process launched the Vietnam War. I think any belief that all the answers to a given problem lie in one certain approach, such as logical-mathematical thinking, can be very dangerous. Current views of intellect need to be leavened with other, more comprehensive points of view.

It is of the utmost importance that we recognize and nurture all of the varied human intelligences and all of the combinations of intelligences. We are all so different largely because we have different combinations of intelligences. If we recognize this, I think we will have at least a better chance of dealing appropriately with the many problems that we face in the world. If we can mobilize the spectrum of human abilities, not only will people feel better about themselves and more competent; it is even possible that they will also feel more engaged and better able to join the rest of the world community in working for the broader good. Perhaps if we can mobilize the full range of human intelligences and ally them to an ethical sense, we can help increase the likelihood of our survival on this planet, and perhaps even contribute to our thriving.

**John White**

# Howard Gardner: The Myth of Multiple Intelligences

## Introduction

. . . MI theory identifies some eight or nine types of intelligence: not only the logico-mathematical and linguistic kinds measured by IQ , but, also musical, spatial, bodily-kinaesthetic, intrapersonal, interpersonal, to which have now been added naturalist and possibly existential intelligences. My question will be: is there good evidence that these intelligences exist? Or are they a myth?

MI theory is all the rage in school reform across the world. I heard recently from James McAleese of Richard Hale School in Hertford that the Canadian province of Quebec has introduced the idea into all its secondary schools. In Britain many schools are using MI as a basis for a more flexible type of teaching and learning, which acknowledges that children have different preferred "learning styles." Not everyone learns best through traditional methods which draw heavily on linguistic and logical skills. So room is made for children who can bring to bear on their learning their ability in music, say, or their kinaesthetic abilities. In history, for example, pupils' work on the Treaty of Versailles might include a conventional essay for the linguistic children and a rap presentation of the treaty for the musical ones. In many schools children are given questionnaires to profile their intelligences. Some schools give their pupils smart cards—the size of credit cards—inscribed with their preferred intelligences.

And MI does appear to deliver the goods in terms of inclusion and raising self-esteem. Pupils who used to think themselves dim can blossom when they find out how bright they are making music or interacting with people. Kinaesthetic learners can now see themselves as "body smart." The idea that intelligence is not necessarily tied to IQ has been a liberating force.

The educational world, including government agencies as well as schools, has gone for MI in a big way. But for the most part it seems to have taken over the ideas without questioning their credentials. MI theory comes to schools "shrink-wrapped", as one teacher put it to me. This is understandable, since schools do not have the time to investigate all the ideas that come their way that look as if they have some mileage in the classroom.

From a Lecture at the Institute of Education, University of London, November 17, 2004.

The idea that children come hard-wired with a whole array of abilities in varying strengths is appealing. But is there any reason to think it true?

Everything turns on the claim that the eight or nine intelligences actually exist. The bare idea that intelligence can take many forms and is not tied to the abstract reasoning tested by IQ is both welcome and true. But it's hardly news. Many philosophers and psychologists have agreed with common sense that intelligence has a lot to do with being flexible in pursuit of one's goals. You want to buy a washing machine and check things out rather than rush into it. You vary your tactics against your opponent when you are playing tennis. Your child is being bullied at school and you work out what's best to do. There are innumerable forms in which intelligence can be displayed. We don't need a new theory to tell us this. Long ago the philosopher Gilbert Ryle reminded us that 'the boxer, the surgeon, the poet and the salesman' engage in their own kinds of intelligent operation, applying 'their special criteria to the performance of their special tasks.' All this is now widely accepted.

This means that there are as many types of human intelligence as there are types of human goals. Gardner has corralled this huge variety into a small number of categories. Is this justified? Is it true that there are just eight or nine intelligences? Or is MI theory a myth? . . .

I'm aware that, if Gardner is right, I'll probably be connecting more with those of you whose preferred learning style is linguistic or logical. But kinaesthetics among you please feel free to walk about the room or express things in mime. Interpersonals are most welcome to discuss the argument with their neighbour as we go along. I thought I'd cracked it for those stronger on the spatial, since I've got some overheads. But then I realized they are mainly filled with words—so I guess the linguistically intelligent will be the winners in this.

## How Do You Know When You've Got an Intelligence?

How does Gardner pick out his intelligences? How does he identify them? In Chapter 4 he writes

> First of all, what are the prerequisites for an intelligence: that is, what are the general desiderata to which a set of intellectual skills ought to conform before that set is worth consideration in the master list of intellectual competences? Second, what are the actual criteria by which we can judge whether a candidate competence, which has passed the "first cut," ought to be invited to join our charmed circle of intelligences?

Identifying an intelligence is thus a two-stage process. First, it has to satisfy the prerequisites; and secondly it has to satisfy the criteria.

### Prerequisites

The first stage is the more important. If a candidate fails here, it stands no chance. So what Gardner says about prerequisites is crucial. He tells us that

> A human intellectual competence must entail a set of skills of problem-solving . . . and must also entail the potential for finding or creating problems. . . . These prerequisites represent my effort to focus on those intellectual strengths that prove of some importance within a cultural context.

He goes on to say that

> a prerequisite for a theory of multiple intelligences, as a whole, is that it captures a reasonably complete gamut of the kinds of abilities valued by human cultures.

### *Failing Candidates*

Which candidates fail and which pass the test? Among failures, Gardner includes the "ability to recognize faces" because it "does not seem highly valued by cultures."

Is this true? If most of us could not recognize the faces of our relatives, friends, colleagues, or political leaders, it is hard to see how social life would be possible.

### *Passing Candidates*

In Gardner 1983 the passing candidates must include the seven intelligences. They must have all been picked out for their problem-solving and problem-creating skills important in human cultures.

Are we talking about all human cultures, most, or only some of them? Gardner is not clear on this.

Neither is there any evidence that he has surveyed a great number of human societies in order to reach this conclusion.

There is a mystery about this "first cut." How is it that recognizing faces fails, but musical ability passes? Gardner does not give us any clear indication.

What he has in mind, I think, is that the ability to recognize faces is not an *intellectual area* that is culturally valued. It's not like mathematics or music or the visual arts. If this is so—and I give further evidence below that it is—then for something to count as an intelligence it has to be a subdivision of the realm of the intellect. It has to be something like a form of knowledge or understanding in the sense used by Paul Hirst in his well-known theory of "forms of knowledge."

If this is right, then the first thing you have to do to pick out an intelligence—as a prerequisite—has nothing to do with empirical investigations of individuals and seeing how their minds or their brains work. It has all to do with reflecting on the social world—specifically that part of the social world concerned with intellectual activities and achievements. To be an intelligence is—so far—the same as being a separable realm of understanding.

I will come back to the "prerequisites" later. As we shall see, they are of pivotal importance.

## Criteria

Once a candidate intelligence has satisfied the prerequisites, it has to meet various criteria. These comprise:

- potential isolation of the area by brain damage
- the existence in it of idiots savants, prodigies and other exceptional individuals
- an identifiable core operation/set of operations
- a distinctive developmental history, along with a definable set of expert "end-state" performances
- an evolutionary history and evolutionary plausibility
- support from experimental psychological tasks
- support from psychometric findings
- susceptibility to encoding in a symbol system.

I examined these problems in a little book I wrote on Gardner's theory in 1998 called *Do Howard Gardner's Multiple Intelligences Add Up?* Here I will simply summarise some main arguments. I begin with specific items. For convenience, I begin with two of them taken together.

> "An identifiable core operation/set of operations"
>
> "A distinctive developmental history, along with a definable set of expert 'end-state' performances"

The interconnectedness of these two can be illustrated by linguistic intelligence. This has as its "core operations" a sensitivity to the meaning of words, to the order among words, to the sounds and rhythms of words, and to the different functions of language. These core operations are seen at work "with special clarity" in the work of the poet. Linguistic intelligence also possesses a distinctive developmental history, culminating in expert "end-state" performances like those of the poet. Other intelligences illustrate the same point.

Gardner's theory of intelligence is developmentalist. Developmentalism is the theory that the biological unfolding between two poles from seed through to mature specimen that we find in the physical world is also found in the mental world. In his criteria, Gardner acknowledges the two poles in the mental case. At one end, there are allegedly genetically given capacities. At the other end is the mature state, the "definable set of expert 'end-state' performances". Gardner is interested in the really high fliers in each area—people like famous poets (linguistic); famous mathematicians (logic-mathematical); famous musicians (musical); famous visual artists; famous dancers, mime-artists (bodily/kinaesthetic); famous politicians (interpersonal); writers like Proust (intrapersonal).

### *Problems in Developmentalism*

Gardner's theory faces an objection besetting all forms of developmentalism. This theory is based on the assumption that the unfolding familiar in the biological realm is also found in the mental. There are two problems about this, one for each of the two poles.

i. First the seed, or initial state. Biological seeds, plant or animal, *have within them the power to unfold* into more complex stages, given appropriate environmental conditions. To locate a parallel initial state in the mental case it is not enough to pick out innately given capacities. There is no doubt that such capacities exist. We are all born with the power to see and hear things, to desire food etc. But these do not have within them the power to *unfold* into more complex forms. They do *change* into more sophisticated versions: the desire for food, for instance, becomes differentiated into desires for hamburgers and ice-cream. But it does not unfold into these. The changes are cultural products: people are socialized into them.

ii. Secondly, the mature state—Gardner's "end-state." We understand this notion well enough in physical contexts. A fully-grown human body or delphinium is one which can grow no further. It can certainly go on *changing*, but the changes are to do with maintenance and deterioration, not further growth. If we apply these ideas to the mind, do we want to say that all human beings have mental ceilings—e.g. in each of Gardner's intelligences—beyond which they cannot progress? Psychologists like Cyril Burt have believed this, but the notion is deeply questionable. I can argue this through further if you wish.

There is also a problem about *what counts* as maturity—the end-state—in the case of the intelligences. With the human body, we know through the use of our senses when maturity has occurred: we can *see* that a person is fully grown. What equivalent is there in the mental realm?

We do not just use our senses. We cannot see a person's intellectual maturity as we can see that he or she is physically fully grown. Significantly, ideas about maturity are likely to be controversial. Some people would understand intellectual maturity in quiz show terms, as being able to marshal and remember heaps of facts; others would emphasize depth of understanding, etc. The judgments lack the consensus found in judgments about fully grown pine trees. This is because we are in the realm of value judgments rather than of observable facts.

Gardner's examples of high levels of development in the intelligences reflect his own value judgments. He has in mind the achievements of selected poets, composers, religious leaders, politicians, scientists, novelists and so on. It is Gardner's value judgments, not his empirical discoveries as a scientist, that are his starting point.

I have tried to show that whether we look towards the beginning or towards the end of the development process, we find apparently insuperable problems in identifying mental counterparts to physical growth. Since developmentalist assumptions are central to Gardner's MI theory, the latter is seriously undermined.

"Susceptibility to encoding in a symbol system"

Gardner writes:

> following my mentor Nelson Goodman and other authorities, I conceive of a symbol as any entity (material or abstract) that can denote

> or refer to any other entity. On this definition, words, pictures, diagrams, numbers, and a host of other entities are readily considered symbols.

It is important to see how wide the range of Gardner's symbols is. They include not only obvious ones like words and mathematical symbols, but also paintings, symphonies, plays, dances and poems. It is because works of art are symbols in his view that he can connect many of his intelligences with their own kind of symbolic entities. For instance, it is not only words which are the symbols associated with linguistic intelligence: this also contains such symbols as poems. Symbols in music include musical works; in spatial intelligence paintings and sculptures, in b/k intelligence dances; in intrapersonal intelligence introspective novels like Proust's. But the notion that a work of art is itself a symbol is problematic in aesthetics. The main difficulty is: what is it symbolizing? Take a work of abstract art. Or a poem by Sylvia Plath. What are these symbols of?

The whole theory of symbolization in art from Suzanne Langer to Nelson Goodman is deeply problematic.

We can discuss this further later if you'd like. For the moment my claim is that this criterion "**susceptibility to encoding in a symbol system**" rests on a highly dubious aesthetic theory. It is a long way from empirical science.

Without going through all the other criteria, a word about two of them.

> "The potential isolation of the area by brain damage"

I think we can take it that there are localized areas of function within the brain. If one part of the brain is damaged, one's sight is impaired, if another, one's ability to move one's left hand. All this shows is that certain physiological necessary conditions of exercising these capacities are absent. It does not help to indicate the existence of separate "intelligences."

Given his developmentalism, one can understand why Gardner should look to brain localization in order to identify intelligences, for he has to provide an account of the "seed" which is to unfold into its mature form, and this seed has to be part of our original constitution. But the kinds of function picked out by brain localization research do not have the power to *unfold* into maturer versions of themselves.

> "The existence, in an area, of idiots savants, prodigies and other exceptional individuals"

Gardner invokes the existence of *idiots savants* to support his theory, but what I know of them does not lead me to think of them as intelligent. What they all have in common is a *mechanical* facility, one which lacks the flexibility of adapting means to ends found in intelligent behaviour.

Prodigies only support Gardner's case if there is good evidence that their talents are innate. But what evidence there is seems to point to acquired abilities.

## Conclusion

It would be natural to think that the "criteria" are all straightforwardly applicable. But this is not so. The criteria to do with development and with symbols presuppose the truth of *theories*—one in psychology, the other in aesthetics—which turn out to be untenable. And this undermines the viability of MI theory as a whole. . . .

My main concern is not with MI theory for its own sake but with its present influence in the educational world. If I am right, the eight or nine intelligences have not been shown to exist. If so, what are the implications for the school reforms based on the theory? As things are now, children are being encouraged to see themselves, in PSHE (Personal, Social and Health Education) lessons and elsewhere, as having innately given strengths in certain areas. This is part of their self-understanding. But if the theory is wrong, they may be getting a false picture of themselves. . . .

# CHALLENGE QUESTIONS

## Is the Theory of Multiple Intelligences Valid?

1. Why might the educational world be drawn toward a theory of multiple intelligences? Support your answer with examples from your own educational experience.
2. What possible dangers could arise from schools applying multiple intelligence theory, especially as described by White?
3. White argues that Gardner's list of intelligences is too restrictive. Can you think of any intelligences that do not appear in Gardner's list? Justify your claim.
4. What is the difference between talent and intelligence? Should intelligence be considered primarily a measure of cognitive and academic abilities? Support your answers.
5. Gardner argues that some intelligences are not covered by IQ tests. How might a psychologist evaluate these intelligences? For example, what kind of test or evaluation would you use to determine an individual's musical intelligence?

# ISSUE 11

## Are the Recovered Memories of Psychological Trauma Valid?

**YES: David H. Gleaves, Steven M. Smith, Lisa D. Butler, and David Spiegel**, from "False and Recovered Memories in the Laboratory and Clinic: A Review of Experimental and Clinical Evidence," *Clinical Psychology: Science and Practice* (Spring 2004)

**NO: John F. Kihlstrom**, from "An Unbalanced Balancing Act: Blocked, Recovered, and False Memories in the Laboratory and Clinic," *Clinical Psychology: Science and Practice* (Spring 2004)

**ISSUE SUMMARY**

**YES:** Psychologist David H. Gleaves and his colleagues use experimental and clinical evidence to argue that blocked and recovered memories of trauma are valid phenomena.

**NO:** Psychologist John F. Kihlstrom challenges the validity of blocked and recovered memories of trauma, arguing that false memories of trauma are damaging both to clients and to those they may accuse of abuse.

Although many of Freud's ideas have been highly criticized in psychology, some of his conceptions have remained as popular as ever in the wider culture. Consider the common notion that people who experience traumatic events sometimes repress or block their memories of these events. Freud theorized that this type of repression is a defense mechanism against the troubling nature of such memories and that repression could lead to a variety of psychological problems. To treat these psychological problems, according to Freud, the patient would need to "recover" these memories or bring them into consciousness.

In recent scholarship the notion that people can recover blocked memories of trauma has been a source of controversy. Research demonstrating that we can create false memories has raised questions about whether the therapies that claim to help people recover memories are actually *creating* the memories. This is clearly a sensitive question. On the one hand, there is great concern about dismissing what may be valid memories of trauma and all that it would mean to a victim. On the other hand, there is equal concern about the damage that creating a false memory might do to those who could be falsely accused of perpetrating abuse.

In the first article, psychologist David H. Gleaves and his colleagues offer a review of the research literature on false, blocked, and recovered memories. They assert that accounts of false recovered memories are grossly exaggerated. Gleaves and colleagues argue that refutations of recovered memories are based less on scientific data and more on anecdotal accounts reported by popular media. Their review of the research suggests that the false memories of trauma are difficult to create and that recovered memories should not be easily dismissed. They point to data that suggests we sometimes do, in fact, block and recover memories, and they argue that this data may apply to memories of trauma as well.

In the second article, psychologist John F. Kihlstrom disputes the claims of Gleaves and colleagues, arguing that their "presentation is seriously unbalanced" and that a truly balanced review of the literature casts doubt on the validity of blocked and recovered memories. According to Kihlstrom, the fact that evidence for falsely recovered memories is anecdotal does not mean that it is poor evidence. He further argues that "research on actual trauma victims has produced hardly a shred of evidence for psychogenic amnesia covering the trauma event itself." Indeed, theories of repression in general should be abandoned for lack of evidence. Kihlstrom asserts that therapists who claim to recover memories are too likely to produce false memories and that they should give up the "clinical folklore" (inspired by Freud) about memory recovery.

**POINT**

- Clinicians have long recognized the reality of blocked and recovered memories.
- In its description of dissociative amnesia, the DSM acknowledges that persons sometimes block memories of traumatic events.
- Although false memories of ordinary events can be planted, it is unlikely that people can develop false memories of trauma.
- Accounts of false recovered memories are based on anecdotal reports and not on empirical findings.
- The concept of "false memory syndrome" is misleading and merely serves to discredit accusations of sexual abuse.

**COUNTERPOINT**

- Stories of blocked and recovered memories are the result of "clinical folklore," not scientific data.
- Emotional arousal releases hormones that improve memory, suggesting that trauma victims are more likely to remember events clearly than to repress them.
- Therapists who believe in repressed memories are likely to plant this notion in their clients, creating conditions where clients are more susceptible to false memories.
- We should not dismiss anecdotal evidence for false recovered memories simply because it is anecdotal.
- False memory syndrome it is real and goes beyond merely having a false memory.

YES ↩ David H. Gleaves, Steven M. Smith, Lisa D. Butler, and David Spiegel

# False and Recovered Memories in the Laboratory and Clinic: A Review of Experimental and Clinical Evidence

Blocked and recovered memories of traumatic events have long been regarded as real phenomena by the mental health profession, our legal system, and the public at large. These phenomena originally were studied by Pierre Janet and Sigmund Freud, and Freud's (1896/1962) "Aetiology of Hysteria" is perhaps the best known early discussion of this topic. In this now famous 1896 address, Freud presented his "Seduction Theory" in which he argued that "hysteria" resulted from repressed memories of childhood sexual trauma. Freud further argued that bringing these memories into consciousness would lead to the alleviation of the hysterical symptom.

Freud subsequently abandoned his seduction theory in favor of his theory of childhood sexual fantasy at a time when he was trying to develop a more general theory of psychopathology designed to account for disorders other than hysteria such as obsessive-compulsive neurosis and schizophrenia. However, the concept of repressed memories of trauma continued to receive attention, particularly in the literature on wartime trauma. For example, Sargant and Slater described a World War II account of 1000 consecutive admissions to a neurological unit. Over 14% of the sample exhibited amnesia, with the severity of amnesia appearing to be associated with the severity of trauma (e.g., 35% of those exposed to severe stress exhibited significant amnesias). Retrieval of these memories of trauma was seen as essential to recovery and was accomplished through the use of psychotherapy, hypnosis, or even drugs such as sodium pentothal.

More recently, reported amnesia and/or subsequent recovery of memories have been found to be relatively common in studies of clinical populations that experienced childhood sexual and physical abuse.

Despite these clinical data, other researchers, clinicians, or journalists have questioned the existence of repressed and recovered memories, challenging the academic community to provide objective evidence of these phenomena and at times going so far as to claim that there is no scientific support for the

From *Clinical Psychology: Science and Practice*, vol. 11, issue 1, March 2004, pp. 3–28 (excerpts).

phenomena. Some have also questioned whether "recovered" memories might actually be confabulated or false memories. Empirical evidence from controlled laboratory studies of nonpatient populations reliably demonstrates the reality of false memories, providing support for this alternative explanation.

The debate over false and recovered memories has polarized the academic and mental health communities into camps that endorse one phenomenon or the other. The controversy also affects the legal system in that it has seen lawsuits based on alleged repressed and recovered memory as well as lawsuits based on alleged implantation of false memories of abuse.

In the present paper we take the position described by Pezdek and Banks as well as others. We acknowledge that under certain circumstances both false and genuine recovered memories may exist. We describe laboratory analogues for both types of experiences. Assuming that both types of phenomena are possible, we suggest that the critical questions are (a) how common is each type of memory phenomenon, (b) what factors lead to the occurrence of each (including under what conditions are each possible and/or likely to occur), and perhaps most importantly, (c) can these two types of memories be distinguished from each other? Toward these goals, we review experimental and clinical data relevant to answering these questions and propose and describe an empirical research protocol that can not only demonstrate both phenomena, but that can also compare the two. Such comparisons can help to determine the causes of these phenomena, discover factors that influence the two, and hopefully reveal signature variables that could provide telltale signs differentiating false memories from recovered ones.

## Theoretical Accounts and Evidence of False Memories

### The Logic of False Memories

A number of researchers have found evidence of "false memories," defined as experiences that to rememberers seem to be memories of events that took place within experiments, but which do not correspond to experimentally presented stimuli. A false memory is not simply any memory error. The term refers to cases in which one appears to experience a memory of an event that did not occur. Memory errors that do not constitute false memories include, for example, retrieval failures, omission errors in recall, and recognition failures. Rather than the absence of memory that is characteristic of omission errors, a false memory involves an experience of remembering a relatively complete episode that did not in fact occur. The difference between accurate and false memories is in the correspondence or non-correspondence of the memory with objective reality.

Human memories constitute evidence of prior experiences, but currently there may be no guarantee of accuracy, however authentic the memories may seem to the rememberer. Studies of the relation between subjective metacog-nitive assessments of one's memory accuracy and objective measures of accuracy have often shown weak or even nonexistent correlations. Even when such correlations are strong, they are by no means perfect, indicating that the accuracy of memories can be misjudged.

## Clinical Evidence for False Memories

Despite recent claims that false memories of sexual abuse and a false-memory syndrome reached epidemic proportions in the 1990s, we found no empirical clinical research to support such a claim. The primary clinical evidence for the existence of false memories of trauma comes mainly from anecdotal reports by either persons who claim to have been falsely accused of sexual abuse or from persons known as "retractors" or "recantors," persons who once reported having had memories of sexual abuse that they now believe to be false. In addition, there are clinical reports (particularly with respect to dissociative identity disorder) that describe admixtures of true and false traumatic memories being recounted by the same patient. Reports of the first type have appeared as books published in the popular literature and have been described in review papers published in the scientific literature. For example, Loftus described having received numerous letters from persons claiming to have been falsely accused of sexual abuse. Anecdotal and case reports of recantors have also recently been published in the popular and scientific literature.

In addition, there have been published discussions of "high profile" cases in which persons claimed that false memories of abuse had been suggested or implanted. One such case occurred in *Ramona v. Ramona* in which a man whose daughter allegedly recovered memories of abuse by him successfully sued his daughter's therapist (against the daughter's wishes) for suggesting or reinforcing false memories. Another often cited case is that of Paul Ingram, a man serving time after confessing to raping his daughters repeatedly. Writers who have cited his case as an example of false memories argue that Ingram's confessions were based on false memories created during interrogation. Thus, in this case, both the alleged victim and the alleged perpetrator are said to have had false memories of nonexistent sexual abuse.

## Experimental Evidence of False Memories

Despite the lack of clinical evidence for a false-memory syndrome epidemic, several lines of experimental research support the conclusion that subjects can be made to report remembering events that did not occur. These include studies of the misinformation effect, hypnotic pseudomemory, failures of reality monitoring, intrusions in schema-guided recall, and intrusions in recall of list words. The putative causes of the false memories in these studies have included overwriting of the original memory trace, which inextricably integrates accurate and inaccurate information, and source monitoring failures that involve such factors as misattributions of familiarity or failures to distinguish perceived events from imagined ones.

The misinformation effect, similar to retroactive interference effects, is generated in three basic steps that include presentation of the original events, intervening events intended to mislead the participant, and a memory test. For example, the participant might witness a videotaped sequence of events, followed by a postevent question that contained a misleading inference. On a later test many participants remember the inferred events as having actually occurred.

In a particularly interesting example of the misinformation effect, the subject is convinced by family members that a fabricated event occurred during the subject's childhood, at which point the subject may report remembering details of what is a fabricated event. Although the validity of Loftus' "lost in the mall study" has been seriously questioned, in part because the misinformation was of a relatively common, plausible, and nontraumatic experience, Pezdek and colleagues replicated the finding to the extent that three of 20 subjects accepted a similar suggestion. However, when a suggestion of a more unusual and possibly traumatic memory analogous to sexual abuse (a rectal enema) was given, none of the subjects adopted the suggestion.

The original explanation of misinformation effects was based upon the notion that related events are not stored faithfully, independently, and veridically, but rather the individual events are used to construct an integrated memory trace that represents the gist or general meaning of the episode. This constructed memory supposedly includes inferences, not only from the original events, but potentially from intervening misleading suggestions. Furthermore, according to this explanation, original events cannot be distinguished from the potentially false inferences in a memory representation. In this view, false memories could include retrieval of false suggestions or inferences, or retrieval of blends of original and intervening (false) information. Alternative explanations of misinformation effects are based upon the presumption that parallel and independent memory traces of original and intervening events are both stored in memory, thereby allowing at least the possibility of later distinguishing original events from inaccurate suggestions and inferences. This theoretical debate has not yet been resolved.

Another experimental methodology for creating and demonstrating false memory, which is a variant of the misinformation approach, involves hypnotically created pseudomemory. In Laurence and Perry's experiment, they hypnotically regressed subjects to a night during the previous week and suggested their having awakened from sleep upon hearing a loud noise. Approximately half of the highly hypnotizable subjects reported the suggested memory as real (although some reported being unsure; also see below discussion for alternative interpretations from Spanos & McLean of these results). Barnier and McConkey extended this line of research by determining that it was hypnotizability rather than induction of a hypnotic trance that better predicted the report of pseudomemory. Dywan and Bowers illustrated another nonhypnotic component that affects findings in studies of hypnotic "misinformation." They found that the use of hypnosis increased conviction that recalled information was correct, but not its accuracy. Accuracy was a product of recall effort: the more information produced, the less likely it was to be accurate, indicating that the increase in productivity occurs at the expense of the strictness of the response criterion. On the one hand, the best recollection is usually not the first one; repeated recall trials produce more accurate information, meaning that at least some accurate information is not immediately available to conscious recall. On the other hand, pressure to recall more information about an event may result in lower overall accuracy of recall.

Another experimental methodology that has been used to demonstrate false memory effects is the reality-monitoring paradigm. Reality monitoring refers to the ability (or inability) to distinguish between memories that were generated from internal and those from external events. In this procedure, participants might be asked to view a mixed list of pictures and words and to form mental images of the referents of the words. On a later memory test the participants are often unable to distinguish between pictures they were shown and those that they generated through mental imagery. This phenomenon has its corollary in the hypnotic phenomenon of "source amnesia," in which an individual will recall some information implanted during hypnosis but will be unable to recall, or will misrepresent, the source, for example it as coming from a prior store of information rather than the recent hypnotic suggestion.

Johnson, Hashtroudi, and Lindsay have explained failures of reality monitoring as examples of more general source-monitoring failures. Source monitoring refers to the ability to correctly attribute the source of a memory. A number of attributes of memories, including contextual, semantic, or perceptual features, potentially can be used to discriminate among different sources of the memories. Johnson et al. claimed that most memory illusions, such as misattributed familiarity, cryptamnesia, and confabulation are due to source monitoring failures. Jacoby's explanation of misattributed familiarity is based upon a distinction between two types of memory, an automatic, unconscious familiarity response, and an intentional, deliberate type of remembering that is under conscious control. When a memory is automatically stimulated without an accompanying conscious respecification of its source, the resultant familiarity might be attributed to an inappropriate source.

Another approach to the study of false memories has been to observe schema-guided recall and recognition. For example, Brewer and Treyens examined false recognition of objects that fit an episodic schema. They found that schema-consistent memories were more likely to be falsely recalled and recognized than schema-inconsistent responses. This is similar to Pezdek et al.'s finding that plausibility and script-relevant knowledge determine the extent to which events can be suggestively implanted in memory.

List-learning techniques have also been used to study false memories. Participants in these paradigms are typically presented with a list of words that are all associatively related to a single nonpresented target word. The critical nonpresented target word is often falsely recalled even though it does not appear on the memorized list. For example, a list might have words associated with the word *spider,* such as *web, insect,* and *arachnid,* but not the word *spider.* Participants often claim to recall *spider* even when they are admonished not to report words that were not on the list. In one variant of this procedure, participants are given a categorized list that contains the most common members of a category except for the most typical category member, which is omitted from the list. Participants often falsely recall the nonpresented category member, and the effect is even stronger if the number of associates is increased or the critical nonpresented word is primed on an unrelated task.

Theoretical accounts of false memories generated in list-learning paradigms include explanations involving implicit associative responses, misattributed source memory, and fuzzy memory traces. The first of these explanations is that when people study a list of words they implicitly think of associates of those words, and memories of the implicit associates are later mistaken for memories of actual list members. This explanation is related to the source-monitoring explanation of false memories in that it supposes that memories of implicit associative responses are not adequately distinguished from memories of physical stimuli. The source monitoring explanation is also useful for explaining primed false memories; memories of primed words are not adequately distinguished from memories of correct list words.

Another theory, the fuzzy-trace explanation of false memories in list-word recall, is that both verbatim and gist memory traces are stored during learning, and false recall can result if memory relies on the inaccurate memory trace representing the gist of the event. Reliance on fuzzygist memory traces rather than veridical verbatim traces, according to this theory, is increased by longer retention intervals, a prediction supported by the results of list-learning studies of false memories. In addition, when memory tests emphasize memory for substance (i.e., meaning), then things that were not previously studied may be easier to endorse on recognition tests than things that were.

## Conclusions and Limitations of Conclusions about False Memory Research

The clinical and experimental research on false memory each has its own strengths and limitations. The most glaring limitation of some *clinical* reports on false memory is that they provide no way of determining if the memories are in fact false. In many cases, the credibility of the source of information needs to be considered. For example, Rubin noted that when the source of information is the parent accused of the abuse, there are numerous alternative interpretations of what may have actually occurred. Rubin noted that "Denial, dynamics of secrecy in incestuous families, behavioral reenactments of childhood victimization, alcohol-induced blackouts, and outright lying" may explain some claims that persons have been falsely accused of abuse. When the data come from a "retractor" they may be more convincing. However, persons with verifiable histories of abuse are known to vacillate between accepting and denying the reality of their memories of abuse and may be vulnerable to suggestions (by family members or lawyers) that their memories are false. It is inconsistent to assume that a memory is credible when someone claims not to have been abused, and to assume that a memory is not credible when someone claims the opposite. However, there are reports in which the history of abuse has been documented, such as L. M. Williams' study in which the episodes were identified through hospital emergency room records of assessment and treatment for abuse.

There are also severe limitations regarding the "high profile" cases that have been presented in the scientific literature. Numerous authors have noted that claims regarding the Ingram case are contradicted by the actual facts. For example, there is testimony from those who initially interviewed Ingram, that he confessed to the sexual abuse the first time he was confronted with the charges, rather than after months of interrogation, suggestions, and pressure, as some commentators have suggested. Olio and Cornell have recently observed that the uncritical acceptance and parroting of the alleged facts of the Ingram case has become "an academic version of an urban legend." Similarly, regarding the *Ramona v. Isabella* case, we refer the reader to Bowman and Mertz's indepth discussion of the case to determine to what degree it should be regarded as evidence supporting the reality of false memories of abuse. This type of data suffer from the same limitation as the clinical data described above; there is not convincing evidence that the memories in question are in fact false.

Another limitation of the clinical data on false memories is that the possible occurrence of such phenomena does not imply the existence of a false-memory syndrome (FMS). The current *Diagnostic and Statistical Manual of Mental Disorders* defines a syndrome as "a grouping of signs and symptoms, based on their frequent co-occurrence, that may suggest a common underlying pathogenesis, course, familial pattern, or treatment selection." Currently there are few or no empirical data supporting the claim that false-memory syndrome exists, mainly because so little research on this issue has been conducted. In one published empirical study that we found, Hovdestad and Kristiansen concluded that, "In sum, the weak evidence for the construct validity of the phenomenon referred to as FMS, together with the finding that few women with recovered memories satisfied the criteria and that women with continuous memories were equally likely to do so, lends little support to the FMS theory." More recently, Dallam concluded that "in the absence of any substantive scientific support, 'False memory Syndrome' is best characterized as a pseu-doscientific syndrome that was developed to defend against claims of child abuse."

Although these conclusions illustrate that data in support of false-memory syndrome are still lacking, objection to the term is not new among the scientific community. As early as 1993, numerous researchers published a formal objection to the term being used in this context arguing that the term false-memory syndrome was really "a non-psychological term originated by a private foundation whose stated purpose is to support accused parents." They urged, "For the sake of intellectual honesty, let's leave the term 'false memory syndrome' to the popular press."

Kihlstrom has more recently attempted to defend the use of the term. Basically his argument was that numerous other writers have used the term "syndrome" in nonscientific context (e.g., the "Lolita syndrome," "sissy boy syndrome," and "China syndrome,"); thus there is no reason to question its use in this case. A related defense (noted by a reviewer of this article) is that criticism of use of the term "syndrome" is simply a red herring, and the critical matter is whether memories are accurate or inaccurate. Although we in general agree with the justification here (that accuracy per se is what is critical), the issue is not a red herring because clearly FMS is being described (a) *as if* it is a scientific diagnosis and form of psychopathology, and (b) as being an entity above and beyond the simple issue of the accuracy of a memory. One needs to look no further than the definition from Kihlstrom quoted on the False Memory Syndrome Foundation web site. He described FMS as a form of psychopathology above and beyond the simple issue of the accuracy of memory. Kihlstrom wrote:

> Note that the syndrome is *not* characterized by false memories as such. We all have memories that are inaccurate. Rather, the *syndrome* may be *diagnosed* when the memory is so deeply ingrained that it orients the individual's entire personality and lifestyle, in turn disrupting all sorts of other adaptive behavior. The analogy to *personality disorder* is intentional. [emphasis added]

Clearly false-memory syndrome is being described as if it is a form of psychopathology much above and beyond the issue of the accuracy of memory. The fact that mental health professionals have even testified in court that plaintiffs in sexual abuse cases suffered from "FMS" is further evidence that the term is being misused. Although research may someday suggest that FMS actually exists, current data do not. Thus, it is at best premature to use the term "false memory syndrome" and we recommend that the term not be used. To thoroughly discuss this issue is beyond the scope of the present paper.

Regarding the experimental research on false memories, these studies make it clear that some persons can be made to report remembering events that did not occur (or objects that were not observed), in settings in which the consequences of a mistake are relatively minor. Reported false memories can be reliably and predictably evoked and studied with a variety of laboratory procedures. Furthermore, the occurrence of false memories does not appear to rely on extraordinary affective states or special cognitive processes; rather, they seem to be produced by the same cognitive mechanisms that produce accurate remembering. However, there are a number of limitations to the conclusions and inferences that can be made from experimental research on false memories. One limitation concerns the degree to which reported false memories reflect genuine alterations in memory (or belief in memory) versus reporting biases. That is, do research participants reporting false memories really believe that what they are reporting are memories, or are their reports due to the demand characteristics of the research? In their study of hypnotizability and pseudomemory Lynn, Weekes, and Milano asked subjects about reported pseudomemories in more than one way. When asked in open-ended style 11.5% of subjects reported actually remembering the suggested event (a phone ringing). However, when actually required (in a forced-choice format) to indicate whether they had heard an actual phone ring or if the ring was suggested, none of the participants exhibited pseudomemory. The findings led the authors to conclude that "Although hypnotic suggestions produce shifts in awareness and attention, subjects are not deluded by suggestions into confusing fantasy with reality."

Similar results were obtained by Barnier and McConkey, who showed participants slides of a purse snatching and then suggested false aspects of the event in the slides (that the attacker wore a scarf and helped the victim pick up flowers). The authors tested for false memories in both formal and informal contexts using high- and low-hypnotizable subjects. Although a sizeable number of the highly hypnotizable subjects reported remembering the false aspects of the events when tested in a formal setting, the majority (13 out of 15 for one memory and 14 out of 15 for another) did *not* exhibit pseudomemory when tested in an informal setting. The authors also collected qualitative data regarding participants' behaviors. Some indicated behavioral compliance. For example, one noted: "I knew he didn't have a scarf. I felt pressured, so I put a scarf on him to give an answer." Response bias does not seem to explain all of the experimental research on false memory, but the degree to which it does should not be minimized and has not been completely determined.

Another limitation of published empirical work concerns the degree to which this research can be generalized and applied to cases of false memories of child sexual abuse or naturally occurring traumatic events. The reliability of producing certain laboratory phenomena, such as optical illusions, is no assurance that the phenomena are common, naturally occurring events. Indeed, Mook suggests that laboratory research best illuminates "what *can* happen, rather than what typically *does*." When the purpose is to predict or explain behavior in the real world, then the generalizability concerns as to the comparability of populations, settings, manipulations, and measurement must be considered. At issue is the fact that the vast majority of the laboratory research on false memories has involved suggesting memories of schema-consistent, mundane events or objects to nonclinical subjects—events which are, in many cases, corroborated by family members—and eliciting false reports with no long-term personal consequences, such as family disruption or a jail term for a family member. In the only study with adult subjects in which the investigators attempted to implant a memory remotely similar to child sexual abuse, they were unsuccessful in doing so.

There are also many ways in which false memory research fails to parallel what may happen in psychotherapy, thus limiting the generalizability of the results. For example, in Loftus's "lost in the mall" study, it was actually the family member, rather than the experimenter, who convinced the subjects of the false childhood memories. The generalizability depends on what this finding actually demonstrates. Is it that therapists can have powerful influence over clients or that parents or other family members can deceive their children? If it is the latter, such results do not support the position that false memories frequently occur in therapy.

In another line of recent laboratory research that more closely mimics a possible psychotherapy situation, Loftus and Mazzoni exposed subjects to a 30-min brief-therapy simulation in which an expert clinician analyzed a dream report that the subject offered. The clinician proposed an interpretation (an "expert personalized suggestion") that the dream indicated that the subject had probably experienced a given event in early childhood (either being lost or being in a dangerous situation). The theme of the interpretation was determined by random assignment, however the interpretation was personalized to build on the dream material that the subject had provided. Results indicated that the majority of subjects were more confident at four-week follow-up that they had experienced these childhood events. It is unknown, however, whether participants also developed false memories of the events that corresponded to their increased confidence.

This distinction between increasing confidence that something has happened and increasing the production of false memories of the event is a potential limitation to the relevance of the recent "imagination inflation" literature to the understanding of false-memory creation. In these studies, having subjects simply imagine events increases their confidence that the events have indeed occurred. However, changing beliefs about the likelihood of the events does not necessarily create memories of the event. In one false-memory study, however, coupling imagination with authoritative suggestion (for an event confirmed by family members) increased false-memory creation over authoritative suggestion alonc, confirming that imagination can facilitate false-memory creation.

For a different reason, laboratory research may *underestimate* the degree of influence and suggestion that may occur in therapy. Contact between experimenter and research participant is generally brief compared to therapist-client contact. In Hyman et al.'s study of false childhood memories, participants only reported false memories after two or three sessions but never did in the first. In the Loftus and Mazzoni study only one experience was interpreted. The possible effects of several weeks or even months of suggestion, or of multiple converging suggestions/interpretations, have not been studied experimentally. Of relevance to the former possible effect, Zaragoza and Mitchell found that repeated exposure to suggestion can increase confidence in and conscious recollections of false memories of witnessing an event.

Experimental studies have not yet determined whether false memories could occur for bizarre or affectively charged events, important concerns to clinical psychologists. It is not yet known whether bizarreness in a memory identifies it as a false memory or an accurate one. The limitation of our understanding of false memories that is most relevant to the present paper is whether accurate and false memories can be distinguished from one another, either by the subject who is remembering, or by an observer. Whether or not there are experiential or behavioral "signatures" that indicate the likelihood that a memory is false or accurate is a critical question that has not been thoroughly addressed by empirical research. To date, findings suggest that memories for true events tend to be described with more words, contain greater clarity of perceptual details, and are held with greater confidence than are false memories. The sensory detail results are similar to those found when experimenters compare remembered versus imagined autobiographical childhood events or childhood events that subjects *remember* happening rather than simply *know* happened.

To summarize, the empirical findings of false memories provide an alternative explanation for memories recovered in therapy, casting some doubt as to the accuracy or reality of the memories. However, the circumstances under which false memories can or are likely to occur have yet to be determined. Furthermore, the existence of false memories does not imply the existence of a syndrome nor does it contradict the possibility that blocked and accurately recovered memories can also occur. We now consider evidence concerning blocked and recovered memories.

## Empirical Evidence and Theories of Memory Blocking and Recovery

### Defining Blocked and Recovered Memories

What we refer to as blocked and recovered memories are cases in which established memories are rendered inaccessible for some period of time, after which the essentially intact memories are retrieved. Memory blocks and the potential recovery of memories are directly relevant to clinical disorders such as post-traumatic stress disorder and the dissociative disorders. Our operational definition of blocked and recovered memories specifies three criteria: (a) There must be corroborating evidence that the event in question was actually experienced by the person, (b) At some later time it must be found that the event cannot be recalled, and (c) After the period of inaccessibility, it must be found that the event can be successfully recalled. Criteria similar to these have also been used by Haber and Haber (1996) and Schooler and colleagues.

### Clinical Evidence of Blocked and Recovered Memories: Dissociative Amnesia

In the current *DSM*, dissociative amnesia is defined as "a reversible memory impairment in which memories of personal experience cannot be retrieved in verbal form." The events that cannot be recalled are "usually of a traumatic or stressful nature" and the inability to remember is "too extensive to be explained by normal forgetfulness."

Although there have been claims that dissociative amnesia is a recently recognized (or invented) phenomenon, it has been recognized by clinicians since the beginning of the 19th century. Dissociative (or psychogenic or hysterical) amnesia was studied and described extensively by Pierre Janet in the 1880s as well as by Freud in some of his early writings. There are also numerous descriptions of dissociative amnesia in the early and recent literature on combat and war trauma and civilian voilance. Modai also described total amnesia for childhood in a survivor of the holocaust. In many of these reports, the authors also described how memory for the traumatic experiences of war could be retrieved through therapy, hypnosis, or even narcosynthesis. These authors did sometimes caution that what was retrieved was often a mixture of accurate memory and fantasy.

More recent research has focused on the presence of amnesia and/or recovered memory for experiences of child sexual abuse (CSA). Recently reported anecdotal, legal, and clinical cases of amnesia and memory recovery offer compelling "existence proof" for these phenomena. D. Brown, Scheflin, and Whitfield recently reviewed the clinical research in this area. They concluded that "In just this past decade alone, 68 research studies have been conducted on naturally occurring dissociative or traumatic amnesia for childhood sexual abuse. Not a single one of the 68 data-based studies failed to find it." Similar conclusions were reached by van der Hart and Nijenhuis and Scheflin and D. Brown in their earlier review of the literature. Critics of these conclusions may point to the report of H. G. Pope, Hudson, Bodkin, and Oliva, who reviewed 63 different studies of victims of non-CSA types of trauma and claimed that they "could not find any clear and unexplained occurrences of amnesia for the traumatic events," though some of the evidence and conclusions presented in this review were disputed by D. Brown et al. More recently, some of D. Brown and colleagues' own evidence and conclusions have also been vigorously challenged. Nonetheless, collectively the clinical evidence does seem to suggest that varying degrees of amnesia for traumatic experiences and subsequent recovery of memory are real phenomena.

## Experimental Evidence for Blocked and Recovered Memory

Critics or skeptics of the concept of recovered memory often claim that there is no experimental (or laboratory) evidence for the concept of recovered memory. Almost invariably, the reference cited for such statements is a literature review by Holmes who concluded that "despite over sixty years of research . . . at the present time there is no controlled laboratory evidence supporting the concept of repression." To thoroughly discuss Holmes's conclusions and the relevance to the recovered memory/false memory controversy would be beyond the scope of this article (see Gleaves, 1996 or Gleaves & Freyd, 1997 for more extensive discussions). The critical point is that Holmes only reviewed evidence for one possible mechanism of memory blocking and recovery (repression), defined in a very specific form.

In reality, empirical evidence of memory blocking (or inhibition) and recovery has come from several experimental paradigms, including spontaneous recovery from retroactive interference, tip-of-the-tongue (TOT) research, blocking in implicit memory, recovery from posthypnotic amnesia, output interference and recovery, retrieval-induced forgetting, directed forgetting and recovery, and memory inhibition through executive control. In each of these cases the memory blocks are more enduring than a few seconds, as is the case with many other empirical findings of temporary inaccessibility, such as negative priming effects, Stroop interference tasks, or inhibitory orthographic priming. We will briefly review each of these areas of empirical research that documents memory blocking and recovery.

*Retroactive interference and spontaneous recovery.* Retroactive interference has been one of the longest standing topics of interest in the experimental study of human memory. When experiences similar to an event in question are stored in memory after the target event, the resultant forgetting of the target event is referred to as retroactive interference. Lengthening the retention interval, however, causes recovery of the forgotten material, suggesting either that associations weakened by retroactive interference somehow recover their strength, or that original associations remain intact and interference only causes temporary inaccessibility. Consistent with the notion that original memories remain intact after retroactive interference are findings from associative-matching tests that show retention of original memories, as well as evidence that original and interfering memories are independent entities. Spontaneous recovery effects in verbal learning and memory have been found with paired associate learning tasks, serial recall, and free recall. These findings show that whatever the mechanisms involved, it is nonetheless clear that learned associations can become temporarily inaccessible and can be recovered at a later time.

*Output interference and reminiscence.* Memory blocking and recovery can be used to explain another interesting conundrum, the question of what causes hypermnesia and reminiscence. Hypermnesia is a net improvement in recall when repeated recall tests are given without extra practice sessions. Reminiscence, a very similar concept, refers to the recovery of unrecalled material, independently of the amount forgotten from one test to the next. These phenomena defy the notion that forgetting increases over time, because more is remembered on later tests.

Hypermnesia and reminiscence can be explained as recovery from initial blocking in recall. That is, when people recall a list of words or pictures, the act of recalling some of the items on the list has the effect of blocking other items that have not yet been recalled. This inhibition or interference has been termed *output interference*. Thus, hypermnesia and reminiscence may occur on a later test because blocks caused by output interference weaken over time, in accordance with predictions of stimulus fluctuation theory. The theory predicts that delaying a second recall test should allow more time for output interference to weaken, and therefore should increase recovery. This prediction was supported by the finding of incubated reminiscence and hypermnesia effects.

Output interference is caused not only by one's own recall efforts, but also by experimenter-provided items from a learned list. The procedure in which the experimenter provides some of the list items as cues on a recall test is called part-list or part-set cueing. Surprisingly, part-list cueing inhibits or interferes with recall of the remainder of the list.

If part-list cueing causes output interference, and if greater initial output interference leads to greater recovery and hypermnesia, then using part-list cues on an initial recall test should increase the hypermnesia observed on a retest. Experiments reported by Basden and Basden, Basden, Basden, and Galloway, and J. M. Brown and Smith supported this prediction; part-list cues caused memory blocking on an initial recall test, and increasing recovery (reminiscence) on a later recall test. An exaggerated version of this part-list cueing procedure constitutes an essential component of the comparative memory paradigm that we report in the present study.

*Directed forgetting.* The directed forgetting paradigm has been used successfully to impair the accessibility of experimentally presented materials. In one version of the directed forgetting paradigm, the list method, experimental participants are told that they can forget the list of words they had just been trying to memorize because, they are told, they will not need to remember that list on a later memory test. Instead, participants are told, they should concentrate on memorizing a second list of words, which are then presented. In the control condition, participants are not given this *forget* instruction. The typical directed forgetting effect is evidenced by two results: (a) the first list is recalled more poorly if forget instructions are given, and (b) the second list is recalled better if the forget instruction is given, presumably due to decreased proactive interference from the forgotten first list.

Bjork and Bjork found that the inaccessibility caused by directed forgetting can be eradicated if experimental participants are re-exposed to some of the forgotten material on a recognition test. In this study Bjork and Bjork found that if they included a few forgotten list-1 words on an intervening recognition test, then directed forgetting effects were not seen on a final recall test. This result constitutes another finding of recovery of memories that had been made inaccessible.

*Posthypnotic amnesia and hypermnesia.* Perhaps the strongest experimental support for blocked and recovered memories comes from the research on hypnotic (or posthypnotic) amnesia and hypermnesia. This body of research shows that when hypnotizable participants are given suggestions during hypnosis to forget some events they have already experienced, memories of those events appear to be blocked or inaccessible. Although the degree of forgetting induced by hypnotic suggestion is often great, it has also been found that the "lost" memories can be largely recovered if the participant is given a prearranged signal to cancel the suggested amnesia. As noted by Evans, "When the experimenter administers a prearranged cue, the critical memories appear to flood back into awareness, and the hitherto amnesic subject is now able to remember the events and experiences clearly and without difficulty."

It is this reversibility of amnesia that makes the hypnotic phenomenon most analogous to blocked and recovered memories of naturally occurring traumatic events. Furthermore, experimental tests of implicit memory suggest that during their period of inaccessibility, memories may indirectly affect experiences and behavior in the same sense that dissociated memories are allegedly assumed to affect behavior even though one may have no explicit memory of the events.

Another aspect of posthypnotic amnesia that makes it a good laboratory model for dissociative amnesia concerns Bowers and Woody's study of hypnotic amnesia and the "paradox of intentional forgetting." This paradox refers to the fact that, in many instances, when someone tries to forget some learned material, the result is an intrusion of the to-be-forgotten material. As noted by Bowers and Woody and known by many clinicians, the very intention to *not* think about something paradoxically can bring the material to mind.

This paradox of intentional forgetting in some ways parallels what is observed with victims of psychological trauma. That is, most put great effort into not thinking about the events in question, but frequently still (or perhaps consequently) experience intrusive thoughts diagnostic criteria for post-traumatic stress disorder include both avoidance (e.g., trying to avoid thinking about the event, amnesia for the experience) and re-experiencing/intrusive symptoms (e.g., intrusive thoughts, nightmares, flashbacks). The fact that many persons with PTSD seem to exhibit this paradoxical inability to forget has led some critics of dissociative amnesia to argue that it is totally inconsistent with what is observed in actual victims of trauma (i.e., actual trauma victims cannot forget). For example, in describing her experiences at a conference for the False Memory Syndrome Foundation, Wylie wrote, "People remember their traumas, speakers point out again and again; their problem is not that they've lost their memories, but that they can't get rid of them—they intrude relentlessly into their daily lives and always have." However, this analysis suggests a fundamental lack of understanding of the clinical phenomenon. The problem in PTSD is not simply a paucity *or* a flooding of memories. Rather it is poor modulation of these emotionally charged memories, such that they are sometimes overwhelming and at other times avoided. Their intrusive strength invites withdrawal, and their reappearance is experienced as an unbidden re-inflicting of the trauma, analogous to the effect of the traumatic event itself, now recapitulated through the nature of its reappearance in memory. As Widiger and Sankis noted, explaining why PTSD is more similar to the dissociative disorders than the anxiety disorders, "difficulty forgetting (or letting go of) a horrifying experience may simply be the opposite side of the same coin of difficulty remembering (accepting or acknowledging) a horrifying experience."

In Bowers and Woody's study, however, they found that hypnotic amnesia was *not* associated with paradoxical effects. They noted that the majority of high-hypnotizable individuals showed no intrusions when administered suggestions for amnesia and concluded that "thought suppression and hypnotic amnesia represent quite different processes." This distinction may be the laboratory analogue of what happens to some victims of trauma. The clinical data on dissociative disorders, some of which we reviewed above, suggest that some persons *are* able to block out trauma memories to varying degrees. Furthermore, the diagnostic criteria for PTSD actually include amnesia. Thus, the above assertion that all trauma victims cannot "get rid of" their traumatic memories appears inaccurate. It would be more accurate to say that victims of trauma experience varying degrees of intrusive memories versus amnesias for the events. A diathesis-stress model has been proposed in which the level of hypnotizabilty (or a related trait) interacts with the nature of the traumatic event to the degree to which memories intrude or are blocked at any given point in time. The level of motivation and the forgetting strategy the person uses may also be factors in determining memory accessibility. . . .

## Theoretical Explanations for Blocked and Recovered Memories

Our brief review of theoretical mechanisms that could cause memory blocking and recovery reveals a number of potential causes of these phenomena that can occur even in simple laboratory situations. Although we make no definitive claims as to which of these mechanisms are at work in naturally occurring cases, it is nonetheless clear that there already exist several possible explanations of blocking and recovery that have been used to explain experimental findings. Theoretical mechanisms that could be used to explain blocked and recovered memories include explanations of hypermnesia, recovery from retrieval inhibition, state-dependent memory, arousal effects, and a special emotion mechanism.

*Repression and hypermnesia.* Erdelyi and Goldberg defined repression as a tendentious rejection from awareness of aversive memories for the purpose of avoiding the painful feelings associated with the rejected memories. This rejection from awareness may or may not occur as a result of unconscious mechanisms, depending upon one's theoretical outlook. The best evidence of the existence of repression, according to Erdelyi and Goldberg, is hypermnesia, a lifting or recovery from the amnesia that is symptomatic of repression. Citing evidence from a broad array of clinical and nonclinical sources, they conclude that most people experience such hypermnesias, recalling events that had previously excluded from consciousness to avoid psychic pain. An alternative explanation, that hypermnesia effects are due not to memory, but rather to a reporting bias, was not supported by the results of Roediger and Payne, who found that the observed level of hypermnesia was not affected by a relaxed reporting criterion, or even by "forced recall" instructions that required experimental participants to guess at to-be-recalled memories once intentional attempts to recall had been exhausted. Although the cognitive mechanisms that give rise to hypermnesia have not yet been conclusively determined, it is conceivable that laboratory-induced and clinically observed hypermnesias have the same causes.

*State dependence.* Mood-dependent memory, sometimes seen as a type of contextual dependence, refers to findings that show that memory of events can be enhanced by reinstating the affective state present when the events were initially experienced. Mood-dependence could be one of the reasons that traumatic memories become blocked from conscious awareness. That is, if the critical events were associated with an extreme or unusual affective state, then dissociation could occur, or become exacerbated, by the low likelihood of reentering that mood state. Bower has proposed this as a possible model of how some memories and identity information could remain inaccessible at times for patients with dissociative identity disorder.

*Interference, inhibition, and spontaneous recovery.* Interference, a classic issue of interest in the experimental study of memory, is forgetting caused by the presence of material in memory that is similar to the target of one's memory search. Mechanisms that have been proposed as underlying interference effects include response competition, occlusion, inhibition, and unlearning. Whereas unlearning refers to a loss of material from memory, response competition, occlusion, and inhibition refer to temporary memory failures. Response competition occurs when the retrieval of one associated response impedes or delays retrieval of another associated response. Occlusion is similar to competition, and refers to forgetting that depends upon the strength of competing associations.

Inhibition, a theoretical mechanism analogous to neural inhibition, refers to a temporary deficiency in one's ability to retrieve material stored in memory. Retrieval inhibition has been suggested as the mechanism responsible for a number of forgetting phenomena, including post-hypnotic amnesia, directed forgetting, retrieval induced forgetting, part-list cueing effects, and memory suppression. In the Anderson and Green study, both associative interference and unlearning of the cue-target association were ruled out as the mechanisms underlying the observed retrieval impairment, providing strong support in this case for the existence of an inhibitory control mechanism inhibiting the unwanted memory itself.

Recovery from interference (or inhibition), sometimes called spontaneous recovery, constitutes the best evidence that interference does not necessarily render memories permanently inaccessible. A theoretical model that explains recovery from retroactive interference originated with Estes' stimulus-sampling theory, and has been developed by several other theoreticians, including Bower, Glenberg, and Mensink and Raaijmakers. The general form of this model states that interfering memories, which are cue-dependent, are rendered inaccessible over time or with contextual changes because temporal/contextual change leads to altered encodings of memory cues. Decreasing the accessibility of competing memories makes the originally blocked memories less inaccessible, thereby increasing the chances of recovering the original memories. This research is consistent with the notion that conflicting memories regarding abusive parents that emerge from victimization and continued dependence on the same people may hamper episodic memory retrieval. This type of model can also be used to explain recovery of memories in other experimental paradigms.

*Mechanisms related to emotion and arousal.* Approaches to repression as forgetting of emotionally traumatic experiences focus more on the traumatic aspects of the phenomenon rather than the resultant amnesia. Experimental evidence of such a putative emotional mechanism is understandably sparse. However, in studies by Loftus and Burns and Christianson and Nilsson, both of which used material that was perhaps as stressful as ethically possible, both found that amnesia was associated with trauma. Although Loftus and Burns concluded that their results suggested that "mentally shocking episodes" possibly disrupt processes related to storage of information in memory, Christianson and Nilsson found amnesia on tests of recall but not recognition, indicating that retrieval rather than storage was affected by the traumatic experience.

## Conclusions and Limitations of Conclusions Regarding Blocked and Recovered Memory

As with the reviewed research on false memory, there are many limitations associated with the clinical and experimental research on blocked and recovered memory. Many of the clinical reports suffer from limitations of retrospective research. In many instances, the alleged events of abuse were not corroborated. When they were, the type of corroborating evidence was sometimes not described and thus is not open to objective evaluation. In some of the research, especially the report by L. M. Williams, one cannot be certain that failure to report memory is due to failure to remember or that failure to remember is due to anything other than normal forgetting, although the documented intensity of the trauma and resulting injury make this explanation less plausible.

Nonetheless, there is an accumulating, if small, store of corroborated and well-documented case studies that may help illuminate the phenomena and inform future research. In fact, in one clinical case study the initial memory recovery event was videotaped and has been examined and evaluated by a variety of commentators. Additionally, clinical studies of the circumstances and triggers of memory recovery have helped to further describe the nature of amnesia and memory recovery in the case of real traumatic memories.

Some of the laboratory research also suffers from limitations. For the same ethical reason that one cannot try to induce false memories of actual sexual trauma, one cannot subject participants to truly traumatic experiences to determine the degree to which persons can block or "repress" these memories. Thus, the degree to which research on blocking and recovery of memory can be generalized to memories of trauma cannot be directly determined.

Some researchers have argued that findings of posthypnotic amnesia are limited no less than are findings of hypnotic pseudomemories. It is not clear to what degree reports of amnesia are due to compliance, role playing, or strategic enactment, although these studies rarely take hypnotizability into account and overemphasize subjects' motivation to "behave like a hypnotized person." As with the research on hypnotically induced false memory, these factors do not appear to account for all of the findings of posthypnotic amnesia. . . .

## Conclusions and Future Directions

When memories of traumatic events appear to be recovered, do such experiences reflect truly recovered memories that are essentially accurate, or are such events likely to be false memories of events that never happened? Although no immediate resolution of this important question is at hand, in the present paper we acknowledge and demonstrate the reality of both recovered and false memories. That is, the conclusion that we want to convey is that there is a wealth of data related to both sides of this controversial coin. Recurrent claims that no data exist that support either of these phenomena are, in our opinion, contradicted by the actual data. Furthermore, we believe that it is also inaccurate to paint this debate (as has been done both in the popular and scientific media) as being the academics against the clinicians with only the clinical data supporting the recovered memory position and the experimental data supporting the false memory position. Research from numerous bodies of experimental research supports the reality of memory blocking and recovery.

The issues that are truly debatable concern what inferences can be drawn from the available data. All of the data are limited to some degree. For ethical reasons, research that would perhaps definitively resolve this controversy cannot be conducted. It is noteworthy that the same ethical limitation applies to both aspects of this topic. That is, it would be unethical to subject research participants (particularly children) to the types of events allegedly associated with dissociative amnesia (i.e., physical and/or sexual traumas). However, it would also be unethical to attempt to create false memories of horrific events in research participants. We are then left with different bodies of research that, each in its own way, is limited in terms of what inferences can be drawn.

Pezdek and Banks described the unavoidable dialectic of "control versus applicability" or that of internal versus external validity. Often the research that has the highest of the former has the least of the latter (or vice-versa), and this appears to be the case when it comes to false versus recovered memory research. We urge researchers to exercise appropriate cautions and to consider seriously both types of validity when interpreting research. We also suggest that there is much room for improvement in terms of finding a balance of the different types of validity. That is, we believe that the external validity of research can be improved without necessarily sacrificing internal validity. Pezdek et al.'s study of the limits of what types of memory can be suggested is an example of a step in the correct direction. Applying controlled experimental paradigms to clinical samples (rather than simply undergraduate students) is another.

Another step in the correct direction was Smith et al.'s attempt to study both false and recovered memories within a single experimental procedure, allowing for the possibility of directly comparing the two phenomena. We believe that the greatest advancements will be made by researchers with interests in studying both phenomena. Unfortunately, few researchers seem interested in doing so. Smith et al. were indeed able to discriminate between false and recovered memories on the basis of metacognitive reports, including confidence ratings (Experiments 1 and 2) and remember/know judgments (Experiment 2). To our knowledge, this was the first experimental attempt to make such a discrimination. Two variables measuring response latencies did not prove to be useful in discriminating the two types of memories. One of the major goals of future research on this topic should be to experimentally test other variables (e.g., emotionality of events, affective states, retention intervals, and personality factors) that might discriminate the two types of memory phenomena.

By exploring these naturalistic phenomena in controlled experimental settings we can learn more about the mechanisms that underlie them. The same signatures that occur in experimental paradigms could be investigated in naturally occurring cases. Retrospective accounts of individuals with histories of memory dissociation and of therapists who have treated such individuals could be examined as a function of evidence that corroborates or falsifies the reality of the recovered memories. The clearest cases of recovered and false memories, as determined by corroborating evidence, would hopefully display the same signatures that can be observed in controlled laboratory studies. Thus, only by returning our attention to those naturalistic contexts, looking for the same patterns identified experimentally, will we learn whether or not the mechanisms we identify in the laboratory are relevant to real life cases of memory blocking and recovery.

John F. Kihlstrom

# An Unbalanced Balancing Act: Blocked, Recovered, and False Memories in the Laboratory and Clinic

In their paper, Gleaves, Smith, Butler, and Spiegel (this issue) draw on clinical and laboratory research to persuade the reader that traumatic memories can be repressed, that recovered memories of trauma are valid, and that false memories of trauma are not too important, thus supporting both the trauma-memory argument and recovered-memory therapy. Although the authors adopt an ostensibly balanced position that "both false and genuine recovered memories may exist," their actual presentation is seriously unbalanced. As a result, the reader is encouraged to discount laboratory evidence of false memories while accepting laboratory evidence of repression and recovered memories, and to discount clinical evidence of false memories while accepting clinical evidence of repression and recovered memories.

## Clinical Studies of False Memories

With respect to false memories, Gleaves et al. discuss the clinical evidence in a little over a page of text. While it may be true that much of this evidence comes in the form of anecdotal case reports published in the popular press, that is no reason to discount them. Journalists, lawyers, judges, and other "laymen" can read and reason too, as exemplified by Frederick Crews, the literary critic whose articles on the "memory wars" did so much to bring our attention to the problems raised by the recovered memory movement, and Dorothy Rabinowitz, the *Wall Street Journal* columnist who won a 2001 Pulitzer Prize in part for her critical commentaries on the "Kelly Michaels" and "Amirault" cases of preschool child sex-abuse allegations. At least responsible journalists are required to confirm their sources before their stories are published. Psychotherapists—or at least psychotherapists of a certain kind—are content with "narrative" or "personal" truth, regardless of the fact of the matter. It took a journalist interviewing a psychiatrist for a literary journal to expose Sybil as, shall we say, misdiagnosed.

From *Clinical Psychology: Science and Practice,* vol. 11, issue 1, March 2004, pp. 34–41. 

What really matters, of course, is not the professional affiliation of the investigator, or the means by which the investigation was published, but the actual evidence produced by the investigation. On this score, Gleaves et al. have remarkably little to say. They do not confront Moira Johnston's account of the Ramona case, a landmark court decision in which practitioners paid heavy penalties and lost their licenses for implanting false memories and which established the precedent, entirely new in tort law, that third parties can sue practitioners for damages caused by malpractice. And although we can quibble about the details of who said what, when, and under what circumstances, can anyone read Lawrence Wright's account of the Paul Ingram case and not come away wondering whether he really participated in hundreds of episodes of ritual infanticide and cannibalism, including the rape of his own children by his poker buddies while their mother watched? Unfortunately, neither of these book-length analyses is even cited by the authors, much less discussed.

Turning to the "professional" literature, Gleaves et al. cite Williams' study as evidence that self-reports of abuse have been independently "documented." But this is something of a red herring because the issue is not whether Williams' survey respondents had been abused. The issue is whether any of them showed trauma-induced amnesia for their abuse. On that matter, Williams' study is simply unconvincing. It is more likely that the events in question were subject to normal forgetting processes or to infantile and childhood amnesia. It is also likely that many informants were simply unwilling to disclose their histories to the interviewer, a common and well-known problem with crime reports of any type.

To my knowledge, nobody has ever claimed that all adult memories of childhood sexual abuse are false, so it should come as no surprise that some such memories can be corroborated. But what are we to do with those self-reports that are not corroborated? Should we simply accept them at face value? Just because some memories are valid does not mean that all memories are valid. But that seems to be the implication of the authors' argument. When therapists speculate that their patients' current problems are causally linked to events in childhood, it would seem that they incur some obligation to determine whether the alleged events actually occurred. But apparently therapists rarely seek independent corroboration of their patients' autobiographical narratives. If indeed there is an absence of clinical literature bearing on the problem of false memory, to a great extent this may be attributed to a sort of "pact of ignorance" between patients, who do not wish to have their self-narratives challenged, and therapists, who have no wish to challenge them.

People can also quibble forever about the scientific status of "false memory syndrome," but no one who uses such concepts as "battered woman syndrome" or "Stockholm syndrome" in clinical discourse should have any principled objection to the term. Still, Gleaves et al. are quite right that the essence of the syndrome is not merely the existence of a false memory. Rather, the syndrome refers to the re-orientation of an individual's identity and personality around a mental representation of his or her personal past—in other words, a memory—that is objectively false. Consider, for example, the well-documented case of Binjamin Wilkomirski, author of the award-winning

Holocaust "memoir" *Fragments*. *Fragments* now appears to have been the work of an author who was actually born in neutral Switzerland to an unmarried Protestant woman and raised and schooled there by foster parents who died before he published his book. Apparently, Wilkomirski incorporated details of the Holocaust gleaned from his voluminous reading into what is essentially a work of the imagination, but one in which he himself devoutly believed. Following a detailed investigation, Wilkomirski's publisher withdrew *Fragments* from publication. Yet, when confronted with the facts, the author angrily replied, "I *am* Binjamin Wilkomirski!" In an interesting twist, at one point a woman who claimed to have been in the camps as a child herself, and to have known Wilkomirski there ("He's my Binje!"), was found to have been born in Tacoma in 1941 and raised in Washington as a foster child by devout Presbyterians.

## Laboratory Studies of False Memories

In stark contrast to their relatively brief overview of the clinical evidence of false memories, Gleaves et al. provide a detailed analysis of laboratory studies of false memories—but one that is written in such a way as to blunt the impact of the laboratory findings and convey the impression that they are not too important for clinicians. For example, the reader is informed that there are several different explanations for both the postevent misinformation effect and the associative-memory illusion—as if that mattered, given that both effects are so robust that they can be demonstrated under classroom conditions. In the final analysis, it is the robust nature of these and similar effects that should give clinicians pause, because the effects are created by the very forces that go on in recovered-memory therapy: the presentation and discussion of themes related to incest, sexual abuse, and the like. In fact, the clinical situation may be even more conducive to the formation of illusory memories than the laboratory.

Instead, we are reassured that because laboratory phenomena do not necessarily occur in the real world, we do not have to worry about them after all. The authors barely mention studies indicating that people with histories of self-reported childhood sexual abuse and other traumas show elevated levels of the associative-memory illusion. Moreover, they push the conclusion that false memories for unusual or infrequent events are difficult to implant, without any mention of later studies that show otherwise. In a psychotherapeutic context, a therapist who believes in both the traumatic etiology of syndromes like anxiety, depression, and eating disorders, as well as the theory of repression, will very likely communicate these ideas to the patient, who may already share them by virtue of exposure to the popular media. Under such circumstances, repressed childhood sexual abuse may become quite plausible indeed.

Despite the authors' efforts to blunt the impact of the laboratory evidence, everything we know about memory from laboratory research suggests that false memories can be a real problem in the clinic, and in the courtroom as well, as indicated, for example, by the extensive literature on false eyewitness identification. This body of memory research is supplemented by a wealth of literature on persuasion, conformity, and other aspects of social influence that are relevant to the therapeutic situation. Psychotherapy, including psychiatry and clinical psychology, must be the only part of healthcare where basic laboratory research is routinely dismissed when inconvenient. Maybe that's why psychotherapy is in the shape it's in.

## Clinical Studies of "Blocked" and "Recovered" Memories

Turning to clinical evidence for "blocked and recovered" memories, Gleaves et al. begin by offering an argument from authority that blocked memories have been recognized by clinicians since the beginning of the 19th century. Unfortunately, they fail to distinguish between clinical folklore, which indeed contains abundant references to repression and other forms of trauma-induced amnesia, and the evidentiary basis for this folklore. While it is true that functional (psychogenic, dissociative) amnesia, fugue, and multiple personality disorder (dissociative identity disorder) have long been recognized in the psychiatric nosology, the evidence for a traumatic etiology in these rarely observed syndromes is remarkably thin. The term "dissociative," as applied to these disorders, is better construed as a descriptive label (referring to loss of conscious access to memory) than any pathological process instigated by trauma.

Gleaves et al. also make reference to the clinical literature on combat trauma—a good rhetorical device, because amnesia has been part of the folklore of war neurosis, and a staple of many movies, since World War I. But this evidence is totally unanalyzed. How well were the clinicians able to rule out brain insult, injury, and disease as causal factors? How well were the clinicians able to independently corroborate the combat memories ostensibly recovered by their patients after hypnosis or narcosynthesis? They also cite the widely discussed case study of Jane Doe as a compelling "existence proof" of recovered memory, despite subsequent evidence that the alleged abuse might not have occurred at all and that Jane Doe's alleged recovery of abuse memories may have been nothing more than her remembering *what she said,* rather than what she experienced, 11 years previously.

Going beyond anecdotal case evidence, Gleaves et al. attempt to bolster their case for trauma-induced amnesia by referring to studies of amnesia for childhood sexual abuse (CSA) reviewed by Brown, Scheflin, and Whitfield, and they quote approvingly those authors' statement that "Not a single one of the 68 databased studies failed to find it." Unfortunately, re-examination of this body of evidence, as well as of studies of trauma other than CSA, shows the facts to be otherwise. All too often, researchers in the area of trauma and memory fail to obtain independent corroboration of the traumatic event in question. Or, when the trauma has been satisfactorily documented, they fail to distinguish memory failure from reporting failure. Or, in cases of genuine forgetting, they fail to distinguish functional amnesia induced by psychological trauma, and presumably mediated by processes such as repression and dissociation, from other causes of forgetting, including normal forgetting over a long retention interval, the effects of infantile and childhood amnesia, and "organic" amnesia associated with brain insult, injury or disease. Nor, in cases where trauma was forgotten and subsequently remembered, do they distinguish memories recovered by the lifting of repression or breaching of dissociation from other causes of remembering, including the normal effects of shifting retrieval cues, reminiscence, and hypermnesia. Nor is there any distinction drawn between the recovery of a forgotten memory of trauma and a reinterpretation of an event that had always been remembered.

These are serious methodological problems, and one or more of them infect every one of the studies in this body of literature. In a particularly revealing exchange, Brown et al. offered nine studies "in favor of the existence of traumatic amnesia," only to have each of these studies systematically dismantled by Piper et al.. Nevertheless, Gleaves et al. conclude that, "collectively the clinical evidence does seem to suggest that varying degrees of amnesia for traumatic experiences and subsequent recovery of memory are real phenomena." It would be more accurate to say that this entire body of research has failed to uncover even a single convincing instance of repressive or dissociative amnesia for trauma.

## Laboratory Studies of "Blocked" and "Recovered" Memories

Turning to laboratory evidence for "blocked and recovered" memory, Gleaves et al. attempt to bolster clinical claims of repression and recovered memory by listing a number of experimental paradigms that show either the blocking or the recovery of memory or both, including spontaneous recovery from retroactive inhibition and the tip-of-the-tongue phenomenon. The fact is that nobody has ever argued that people cannot intentionally forget things, nor has anybody ever argued that people cannot forget something they once remembered and then remember it again later. The real question is whether the laboratory evidence of "blocked and recovered" memories cited by Gleaves et al. supports the idea that traumatic memories can be blocked by such psychological processes as repression and dissociation (however broadly defined), or that recovered-memory therapy can generate valid memories of traumatic events.

Consider, for example, the authors' statement that studies by Loftus and Burns and Christianson and Nilsson "both found that amnesia was associated with trauma." In fact, they found nothing of the sort. In the Loftus and Burns study, for example, subjects in the violent condition showed an average recall of 75.6% correct across the 17 items tested, compared to 80.9% in the nonviolent control group. Both studies did find impairments of memory for peripheral details of an event, in line with the Yerkes-Dodson law. But none of the subjects forgot central details, just as no trauma victim who was old enough to remember (and not brain damaged) was amnesic for his or her experiences in the clinical studies reviewed earlier.

Omitted from this discussion is the wealth of laboratory research, including studies of nonhuman animals employing more stressful conditions than can be used with humans, showing conclusively that emotional arousal leading to the release of stress hormones actually improves memory, at least so far as the central details of the arousing event are concerned. The well-known relation between arousal and memory can easily account for the "un-forgettable" memories suffered by those with posttraumatic stress disorder, but it cannot account for the repressive and dissociative amnesias claimed by some patients and their therapists.

Consider, too, the authors' favorable discussion of the study by Anderson and Green, which has also been touted elsewhere as evidence for Freud's concept of repression. In fact, it is woefully inadequate for this purpose. The memories in this study were pairs of innocuous words, deliberately suppressed by the subjects at the request of the experimenter. But even after 16 suppression trials, the average subject still recalled more than 70% of the targets. There was no evidence presented of persisting unconscious influence of the suppressed items, and there was no evidence that the "amnesia" could be "reversed." Moreover, it is extremely doubtful that any of the subjects were induced to forget that they had participated in a laboratory experiment. The fact is, as the clinical research cited above documents convincingly, the vast majority of trauma victims remember what happened to them all too well. The Anderson and Green study is an interesting contribution to an already extensive literature on the self-regulation of memory, but as support for Freudian repression its reach far exceeds its grasp.

Gleaves et al. also review a laboratory study that combined the Anderson and Green retrieval-inhibition paradigm with the Roediger and McDermott false-memory paradigm in an attempt to uncover features that might discriminate between continuously remembered, blocked but accurately recovered, and false-created memories. Of course, the clinically important issue is not the nomothetic question of how these classes of memories might be distinguished statistically in the aggregate. Rather, it is the idiographic question of whether any discriminanda are reliable enough to be used to evaluate individual memories in the absence of independent corroboration. In this respect, previous attempts to distinguish memories that are the product of experience from those that are the product of imagination hold out little hope. In any event, the principal conclusion from this research was that continuous and recovered memories were associated with higher confidence levels than false memories (dichotomous remember-know judgments are highly correlated with confidence). But surely the authors cannot be suggesting that clinicians use confidence levels as a proxy for accuracy in memory. The weakness of the relationship between accuracy and confidence is one of the best-documented phenomena in the 100-year history of eyewitness memory research. If confidence were an adequate criterion for validity, Binjamin Wilkomirski might have gotten a Pulitzer Prize for history.

The irony of this last section should not go unnoticed: Gleaves himself was among the first to complain when Roediger and McDermott suggested that their laboratory paradigm had any bearing on the problem of recovered memories in the clinic. If Gleaves et al. are going to discount and dismiss laboratory evidence of false memories, as they seek to do earlier in their paper, why are they so ready to accept laboratory evidence of "blocked and recovered" memories later? The bottom line is that, more than 100 years after Janet and Freud, the proponents of the trauma-memory argument and recovered-memory therapy can point to only a handful of clinical cases to support their views, and even these cases are ambiguous. Theirs is a laboratory model in search of a clinical phenomenon. The irony goes even further, because Gleaves et al. call on researchers and theorists to "[return] our attention to . . . naturalistic contexts" and "real life cases of memory blocking and recovery," as if the laboratory research they have reviewed at such length, including their own, is irrelevant after all.

## Memory in Science and in Practice

The fact is, there has been plenty of attention to naturalistic contexts in research on trauma and memory. Unfortunately, the clinical research purporting to demonstrate the blocking and recovery of traumatic memories is fatally flawed, in many cases due to a failure to demonstrate either that the events in question actually occurred or that the person was actually amnesic. Moreover, research on actual trauma victims has produced hardly a shred of evidence for psychogenic amnesia covering the traumatic event itself. Perhaps, after more than 100 years, we should simply declare the trauma-memory argument bankrupt and recovered-memory therapy passé. This would allow us to break the Freudian death-grip on clinical practice once and for all and move psychotherapy into the here and now, where patients' problems actually exist, and where their problems must be resolved. Because the status and autonomy of clinical psychology rests on the assumption that its principles and methods are scientifically validated, continued reliance on clinical folklore with respect to trauma, memory, and repression can only serve to undermine the profession.

# CHALLENGE QUESTIONS

1. Gleaves and his colleagues are critical of anecdotal evidence for falsely recovered memories as reported by journalists, but they seem to be more accepting of anecdotal accounts from clinicians of blocked and recovered memories of trauma. Kihlstrom, on the other hand, is much more generous toward the journalistic and clinical accounts. How much stock can we place in these sorts of anecdotal evidence? How trustworthy are these sources? Why or why not?
2. Coming down on either side of this issue carries certain risks. Affirming the validity of blocked and recovered memories runs the risk of falsely "traumatizing" clients who never actually experienced trauma and falsely accusing purported perpetrators of these traumas. Denying the validity of blocked and recovered memories runs the risk of dismissing actual trauma and its real impact on clients' lives, as well as covering the crime of perpetrators. Do the risks of one side outweigh the risks of the other? Are there ways we might balance these risks? Does evidence from either side make you more willing to take certain risks?
3. If a clinician sees a client who presents with symptoms that are consistent with those often seen in victims of trauma, but this client reports having no traumatic experience, how should the clinician proceed? Based on the evidence presented in these readings, should the clinician consider exploring with the client the possibility of repressed memories of trauma?
4. What sorts of experiments might researchers design in order to more conclusively determine whether repression and recovery of traumatic memories is real? If false recovered memories of trauma *are* real, what ethical considerations would researchers need to consider?
5. Elizabeth Loftus, among other cognitive researchers, is noted for having demonstrated empirically the variability of human memory. Review some of these findings and describe the implications they have for the issue of recovered memories.

# *Internet References . . .*

## Mental Health Infosource: Disorders

This no-nonsense page lists links to pages dealing with psychological disorders, including anxiety, panic, phobic disorders, schizophrenia, and violent/self-destructive behaviors.

**http://www.mhsource.com/disorders**

## Wikipedia: The Free Encyclopedia

An online encyclopedia, this site includes information on a variety of topics. This particular link contains information on ADHD and provides a forum for discussion.

**http://en.wikipedia.org/wiki/Attention_deficit_hyperactivity_disorder**

## Self-Esteem

The self-esteem movement has a substantial following on the Internet, and the National Association of Self-Esteem, one of the leading organizations in the self-esteem movement, hosts this webpage.

**http://www.self-esteem-nase.org**

# UNIT 5

# Mental Health

*A mental disorder is often defined as a pattern of thinking or behavior that is either disruptive to others or harmful to the person with the disorder. This definition seems straightforward, yet there is considerable debate about whether some disorders truly exist. For example, does a child's disruptive behavior and short attention span unquestionably warrant that he or she be diagnosed with Attention-Deficit Hyperactive Disorder (ADHD)? Many psychological disorders, including ADHD, are treated with medications that can have dangerous side effects. Could some of these side effects be so problematic that the medications are unsafe? Some psychologists claim, for example, that antidepressants make patients suicidal, while others argue that it's difficult for patients to control their depression without antidepressants. How do you balance a drug's good and bad effects? And what happens when the person is not diagnosed at all? A learning disability may not have as severe an impact as an "official" diagnosis, but it can still cause major disruptions in an individual's life. How should these conditions be best understood and treated? Is a learning disability the equivalent of a brain deficiency?*

- Is Attention-Deficit Hyperactivity Disorder (ADHD) a Real Disorder?
- Does Taking Antidepressants Lead to Suicide?
- Do Brain Deficiencies Determine Learning Disabilities?

# ISSUE 12

## Is Attention-Deficit Hyperactivity Disorder (ADHD) a Real Disorder?

**YES: National Institute of Mental Health**, from *Attention Deficit Hyperactivity Disorder* (NIH Publication No. 3572), Bethesda, MD: National Institute of Mental Health, U.S. Department of Health and Human Services (2006)

**NO: Rogers H. Wright**, from "Attention Deficit Hyperactivity Disorder: What It Is and What It Is Not," in Rogers H. Wright and Nicholas A. Cummings, eds., *Destructive Trends in Mental Health: The Well Intentioned Path to Harm* (Routledge, 2005)

### ISSUE SUMMARY

**YES:** The National Institute of Mental Health asserts that ADHD is a real disorder that merits special consideration and treatment.

**NO:** Psychologist Rogers H. Wright argues that ADHD is not a real disorder, but rather a "fad diagnosis" that has resulted in the misdiagnosis and overmedication of children.

Diagnosis presents considerable challenges for mental health professionals. The *Diagnostic and Statistical Manual (DSM),* now in its fourth edition, defines widely recognized disorders in terms of clusters of symptoms that typically characterize these disorders. Because mental disorders are usually defined in terms of symptoms, there has been significant room for debate as to which groupings of symptoms constitute legitimate disorders that merit professional attention. Indeed, through its multiple revisions the *DSM* has added some disorders, redefined others, and set aside yet others as these diagnostic debates have shifted the ways we understand mental disorders.

Attention-Deficit Hypractivity Disorder, or ADHD, has been a particularly controversial diagnosis from the time it first appeared in the *DSM-III* nearly 30 years ago. Parents, teachers, psychologists, legislators, and even celebrities have debated not only whether ADHD is a real disorder but also whether the pharmacological treatments that are frequently prescribed are appropriate. Some people worry that we are pathologizing behaviors that are normal and typical of young children (e.g., curiosity, exploration, fidgetiness). Others worry that dismissing the diagnosis and leaving affected children untreated will place these children at a social, academic, and emotional disadvantage.

In the first selection, the National Institute of Mental Health (NIMH) argues that ADHD is a neurologically-based disorder that affects 3–5% of school-age children. According to the NIMH, we can all be occasionally distracted, impulsive, and hyperactive. However, the scientists at the NIMH assert that children with ADHD struggle not only with these sorts of behaviors in greater frequency and intensity but also in a manner that is inappropriate for their age group. Moreover, the NIMH argues that there are treatments, which typically should include medicine, that will prevent greater problems in a child's later life.

In the second article, psychologist Rogers H. Wright contends that ADHD is not a real disorder, but rather a "fad diagnosis." According to Wright, there are a number of complex reasons why a child may show distractibility and/or hyperactivity other than ADHD. Wright discusses how stress and fatigue in children can produce these symptoms as well as neurological and/or emotional problems. Wright argues that the diagnosis of ADHD can distract mental health professionals from assessing for these other possible causes of distractibility and hyperactivity, leading to misdiagnosis and inappropriate treatments.

**POINT**

- There is mounting research evidence that ADHD is a diagnosable disorder that is neurologically based and strongly linked to genetics.
- Hyperactivity and distractibility are common among all children, but these symptoms are more pervasive and inappropriate in children with ADHD.
- ADHD can be diagnosed by assessing whether a person's behavior matches the criteria indicated by the DSM-IV-TR for ADHD.
- Research suggests that the best treatments for ADHD should include medication as part of their regimen.

**COUNTERPOINT**

- ADHD is a "fad diagnosis" that does not exist, like other similar diagnoses that have come and gone.
- Even when symptoms are more pervasive and inappropriate, these are more often signs of excessive fatigue or stress.
- The cluster of symptoms attributed to ADHD leads mental health professionals to treat a diverse group of people as having a single problem that requires a single solution.
- Pharmaceutical treatments for ADHD can create problems and are often unnecessary when the true cause of symptoms is understood.

**National Institute of Mental Health**

# Attention Deficit Hyperactivity Disorder

Attention Deficit Hyperactivity Disorder (ADHD) is a condition that becomes apparent in some children in the preschool and early school years. It is hard for these children to control their behavior and/or pay attention. It is estimated that between 3 and 5 percent of children have attention deficit hyperactivity disorder (ADHD), or approximately 2 million children in the United States. This means that in a classroom of 25 to 30 children, it is likely that at least one will have ADHD.

A child with ADHD faces a difficult but not insurmountable task ahead. In order to achieve his or her full potential, he or she should receive help, guidance, and understanding from parents, guidance counselors, and the public education system.

## Symptoms

The principle characteristics of ADHD are inattention, hyperactivity, and impulsivity. These symptoms appear early in a child's life. Because many normal children may have these symptoms, but at a low level, or the symptoms may be caused by another disorder, it is important that the child receive a thorough examination and appropriate diagnosis by a well qualified professional. Symptoms of ADHD will appear over the course of many months, often with the symptoms of impulsiveness and hyperactivity preceding those of inattention that may not emerge for a year or more. Different symptoms may appear in different settings, depending on the demands the situation may pose for the child's self-control. A child who "can't sit still" or is otherwise disruptive will be noticeable in school, but the inattentive daydreamer may be overlooked. The impulsive child who acts before thinking may be considered just a "discipline problem," while the child who is passive or sluggish may be viewed as merely unmotivated. Yet both may have different types of ADHD. All children are sometimes restless, sometimes act without thinking, sometimes daydream the time away. When the child's hyperactivity, distractibility, poor concentration, or impulsivity begin to affect performance in school, social relationships with other children, or behavior at home, ADHD may be suspected. But because the symptoms vary so much across settings, ADHD is not easy to diagnose. This is especially true when inattentiveness is the primary symptom.

From *National Institute of Mental Health,* NIH Publication No. 3572, 2006. Published by The National Institute of Mental Health. www.nimh.nih.gov

According to the most recent version of the Diagnostic and Statistical Manual of Mental Disorder (DSM-IV-TR), there are three patterns of behavior that indicate ADHD. People with ADHD may show several signs of being consistently inattentive. They may have a pattern of being hyperactive and impulsive far more than others of their age. Or they may show all three types of behavior. This means that there are three subtypes of ADHD recognized by professionals. These are the predominantly hyperactive-impulsive type (that does not show significant inattention); the predominantly inattentive type (that does not show significant hyperactive-impulsive behavior) sometimes called ADD—an outdated term for this entire disorder; and the combined type (that displays both inattentive and hyperactive-impulsive symptoms).

## Hyperactivity-Impulsivity

Some signs of hyperactivity-impulsivity are:

- Feeling restless, often fidgeting with hands or feet, or squirming while seated
- Running, climbing, or leaving a seat in situations where sitting or quiet behavior is expected
- Blurting out answers before hearing the whole question
- Having difficulty waiting in line or taking turns.

## Inattention

The DSM-IV-TR gives these signs of inattention.

- Often becoming easily distracted by irrelevant sights and sounds
- Often failing to pay attention to details and making careless mistakes
- Rarely following instructions carefully and completely losing or forgetting things like toys, or pencils, books, and tools needed for a task
- Often skipping from one uncompleted activity to another.

## Is It Really ADHD?

Not everyone who is overly hyperactive, inattentive, or impulsive has ADHD. Since most people sometimes blurt out things they didn't mean to say, or jump from one task to another, or become disorganized and forgetful, how can specialists tell if the problem is ADHD?

Because everyone shows some of these behaviors at times, the diagnosis requires that such behavior be demonstrated to a degree that is inappropriate for the person's age. The diagnostic guidelines also contain specific requirements for determining when the symptoms indicate ADHD. The behaviors must appear early in life, before age 7, and continue for at least 6 months. Above all, the behaviors must create a real handicap in at least two areas of a person's life such as in the schoolroom, on the playground, at home, in the community, or in social settings. So someone who shows some symptoms but whose schoolwork or friendships are not impaired by these behaviors would not be diagnosed with ADHD. Nor would a child who seems overly active on the playground but functions well elsewhere receive an ADHD diagnosis.

To assess whether a child has ADHD, specialists consider several critical questions: Are these behaviors excessive, long-term, and pervasive? That is, do they occur more often than in other children the same age? Are they a continuous problem, not just a response to a temporary situation? Do the behaviors occur in several settings or only in one specific place like the playground or in the schoolroom? The person's pattern of behavior is compared against a set of criteria and characteristics of the disorder as listed in the DSM-IV-TR.

## Diagnosis

### Professionals Who Make the Diagnosis

If ADHD is suspected, to whom can the family turn? What kinds of specialists do they need?

Ideally, the diagnosis should be made by a professional in your area with training in ADHD or in the diagnosis of mental disorders. Child psychiatrists and psychologists, developmental/behavioral pediatricians, or behavioral neurologists are those most often trained in differential diagnosis. Clinical social workers may also have such training. The family can start by talking with the child's pediatrician or their family doctor. Some pediatricians may do the assessment themselves, but often they refer the family to an appropriate mental health specialist they know and trust. In addition, state and local agencies that serve families and children . . . can help identify appropriate specialists.

Within each specialty, individual doctors and mental health professionals differ in their experiences with ADHD. So in selecting a specialist, it's important to find someone with specific training and experience in diagnosing and treating the disorder.

Whatever the specialist's expertise, his or her first task is to gather information that will rule out other possible reasons for the child's behavior. Among possible causes of ADHD-like behavior are the following:

- A sudden change in the child's life—the death of a parent or grandparent; parents' divorce; a parent's job loss.
- Undetected seizures, such as in petit mal or temporal lobe seizures
- A middle ear infection that causes intermittent hearing problems
- Medical disorders that may affect brain functioning
- Underachievement caused by learning disability
- Anxiety or depression

Next the specialist gathers information on the child's ongoing behavior in order to compare these behaviors to the symptoms and diagnostic criteria listed in the DSM-IV-TR. This also involves talking with the child and, if possible, observing the child in class and other settings.

The child's teachers, past and present, are asked to rate their observations of the child's behavior on standardized evaluation forms, known as behavior rating scales, to compare the child's behavior to that of other children the same age.

The specialist interviews the child's teachers and parents, and may contact other people who know the child well, such as coaches or baby-sitters. Parents are asked to describe their child's behavior in a variety of situations. They may also fill out a rating scale to indicate how severe and frequent the behaviors seem to be.

In most cases, the child will be evaluated for social adjustment and mental health. Tests of intelligence and learning achievement may be given to see if the child has a learning disability and whether the disability is in one or more subjects.

The specialist then pieces together a profile of the child's behavior.

A correct diagnosis often resolves confusion about the reasons for the child's problems that lets parents and child move forward in their lives with more accurate information on what is wrong and what can be done to help. Once the disorder is diagnosed, the child and family can begin to receive whatever combination of educational, medical, and emotional help they need. This may include providing recommendations to school staff, seeking out a more appropriate classroom setting, selecting the right medication, and helping parents to manage their child's behavior.

## What Causes ADHD?

One of the first questions a parent will have is "Why? What went wrong?" "Did I do something to cause this?" There is little compelling evidence at this time that ADHD can arise purely from social factors or child-rearing methods. Most substantiated causes appear to fall in the realm of neurobiology and genetics. This is not to say that environmental factors may not influence the severity of the disorder, and especially the degree of impairment and suffering the child may experience, but that such factors do not seem to give rise to the condition by themselves.

The parents' focus should be on looking forward and finding the best possible way to help their child. Scientists are studying causes in an effort to identify better ways to treat, and perhaps someday, to prevent ADHD. They are finding more and more evidence that ADHD does not stem from home environment, but from biological causes. Knowing this can remove a huge burden of guilt from parents who might blame themselves for their child's behavior.

**Genetics.** Attention disorders often run in families, so there are likely to be genetic influences. Studies indicate that 25 percent of the close relatives in the families of ADHD children also have ADHD, whereas the rate is about 5 percent in the general population. Many studies of twins now show that a strong genetic influence exists in the disorder.

Researchers continue to study the genetic contribution to ADHD and to identify the genes that cause a person to be susceptible to ADHD. Since its inception in 1999, the Attention-Deficit Hyperactivity Disorder Molecular

Genetics Network has served as a way for researchers to share findings regarding possible genetic influences on ADHD.

**Recent Studies on Causes of ADHD.** Some knowledge of the structure of the brain is helpful in understanding the research scientists are doing in searching for a physical basis for attention deficit hyperactivity disorder. One part of the brain that scientists have focused on in their search is the frontal lobes of the cerebrum. The frontal lobes allow us to solve problems, plan ahead, understand the behavior of others, and restrain our impulses. The two frontal lobes, the right and the left, communicate with each other through the corpus callosum, (nerve fibers that connect the right and left frontal lobes).

The basal ganglia are the interconnected gray masses deep in the cerebral hemisphere that serve as the connection between the cerebrum and the cerebellum and, with the cerebellum are responsible for motor coordination. The cerebellum is divided into three parts. The middle part is called the vermis.

All of these parts of the brain have been studied through the use of various methods for seeing into or imaging the brain. These methods include functional magnetic resonance imaging (fMRI), positron emission tomography (PET), and single photon emission computed tomography (SPECT). The main or central psychological deficits in those with ADHD have been linked through these studies. By 2002 the researchers in the NIMH Child Psychiatry Branch had studied 152 boys and girls with ADHD, matched with 139 age- and gender-matched controls without ADHD. The children were scanned at least twice, some as many as four times over a decade. As a group, the ADHD children showed 3-4 percent smaller brain volumes in all regions—the frontal lobes, temporal gray matter, caudate nucleus, and cerebellum.

This study also showed that the ADHD children who were on medication had a white matter volume that did not differ from that of controls. Those never-medicated patients had an abnormally small volume of white matter. The white matter consists of fibers that establish long-distance connections between brain regions. It normally thickens as a child grows older and the brain matures.

## The Treatment of ADHD

Every family wants to determine what treatment will be most effective for their child. This question needs to be answered by each family in consultation with their health care professional. To help families make this important decision, the National Institute of Mental Health (NIMH) has funded many studies of treatments for ADHD and has conducted the most intensive study ever undertaken for evaluating the treatment of this disorder. This study is known as the Multimodal Treatment Study of Children with Attention Deficit Hyperactivity Disorder (MTA).

The MTA study included 579 (95-98 at each of 6 treatment sites) elementary school boys and girls with ADHD, randomly assigning them to one of four treatment programs: (1) medication management alone; (2) behavioral treatment alone; (3) a combination of both; or (4) routine community care.

In each of the study sites, three groups were treated for the first 14 months in a specified protocol and the fourth group was referred for community treatment of the parents' choosing. All of the children were reassessed regularly throughout the study period. An essential part of the program was the cooperation of the schools, including principals and teachers. Both teachers and parents rated the children on hyperactivity, impulsivity, and inattention, and symptoms of anxiety and depression, as well as social skills.

The children in two groups (medication management alone and the combination treatment) were seen monthly for one-half hour at each medication visit. During the treatment visits, the prescribing physician spoke with the parent, met with the child, and sought to determine any concerns that the family might have regarding the medication or the child's ADHD-related difficulties. The physicians, in addition, sought input from the teachers on a monthly basis. The physicians in the medication-only group did not provide behavioral therapy but did advise the parents when necessary concerning any problems the child might have.

In the behavior treatment-only group, families met up to 35 times with a behavior therapist, mostly in group sessions. These therapists also made repeated visits to schools to consult with children's teachers and to supervise a special aide assigned to each child in the group. In addition, children attended a special 8-week summer treatment program where they worked on academic, social, and sports skills, and where intensive behavioral therapy was delivered to assist children in improving their behavior.

Children in the combined therapy group received both treatments, that is, all the same assistance that the medication-only received, as well as all of the behavior therapy treatments.

In routine community care, the children saw the community-treatment doctor of their parents' choice one to two times per year for short periods of time. Also, the community-treatment doctor did not have any interaction with the teachers.

The results of the study indicated that long-term combination treatments and the medication-management alone were superior to intensive behavioral treatment and routine community treatment. And in some areas—anxiety, academic performance, oppositionality, parent-child relations, and social skills—the combined treatment was usually superior. Another advantage of combined treatment was that children could be successfully treated with lower doses of medicine, compared with the medication-only group.

## Medications

For decades, medications have been used to treat the symptoms of ADHD.

The medications that seem to be the most effective are a class of drugs known as stimulants.

Some people get better results from one medication, some from another. It is important to work with the prescribing physician to find the right medication and the right dosage. For many people, the stimulants dramatically reduce their hyperactivity and impulsivity and improve their ability to focus, work, and learn. The medications may also improve physical coordination, such as that needed in handwriting and in sports.

The stimulant drugs, when used with medical supervision, are usually considered quite safe. . . . [T]o date there is no convincing evidence that stimulant medications, when used for treatment of ADHD, cause drug abuse or dependence. A review of all long-term studies on stimulant medication and substance abuse, conducted by researchers at Massachusetts General Hospital and Harvard Medical School, found that teenagers with ADHD who remained on their medication during the teen years had a lower likelihood of substance use or abuse than did ADHD adolescents who were not taking medications.

The stimulant drugs come in long- and short-term forms. The newer sustained-release stimulants can be taken before school and are long-lasting so that the child does not need to go to the school nurse every day for a pill. The doctor can discuss with the parents the child's needs and decide which preparation to use and whether the child needs to take the medicine during school hours only or in the evening and weekends too.

About one out of ten children is not helped by a stimulant medication. Other types of medication may be used if stimulants don't work or if the ADHD occurs with another disorder. Antidepressants and other medications can help control accompanying depression or anxiety.

## Side Effects of the Medications

Most side effects of the stimulant medications are minor and are usually related to the dosage of the medication being taken. Higher doses produce more side effects. The most common side effects are decreased appetite, insomnia, increased anxiety and/or irritability. Some children report mild stomach aches or headaches.

When a child's schoolwork and behavior improve soon after starting medication, the child, parents, and teachers tend to applaud the drug for causing the sudden changes. Unfortunately, when people see such immediate improvement, they often think medication is all that's needed. But medications don't cure ADHD; they only control the symptoms on the day they are taken. Although the medications help the child pay better attention and complete school work, they can't increase knowledge or improve academic skills. The medications help the child to use those skills he or she already possesses.

Behavioral therapy, emotional counseling, and practical support will help ADHD children cope with everyday problems and feel better about themselves.

### *Facts to Remember about Medication for ADHD*

- Medications for ADHD help many children focus and be more successful at school, home, and play. Avoiding negative experiences now may actually help prevent addictions and other emotional problems later.
- About 80 percent of children who need medication for ADHD still need it as teenagers. Over 50 percent need medication as adults.

## The Family and the ADHD Child

Medication can help the ADHD child in everyday life. He or she may be better able to control some of the behavior problems that have led to trouble with parents and siblings. But it takes time to undo the frustration, blame, and anger that may have gone on for so long. Both parents and children may need special help to develop techniques for managing the patterns of behavior. In such cases, mental health professionals can counsel the child and the family, helping them to develop new skills, attitudes, and ways of relating to each other. In individual counseling, the therapist helps children with ADHD learn to feel better about themselves. The therapist can also help them to identify and build on their strengths, cope with daily problems, and control their attention and aggression. Sometimes only the child with ADHD needs counseling support. But in many cases, because the problem affects the family as a whole, the entire family may need help. The therapist assists the family in finding better ways to handle the disruptive behaviors and promote change. If the child is young, most of the therapist's work is with the parents, teaching them techniques for coping with and improving their child's behavior.

Several intervention approaches arc available. Knowing something about the various types of interventions makes it easier for families to choose a therapist that is right for their needs.

**Psychotherapy** works to help people with ADHD to like and accept themselves despite their disorder. It does not address the symptoms or underlying causes of the disorder. In psychotherapy, patients talk with the therapist about upsetting thoughts and feelings, explore self-defeating patterns of behavior, and learn alternative ways to handle their emotions. As they talk, the therapist tries to help them understand how they can change or better cope with their disorder.

**Behavioral therapy (BT)** helps people develop more effective ways to work on immediate issues. Rather than helping the child understand his or her feelings and actions, it helps directly in changing their thinking and coping and thus may lead to changes in behavior. The support might be practical assistance, like help in organizing tasks or schoolwork or dealing with emotionally charged events. Or the support might be in self-monitoring one's own behavior and giving self-praise or rewards for acting in a desired way such as controlling anger or thinking before acting.

**Social skills training** can also help children learn new behaviors. In social skills training, the therapist discusses and models appropriate behaviors important in developing and maintaining social relationships, like waiting for a turn, sharing toys, asking for help, or responding to teasing, then gives children a chance to practice. For example, a child might learn to "read" other people's facial expression and tone of voice in order to respond appropriately. Social skills training helps the child to develop better ways to play and work with other children.

# Attention Deficit Hyperactivity Disorder in Adults

Attention Deficit Hyperactivity Disorder is a highly publicized childhood disorder that affects approximately 3 to 5 percent of all children. What is much less well known is the probability that, of children who have ADHD, many will still have it as adults. Several studies done in recent years estimate that between 30 percent and 70 percent of children with ADHD continue to exhibit symptoms in the adult years.

Typically, adults with ADHD are unaware that they have this disorder—they often just feel that it's impossible to get organized, to stick to a job, to keep an appointment. The everyday tasks of getting up, getting dressed and ready for the day's work, getting to work on time, and being productive on the job can be major challenges for the ADD adult.

## Diagnosing ADHD in an Adult

Diagnosing an adult with ADHD is not easy. Many times, when a child is diagnosed with the disorder, a parent will recognize that he or she has many of the same symptoms the child has and, for the first time, will begin to understand some of the traits that have given him or her trouble for years—distractability, impulsivity, restlessness. Other adults will seek professional help for depression or anxiety and will find out that the root cause of some of their emotional problems is ADHD. They may have a history of school failures or problems at work. Often they have been involved in frequent automobile accidents.

To be diagnosed with ADHD, an adult must have childhood-onset, persistent, and current symptoms. The accuracy of the diagnosis of adult ADHD is of utmost importance and should be made by a clinician with expertise in the area of attention dysfunction. For an accurate diagnosis, a history of the patient's childhood behavior, together with an interview with his life partner, a parent, close friend or other close associate, will be needed. A physical examination and psychological tests should also be given. Comorbidity with other conditions may exist such as specific learning disabilities, anxiety, or affective disorders.

A correct diagnosis of ADHD can bring a sense of relief. The individual has brought into adulthood many negative perceptions of himself that may have led to low esteem. Now he can begin to understand why he has some of his problems and can begin to face them.

**Rogers H. Wright**

# Attention Deficit Hyperactivity Disorder: What It Is and What It Is Not

It is almost axiomatic in the mental health field that fads will occur in the "diagnosis" and treatment of various types of behavioral aberrations, some of which border on being mere discomforts. Although the same faddism exists to some degree in physical medicine, its appearance is not nearly as blatant, perhaps in part because physical medicine is more soundly grounded in the physical sciences than are diagnoses in the mental health field. These fads spill over into the general culture, where direct marketing often takes place. One has to spend only a brief period in front of a television set during prime time to discover ADHD (Attention Deficit Hyperactivity Disorder), SAD (Social Anxiety Disorder), or IBS (Irritable Bowl Syndrome). Even when purporting to be informational, these are more or less disguised commercials, inasmuch as they posit a cure that varies with the drug manufacturer sponsoring the television ad.

The other certainty is that these "diagnoses" will fall from usage as other fads emerge, as was the case a decade or so ago with the disappearance of a once-common designation for what is now sometimes called ADHD. That passing fad was known as minimal brain syndrome (MBS) and/or food disorder (ostensibly from red dye or other food additives). From this author's perspective, these fad "diagnoses" don't really exist. Other writers in this volume (e.g., Cummings, Rosemond, and Wright) have commented on the slipperiness of these "diagnoses"—that is, the elevation of a symptom and/or its description to the level of a disorder or syndrome—and the concomitant tendency to overmedicate for these nonexistent maladies.

## Children and ADHD

Certainly, there are deficiencies of attention and hyperactivity, but such behavioral aberrancies are most often indicative of a transitory state or condition within the organism. They are not in and of themselves indicative of a "disorder." Every parent has noticed, particularly with younger children, that toward the end of an especially exciting and fatiguing day children are literally

From *Destructive Trends In Mental Health: The Well Intentioned Path To Harm,* (Routledge 2005) pp. 129–141. 

"ricocheting off the walls." Although this behavior may in the broadest sense be classifiable as hyperactivity, it is generally pathognomonic of nothing more than excessive fatigue, for which the treatment of choice is a good night's sleep. Distractibility (attention deficit) is a frequent concomitant of excessive fatigue, particularly with children under five years of age, and can even be seen in adults if fatigue levels are extreme or if stress is prolonged. However, such "symptoms" in these contexts do not rise to the level of a treatable disorder.

Conversely, when distractibility and/or hyperactivity characterize the child's everyday behavior (especially if accompanied by factors such as delayed development, learning difficulties, impaired motor skills, and impaired judgment), they may be indicative of either a neurological disorder or of developing emotional difficulties. However, after nearly fifty years of diagnosing and treating several thousand such problems, it is my considered judgment that the distractibility and hyperactivity seen in such children is not the same as the distractibility and hyperactivity in children currently diagnosed as having ADHD. Furthermore, the hyperactivity/distractibility seen in the non-ADHD children described above is qualitatively and quantitatively different, depending on whether it is caused by incipient emotional maldevelopment (functional; i.e., nonorganic) or whether it is due to neurological involvement.

It is also notable that most children whose distractibility and/or hyperactivity is occasioned by emotional distress do not show either the kind or degree of learning disability, delayed genetic development, poor judgment, and impaired motor skills that are seen in children whose "distractibility/hyperactivity" is occasioned by neurological involvement. Only in children with the severest forms of emotional disturbance does one see the kind of developmental delays and impaired behavioral controls that are more reflective of neurological involvement (or what was known as MBS until the ADHD fad took hold). Differentiating the child with actual neurological involvement from the child that has emotionally based distractibility is neither simple nor easy to do, especially if the behavioral (as opposed to neurological) involvement is severe.

A major and profound disservice occasioned by the current fad of elevating nonspecific symptoms such as anxiety and hyperactivity to the level of a syndrome or disorder and then diagnosing ADD/ADHD is that we lump together individuals with very different needs and very different problems. We then attempt to treat the problem(s) with a single entity, resulting in a one-pill-fits-all response. It is also unfortunately the case that many mental health providers (e.g., child psychiatrists, child psychologists, child social workers), as well as many general care practitioners (e.g., pediatricians and internists), are not competent to make such discriminations alone. Therefore, it follows that such practitioners are not trained and equipped to provide ongoing care, even when an appropriate diagnosis has been made.

To add to an already complicated situation, the symptom picture in children tends to change with time and maturation. Children with neurological involvement typically tend to improve spontaneously over time, so that the symptoms of distractibility and hyperactivity often represent diminished components in the clinical picture. Conversely, children whose distractibility and hyperactivity are emotionally determined typically have symptoms that tend to intensify or be accompanied/replaced by even more dramatic indices of emotional distress.

## Management of Children Exhibiting "ADHD" According to Etiology

It is apparent that somewhat superficially similar presenting complaints (i.e., distractibility and hyperactivity) may reflect two very different causative factors, and that the successful treatment and management of the complaint should vary according to the underlying causation. Neurological damage can stem from a number of causative factors during pregnancy or the birth process, and a successful remedial program may require the combined knowledge of the child's pediatrician, a neuropsychologist specializing in the diagnosis and treatment of children, and a child neurologist. In these cases appropriate medication for the child is often very helpful.

Psychotherapy for the child (particularly younger children) is, in this writer's experience, largely a waste of time. On the other hand, remedial training in visual perception, motor activities, visual—motor integration, spatial relations, numerical skills, and reading and writing may be crucial in alleviating or at least diminishing the impact of symptoms. Deficits in these skills can be major contributors to the hyperactivity and distractibility so frequently identified with such children. Counseling and psychotherapeutic work with the parents is very important and should always be a part of an integrated therapeutic program. Such children need to be followed by an attending pediatrician, a child neurologist, a child neuropsychologist, and an educational therapist, bearing in mind that treatment needs change throughout the span of remediation. For example, medication levels and regimens may need to be adjusted, and training programs will constantly need to be revised or elaborated.

It is also noteworthy that so-called tranquilizing medication with these children typically produces an adverse effect. This writer remembers a situation that occurred early in his practice, a case he has used repeatedly to alert fledgling clinicians to the importance of a comprehensive initial evaluation and ongoing supervision in the development of neurologically involved children.

John, a two-and-a-half-year-old boy, was referred by his pediatrician for evaluation of extreme hyperactivity, distractibility, and mild developmental delay. The psychological evaluation elicited evidence of visual perceptual impairment in a context of impaired visual motor integration, a finding suggestive of an irritative focus in the parietal-occipital areas of the brain. This finding was later corroborated by a child neurologist, and John was placed on dilantin and phenobarbital. A developmental training program was instituted, and the parents began participation in a group specifically designed for the parents of brain-injured children. Over the next couple of years, the patient's progress was excellent, and his development and learning difficulties were singularly diminished. The parents were comfortable with John's progress and with their ability to manage it, so they decided to have a long-wanted additional child. In the meantime, the father's work necessitated moving to another location, leading to a change of obstetrician and pediatrician.

The second pregnancy proceeded uneventfully and eventuated in the birth of a second boy. Shortly after the mother returned home with the new infant, John began to regress, exhibiting a number of prior symptoms such as hyperactivity and distractibility, as well as problems in behavioral control. The new pediatrician referred the family to a child psychiatrist, who promptly placed John on a tranquilizer. Shortly thereafter, John's academic performance began to deteriorate dramatically, and his school counseled the parents about the possibility that he had been promoted too rapidly and "could not handle work at this grade level."

At this point, the parents again contacted this writer, primarily out of concern for John's diminished academic performance. Because it had been more than two years since John had been formally evaluated, I advised the parents that another comprehensive evaluation was indicated. The parents agreed, and a full diagnostic battery was administered to John, the results of which were then compared to his prior performance. It immediately became apparent that he was not functioning at grade level, and that the overall level of his functioning had deteriorated dramatically.

In his initial evaluation, John's functional level had been in the Bright Normal range (i.e., overall IQ of 110 to 119), whereas his current functioning placed him at the Borderline Mentally Retarded level (IQ below 60). The history revealed nothing of significance other than the behavioral regression after the birth of the sibling and the introduction of the new medication. I advised the parents that I thought the child was being erroneously medicated, with consequent diminution of his intellectual efficiency, and that the supposition could be tested by asking the attending child psychiatrist to diminish John's medication to see if the child's performance improved.

The attending child psychiatrist was quite upset by the recommendations and the implications thereof and threatened to sue me for "practicing medicine without a license." I informed the physician that I was not practicing medicine but rather neuropsychology, along with deductive reasoning known as "common sense," which we could test by appropriately reducing John's dosage level for a month and then retesting him. Faced with the alternative of a legal action for slander or libel for having accused this neuropsychologist of a felony, the child psychiatrist agreed.

Upon retesting a month later, the child's performance level had returned to Bright Normal, and his academic performance and behavior in school had improved dramatically. By this time approximately six to eight months had elapsed since the birth of the sibling, and John had become accustomed to his new brother. All concerned agreed that the medication had not been helpful and that the child should continue for another three to six months without medication. Subsequent contact with the parents some six months later indicated that John was doing well at school. The parents were quite comfortable with the behavioral management skills they had learned, which enabled them to handle a child with an underlying neurological handicap.

As noted earlier, the marked distractibility and/or hyperactivity in children with neurological involvement tends to diminish through adolescence, especially after puberty, as do many of the other symptoms. As a consequence, these children present a very different clinical picture in adolescence and adulthood. Typically, they are characterized by impulsivity, at times poor judgment, and excessive fatigability. It is generally only under the circumstances of extreme fatigue (or other stress) that one will see fairly dramatic degrees of distractibility and hyperactivity. Thus, an appropriate diagnosis leading to productive intervention is difficult to make.

Conversely, children who exhibit the symptoms of distractibility and hyperactivity on an emotional basis typically do not show the diminution of symptomatology with increasing age. In fact, the symptoms may intensify and/or be replaced by even more dramatic symptoms, especially during puberty and adolescence. It should also be emphasized that the kind of distractibility and hyperactivity exhibited by the emotionally disturbed youngster is very different in quality and quantity from that of a youngster whose hyperactivity and distractibility has a neurological basis. Unfortunately, it is also frequently the case that a youngster with a neurological handicap may have significant emotional problems overlaying the basic neurological problems, making diagnosis even more complicated. But the overriding problem confronting parents today is the misdiagnosis of emotionally-based symptoms that brings the recommendation of unwarranted medication.

In the largest study of its kind, Cummings and Wiggins retrospectively examined the records of 168,113 children and adolescents who had been referred and treated over a four-year period in a national behavioral health provider operating in thirty-nine states. Before beginning treatment, sixty-one percent of the males and twenty-three percent of the females were taking psychotropic medication for ADD/ADHD by a psychiatrist, a pediatrician, or a primary care physician. Most of them lived in a single-parent home, and lacked an effective father figure or were subjected to negative and frequently abusive male role models. Behavioral interventions included a compassionate but firm male therapist and the introduction of positive male role models (e.g., fathers, Big Brothers, coaches, Sunday school teachers, etc.) into the child's life. Counseling focused on helping parents understand what constitutes the behavior of a normal boy.

After an average of nearly eleven treatments with the parent and approximately six with the child, the percentage of boys on medication was reduced from sixty-one percent to eleven percent, and the percentage of girls on medication went from twenty-three percent to two percent. These dramatic results occurred despite very strict requirements for discontinuing the medication, which seems to point to an alarming overdiagnosis and overmedication of ADD/ADHD and greater efficacy of behavioral interventions than is generally believed to be the case by the mental health community.

## Adult ADHD

The wholesale invasion of ADHD in childhood and adolescence is accompanied by a concurrent explosion of such diagnoses into adulthood. One cannot watch television without being bombarded by the direct marketing that asks: "Do you find it difficult to finish a task at work? Do you frequently find yourself daydreaming or distracted? You may be suffering from ADD. Consult your physician or WebMD." Of course, adult ADD exists; children with real ADD will grow into adulthood. But the symptoms described in this aggressive TV marketing are more reflective of boredom, the mid-day blahs, job dissatisfaction, or stress than a syndrome or disorder requiring treatment.

Unfortunately, treatment interventions focused primarily on medication and based on such ethereal and universal symptoms promise an instant "cure" for the patient who now does not have to confront possible unhappiness or stress. Such simple solutions also find great favor with the insurers and HMOs that look for the cheapest treatment. Persons exhibiting "symptoms" are more likely to benefit from a variety of behavioral interventions ranging from vocational counseling for job dissatisfaction and marital counseling for an unhappy marriage, to psychotherapy for underlying emotional stress, anxiety, or depression. Such interventions tend to be time-consuming and costly, with the consequence that the patients may inadvertently ally themselves with managed care companies devoted to the principle that the least expensive treatment is the treatment of choice.

Distractibility and hyperactivity of the type that we have called the "real ADHD" does exist in adults. However, in general, symptoms are much more subtle and, in many if not most cases, overshadowed by other symptoms. Thus, if mentioned at all, distractibility and hyperactivity are rarely significant presenting complaints. Such things as poor judgment, behavioral difficulties, forgetting, difficulties in reading/calculating, and getting lost are typically pre-eminent in the adult patient's presenting complaints. These usually become apparent in adulthood after an accident, strokes (CVA), infections of the brain, and other such events. The very drama of the causative factor typically makes the diagnosis apparent, and treatment providers are "tuned in" to anticipate sequellae secondary to neurological damage: intellectual and/or judgmental deficits, behavioral change, impulsivity, and motor impairment.

It should be emphasized that hyperactivity and distractibility, although present, are less dramatic symptoms that are understandably of less concern to the patient. Furthermore, they often diminish rapidly in the first eighteen months following the neurological event. Even then, the major constellation of symptoms may not be sufficiently dramatic to alert attending medical personnel as to the primary cause of the patient's complaints. This is particularly true of contrecoup lesions occurring most frequently in auto accidents.

Although circumstances resulting in contrecoup damage are frequent and often missed, there are also other, even more significant, types of neurological involvement that may also pass unnoticed. These include early-onset Alzheimer's disease beginning at age fifty and cerebral toxicity resulting from inappropriate medication in the elderly, which is usually misdiagnosed as incipient Alzheimer's. Expectation can unfortunately contribute not only to a misdiagnosis, but also failure to order tests that might elicit the underlying condition. In addition, the converse may infrequently occur: Neurological involvement may be anticipated but is not demonstrable and does not exist. Three illustrative cases follow.

*Case 1*

Bill, a young construction worker, received notice of his imminent induction into the armed services. Right after lunch on a Friday afternoon, a large section of 2 × 4 lumber dropped from the second story of a work site, striking him butt-first in the right anterior temporal region of the head. He was unconscious for a short period of time, quickly recovered consciousness, and showed no apparent ill effects from the blow. He refused hospitalization, and was taken by his employer to his home.

On the following Monday, Bill phoned his employer saying that he was still "not feeling too good," and given the imminence of his induction into the Army, he "was just going to goof off" until he was "called up." The employer had no further contact with Bill, who was inducted into the Army, where he almost immediately began to have difficulty, primarily of a behavioral type. Throughout his basic training, he tended to be impulsive and to use poor judgment, and he was constantly getting into fights with his companions. He barely made it through training and was shipped overseas where he was assigned to a unit whose primary duty was guard duty.

Throughout his training and his subsequent duty assignment, Bill was a frequent attendee at sick call with consistent complaints of headache, earning him the reputation of "goof-off." His military career was terminated shortly after an apparently unprovoked attack on the officer in charge of the guard detail to which Bill was assigned. After a short detention in the stockade, he was discharged from the Army. His headaches and impulsivity continued into civilian life and prompted Bill to seek medical assistance through the Veterans Administration. The VA clinic's case study included neurological screening tests that were strongly suggestive of brain involvement. Consequently, he was given a full psychological work-up, which revealed intellectual impairment attendant to temporal lobe damage.

Subsequent neurological and encephalographic studies were consistent with the neuropsychological conclusions, and indicated a major focus in the anterior temporal area of the brain. A careful and detailed history was taken, and the incident of the blow to the head was elicited. This case suggests that even though Bill refused hospitalization, because of the severity of the blow it would have been prudent for the employer to insist on a thorough evaluation.

*Case 2*

James, a man in his late forties, was the son of a Southern sharecropper. Upon graduation from high school, he attended the Tuskegee Institute for a short period before he was drafted into the armed forces. James had a productive military career and upon his discharge moved to California, got married, and proceeded to raise his family. He had trained himself as a finish carpenter and cabinetmaker. His work was highly regarded, and his annual income was well above the average for his field. One of his three children was a college graduate, a second was well along in college, and the third was graduating from high school. James owned his own home and enjoyed a fine reputation as a contributing citizen of his community.

While at work installing a complicated newel post and banister, James became disoriented and tumbled from a stair landing, falling some five feet and landing primarily on his head and shoulders but experiencing no apparent loss of consciousness. He was taken to a hospital for evaluation but was released with no significant findings. Almost immediately thereafter, he began to have difficulty at work. He would become disoriented, could not tell left from right, and made frequent mistakes in measuring, sawing, and fitting even simple elements. Before the accident he seldom if ever missed work, but now he became a frequent absentee. The quality of his work deteriorated and his income plummeted. He sought medical advice and was given a small stipend under the Workers Compensation program.

Over several weeks, he demonstrated no progress, and the attending neurologist and neurosurgeon referred him for neuropsychodiagnostic evaluation as a possible malingerer. The neuropsychologist noted that James' current status was completely at odds with his prior history, and not at all consistent with malingering. For example, the evaluation revealed that this highly skilled cabinetmaker, to his embarrassment, could no longer answer the question, "How many inches are there in two and a half feet?" The neuropsychological finding of pervasive occipital-parietal involvement was subsequently corroborated by electroencephalographic study.

### *Case 3*

An airline captain driving along Wilshire Boulevard in Los Angeles lost consciousness when he experienced a spontaneous cerebral hemorrhage. He was immediately taken to a nearby major hospital where he received immediate and continuing care. Subsequently, a subdural hematoma developed, requiring surgical intervention. The captain recovered and showed no clinically significant signs of neurological involvement. An immediate post-recovery issue was the possibility of being returned to flight status. The attending neurosurgeon referred the patient for a comprehensive neuropsychological evaluation that found no indication of residual neurological deficit. Consequently, the neuropsychologist and the attending neurosurgeon recommended return to flight status.

In summary, in none of the foregoing situations was attention deficit or hyperactivity a significant presenting complaint, although the presence of both was clinically demonstrable at various times in the posttraumatic period. Yet the failure to recognize their presence would not have had a negative impact on treatment planning and or management in any of the three cases. Conversely, if excessive focus on the possible "attention deficits and/or hyperactivity disorder" dictated the nature of the therapeutic intervention, a significant disservice to each of these patients would have resulted.

Traditionally when distractibility and/or hyperactivity are prominent parts of the presenting complaint, the mental health provider directs diagnostic energies toward ascertaining the underlying source of these dysphoric experiences. The distractibility and hyperactivity would have been viewed as secondary symptoms to be tolerated, if possible, until the resolution of the underlying problem resulted in their alleviation. In situations where the symptoms were so extreme as to be significantly debilitating, the mental health provider might reluctantly attempt to provide some symptom relief. However, in such cases this was done with the certain knowledge that it was an expedient, and was not addressing causation.

Times have changed dramatically, reflecting the interaction of a number of factors such as competition and cost controls. With the emergence of a plethora of mental health service providers, psychiatry opted to "remedicalize," essentially abandoning what it refers to as "talk therapy" in favor of medicating questionable syndromes and disorders. Psychology, pushed by its academic wing, could never decide what level of training was sufficient for independent mental health service delivery (i.e., master's versus doctoral degrees), and graduate-level training programs began to turn out hordes of master's-level providers in counseling, social work, education, and school psychology.

Meanwhile, the inclusion of mental health benefits in pre-paid health programs broadened consumption and brought about managed care as a means of reducing consumption of all kinds of health services, including behavioral health services. When the American public's impatience with time-consuming processes is added to managed care's limiting of services in the context of a glut of mental health providers the scene is set for considerable mischief. Add to this brew the fact that psychiatry holds a virtual medication-prescribing monopoly in mental health and that drug manufacturers are constantly developing and marketing new magic pills, it all adds up to an environment that encourages the "discovery" of yet another syndrome or disorder for which treatment is necessary.

## Summary

When hyperactivity and/or distractibility is truly one of the presenting symptoms, it is indicative of a complex situation that warrants extensive and thoughtful evaluation, and, more often than not, complex and comprehensive treatment planning from the perspective of a variety of specialists. In situations where the attention deficit and/or hyperactivity reflects problems in parenting, chemotherapeutic intervention for the child is likely to be, at best, no more than palliative and, at worse, may succeed in considerably complicating the situation. In this writer's experience, chemotherapeutic intervention for emotionally disturbed children is a last resort and of minimal value in addressing the overall problem. Psychotherapeutic intervention with the parents, which may or may not include the child, is more often than not the treatment of choice. This is a judgment that is best made only after exhaustive study by pediatrics, psychology, neurology, and perhaps, last of all, psychiatry, which so often seems all too eager to overmedicate. . . .

Where the presenting complaints of hyperactivity and distractibility are in a context of delayed development, excessive fatigability, learning deficits, and other such signs, the complexity of the diagnostic problem is substantially increased. In such circumstances, it is absolutely not in the child's best interest to limit the diagnostic evaluation to a single specialty. With the increasing evidence that neurological involvement can follow any number of prenatal and postnatal exposures, wise and caring parents will insist on a comprehensive evaluation by specialists in pediatrics, child neurology, and child neuropsychology. More often than not, if medication is indicated, it will be of a type quite different than what is used in the management of so-called ADHD.

Furthermore, treatment intervention and case management will likely involve skilled educational training of the specialized type developed for use with the brain-injured child. In the case of a friendly pediatrician, a concerned psychologist, or a caring child psychiatrist, any or all attempting unilaterally to diagnose and/or manage the treatment regimen, the concerned and caring parent is well advised to promptly seek additional opinions. For a comprehensive description of the type of evaluation that is most productive in the management of children of this kind.

# CHALLENGE QUESTIONS

## Is Attention-Deficit Hyperactivity Disorder (ADHD) a Real Disorder?

1. According to these authors, how does normal distractibility differ from disordered distractibility? What motivations might some people have to label normal distractibility as a disorder?
2. Wright argues that medication can often create problems whereas NIMH suggests that medication might be necessary to treat ADHD. What are the risks and benefits of pharmacological treatment? What are the risks and benefits of eschewing pharmacological treatment?
3. Based on your readings, do you believe that ADHD is a real disorder? Why or why not? What does it mean if ADHD is or is not a real disorder?
4. There are many people involved in the question of ADHD's legitimacy as a disorder, including children themselves, parents, doctors, psychologists, politicians, and the media. Who should decide whether ADHD is a real disorder? Might any of these groups have motives that could bias them toward one conclusion or the other?

# ISSUE 13

## Does Taking Antidepressants Lead to Suicide?

**YES: David Healy and Chris Whitaker**, from "Antidepressants and Suicide: Risk-Benefit Conundrums," *Journal of Psychiatry & Neuroscience* (September 2003)

**NO: Yvon D. Lapierre**, from "Suicidality with Selective Serotonin Reuptake Inhibitors: Valid Claim?" *Journal of Psychiatry & Neuroscience* (September 2003)

### ISSUE SUMMARY

**YES:** Psychiatrist David Healy and statistician Chris Whitaker argue that psychological research reveals a significant number of suicidal acts by individuals taking antidepressants and, thus, they recommend stricter controls on these drugs.

**NO:** In response, psychiatrist Yvon D. Lapierre maintains that the research on suicidality and antidepressants is unconvincing, recommending that conclusions from these findings should be severely limited.

Drugs for depression have become so familiar and are used so frequently in our society that their safety has been almost taken for granted. It was surprising, then, when recent research findings seemed to indicate that suicide is a possible effect of a certain class of antidepressants—specifically, selective serotonin reuptake inhibitors, or SSRIs. Almost immediately, the defenders of these drugs offered another explanation: These findings are the result of an increase in the number people with depression and not an effect of anti-depressants. In other words, because suicide is a risk for people with depression, an increase in the number of depressed people accounts for the increase in the number of suicides.

The problem is that the Food and Drug Administration (FDA) does not seem to agree with this explanation. Recently, it ordered manufacturers of all antidepressants, not just SSRIs, to include a "black box" warning on their labels—the most serious caution the government can require. This warning alerts people to the increased risk of suicide among children and adolescents taking antidepressant medication. This move by the FDA means the U.S. government believes that current evidence is sufficient to take serious action. Some health professionals fear that people might misinterpret this serious action and resist seeking treatment for depression altogether.

The first article supports the FDA decision. Looking at figures from randomized controlled trials (RCTs)—the gold-standard of research designs—David Healy and Chris Whitaker found too many suicidal acts among people on antidepressants, especially when compared with people using placebos (drugs that have no treatment effect). While the authors agree these studies show that SSRIs do reduce suicidality in some patients, they argue that there is a net increase in suicidal acts associated with their use. In other words, more people are ultimately harmed than helped. Still, Healy and Whitaker do not recommend that people stop taking antidepressants. They do, however, believe that warnings and monitoring of antidepressants are necessary to reduce the overall risk of suicide.

In response, Yvon D. Lapierre disagrees with Healy and Whitaker's contention that antidepressants increase the risk of suicide. He notes the number of methodological problems and biases with the studies Healy and Whitaker used to support their conclusions. He also points to other studies that just as strongly indicate that suicidal thoughts are lessened by the same drugs. He admits that the research as a whole has yielded mixed findings. Still, this is all the more reason to avoid hastily concluding that antidepressants lead to suicide. The conclusions of Healy and Whitaker, therefore, are premature.

**POINT**

- Studies show an increase in suicidal acts when people take antidepressants.
- Studies that claim a reduction of suicidality in some patients ignore how the same treatment can produce suicidality in others.
- Clinicians should be more vigilant and restrict treatment for those most at risk for suicide.
- Consumers and clinicians should be warned about the dangers of antidepressants.

**COUNTERPOINT**

- The inherent biases of these studies decrease the ability to draw valid conclusions.
- Studies strongly suggest that antidepressants decrease suicidal thoughts in some patients.
- Suicide is already recognized among clinicians as a major risk of depression.
- Because results of clinical studies are inconclusive, more research should be conducted before serious action is taken.

YES 

**David Healy and Chris Whitaker**

# Antidepressants and Suicide: Risk–Benefit Conundrums

## Introduction

. . . The debate regarding selective serotonin reuptake inhibitors (SSRIs) and suicide started in 1990, when Teicher, Glod and Cole described 6 cases in which intense suicidal preoccupation emerged during fluoxetine treatment. This paper was followed by others, which, combined, provided evidence of dose–response, challenge, dechallenge and rechallenge relations, as well as the emergence of an agreed mechanism by which the effects were mediated and demonstrations that interventions in the process could ameliorate the problems. A subsequent series of reports on the effects of sertraline and paroxetine on suicidality and akathisia pointed to SSRI-induced suicidality being a class effect rather than something confined to fluoxetine.

An induction of suicidality by SSRIs, therefore, had apparently been convincingly demonstrated according to conventional criteria for establishing cause and effect relations between drugs and adverse events, as laid out by clinical trial methodologists, company investigators, medico-legal authorities and the federal courts. Far less consistent evidence led the Medicines Control Agency in Britain in 1988 to state unambiguously that benzodiazepines can trigger suicide.

Specifically designed randomized controlled trials (RCTs) on depression-related suicidality at this time would have established the rates at which this seemingly new phenomenon might be happening. However, no such studies have ever been undertaken. This review, therefore, will in lieu cover the RCT data on newly released antidepressants and suicidal acts, the meta-analyses of efficacy studies in depression that have been brought to bear on the question and relevant epidemiological studies.

## Efficacy Studies

In lieu of specifically designed RCTs, the RCTs that formed the basis for the licence application for recent antidepressants are one source of data. Khan and colleagues recently analyzed RCT data to assess whether it was ethical to continue using placebos in antidepresant trials. Although the U.S. Food and Drug

From *Journal of Psychiatry & Neuroscience,* 28(5), September 2003, pp. 331–337 (refs. omitted). 

Administration (FDA), in general, recommends that data from clinical trials be analyzed both in terms of absolute numbers and patient exposure years (PEY), given that an assessment of the hazards posed by placebo was the object of this study, the investigators appropriately analyzed the figures in terms of PEY only. Khan et al. found an excess of suicidal acts by individuals taking antidepressants compared with placebo, and this was also replicated in another analysis, but the rates of suicidal acts in patients taking antidepressants and those taking placebo were not significantly different in these analyses. Yet, another study reported that rates of suicidal acts of patients taking antidepressants for longer durations may, in fact, fall relative to placebo, which might be expected because longer term studies will select patients suited to the agent being investigated.

Although an analysis in terms of PEYs may be appropriate for an assessment of the risk of exposure to placebo, it is inappropriate for the assessment of a problem that clinical studies had clearly linked to the first weeks of active therapy. An analysis of suicidal acts on the basis of duration of exposure systematically selects patients who do not have the problem under investigation, because those with the problem often drop out of the trial, whereas others who do well are kept on treatment for months or more on grounds of compassionate use.

The data presented by Khan and colleagues has accordingly been modified here in 4 respects (Table 1). First, suicides and suicidal acts are presented in terms of absolute numbers of patients. Second, on the basis of an FDA paroxetine safety review and FDA statistical reviews on sertraline, it is clear that some of the suicides and suicidal acts categorized as occurring while patients were taking placebo actually occurred during a placebo washout period; placebo and washout suicides are therefore distinguished here. Third, data for citalopram, from another article by Khan et al., are included (although no details about the validity of assignments to placebo are available). Fourth, fluoxetine data from public domain documents are presented, again dividing the data into placebo and washout period suicidal acts, along with data for venlafaxine.

When washout and placebo data are separated and analyzed in terms of suicidal acts per patient (excluding missing bupropion data) using an exact Mantel–Haenszel procedure with a 1-tailed test for significance, the odds ratio of a suicide while taking these new antidepressants as a group compared with placebo is 4.40 (95% confidence interval [CI] 1.32–infinity; $p = 0.0125$). The odds ratio for a suicidal act while taking these antidepressants compared with placebo is 2.39 (95% CI 1.66–infinity; $p \leq 0.0001$). The odds ratio for a completed suicide while taking an SSRI antidepressant (including venlafaxine) compared with placebo is 2.46 (95% CI 0.71–infinity; $p = 0.16$), and the odds ratio for a suicidal act while taking SSRIs compared with placebo is 2.22 (95% CI 1.47–infinity; $p \leq 0.001$).

If washout suicidal acts are included with placebo, as the companies appear to have done, but adjusting the denominator appropriately, the relative risk of suicidal acts while taking sertraline, paroxetine or fluoxetine compared with placebo becomes significant, with figures ranging from 3.0 for sertraline to over 10.0 for fluoxetine.

*Table 1*

**Incidence of Suicides and Suicide Attempts in Antidepressant Trials from Khan et al. and Kirsch et al.**

| Treatment | No. of Patients | No. of Suicides | No. of Suicide Attempts | Suicides and Attempts, % |
|---|---|---|---|---|
| Sertraline hydrochloride* | 2053 | 2 | 7 | 0.44 |
| Active comparator | 595 | 0 | 1 | 0.17 |
| Placebo | 786 | 0 | 2 | 0.25 |
| Placebo washout | | 0 | 3 | |
| Paroxetine hydrochloride* | 2963 | 5 | 40 | 1.52 |
| Active comparator | 1151 | 3 | 12 | 1.30 |
| Placebo | 554 | 0 | 3 | 0.54 |
| Placebo washout | | 2 | 2 | |
| Nefazodone hydrochloride | 3496 | 9 | 12 | 0.60 |
| Active comparator | 958 | 0 | 6 | 0.63 |
| Placebo | 875 | 0 | 1 | 0.11 |
| Mirtazapine | 2425 | 8 | 29 | 1.53 |
| Active comparator | 977 | 2 | 5 | 0.72 |
| Placebo | 494 | 0 | 3 | 0.61 |
| Bupropion hydrochloride | 1942 | 3 | — | |
| Placebo | 370 | 0 | — | |
| Citalopram* | 4168 | 8 | 91 | 2.38 |
| Placebo | 691 | 1 | 10 | 1.59 |
| Fluoxetine* | 1427 | 1 | 12 | 0.91 |
| Placebo | 370 | 0 | 0 | 0 |
| Placebo washout | | 1 | 0 | |
| Venlafaxine* | 3082 | 7 | 36 | 1.40 |
| Placebo | 739 | 1 | 2 | 0.41 |
| **All investigational drugs** | 21556 | 43 | 232 | 1.28 |
| **All SSRIs*** | 13693 | 23 | 186 | 1.53 |
| Active comparators | 3681 | 5 | 24 | 0.79 |
| Total placebo | 4879 | 2 | 21 | 0.47 |
| SSRI trial placebo | 3140 | 2 | 16 | 0.57 |

*SSRI = selective serotonin reuptake inhibitor.

Other data sets yield similar findings. For instance, in Pierre Fabre's clinical trial database of approximately 8000 patients, the rate for suicidal acts by those taking SSRIs appears to be 3 times the rate for other antidepressants. However, these other data sets include a mixture of trials. The current analysis limits the number of studies but ensures that they are roughly comparable, and the selection of studies is based on regulatory requirements rather than individual bias.

## Meta- and Other Analyses of SSRIs and Suicidal Acts

In addition to the RCT data indicating an excess of suicidal acts by those taking SSRIs, the clinical trials on zimelidine, the first SSRI, suggested there were more suicide attempts by patients taking it than by those taking comparators, but Montgomery and colleagues reported that although this might be the case, zimelidine appeared to do better than comparators in reducing already existing suicidal thoughts. A similar analysis demonstrated lower suicide attempt rates for those taking fluvoxamine than the comparators in clinical trials. Problems with paroxetine led to similar analyses and similar claims.

The best-known analysis of this type was published by Eli Lilly after the controversy with fluoxetine emerged; from the analysis of pooled data from 17 double-blind clinical trials in patients with major depressive disorder, the authors concluded that "data from these trials do not show that fluoxetine is associated with an increased risk of suicidal acts or emergence of substantial suicidal thoughts among depressed patients." There are a number of methodological problems with Lilly's analysis, however, and these apply to some extent to all other such exercises. First, none of the studies in the analysis were designed to test whether fluoxetine could be associated with the emergence of suicidality. In the case of fluoxetine, all of the studies had been conducted before concerns of suicide induction had arisen. Some of the studies used in the analysis had, in fact, been rejected by the FDA. Second, only 3067 patients of the approximately 26,000 patients entered into clinical trials of fluoxetine were included in this meta-analysis. Third, no mention was made of the fact that benzodiazepines had been coprescribed in the clinical trial program to minimize the agitation that Lilly recognized fluoxetine could cause. Fourth, no reference was made to the 5% of patients who dropped out because of anxiety and agitation. Given that this was arguably the very problem that was at the heart of the issue, the handling of this issue was not reassuring. The 5% dropout rate for agitation or akathisia holds true for other SSRIs as well, and the differences between SSRIs and placebo are statistically significant. Given that the *Diagnostic and Statistical Manual of Mental Disorders, fourth edition, text revision* (DSM-IV-TR) has connected akathisia with suicide risk, this point is of importance.

Finally, this and other analyses depend critically on item 3 (i.e., suicide) of the Hamilton Rating Scale for Depression; this approach to the problem is one that FDA officials, Lilly personnel and Lilly's consultants agreed was methodologically unsatisfactory. The argument in these meta-analyses has, broadly speaking, been that in the randomized trials, the SSRI reduced suicidality on item 3 and that there was no emergence of suicidality, as measured by this item. To claim that the prevention of or reduction of suicidality in some patients in some way means that treatment cannot produce suicidality in others is a logical non sequitur. The argument that item 3 would pick up emergent suicidality in studies run by clinicians who are not aware of this possible adverse effect has no evidence to support it.

Despite these methodological caveats, the claim that SSRIs reduce suicidality in some patients appears strong. However, insofar as SSRIs reduce suicidal acts in some, if there is a net increase in suicidal acts associated with SSRI treatment in these same trials, the extent to which SSRIs cause problems for some patients must be greater than is apparent from considering the raw data.

## Epidemiological Studies

Epidemiology traditionally involves the study of representative samples of the population and requires a specification of the methods used to make the sample representative. A series of what have been termed epidemiological studies have been appealed to in this debate. The first is a 1-column letter involving no suicides. The second is a selective retrospective postmarketing chart review involving no suicides, which analyzed by the American College of Neuropsychopharmacology, the FDA and others, shows a 3-fold increased relative risk of emergent suicidality for fluoxetine versus other antidepressants.

A third study was conducted by Warshaw and Keller on patients with anxiety disorder, in which the only suicide was committed by a patient taking fluoxetine. However, only 192 of the 654 patients in this study received fluoxetine. This, therefore, was not a study designed to test fluoxetine's capacity to induce suicidality. In a fourth study of 643 patients, conceived 20 years before fluoxetine was launched and instituted 10 years before launch, only 185 patients received fluoxetine at any point. This was clearly not a study designed to establish whether fluoxetine might induce suicidality. None of these studies fit the definition of epidemiology offered above.

Although not properly epidemiological, 2 post-marketing surveillance studies that compared SSRI with non-SSRI antidepressants found a higher rate of induction of suicidal ideation for those taking SSRIs, although not in the rates of suicidal acts or suicides.

In a more standard epidemiological study of 222 suicides, Donovan et al. reported that 41 of those suicides were committed by people who had been taking an antidepressant in the month before their suicide; there was a statistically significant doubling of the relative risk of suicide in those taking SSRIs compared with tricyclic antidepressants. In a further epidemiological study of 2776 acts of deliberate self-harm, Donovan et al. found a doubling of the risk for deliberate self-harm for those taking SSRIs compared with other antidepressants.

A set of post-marketing surveillance studies carried out in primary care in the United Kingdom by the Drug Safety Research Unit (DSRU) recorded 110 suicides in over 50,000 patients being treated by general practitioners in Britain. The DSRU methodology has since been applied to mirtazapine, where there have been 13 suicides reported in a population of 13,554 patients. This permits the comparisons outlined in Table 2.

A further study from British primary care was undertaken by Jick and colleagues, who investigated the rate and means of suicide among people taking common antidepressants. They reported 143 suicides among 172,580 patients taking antidepressants and found a statistically significant doubling of the relative risk of suicide with fluoxetine compared with the reference antidepressant, dothiepin, when calculated in terms of patient exposure years.

*Table 2*

**Drug Safety Research Unit Studies of Selective Serotonin Reuptake Inhibitors (SSRIs) and Mirtazapine in Primary Care Practice in the United Kingdom**

| Drug | No. of Patients | No. of Suicides | Suicides/100,000 Patients (and 95% confidence interval) | |
|---|---|---|---|---|
| Fluoxetine | 12692 | 31 | 244 | (168–340) |
| Sertraline | 12734 | 22 | 173 | (110–255) |
| Paroxetine | 13741 | 37 | 269 | (192–365) |
| Fluvoxamine | 10983 | 20 | 182 | (114–274) |
| Total SSRIs | 50150 | 110 | 219 | |
| Mirtazapine | 13554 | 13 | 96 | (53–158) |

Controlling for confounding factors such as age, sex and previous suicide attempts left the relative risk at 2.1 times greater for fluoxetine than for dothiepin and greater than any other antidepressant studied, although statistical significance was lost in the process. Of further note are the elevated figures for mianserin and trazodone, which are closely related pharmacologically to mirtazapine and nefazodone. Controlling for confounding factors in the case of mianserin and trazodone, however, led to a reduction in the relative risk of these agents compared with dothiepin.

To provide comparability with other figures, I have recalculated these data in terms of absolute numbers and separated the data for fluoxetine (Table 3). The data in the Jick study, however, only allow comparisons between antidepressants. They shed no light on the differences between treatment with antidepressants and non-treatment or on the efficacy of antidepressants in reducing suicide risk in primary care. The traditional figures with which the DSRU studies and the Jick study might be compared are a 15% lifetime risk for suicide for affective disorders. This would be inappropriate, however, because this 15% figure was derived from patients with melancholic depression in hospital in the pre-antidepressant era.

There are very few empirical figures available for suicide rates in primary care depression, the sample from which the Jick et al. and DSRU data come. One study from Sweden reports a suicide rate of 0 per 100,000 patients in non-hospitalized depression. Another primary care study from the Netherlands gives a suicide rate of 33 per 100,000 patient years. Finally, Simon and VonKorff in a study of suicide mortality among individuals treated for depression in Puget Sound, Wash., reported 36 suicides in 62,159 patient years. The suicide risk per 100,000 patient years was 64 among those who received outpatient specialty mental health treatment, 43 among those treated with antidepressant medications in primary care and 0 among those treated in primary care without antidepressants.

*Table 3*

**Suicides Rates of Patients Taking Antidepressants in Primary Care Settings in the United Kingdom***

| Drug | Suicides/100,000 Patients (and 95% CI) | | No. Suicides/No. Patients |
|---|---|---|---|
| Dothiepin | 70 | (53–91) | 52/74 340 |
| Lofepramine | 26 | (8–61) | 4/15 177 |
| Amitriptyline | 60 | (41–84) | 29/48 580 |
| Clomipramine | 80 | (38–144) | 9/11 239 |
| Impiramine | 47 | (20–90) | 7/15 009 |
| Doxepin | 69 | (17–180) | 3/4 329 |
| Flupenthixol | 78 | (43–129) | 13/16 599 |
| Trazodone | 99 | (31–230) | 4/4049 |
| Mianserin | 166 | (86–285) | 11/6609 |
| Fluoxetine | 93 | | 11/11 860 |
| **Total excluding fluoxetine** | **67** | | **132/195 931** |

*Note:* CI = confidence interval.

* From jick et al.

Utilizing a database of 2.5 million person years and 212 suicides from North Staffordshire, Boardman and Healy modeled the rate for suicide in treated or untreated depression and found it to be of the order of 68/100,000 patient years for all affective disorders. This rate gives an upper limit on the suicide rate in mood disorders that is compatible with observed national rates of suicide in the United Kingdom. Boardman and Healy estimate a rate of 27 suicides per 100,000 patients per annum for primary care primary affective disorders. Possible relative risks for SSRIs from the DSRU studies set against these figures and the findings from the Jick study for all antidepressants excluding fluoxetine are presented in Table 4.

Comparing the figures for SSRIs from Table 2 with those for the non-SSRI antidepressants from the Jick study gives a mean figure for non-SSRI antidepressants of 68 suicides per 100,000 patients exposed compared with a figure of 212 suicides for the SSRI group. Based on an analysis of 249,803 exposures to antidepressants, therefore, the broad relative risk on SSRI antidepressants compared with non-SSRI antidepressants or even non-treatment is 234/68 or 3.44.

There are 2 points of note. First, these low rates for suicide in untreated primary care mood disorder populations are consistent with the rate of 0 suicides in those taking placebo in antidepressant RCTs. Second, correcting the DSRU figures for exposure lengths gives figures for suicides on sertraline and paroxetine comparable to those reported from RCTs by Khan et al.

*Table 4*

**Relative Risk (RR) of Suicide While Taking SSRIs (from DSRU Studies) Compared with General Risk of Suicide in UK Primary Care Primary Affective Disorders and in UK Primary Care Depression Treated with Non-SSRI Antidepressants**

| Drug | RR from DSRU Sample Compared with Primary Care Sample | RR from DSRU Sample Compared with Primary Care Depression Sample Treated with Non-SSRI Antidepressants |
|---|---|---|
| Sertraline | 6.4 | 2.54 |
| Fluoxetine | 9.2 | 3.59 |
| Paroxetine | 10.2 | 3.96 |
| **Total SSRI** | **8.3** | **3.44** |

*Note:* DSRU = Drug Safely Research Unit.

## Conclusion

Since antidepressant drug treatments were introduced, there have been concerns that their use may lead to suicide. Hitherto, there has been a legitimate public health concern that the debate about possible hazards might deter people at risk from suicide from seeking treatment, possibly leading to an increased number of suicides. The data reviewed here, however, suggest that warnings and monitoring are more likely to reduce overall risks or that at least we should adopt a position of clinical equipoise on this issue and resolve it by means of further study rather than on the basis of speculation.

The evidence that antidepressants may reduce suicide risk is strong from both clinical practice and RCTs. An optimal suicide reduction strategy would probably involve the monitored treatment of all patients and some restriction of treatment for those most at risk of suicide. In addition, given evidence that particular personality types suit particular selective agents and that mismatching patients and treatments can cause problems, further exploration of this area would seem called for.

**Yvon D. Lapierre**

# Suicidality with Selective Serotonin Reuptake Inhibitors: Valid Claim?

## Introduction

. . . A plethora of new antidepressants followed the introduction of the selective serotonin reuptake inhibitors (SSRIs) with the associated claims of their relative innocuity compared with the previous generation of tricyclics antidepressants (TCAs) and monoamine oxidase inhibitors. These claims seem to have reached their high point, and SSRIs as well as other antidepressants are now undergoing a second phase of critical review. This reappraisal of antidepressants addresses not only the claims of efficacy but also those related to side effects and to the toxicological profiles of the old as well as of the newer products. These have challenged long-held views and have brought to light new findings that would most likely not have come about otherwise. Invariably, in such circumstances, the pendular shift of attitudes can easily lead to exaggerated claims toward the negative and unwanted effects to the point of discarding previously demonstrated positive findings. It is then necessary to have a critical and balanced expression of opinions and analytic reviews of the available data to arrive at a just appraisal of reality.

The risk of suicide has remained at around 15% in patients with mental disorders, with only a marginal decline of suicide rate since the advent of antidepressants. Over 50% of those who commit suicide have an associated mood disorder, which is usually depression. Long-term follow-up shows that this is more pronounced in unipolar depressives and that treatment lessens the risk somewhat, but it still remains above the norm.

One considerably controversial issue has been the risk of suicide in relation to SSRI antidepressants. The issue arose from a series of case reports of patients who developed intense suicidal preoccupations and intense thoughts of self-harm while taking antidepressants. The initial reports implicated fluoxetine, and this was followed by reports suggesting a similar phenomenon with other SSRIs, thus leading to the speculation of a class effect.

Retrospective analyses of some randomized controlled trials (RCTs) on SSRIs suggest that the incidence of suicide may be higher in patients undergoing treatment with this new class of antidepressant, but any conclusion is still

From *Journal of Psychiatry & Neuroscience,* vol. 28, no. 5, September 2003, pp. 340–347 (refs. omitted). 

uncertain. This leads to the purpose of this duo of papers (Healy and Whitaker and this one), where facts may be submitted to different views and interpretation. Healy and Whitaker's contention is that SSRIs are conductive to an increased risk of suicide; this author disagrees.

The first question that arises is whether there is a temporal cause–effect relation between the administration of a specific drug and the development of suicidal ideation and of suicide. The order of such a cause and effect relation may then be examined and attributed, if applicable, as either a primary drug effect, a paradoxical drug effect, an expected side effect of the drug or, finally, an action that may be secondary to a side effect of the compound. A second issue to be addressed is whether this effect is drug specific or class specific. The question of validity of any imputed causality must be critically re-evaluated throughout this process. Once these issues are clarified, strategies that would improve the outcome of treatment for patients with depression may arise.

This paper will address the problem by first looking at issues of efficacy and suicide data and then discussing the case for the alleged link between suicide and SSRI and other antidepressant therapies.

## Efficacy Issues

The efficacy of a widely used intervention may be evaluated by assessing its impact on the population at large through epidemiological approaches and then on the experiences obtained from clinical trials and clinical practice.

Epidemiological observations suggest that there has been a gradual increase in the incidence of depression in post-World War II generations. There are indications that this illness will become an ever-increasing burden of disability in Western societies. Given that depression is the predominant risk factor for suicide, one would expect that with the increased numbers of depressed individuals, there would be an increase in suicide rates. Furthermore, if there is validity to the claim that SSRIs play a causative role in suicide, there would be an even greater increase in suicide rates since the advent of these drugs. Although this may not have materialized as such, these speculations are not necessarily dismissed as being completely invalid.

Epidemiological studies on the issue of antidepressant treatment and suicide have been conducted in a number of countries. In Italy, there was found to be a possible relation between increased SSRI use from 1988 to 1996 and suicide rate. There was a slight increase in suicide rates for men but a more pronounced decrease for women; however, these changes were not significant. In Sweden, from 1976 to 1996, increased utilization of antidepressants paralleled a decrease in suicide rates. In Finland, the increased use of SSRIs coincided with a decrease in suicide mortality, as well as with an increase in the incidence of fatal overdoses with TCAs. The tricyclics accounted for 82% of suicides by antidepressant overdose.

In the National Institute of Mental Health Collaborative Depression Study, Leon et al. assessed the possibility of an increased suicidal risk associated with the SSRI fluoxetine. In the 185 patients in follow-up, there was a trend for a decrease in the number of suicide attempts compared with patients receiving other treatments. Although this cohort was at higher risk because of a history of repeated suicide attempts, treatment with fluoxetine resulted in a nonsignificant reduction of attempts in these patients.

The findings of these epidemiological studies do not provide any indication that the use of antidepressants, and more specifically SSRIs, contribute to an increased risk of suicide in population bases or in depressed populations.

The main sources of information on psychopharmacological agents are the data from clinical trials. Then, post-marketing studies are intended to provide the alerts on safety and potentially new indications for the drug. Both of these sources have limitations and biases, however, inevitably adding fuel to the present debate.

Given that RCTs are designed to primarily identify clinical efficacy and acute or short-term safety of antidepressants, there are limitations on the gathering of exhaustive data on unwanted side effects. The selection of patients for an RCT generally excludes those who are considered to be at risk for suicide. This is usually determined clinically, and the judgment is based on clinical indicators that have, in past experience, been associated with increased risk. Up to 80% of depressed patients may experience thoughts of suicide, and there is a greater than 15% risk of suicide with depression, making the elucidation of suicidal thoughts and intent increasingly relevant to a valid assessment of risk.

This rationale is based on the premise that suicidal ideation is the precursor to and is likely to lead to suicidal acting out. Suicidal acts in the recent past, as well as a number of other associated factors, contribute to the evaluation of risk and the decision of inclusion or exclusion. This inevitably leads to a skewed population, where those appearing to be most clearly at risk and those more severely depressed are often excluded.

The experimental design most often used is a single-blind placebo-washout phase followed by a double-blind randomized phase with a placebo control, a standard active treatment control and an experimental treatment arm. Because of the pressures against the use of placebo in RCTs, as well as cost considerations, there is a trend toward having unbalanced groups, with fewer subjects in the placebo and control arms. This results in reduced statistical power and the need for more patients in the studies and has contributed to increasing numbers of multicentre trials to meet these and other exigencies.

The end point of an RCT is time limited, and the criteria of successful outcome are based on clinical evaluations that of necessity are quantified using rating scales and focus on the immediate objective. They then have limited retrospective applicability and intrinsic limitations when explored retroactively for other purposes. This does not necessarily invalidate subsequent retrospective studies, but one must consider that there are limits on conclusions that can be reached because of these limitations and other biases. To mention but a few that may be relevant to the issue at hand, patient selection, diagnostic considerations and statistical limitations come to mind.

A similar pattern of biases occurs in post-marketing surveillance studies. The source of data varies from one jurisdiction to the next, as do the methods and obligations to report adverse events. Clinicians are known to adopt different prescribing patterns for patients presenting more severe states of depression and for those considered to be at greater risk for suicide. The former group are more likely to receive a TCA, whereas the latter are more likely to receive a "safer-in-overdose" SSRI. Thus, a significant bias in patient selection arises in the evaluation of suicidal risk under one form of treatment or another.

Suicidality and suicide should be distinguished. Thoughts of suicide are not uncommon in the general population but become problematic if they are too frequent, intense or commanding and lead to greater risk of acting on the ideation. Most suicides are preceded by increases in suicidal ideation. Thus, this becomes an important consideration in the assessment of suicide risk. On the other hand, suicidal ideation as such cannot be totally equated to suicidal behaviour.

Conditions favourable to acting on the ideation, such as increased impulsivity or a high level of anxiety and agitation, increase the risk of suicide. The suicidal tendencies item of the Hamilton Rating Scale for Depression is the instrument for quantification of suicidality in RCTs. It allows for a certain degree of quantification on the seriousness of suicidal tendencies and emphasizes mainly suicidal ideation as such. It is not meant to clearly discriminate and quantify the nuances of suicidality to allow for definitive conclusions to be drawn on the severity of the suicidal risk. However, it is probably the most widely used rating scale for RCTs on depression and has become the standard instrument for the analysis of the many features of this illness and for assessing change at different intervals during a clinical trial.

Meta-analyses of RCTs have yielded conflicting results. The short duration of RCTs, which are the basis of these meta-analyses, may not provide valid long-term data, but they do contribute to an understanding of acute therapeutic effects. There is an inherent deficiency in meta-analyses because of the intrinsic limitations of post hoc analyses. Nevertheless, a few of these reports suggested that fluoxetine was associated with a greater incidence of suicidal thoughts. This was followed by other reports suggesting that sertraline, fluvoxamine, paroxetine and citalopram produced similar effects. This led to the speculation of a class effect of SSRIs. On the other hand, there are meta-analytic and other types of studies that just as strongly suggest that emergent suicidal ideation was lessened by these same SSRIs. In the Verkes et al. study, the findings are more convincing because of the high-risk population involved. Others have suggested that, not only do SSRIs reduce suicidal ideation, but the symptom is increased in patients taking norepinephrine reuptake inhibitors.

A meta-analytic study of treatment with fluoxetine, tricyclic antidepressants are placebo in large samples of patients with mood disorders ($n$ = 5655) and non-mood disorders ($n$ = 4959) did not identify statistically significant differences in emergent suicidal thoughts between groups, and there were no suicides in the non-mood disorder group. These data do not support a suicidogenic effect of SSRIs or TCAs.

Firm conclusions on suicidality and SSRIs based on these findings should be guarded at this point. Suffice it to say that the evidence to suggest that SSRIs generally reduce suicidality is more convincing than that supporting the contrary.

## Suicide

The risk of a depressed patient committing suicide with prescribed antidepressants has been a long-standing concern of clinicians treating depressed patients. This was particularly significant with the older generation tricyclics and was one reason to advocate the use of the newer agents (because of their reported lower lethal potential in overdose). On the other hand, it is surprisingly rare for patients to use prescribed antidepressants for suicidal purposes. Data on the agents used for suicide from a number of countries suggest that only about 5% of overdoses are with antidepressants (range 1%–8%). An outlier appears to be the United Kingdom, with reports of 14%. Men commit suicide by overdose much less frequently than women. An important finding in these reports is that patients tend to use previously prescribed, undiscarded antidepressants as their drug of choice. This points to the important role of therapeutic failure in a number of patients who commit suicide.

The advent of the SSRIs brought a renewed impetus in physician and public education on depressive disorders to not only raise professional and public awareness of depression but also publicize the profile of the new antidepressants in their treatment. This, in addition to other factors, has led to many of these educational activities being sponsored by the pharmaceutical industry, with the inevitable ensuing risk of bias. These efforts have certainly contributed to a heightened awareness of depression by professionals and to less reluctance in using antidepressants because of improved safety profiles with equivalent efficacy.

Although antidepressants have been pivotal in the treatment of depression for more than 4 decades, a number of unanswered questions remain. The therapeutic superiority of antidepressants has been taken for granted despite the inconsistent robustness in many controlled studies, where their superiority over placebo is not always clearly demonstrated. Recent data on the latest generation of antidepressants, the SSRIs and serotonin–norepinephrine reuptake inhibitors suggest that only 48% of placebo-controlled studies show a consistent statistically significant superiority of the antidepressant over placebo. This figure may be inferior to the generally accepted greater success rate and emphasizes the need for individualized therapeutic strategies. This becomes critical for poor responders, where the limitations of available treatments become obvious. Depression is the main risk factor for suicide, the final and fatal outcome of non-response to treatment. If, as is suggested by some, the risk of suicide is increased by antidepressants, which are considered to be the cornerstone and most widely accepted treatment for depression, the use of such agents would obviously necessitate a critical re-evaluation.

Suicidality and suicidal actions induced de novo by SSRIs was suggested by a few clinical papers that followed Teicher's initial case report. Because of the paradoxical nature of these observations, a number of retrospective analyses of large cohorts were then conducted. The analyses of the US Food and Drug Administration database by Kahn et al. looked at suicidality and suicide rates in a cohort of 23,201 patients participating in clinical trials of antidepressants. Overall suicide rates for patients were 627/100,000 compared with a general population rate of 11/100,000. There were no significant differences between rates for placebo, comparator drugs and new-generation investigational drugs. The mortality rates ranged from 0.19% for placebo to 0.14% for the investigational drugs and 0.11% for the active comparators. There were no significant differences in patient exposure years between these 3 groups, although the numerical values were higher for the antidepressant groups. The attempted suicide rate ranged from 0.66% for the investigational drugs to 1.37% for the comparators to 1.39% for placebo (no significant differences). Patient exposure years also did not differ significantly. These findings do not provide information on the duration of exposure to treatment but include the data on all patients who participated in the trials and are thus quite representative of short-term studies. Patient exposure years, which cumulates the duration of treatment and the number of patients treated, did not show differences either. These data do not support the suggestion that SSRIs add to suicide risk.

A similar study was done in the Netherlands by Storosum et al. on data submitted to the Medicines Evaluation Board of the Netherlands for 12,246 patients treated in short-term (< 8 wk) clinical trials. Attempts at suicide occurred in 0.4% of patients in both placebo and active drug groups. Completed suicide occurred in 0.1% of patients in both placebo and active treatment groups. In longer-term studies (> 8 wk) involving 1949 patients, attempted suicide occurred in 0.7% of patients in both groups, and completed suicides occurred in 0.2% (2 patients) of the active drug group (no significant difference). These results also do not support a suicidogenic effect of these antidepressants.

Donovan et al. reviewed 222 suicides that occurred in a 4-year period in 3 different regions of the United Kingdom. Of these, 83% had been diagnosed with depression in the past and 56% had been prescribed antidepressants in the previous year; 41 had been prescribed a TCA and 13 an SSRI within 1 month of their suicide, and these formed the main cohort of the study. On the basis of the relative proportion of prescriptions in these regions, the authors concluded that the risk of suicide is greater with SSRIs than with TCAs. An important variable that may have skewed these findings is that those taking SSRIs included most of the patients who had a recent history of deliberate self harm, which in itself is recognized as an important predictor of suicide. It is thus difficult to make any definitive conclusions from these findings because the inherent biases in patient selection for treatment force the results and conclusions.

More recently, Oquendo et al. reported on 136 depressed patients who were discharged from hospital after a major depressive episode and were followed in community settings for 24 months; 15% of patients attempted suicide during the 2 years, and 50% of these attempts occurred during the first 5 months of follow-up. Treatment was in a naturalistic setting and was monitored regularly. The medications administered were mainly the new-generation antidepressants. A critical review of the dosage administered considered it to be adequate in only 9 (43%) of the patients at the time of attempted suicide. Four of these patients had relapsed into a recurrence of depression. These findings elicit a number of questions such as the importance of treatment resistance, history of suicide attempts, components of adequate treatment, adequacy of drug treatment and compliance.

The case put forth in the first of this duo of papers is beguiling. It is indeed seductive to use legal precedents and the court of public opinion to evaluate the scientific merit and withdrawal of a therapeutic agent. However, it remains paramount that methodology not be changed to lead to selective data. For this reason, it is not appropriate in these instances to allow the bias introduced by separating placebo washout out of the trial data, especially if "intent to treat" and last observation carried forward data are to serve as the basis of outcome analyses.

It is not appropriate to agree with the statement that clinicians would not be vigilant to the risk of suicide in antidepressant RCTs, because suicide is universally recognized as the major complication of depression. Although antidepressant RCTs are not designed to evaluate suicide risk, disregarding the data generated is as inappropriate as disregarding the data collected for the study's designed purpose.

## Discussion

SSRI antidepressants as a class are among the most frequently prescribed drugs in the Western world. Their applications have broadened from their initial indication in depression to a number of other psychiatric conditions such as obsessive–compulsive disorder, generalized anxiety disorder and, more recently, late luteal phase disorder. This provides a wide spectrum of conditions under which the SSRIs are administered and allows for a much broader clinical experience for the appraisal of the drugs in question. There have not been any reports of suicide in patients taking SSRIs for these other conditions.

Suicide is a leading public health problem in all societies. It is estimated that known suicides account for 1 million deaths worldwide annually. Given that depression is a significant factor in nearly 50% of these cases, the treatment of depression merits critical appraisal, especially if this treatment contributes further to suicidal behaviour, as has been suggested. This partly explains the reaction to the initial reports of increased suicidality during treatment with fluoxetine and then with the other SSRIs. These reports have led to a healthy second look at the available data and to the pursuit of additional studies and observations.

Clinical studies and meta-analyses indicate that an overwhelming number of patients experience a decrease in suicidal ideation while taking SSRIs. The fact that these meta-analyses were based on data collected primarily to demonstrate efficacy does not diminish their validity. Although the method of evaluation has been criticized (i.e., a single item on the HAM-D) and the evidence of decreased suicidality admittedly not highly nuanced, the data still reflect the observed clinical reality. A decrease in suicidality must be considered to reflect an improvement in the depressed condition.

Despite the availability of less toxic antidepressant drugs, the increasing use of antidepressants has not consistently been associated with a significant decline in suicide rates. As the SSRIs gain popularity, the use of the older TCAs as instruments of suicide by overdose has decreased. However, other more violent means are resorted to, thus indirectly reducing the positive safety impact of the SSRIs. It would be simplistic to make conclusions on single causality in suicidal behaviour without recognizing the complexities of the behaviour and circumstances that lead to the outcome.

Although evidence from large studies points to a reduction in suicidal ideation, the few reports of the appearance of intense suicidal thoughts in a few patients must not pass unnoticed. There were sporadic reports of suicidality with zimelidine, the first SSRI. This did not hold up to statistical testing and, because the drug was discontinued shortly after being launched, there was no follow-up. There were no major concerns at this time because most patients experienced an improvement in suicidal thoughts. A sporadic paradoxical effect to a psychotropic agent is a well-known phenomenon. It is well documented with antipsychotic agents such as the phenothiazines, where excitement and even worsening of the psychotic disorder have been observed. These are rare events but must be kept in mind so they will be recognized when they do occur. It is also essential to recognize that the emergence of suicidal thoughts may simply be attributable to underlying psychopathology.

Studies of fluoxetine have reported that this drug, in addition to causing some increase in agitation in some patients, may also cause akathisia. High levels of anxiety and agitation are known to accompany increased suicidal behaviour. In such a situation, the behaviour would be secondary to a side effect of the drug, rather than to its primary action.

Post hoc studies have intrinsic limitations but can shed some light on the understanding of this issue. The findings of Donovan and colleagues suggest that the increased risk of suicide is to a great extent explained by patient selection in some clinical studies. They did not factor in deliberate self-harm in the attribution of patients in their study. The increased risk of suicidality in patients with a history of repeated deliberate self-harm is well known. Even if these patients had been screened as not being actively suicidal at the onset of a trial, they were nevertheless still at higher risk subsequently. This type of susceptibility bias was very much present in the Leon et al. study and in that by Donovan et al.

A common deficiency in many studies of the treatment of depression is a consideration of unipolarity or bipolarity. The latter is readily missed for a number of reasons but, because the condition is not uncommon and requires adapted treatment with mood stabilizers, a greater risk of suicide may appear in these patients than in undertreated patients.

Despite anecdotal reports implicating most of the SSRIs, a drug-specific or class effect is not substantiated. Unfortunately, SSRIs have not been compared critically with other classes of antidepressants. On the other hand, the common pharmacological action of serotonin reuptake inhibition does not explain all of the actions of these drugs. A comparison of fluoxetine with its activating properties and citalopram with its more sedating profile illustrates the different effects SSRIs can have. Fluoxetine is known to occasionally cause some agitation. This may be experienced independently from akathisia which may, albeit rarely, also result from fluoxetine. The combination of the 2 (i.e, akathisia and agitation) has been associated with increased suicidal tendencies in depressed patients, but it is unlikely that this would support a class effect or phenomenon. It is more likely a consequence of a rare side effect of the drug.

A pharmacological explanation for a rare event is difficult to establish because it is, by definition, unpredictable. However, it is not beyond the realm of possibility and merits further exploration, although it is unlikely to attract interest simply because of the rarity of the event and the unpredictability of a host of variables.

## Conclusion

Any conclusions based on these few reports of sporadic cases of increased suicidality with SSRIs must be limited and highly tentative. The most these cases can suggest is an individual paradoxical effect, and these can be compared with the large number of patients who experience a diminution of suicidality and an improvement in depression. Another significant factor is that as the use of these antidepressants has broadened, the initial reports have not been followed by an increasing number of cases. Results of clinical studies are inconclusive, with some supporting a link and others refuting one. However, the awareness of the possibility of increased suicidality with SSRI treatment must be taken in the context of the risk of suicide in treating depression with any other antidepressant. Suicide is an inherent risk in the context of depression but this should not deter from adequate treatment.

A review of this issue serves as a reminder of the basic principles of good therapeutics that recommend that the complete profile of the drug be taken into account when selecting a pharmacotherapeutic agent. Once the primary (desired) and secondary (unwanted or not) effects have been fully considered, the total profile of the drug can be tailored to the clinical profile of an individual patient.

The newer SSRI antidepressants were never considered to be superior in efficacy to the TCAs, but their entry into the therapeutics of depression has reduced the risk of iatrogenic intoxication and, most likely, the overall risk of suicidal outcome in adequately treated patients. There is, at this time, insufficient evidence to claim that they lead to suicide.

# CHALLENGE QUESTIONS

## Does Taking Antidepressants Lead to Suicide?

1. How would you account for the major differences in the results of the studies that Healy/Whitaker and Lapierre present?
2. From the data presented, do you think antidepressants pose a risk for suicide? Support your answer.
3. If you were the parent of a child, under what circumstances would you permit him or her to take antidepressants? Justify your answer with information from the two articles.
4. One of the issues that separates these two sets of authors is whether the data are "sufficient." Interview two faculty members from the psychology department to find out how they would know when the data are sufficient for action, such as the black box warning on antidepressants.
5. There was some discussion about taking SSRI drugs off the market when the potential for suicide was revealed. Why do you think the FDA did not do so? Do you agree? Support your opinion.

# ISSUE 14

## Do Brain Deficiencies Determine Learning Disabilities?

**YES: Sally E. Shaywitz and Bennett A. Shaywitz**, from "Reading Disability and the Brain," *Educational Leadership* (March 2004)

**NO: Gerald Coles**, from "Danger in the Classroom: 'Brain Glitch' Research and Learning to Read," *Phi Delta Kappan* (January 2004)

### ISSUE SUMMARY

**YES:** Sally and Bennett Shaywitz, codirectors of the National Institute of Child Health and Human Development, suggest that reading disabilities stem from "brain glitches".

**NO:** Educational psychologist Gerald Coles believes that learning "disabilities" come from myriad sources, and each source needs to be considered when diagnosing and treating disabilities.

The prominent federal program No Child Left Behind includes the educational objective that *all* children will learn to read by the end of third grade. It also assumes that this goal can be accomplished through the use of "effective, research-based reading programs." While the motives of this program are surely laudable, is this lofty ideal possible? Many scholars are skeptical because there seems to be such a wide range of abilities and situations among children. Some situations include economic, emotional, and cultural impediments that prevent children from reaching this goal. Perhaps more importantly, many children have learning disabilities, a broad group of diagnoses generally referring to difficulty in one or more areas related to learning, such as reading or math.

The issue in question here is whether this latter problem, the issue of learning disabilities, is the result of a malfunctioning brain. Many neuroscientists, psychologists, and others believe that the solutions to reading and other learning disabilities can be found in the brain itself. They conduct various studies to examine brain functions, look for which specific areas of the brain are used in reading and learning, and attempt to understand the neurological differences between good readers and poor readers. In another camp are experts who believe that, while brain functioning is important, and indeed malfunctioning physiology may impede normal learning ability in some cases, there are other influential factors. From this position, each case of "learning disability" should be carefully examined to discover its true origins, and each child should receive the help appropriate to his/her particular problem.

Sally and Bennett Shaywitz are prolific researchers and writers in the area of learning and development. They have also been instrumental in establishing the No Child Left Behind reading program. Their fundamental assertion in the first article is, "Spoken language is instinctive—built into our genes and hardwired in our brains." According to these researchers, reading and language actually *originate* in our neural networks. Therefore, reading disabilities occur when the "wiring" malfunctions in the particular area of the brain responsible for reading. Their research, which uses functional MRI (fMRI) scans to examine different regions of the brain, found what they call brain "glitches"; places where the brains of people with learning disabilities seem to function differently than those of people without disabilities.

In stark contrast to the Shaywitzes, Dr. Coles is highly critical of brain-based explanations. He holds that reading problems can come from social, cultural, economic, and other factors, and there is no way to distinguish those who have abnormal brains from those who are simply poor readers. As a consequence, many disadvantaged children are incorrectly classified as learning disabled. "Never have these 'brain glitch' explanations been more pervasively intrusive for all beginning readers and their teachers across the nation. . . . This work is a danger . . . both because it applies unproven labels to an ever-larger number of children and because it promotes a single kind of instruction that . . . contains no promise for leaving no beginning reader behind." He concludes that little the Shaywitzes say has been proven and that care should be taken not to adopt a one-size-fits-all program to improve reading when there are so many different reasons for poor reading.

| POINT | COUNTERPOINT |
|---|---|
| • fMRI scans can identify areas in the brain that malfunction during reading. | • fMRI scans track blood flow and active engagement of the brain, not malfunction. |
| • To learn to read, beginners must learn the phonetic code and develop phonetic awareness. | • There are many different styles of readers, some phonetic and some not. |
| • Dyslexia and other reading disabilities have their origin in the brain. | • Many other sources of stress can hinder early reading development. |
| • Different areas of the brain have specialized functions, and specific operations happen in those areas. | • All neurological functions work through a network involving many different parts of the brain. |

**Sally E. Shaywitz and Bennett A. Shaywitz**

# Reading Disability and the Brain

The past decade has witnessed extraordinary progress in our understanding of the nature of reading and reading difficulties. Never before have rigorous science (including neuroscience) and classroom instruction in reading been so closely linked. For the first time, educators can turn to well-designed, scientific studies to determine the most effective ways to teach reading to beginning readers, including those with reading disability (National Reading Panel, 2000).

What does the evidence tell us? Several lines of investigation have found that reading originates in and relies on the brain systems used for spoken language. In addition, accumulating evidence sheds light on the nature of reading disability, including its definition, prevalence, longitudinal course, and probable causes. Although the work is relatively new, we have already made great progress in identifying the neural systems used for reading, identifying a disruption in these systems in struggling readers, and understanding the neural mechanisms associated with the development of fluent reading.

## Reading and Spoken Language

Spoken language is instinctive—built into our genes and hardwired in our brains. Learning to read requires us to take advantage of what nature has provided: a biological module for language.

For the object of the reader's attention (print) to gain entry into the language module, a truly extraordinary transformation must occur. The reader must convert the print on the page into a linguistic code: the phonetic code, the only code recognized and accepted by the language system. Unless the reader-to-be can convert the printed characters on the page into the phonetic code, these letters remain just a bunch of lines and circles, totally devoid of meaning. The written symbols have no inherent meaning of their own but stand, rather, as surrogates for the sounds of speech.

To break the code, the first step beginning readers must take involves spoken language. Readers must develop *phonemic awareness*. They must discover that the words they hear come apart into smaller pieces of sound.

On the basis of highly reliable scientific evidence, investigators in the field have now reached a strong consensus: Reading reflects language, and reading disability reflects a deficit within the language system. Results from

As seen in *Educational Leadership*, March 2004, based on the book *Overcoming Dyslexia* by Sally E. Shaywitz (Knopf, 2003). Grateful acknowledgement is made to Sally Shaywitz, c/o Writers' Representatives LLC (to whom all inquiries should be directed for permission to reprint).

large and well-studied populations with reading disability confirm that in young school-age children and in adolescents, a weakness in accessing the sounds of spoken language represents the most robust and specific correlate of reading disability. Such findings form the foundation for the most successful, evidence-based interventions designed to improve reading (National Reading Panel, 2000).

# Understanding Reading Disability

Reading disability, or *developmental dyslexia*, is characterized by an unexpected difficulty in reading in children and adults who otherwise possess the intelligence, motivation, and education necessary for developing accurate and fluent reading. Dyslexia is the most common and most carefully studied of the learning disabilities, affecting 80 percent of all individuals identified as learning disabled and an estimated 5–17 percent of all children and adults in the United States.

## Incidence and Distribution of Dyslexia

Recent epidemiological data indicate that like hypertension and obesity, reading ability occurs along a continuum. Reading disability falls on the left side of the bell-shaped curve representing the normal distribution of reading ability.

Dyslexia runs in families: One-fourth to one-half of all children who have a parent with dyslexia also have the disorder, and if dyslexia affects one child in the family, it is likely to affect half of his or her siblings. Recent studies have identified a number of genes involved in dyslexia.

Good evidence, based on surveys of randomly selected populations of children, now indicates that dyslexia affects boys and girls equally. Apparently, the long-held belief that only boys suffer from dyslexia reflected bias in school-identified samples: The more disruptive behavior of boys results in their being referred for evaluation more often, whereas girls who struggle to read are more likely to sit quietly in their seats and thus be overlooked.

Longitudinal studies indicate that dyslexia is a persistent, chronic condition rather than a transient "developmental lag." Children do not outgrow reading difficulties. The evidence-based interventions now available, however, can result in improved reading in virtually all children.

## Neurobiological Origins of Dyslexia

For more than a century, physicians and scientists have suspected that dyslexia has neurobiological origins. Until recently, however, they had no way to examine the brain systems that we use while reading. Within the last decade, the dream of scientists, educators, and struggling readers has come true: New advances in technology enable us to view the working brain as it attempts to read.

Perhaps the most convincing evidence for a neurobiological basis of dyslexia comes from the rapidly accumulating and converging data from functional brain imaging investigations. The process of functional brain imaging is quite simple. When we ask an individual to perform a discrete cognitive task, that task places processing demands on specific neural systems in the brain. Through such techniques as functional magnetic resonance imaging (fMRI), we can measure the changes that take place in neural activity in particular brain regions as the brain meets those demands. Because fMRI uses no ionizing radiation and requires no injections, it is noninvasive and safe. We can use it to examine children or adults on multiple occasions.

Using functional brain imaging, scientists around the world have discovered not only the brain basis of reading but also a glitch in the neural circuitry for reading in children and adults who struggle to read. Our studies and those of other investigators have identified three regions involved in reading, all located on the left side of the brain. In the front of the brain, Broca's area (technically the inferior frontal gyrus) is involved in articulation and word analysis. Two areas located in the back of the brain are involved in word analysis (the parieto-temporal region) and in fluent reading (the occipito-temporal region, also referred to as the word form area).

Studies of dyslexic readers document an underactivation of the two systems in the back of the brain together with an overactivation of Broca's area in the front of the brain. The struggling readers appear to be turning to the frontal region, which is responsible for articulating spoken words, to compensate for the fault in the systems in the back of the brain.

Researchers have observed this neurobiological signature of dyslexic readers across cultures and across different languages. The observation of this same pattern in both children and adults supports the view that reading difficulties, including the neural disruption, do not go away with maturity. To prevent failure for students with a reading disability, we must identify the disability early and provide effective reading programs to address the students' needs.

## The Importance of Fluency

In addition to identifying the neural systems used for reading, research has now revealed which systems the brain uses in two important phases in the acquisition of literacy.

Beginning reading—breaking the code by slowly, analytically sounding out words—calls on areas in the front of the brain (Broca's area) and in the back of the brain (the parieto-temporal region).

But an equally important phase in reading is fluency—rapid, automatic reading that does not require attention or effort. A fluent reader looks at a printed word and instantly knows all the important information about that word. Fluent reading develops as the reader builds brain connections that eventually represent an exact replica of the word—a replica that has integrated the word's pronunciation, spelling, and meaning.

Fluency occurs step-by-step. After systematically learning letters and their sounds, children go on to apply this knowledge to sound out words slowly and analytically. For example, for the word "back," a child may initially represent the word by its initial and final consonants: "b—k." As the child progresses, he begins to fill in the interior vowels, first making some errors—reading "back" as "bock" or "beak," for example—and eventually sounding out the word correctly. Part of the process of becoming a skilled reader is forming successively more detailed and complete representations of familiar words.

After the child has read the word "back" correctly over and over again, his brain has built and reinforced an exact model of the word. He now reads that word fluently—accurately, rapidly, and effortlessly. Fluency pulls us into reading. A student who reads fluently reads for pleasure and for information; a student who is not fluent will probably avoid reading.

In a study involving 144 children, we identified the brain region that makes it possible for skilled readers to read automatically. We found that the more proficiently a child read, the more he or she activated the occipito-temporal region (or word form area) in the back of the brain. Other investigators have observed that this brain region responds to words that are presented rapidly. Once a word is represented in the word form area, the reader recognizes that word instantly and effortlessly. This word form system appears to predominate when a reader has become fluent. As a result of this finding, we now know that development of the word form area in the left side of the brain is a key component in becoming a skilled, fluent reader.

## Helping Struggling Readers Become More Fluent

Our study of 144 children also revealed that struggling readers compensate as they get older, developing alternate reading systems in the front of the brain and in the *right* side of the brain—a functioning system, but, alas, not an automatic one. These readers do not develop the critical left-side word form region necessary for rapid, automatic reading. Instead, they call on the alternate secondary pathways. This strategy enables them to read, but much more slowly and with greater effort than their classmates.

This research evidence of a disruption in the normal reading pathways provides a neurobiological target for reading interventions. In a new study, we hypothesized that an evidence-based, phonologically mediated reading intervention would help dyslexic readers develop the fast-paced word form systems serving skilled reading, thus improving their reading accuracy and fluency. Under the supervision of Syracuse University professor Benita Blachman, we provided 2nd and 3rd grade struggling readers daily with 50 minutes of individual tutoring that was systematic and explicit, focusing on helping the students understand the *alphabetic principle,* or how letters and combinations of letters represent the sounds of speech.

Students received eight months (105 hours) of intervention during the school year in addition to their regular classroom reading instruction. The experimental intervention replaced any additional reading help that the students might have received in school. Certified teachers who had taken part in an intensive training program provided the tutoring.

Immediately after the yearlong intervention, students in the experiment made significant gains in reading fluency and demonstrated increased activation in left hemisphere regions, including the inferior frontal gyrus and the parieto-temporal region. One year after the experimental intervention ended, these students were reading accurately and fluently and were activating all three left-side brain regions used by good readers. A control group of struggling readers receiving school-based, primarily nonphonological reading instruction had not activated these reading systems.

These data demonstrate that an intensive, evidence-based reading intervention brings about significant and durable changes in brain organization so that struggling readers' brain activation patterns come to resemble those of typical readers. If we provide intervention at an early age, then we can improve reading fluency and facilitate the development of the neural systems that underlie skilled reading.

## Evidence-Based Effective Reading Instruction

In addition to new neurological research on the nature of reading, educators can draw on a body of rigorous, well-designed, scientific studies to guide reading instruction. In 1998, the U.S. Congress mandated the National Reading Panel to develop rigorous scientific criteria for evaluating reading research, apply these criteria to existing reading research, identify the most effective teaching methods, and then make findings accessible for parents and teachers. As a member of the Panel, I can attest to its diligence. After two years of work, the Panel issued its report (2000).

The major findings of the report indicate that in order to read, all children must be taught alphabetics, comprising phonemic awareness and phonics; reading fluency; vocabulary; and strategies for reading comprehension. These elements must be taught systematically, comprehensively, and explicitly; it is inadequate to present the foundational skills of phonemic awareness and phonics incidentally, casually, or fragmentally. Children do not learn how letters represent sounds by osmosis; we must teach them this skill explicitly. Once a child has mastered these foundational skills, he or she must be taught how to read words fluently.

Good evidence now indicates that we can teach reading fluency by means of repeated oral reading with feedback and guidance. Using these methods, we can teach almost every child to read. It is crucial to align all components of a program with one another—for example, to provide so-called decodable booklets that give the student practice in the specific letter-sound linkages we are teaching. The use of decodable booklets enables the repeated practice necessary to build the automatic systems in the word form region that lead to fluent reading.

## Neuroscience and Reading Research Agree

We are now in an era of evidence-based education. Objective scientific evidence—provided by brain imaging studies and by the National Reading Panel's rigorous scientific review of the literature—has replaced reliance on philosophy or opinion.

In considering a reading program, educators should ask several key questions:

- Is there scientific evidence that the program is effective?
- Was the program or its methodology reviewed by the National Reading Panel?
- In reading instruction, are phonemic awareness and phonics taught systematically and explicitly?
- How are students taught to approach an unfamiliar word? Do they feel empowered to try to analyze and sound out an unknown word first rather than guess the word from the pictures or context?
- Does the program also include plenty of opportunities for students to practice reading, develop fluency, build vocabulary, develop reading comprehension strategies, write, and listen to and discuss stories?

Children are only 7 or 8 years old once in their lifetime. We cannot risk teaching students with unproven programs. We now have the scientific knowledge to ensure that almost every child can become a successful reader. Awareness of the new scientific knowledge about reading should encourage educators to insist that reading programs used in their schools reflect what we know about the science of reading and about effective reading instruction.

**Gerald Coles**

# Danger in the Classroom: 'Brain Glitch' Research and Learning to Read

Did you know that recent studies of the brain and reading support the reading instruction mandated in George W. Bush's No Child Left Behind (NCLB) legislation? And did you know that this research also supports the legislation he has proposed to dismantle Head Start's comprehensive approach to preschool education? And were you aware that, thanks to this brain research, we now know how children learn to read and which areas of the brain must first be stocked to promote skilled reading? Did you realize that we now have strong brain-based evidence that the best reading instruction is heavily prescriptive, skills-emphasis, building-blocks teaching that starts with small pieces of written language and proceeds to larger ones—and teachers are fortunate because these features are contained in reading programs like Open Court?

You didn't know all that? Good, because none of it is true, although you would never know that if you just listened to the President, the educators and assorted researchers who support his educational agenda, and the media who repeat their assertions.

Over 25 years ago, when I began appraising theories about faulty brain wiring in beginning readers, my criticism of the research then being conducted was limited to ersatz explanations of so-called brain dysfunctions in children called "learning disabled," "reading disabled," or "dyslexic." Contrary to the assertions made then, the research had never shown that the overwhelming number of these children did not have normal brains. Certainly a portion of poor readers had problems that were the result of exposure to such toxins as lead and cadmium, to food additives, and to other environmental influences. But, I argued, there was no evidence that they accounted for more than a small portion of the large numbers of children given these labels and shunted into special education programs.

At some point, thanks to increased, widespread criticism of these "brain-based" explanations, I had thought a change had started toward more informed, measured interpretations. However, my naive thinking has long been gone. Not only are explanations about "brain glitches," to use the term employed by reading researcher Sally Shaywitz, now being applied more forcefully to "dyslexics," but they have also been reworked to explain how all children learn to read, what single method of instruction must be used to teach them, and why the single method mandated in Bush's Reading First, part of the NCLB legislation, is a wise, scientifically based choice. Thus never have these "brain glitch" explanations been more pervasively intrusive for all beginning readers and their teachers in classrooms across the nation. . . .

A new best seller, *Overcoming Dyslexia*, by Sally Shaywitz, who has received considerable NICHD [National Institutes of Child Health and Human Development] funding for her research, claims to present "the advances in brain science" that inform what "at last we know," which are "the specific steps a child or adult must take to build and then reinforce the neural pathways deep within the brain for skilled reading." Shaywitz served on the panel whose findings, she proudly explains to readers, "are now part of the groundbreaking No Child Left Behind Legislation." . . .

In this article I will argue that, despite all the unbridled assertions about the wonder of it all, this new "brain glitch" research is theoretically, empirically, and conceptually deficient, as was the deficit-driven work that preceded it by decades. . . . More than ever, claims about the research constitute an ideological barrier to a sounder understanding of the connections between brain activity and learning to read. More than ever, this work is a danger in the classroom both because it applies unproven labels to an ever-larger number of children and because it promotes a single kind of instruction that, based on the actual empirical evidence mustered for it, contains no promise for leaving no beginning reader behind. To all of this, add the false and cruel expectations that these claims generate in parents.

To help illustrate my critique, I will use as an example a recent, highly publicized study on reading and brain activity whose co-authors include Reid Lyon, Sally Shaywitz, and several other researchers whose work argues for building-blocks teaching and has been used as evidence for Reading First instruction. (For convenience I call it the Shaywitz/Lyon study).

## Is the Brain "Reading"?

Functional magnetic resonance imagery (fMRI) is a valuable diagnostic and investigative technology that can measure blood flow in the brain and thereby provide information about certain kinds of brain activity when someone is performing a task. However, like every technology used in research, its value and the information it produces are never better than the initial theory and concepts that steer its application. Perhaps the biggest misrepresentation in the "brain glitch" research is that the color scans produced by fMRI provide information about "reading." In fact, they provide no such thing, because the "reading" tasks under study are largely a person's performance on simple sound and sound/symbol (phonics) tasks with words and parts of words, rather than performance in reading as conventionally defined, that is, reading and comprehending sentences and paragraphs. (The same misrepresentation appears in claims about "reading" contained in the report of the National Reading Panel, the chief research document cited in the Reading First legislation.)

The puny definition of reading used in this research appears not to concern the investigators, though, because they design their studies on the assumption that these simple tasks involving words and parts of words embrace the core requirements for beginning readers: that is, mastery of phonological awareness (distinguishing and manipulating sounds in words) and sound/symbol relationships. As the Shaywitz/Lyon study explains, there is now "a strong consensus" (that is, a broad unanimity of professional opinion) that phonological awareness is the first building block within the sequence and that reading disability reflects a deficit in this "lower level component" of "the language system." Only after mastering this component can beginning readers effectively continue to master other reading skills.

That's the claim. The reality is that the so-called strong consensus does not exist. I and others have published thorough research reviews that critique—and dismiss—the "lower level component" model and the supposed empirical evidence showing the superior effect of early, direct, and intensive instruction in word sounds on later reading. As I have also argued, this narrow, do-as-you're-told instruction not only pushes aside numerous issues that bear on beginning literacy—such as children's backgrounds, interests, problem-solving approaches, and definitions of "reading"—it also masquerades as a bootstrap policy solution for poor children that takes off the table all other policies required to address the many needs that influence learning success or failure. However, for the advocates of this "strong consensus," especially those linked to the political power pushing these claims, conflicting views are never allowed to ruffle their harmony.

Hence, an experiment, such as those reported in the Shaywitz/Lyon study, can be designed in which subjects do "lower level component" tasks, such as deciding if nonwords rhyme ("Do leat and bete rhyme?") or making judgments requiring both phonological and semantic knowledge ("Are corn and rice in the same category?"), and the researchers can claim that the data generated tell us a great deal about "reading," the reading process, and the best kinds of instruction. The conclusions in this work display no awareness of the self-fulfilling prophecy at play when the research focuses solely on "lower level components" decontextualized from a full appraisal of reading, uses no other model of reading and instruction, and then concludes that these components are the initial and key ones in learning to read.

## A Real "Brain Glitch"?

Looking more deeply into the research design of the "brain glitch" studies, we find a problem that dyslexia researchers have long encountered but not overcome when organizing an experiment so that data on brain activity can be meaningfully interpreted: the experiment must start by grouping dyslexics separately from other kinds of poor readers. This distinction is required because even in studies using the fMRI, the data are about brain activity associated with the word-level tasks, not about micro brain damage. Therefore, fMRI differences in brain activity among a group of unsorted poor readers would not provide information about the cause and meaning of the various differences in activity.

To solve the problem, these studies and previous ones employing simpler technologies try first to separate from a group of poor readers those whose problems are assumed to have non-neurological causes, such as emotional, familial, social class, and similar "exclusionary" influences, as they have been called. If these poor readers are excluded, researchers have reasoned, the probability is high that the reading problems of those who remain are caused by a "brain glitch." While this might make sense in theory, in practice it has not worked, because researchers have not created evaluation methods and criteria for separating the two groups of poor readers.

Even worse, for decades, researchers have frequently stated that they have used a thorough process of distinguishing between the two groups, but the assertion has rarely been accompanied by evidence. In the Shaywitz/Lyon study, for example, dyslexics were supposedly identified after the researchers had determined that the subjects' reading problems were not caused by emotional problems or "social, cultural, or economic disadvantage." Yet the researchers, so dedicated to obtaining and reporting a surfeit of brain data, offered not a whit of information on this process of elimination. Presumably, readers of the published study were expected to accept without question the assertion that genuine dyslexics had been identified and that these children could then be compared to "nonimpaired" readers (an odd term, since it refers to normal or average readers but is used in the study to underline a priori the assumption that the dyslexics' brains were impaired).

The need to provide evidence of thorough appraisals of the roots of subjects' reading problems is usually obvious to anyone who has actually taught poor readers and, therefore, knows that there can be numerous contextual causes of poor reading in middle-class children that will not be readily apparent. In my extensive work with children, young adults, and adults with severe reading problems, I have found that causes can be uncovered only after spending considerable time *both* evaluating and teaching a student, with the latter especially necessary. Poor teaching—such as using a one-size-fits-all reading program, insufficient individualized instruction, too much phonics, too little phonics—is just one of the many influences that can produce reading problems in a variety of ways, but those problems will not be apparent without thorough analysis of a person's instructional history and current active reading.

Many unusual family circumstances and stresses can impair a child's early reading progress. A parent losing a job, a family moving to another city in the middle of the first grade, overworked parents, grandparents dying around the time a child began school are all examples of problems I have identified. These experiences hinder reading development by distracting and stressing a child, but they are not overt "emotional" problems. Even when a poor reader comes from a family that appears "normal," only an extensive exploration of the family dynamics can determine whether this appearance might cloak problems that have affected a child's beginning reading.

By not providing criteria and evidence that the "dyslexics" are different from other poor readers, the brain research studies use another self-serving, self-fulfilling prophecy: because the fMRI shows differences in brain activity between "dyslexic" and "nonimpaired" readers, the differences in brain activity must be visual demonstrations of impairment and nonimpairment. How do we know the fMRI data reveal impairment? Because one of the groups was initially identified as impaired. How do we know the group was impaired? Because the group was first identified as impaired and the fMRI data corroborated the impairment. No other explanations can explain the dyslexics' different brain activity. Impaired, for sure! No question about it. . . .

## Fixing the "Brain Glitch"

Beyond finding "brain glitches," researchers have reported other good news: building-block skills instruction can remedy the glitch. "An effective reading program" can produce "brain repair," Shaywitz reports. "The brain can be rewired". . . .

Nearly 20 years ago, Leonide Goldstein and I published a study on differences in brain hemisphere activation in adult beginning readers as they were learning to read. We found that these adults, when they were poor readers or nonreaders, did, indeed, demonstrate brain activation that was different from that found among good readers. However, as their reading improved, through the use of a holistic, comprehensive teaching approach over many months, their brain activation changed toward that commonly found in good readers. We interpreted these data as evidence that new knowledge and competencies were linked to concomitant changes in brain structure and functioning, as one would expect for *all kinds of learning*. There was nothing in the data to suggest that these beginning readers started learning to read with anything other than normal brains that were configured as they were at the beginning of the study because the students had not learned to read; no data suggested that the educational intervention we provided somehow repaired or circumvented dysfunctional brain areas.

To restate a central point for appraising these glitch-fixing interventions: although researchers insist that the training programs they use repair or ameliorate brain hardware or glitches, there is no evidence in any of their studies that this rewiring was different from that which is concomitant with the learning that continues throughout our learning lives. Nor does this so-called repair demonstrate that phonological processing is the *initial* key component in learning to read. The subjects apparently lacked this ability and then learned this ability, and their brain processing changed accordingly. Using modern technology to identify and track brain changes related to changes in reading ability is an extraordinary achievement. Using the achievement for ideological ends is not.

## Emotionless "Cognition"

Like the assumed "consensus" on building-blocks instruction, "brain glitch" research assumes that cognition—that is, the process that creates images, concepts, and mental operations—is not a construct but an independent reality that actually describes the brain processes associated with reading. Ignored in this assumption is the ever-growing evidence suggesting that thinking is an inseparable interaction of both cognition and emotion (feelings, desires, enthusiasms, antipathies, etc.) . . . .

Unfortunately, none of this new perspective on the "continuous and interwoven cognitive-emotional fugue" . . . has entered the "brain glitch" research. As a result, the question of whether diminished activity in a portion of the brain of someone doing a reading task might be a consequence of an emotional response, in that emotional memories can exert a powerful influence on "thought processes," remains unaddressed. By purging emotions and focusing only on cognition, the "brain glitch" research also purges the alternative: a holistic instructional approach based on the assumption that classrooms are filled with whole children for whom learning is always grounded in the fugue of cognition and affect.

## How the Brain Works: Modules?

The interrelationships and interactions missing from the narrow cognitive model of "brain glitch" research lead us to a final concern. A chief premise of this research holds that the brain has specific modules for specialized operations that work in sequence with other modules in learning written language and that foremost of these is at least one module that can process basic sound and sound/symbol skills. This kind of modular model has a certain palpable, visual appeal (not unlike "building-blocks instruction"), but the actual existence of such modules is a theory, not a fact, that has increasingly been questioned. Most likely, the modular model is not one that explains how the brain actually works.

For instance, Merlin Donald, a psychologist who has written extensively on human consciousness, rejects the explanation that modules perform "specialized operations," such as deciphering portions of language. While language areas of the brain, such as those related to aspects of reading, are important in processing particular functions, all are intertwined in extensive networks (a polyphony) of brain areas that are simultaneously and interactively communicating and constructing and reconstructing particular areas within the whole. Yes, the brain has fundamental mechanisms for beginning to learn written language, but it does not begin with a "fixed pattern of connectivity." Instead, the "connectivity pattern is set by experience" with "countless interconnection points, or synapses, which connect neurons to one another in various patterns." In other words, learning and experience create and shape the brain's circuits and how they are used in learning to read; the circuits are not predetermined.

Linguist Philip Lieberman has also criticized modular explanations, calling them "neophrenological theories," that is, theories that "map complex behaviors to localized regions of the brain, on the assumption that a particular part of the brain regulates an aspect of behavior." In these theories, he remarks, the functional organization of the brain is run by "a set of petty bureaucrats each of which controls a behavior." Like Donald, Lieberman proposes that converging behavioral and neurobiological data indicate that human language is composed not of a hierarchical system but of neural networks, including the traditional cortical "language" areas (Broca's and Wernicke's areas), formed through circuits that link populations of neurons in neuroanatomical structures that are distributed throughout the brain. Lieberman stresses, "Although specific operations may be performed in particular parts of the brain, these operations must be integrated into a *network* that regulates an observable aspect of behavior. And so, a particular aspect of behavior usually involves activity in neuroanatomical structures distributed throughout the brain" (emphasis in original). . . .

The view of a "connectivity pattern" that emerges and is activated as children learn to read contrasts with the model of step-by-step progression from module to module. If the former is an accurate model of brain organization and functioning, it suggests that the connectivity pattern should be the focus of research because only by looking at the overall pattern can researchers begin to determine the functioning and interrelationships of any part and the causal, consequential, or interactive function of that part within the entire pattern.

From the perspective of a connectivity pattern model, not only do the brain areas involved in grasping the sound/symbol correspondence *not* have to be primed first before other areas of the pattern can become effectively operable, the creation and functioning of these areas depends on connections within the entire pattern. And because the pattern is not innately fixed, if instruction were to stimulate certain areas more than others, a particular connectivity pattern would emerge. That specific pattern, however, might not necessarily be the sole one required for reading success and might not be superior to other connectivity patterns. Moreover, a more complex connectivity pattern could be created through richer written language learning. None of this is addressed in the "brain glitch" research.

## Conclusion

Philip Lieberman offers a caveat worth emphasizing when appraising "brain glitch" research, learning to read, and the Bush agenda for education: "We must remember that we stand on the threshold of an understanding of how brains really work. The greatest danger perhaps rests in making claims that are not supported by data." Unfortunately, not only have "brain glitch" researchers seldom been guided by such a caveat, they have tended to misconstrue the data and have drawn conclusions that serve to justify unwarranted beliefs, instructional policy, and the politics that have driven the research in the first place. . . .

For research on the brain and reading to become productive, what is needed most is the discarding of fundamental assumptions that have not been validated. Building-blocks instruction has not been proved to be the best way to teach reading. Phonological awareness has not been proved to be the initial, essential component that determines reading success. Thinking does not involve "cognition" alone. The modular organization of the brain is, at best, a disputed theory. Brain activation differences do not necessarily reflect "brain glitches." Dyslexia remains no more a proven malady among a substantial percentage of beginning readers than when Glasgow ophthalmologist James Hinshelwood first discussed it as "congenital word-blindness" at the end of the 19th century.

To make research on the brain and reading work, it must be informed by the complexity of reading acquisition, and it must begin to address such questions as: Will alternative teaching approaches configure brain activity in alternative ways? Will children's differing assumptions about what it means to "read" correspond to differing brain activity and organization? How do different aspects of reading, such as comprehension, syntax, and word analysis, interact in certain reading tasks and what kinds of brain activity do the interactions produce? How does the knowledge children bring to literacy learning affect brain activity?

These and similar questions can begin to contribute to a better understanding of the relationship between brain function and reading acquisition, which in turn can help promote ecological approaches that are grounded in an understanding of the unified interrelationships of brain, active child, and learning environment. They can also begin to help identify genuine brain-related reading impairments. Developing this kind of understanding of integrated interrelationships will require that we eschew views that are either "brain based" or conceive of the brain as an extraneous "black box."

By adding to the current pretensions about the superiority of one brand of "scientifically based" reading instruction, "brain glitch" research remains a danger in the classroom. Unfortunately, because of the political power connected to this sham science and brainless instruction, a mighty effort is required to end that danger.

# CHALLENGE QUESTIONS

## Do Brain Deficiencies Determine Learning Disabilities?

1. What is a learning disability? Where do they come from? How are they identified?
2. Can fMRI scans help neuroscientists and psychologists understand and treat learning disabilities? How? Cite some evidence.
3. How might a generalized reading program, such as that proposed by the Shayitzes, be beneficial? Could it be harmful? How?
4. Explain Dr. Coles's concern about distinguishing between poor readers with brain malfunction and those with non-neurological problems. What are the self-fulfilling prophecies he describes?
5. According to the Shaywitzes, what are the glitches in the brains of poor readers? Do you agree that all poor readers have brain glitches? Why or why not?

# Internet References . . .

## PrescribingPsychologist.com

PrescribingPsychologist.com provides information and links regarding the prescription privilege debate.

**http://www.prescribingpsychologist.com**

## Psychotherapy Links

This directory of psychotherapy websites is sponsored by the University of Western Ontario Department of Psychiatry.

**http://www.aboutpsychotherapy.com/**

## Association for Gay, Lesbian, and Bisexual Issues in Counseling

This is the website of the Association for Gay, Lesbian, and Bisexual Issues in Counseling, a division of the American Counseling Association that works toward educating mental health service providers about issues faced by gay, lesbian, bisexual, and transgendered individuals.

**http://www.aglbic.org**

# UNIT 6

## Social Psychology

*Social psychology is the study of humans in their social environments. For example, a social psychologist might ask how the social environment of torture affects a prisoner. Is coercive interrogation (possibly torture) a good method of gaining important information, or is it a waste of time that only does psychological harm? What can psychologists contribute to these questions? Can not only real-life violence and abuse affect children, but can virtual violence, such as that depicted in video games, also affect children? Does playing a violent video game make children more prone to aggressive behavior? What about the relatively recent changes in our social environment? Some psychologists have pointed to the recent upsurge of sexually explicit "societal and cultural messages" on the Internet and other media. Could this upsurge lead to problems, such as pornography addiction and sexual addictions in general? Do such addictions even exist? If so, can they be treated with addiction treatments, such as the 12-step model used to treat alcoholics?*

# ISSUE 15

## Should Psychologists Abstain from Involvement in Coercive Interrogations?

**YES: Mark Costanza, Ellen Gerrity, and M. Brinton Lykes,** from "Psychologists and the Use of Torture in Interrogations." *Analyses of Social Issues and Public Policy (ASAP)* (December 2007)

**NO: Kirk M. Hubbard,** from "Psychologists and Interrogations: What's Torture Got to Do with It?" *Analyses of Social Issues and Public Policy (ASAP)* (December, 2007)

### ISSUE SUMMARY

**YES:** Psychologists Mark Costanzo, Ellen Gerrity, and M. Brinton Lykes assert that all psychologists should be banned from any involvement in interrogations that involve torture or other unethical forms of coercion.

**NO:** Psychologist and intelligence consultant Kirk M. Hubbard argues that a ban on a psychologist's involvement in coercive interrogations would overly restrict the ways in which psychologists can ethically contribute to their country's intelligence needs.

Psychologists have long been noted for their productive interviews. This skill is, in some sense, the root of psychotherapy. In recent years, however, an ethical dilemma has emerged regarding particular interviews—"coercive interrogations." As reports of prisoner abuse at Abu Ghraib and Guantanamo Bay emerged, many Americans became concerned about the way the government was treating detainees. Many in the psychological community were concerned that psychologists were serving as consultants and perhaps even participating in coercive interrogations, recommending or using techniques that many considered to be torture. They called for the American Psychological Association (APA) to prohibit member psychologists from any involvement in coercive interrogations, claiming that such involvement would violate a psychologist's ethical commitment to "first do no harm."

Other psychologists, however, have worried that the APA barring members from such interrogations would be a hasty move. These psychologists have argued that APA members should be involved in planning interrogations precisely because their expertise can guide interrogators to use coercion ethically. Moreover, the ethical commitment to "first do no harm" could be applied to keeping the United States from harm. Indeed, some psychologists have argued that their primary duty is to prevent harm to their country and that they do not have the same duty to protect their country's enemies.

In the first article, psychologists Mark Costanzo, Ellen Gerrity, and M. Brinton Lykes make the case for prohibiting psychologists from involvement in coercive interrogations. They explain that coercive interrogation techniques, such as torture, are banned by professional organizations like the APA and are violations of US and international law. Further, they argue the research literature shows that coercion is not an effective interrogation technique and its poor results cannot justify its harmful impact. Costanzo and colleagues describe how "torture has long-term negative consequences for the mental health of both survivors and perpetrators of torture." They argue that the harmful nature and ineffectiveness of coercive interrogations require an explicit ban of psychologists' involvement in such practices.

In the second article, psychologist and intelligence consultant Kirk M. Hubbard argues that a ban on psychologists' involvement in torture is unnecessary, because torture is illegal and thus is already prohibited. Indeed, there is no evidence, according to Hubbard, that psychologists have been involved in torture. Hubbard asserts that providing formal restrictions on psychologists' involvement in interrogations will hamper what psychologists can legitimately lend to legal interrogations. He asks, "how is psychology accountable to society—should it withhold information about ways in which to protect our population or to influence terrorists to disclose information?" Because terrorists "do not care if they live or die and have no fear of prison," they "have little or no incentive to work with interrogators." Hubbard calls upon psychologists to become *more* involved in research and consultation about interrogating terrorists to develop effective and humane methods for obtaining information that will protect their country.

| POINT | COUNTERPOINT |
|---|---|
| • "Psychologists should be expressly prohibited from using their expertise to participate in interrogations that make use of torture." | • Because torture is illegal, psychologists are already barred from participation. |
| • "Torture is ineffective as a means of extracting reliable information and likely leads to faulty intelligence." | • Legal coercion may be necessary for interrogating terrorists, given their decreased motivation to comply. |
| • The "ticking time bomb scenario" gives a false air of justification to coercive interrogation methods. | • The "ticking time bomb scenario" is real and has already occurred. |
| • Psychologists have a duty to do no harm at all costs, even to detainees who potentially threaten their country. | • Psychologists have a duty to provide their expertise where it might be instrumental in defending their country. |

YES 

**Mark Costanzo, Ellen Gerrity and M. Brinton Lykes**

# Psychologists and the Use of Torture in Interrogations

*This article argues that psychologists should not be involved in interrogations that make use of torture or other forms of cruel, inhumane, or degrading treatment. The use of torture is first evaluated in light of professional ethics codes and international law. Next, research on interrogations and false confessions is reviewed and its relevance for torture-based interrogations is explored. Finally, research on the negative mental health consequences of torture for survivors and perpetrators is summarized. Based on our review, we conclude that psychologists' involvement in designing, assisting with, or participating in interrogations that make use of torture or other forms of cruel, inhumane, or degrading treatment is a violation of fundamental ethical principles, a violation of international and domestic law, and an ineffective means of extracting reliable information. Torture produces severe and lasting trauma as well as other negative consequences for individuals and for the societies that support it. The article concludes with several recommendations about how APA and other professional organizations should respond to the involvement of psychologists in interrogations that make use of torture or other forms of cruel, inhumane, or degrading treatment.*

The United States and its military should immediately ban the use of torture, and psychologists should be expressly prohibited from using their expertise to plan, design, assist, or participate in interrogations that make use of torture and other forms of cruel, inhumane, or degrading treatment. The use of torture as an interrogation device is contrary to ethical standards of conduct for psychologists and is in violation of international law. Torture is ineffective as a means of extracting reliable information, and likely leads to faulty intelligence. Torture has long-term negative consequences for the mental health of both survivors and perpetrators of torture. The use of torture has far-reaching consequences for American citizens: it damages the reputation of the United States, creates hostility toward our troops, provides a pretext for cruelty against U.S. soldiers and citizens, places the United States in the company of some of the most oppressive regimes in the world, and undermines the credibility of the United States when it argues for international human rights.

From *Analyses of Social Issues and Public Policy,* 7(1), December 2007, pp. 7–16. 

## 1. Torture as a Violation of Professional Codes of Conduct

The American Psychological Association's *Ethical Principles of Psychologists and Code of Conduct* encourages psychologists to, " . . . strive to benefit those with whom they work and take care to do no harm." These guidelines incorporate *basic principles* or *moral imperatives* that guide behavior as well as specific *codes of conduct* describing what psychologists *can* or *cannot* do and are, therefore, directly applicable to the participation of psychologists in torture or in interrogation situations involving harm. Psychologists, physicians, and other health and mental health professionals are also guided by international and interprofessional codes of ethics and organizational resolutions, such as the 1985 joint statement against torture issued by the American Psychiatric Association and the American Psychological Association. In 1986, the American Psychological Association passed a *Resolution against Torture and Other Cruel, Inhuman, or Degrading Treatment.* Both statements "condemn torture wherever it occurs."

The International Union of Psychological Science (IUPsyS), the International Association of Applied Psychology (IAAP), and the International Association for Cross-Cultural Psychology (IACCP) are collaborating in the development of a Universal Declaration of Ethical Principles for Psychologists. They have identified "principles and values that provide a common moral framework . . . [to] "guide the development of differing standards as appropriate for differing cultural contexts" (www.am.org/iupsys/ethintro). An analysis of eight current ethical codes identified across multiple continents revealed five cross-cutting principles: (1) respect for the dignity and rights of persons, (2) caring for others and concern for their welfare, (3) competence, (4) integrity, and (5) professional, scientific, and social responsibility. Sinclair traced the origins of these eight codes to 12 documents including the Code of Hammurabi (Babylon, circa 1795–1750 BC), the Ayurvedic Instruction (India, circa 500–300 BC), the Hippocratic Oath (Greece, circa 400 BC), the (First) American Medical Association Code of Ethics (1847 AD), and the Nuremberg Code of Ethics in Medical Research (1948 AD). Among the ethical principles proposed as universal for all psychologists is that they "uphold the value of taking care to do no harm to individuals, families, groups, and communities."

A wide range of declarations, conventions, and principles govern the conduct of doctors and all health professionals in the context of torture (e.g., the World Medical Association's (1975) Tokyo Declaration), including the establishment of international standards for medical assessments of allegations of torture (e.g., the *Manual on the Effective Investigation and Documentation of Torture and Other Cruel, Inhuman or Degrading Treatment or Punishment (Istanbul Protocol),* United Nations, 1999). Specific restrictions prohibiting the participation of medical personnel in torture and degrading interrogation practices were established in the 1982 United Nations' "*Principles of Medical Ethics* (United Nations, 1982)." The World Medical Association has also established that it is not ethically appropriate for physicians or other health professionals to serve as consultants or advisors in interrogation.

Psychologists can find themselves in contexts where expected professional and ethical conduct and the protection of human rights conflict with compliance with government policies and practices. A 2002 report of Physicians for Human Rights described this "dual loyalty" now confronting a growing number of health professionals within and outside of the Armed Forces. This tension is particularly acute when such policies and practices run counter to international declarations, laws, and conventions that protect human rights (see, for example, the report of Army Regulation-15, 2005).

## 2. Torture as a Violation of Law

As citizens, psychologists in the United States are required to observe a wide range of international and national treaties, conventions, and laws that prohibit torture. The *Universal Declaration of Human Rights* (United Nations, 1948) and the *International Covenant on Civil and Political Rights* (United Nations, adopted in 1966, entered into force, 1976), alongside six other core international human rights treaties, constitute an international "bill of human rights" that guarantees freedom from torture and cruel, inhuman, or degrading treatment (see Article 5 of the Universal Declaration on Human Rights).

Article 1 of the UN *Convention against Torture and other Cruel, Inhuman or Degrading Treatment (CAT),* (United Nations, 1984, 1987), which was signed by the United States in 1988 and ratified in 1994, defines torture during interrogation as:

> Any act by which severe pain or suffering, whether physical or mental, is intentionally inflicted on a person for such purposes as obtaining from him or a third person information or a confession . . . when such pain or suffering is inflicted by or at the instigation of or with the consent or acquiescence of a public official or other person acting in an official capacity.

Article 2 (2) of the Convention outlines specific additional prohibitions and obligations of states that: "No exceptional circumstances whatsoever, whether a state of war or a threat of war, internal political instability or any other public emergency, may be invoked as a justification of torture". . . .

Multiple U.S. laws and resolutions, including the U.S. Bill of Rights, the U.S. Constitution, and the joint congressional resolution opposing torture that was signed into law by President Reagan on October 4, 1984 (United States Congress, 1984), prohibit cruel, inhuman, or degrading treatment or torture. Other conventions to which the United States subscribes prohibit any form of torture as a means of gathering information in times of war (see, for example, the *Geneva Conventions* (1949) and the *European Convention (1989)* relative to the treatment of prisoners of war and to the prevention of torture. In this tradition, Senator John McCain's Amendment (section 1403 of H.R. 1815), approved by the U.S. Congress and signed by President Bush at the end of 2005, prohibits torture and cruel, inhumane, and degrading treatment. However, President Bush's less widely publicized accompanying "signing statement" indicated that he would interpret the law in a manner consistent with his presidential powers, re-igniting debate in many circles within and beyond government. The inconclusiveness of debates among branches of government, and the condemnation of the United States's treatment of prisoners at Guantánamo and Abu Ghraib by foreign governments as well as the UN Committee Against Torture, underscore the urgent need to clarify ethical guidelines for psychologists.

## 3. Research on Interrogations and the Utility of Torture as an Interrogation Tool

Although the primary purpose of torture is to terrorize a group and break the resistance of an enemy, the use of torture is frequently justified as an interrogation device. However, there is no evidence that torture is an effective means of gathering reliable information. Many survivors of torture report they that would have said anything to "make the torture stop." Those who make the claim that "torture works" offer as evidence only unverifiable anecdotal accounts. Even if there are cases where torture may have preceded the disclosure of useful information, it is impossible to know whether less coercive forms of interrogation might have yielded the same or even better results.

Because torture-based interrogations are generally conducted in secret, there is no systematic research on the relationship between torture and false confessions. However, there is irrefutable evidence from the civilian criminal justice system that techniques *less coercive* than torture have produced verifiably false confessions in a surprising number of cases. An analysis of DNA exonerations of innocent but wrongly convicted criminal suspects revealed that false confessions are the second most frequent cause of wrongful convictions, accounting for 24% of the total (see www.innocenceproject.org). In a recent large-scale study, Drizin and Leo identified 125 proven false confessions over a 30-year period. Two characteristics of these known false confessions are notable. First, they tended to occur in the most serious cases—81% confessed to the crime of murder, and another 9% confessed to the crime of rape. Second, because only *proven* false confessions were included (e.g., cases where the confessor was exonerated by DNA evidence or cases where the alleged crime never occurred), the actual number of false confessions is likely to be substantially higher. Military action based on false information extracted through the use of torture has the potential to jeopardize the lives of military personnel and civilians.

The defining feature of an interrogation is the presumption that a suspect is lying or withholding vital information. If torture is an available option, interrogators are likely to resort to torture when they believe a suspect is lying about what he or she knows or does not know. However, there is no reason to believe that interrogators are able to tell whether or not a suspect is lying. Indeed, there is considerable research demonstrating that trained interrogators are *not* accurate in judging the truthfulness of the suspects they interrogate. Overall, people with relevant professional training (e.g., interrogators, polygraphers, customs officers) are able to detect deception at a level only slightly above chance. Moreover, some researchers have identified a troubling perceptual bias among people who have received interrogation training—an increased tendency to believe that others are lying to them. In addition, although specialized training in interrogation techniques does not improve the ability to discern lying, it does increase the confidence of interrogators in their ability to tell whether a suspect is lying or withholding information. The presumption that a suspect is lying, in combination with the overconfidence produced by interrogation training, leads to a biased style of questioning which seeks to confirm guilt while ignoring or discounting information that suggests that a suspect is being truthful. There is also evidence that interrogators become most coercive when questioning innocent suspects, because truthful suspects are regarded as resistant and defiant. Thus, interrogators may be especially likely to resort to torture when faced with persistent denials by innocent suspects. Under such conditions, torture may be used to punish a suspect or as an expression of frustration and desperation on the part of the interrogator. More broadly, there is substantial evidence that judgments about others are influenced by conscious and nonconscious stereotyping and prejudice. Prejudice may lead interrogators to target suspects for torture based on physical appearance, ethnicity, or erroneous stereotypes about behavioral cues.

Unless local authorities (e.g., commanders in charge of a military detention facility) explicitly prohibit the use of torture in interrogations, the risk of torture will be unacceptably high. Decades of research by social psychologists has demonstrated that strong situational forces can overwhelm people's better impulses and cause good people to treat others cruelly. These forces include the presence of an authority figure who appears to sanction the use of cruelty, and a large power disparity between groups, such as the disparity that exists between prisoners and guards. In addition, the dehumanization and demonization of the enemy that occurs during times of intense group conflict—particularly during times of war—reduce inhibitions against cruelty. All of these conditions, combined with the stresses of long-term confinement, appear to have been present at Abu Ghraib. The well-documented reports of torture at the Abu Ghraib and Guantanamo Bay facilities serve as disturbing reminders that it is essential for military authorities to issue clear directives about unacceptable practices in the interrogation of prisoners. These directives need to be combined with effective monitoring of military detention facilities, especially during times of war.

In an effort to circumvent ethical concerns and the lack of evidence about the effectiveness of torture, advocates of the use of torture often resort to hypothetical arguments such as the "ticking time bomb scenario." This frequently used justification for the use of torture as an interrogation tactic presupposes that the United States has in its custody a terrorist who has knowledge of the location of a time bomb that will soon explode and kill thousands of innocent people. Embedded in this implausible scenario are several questionable assumptions: that it is known for certain that the suspect possesses specific "actionable" knowledge that would avert the disaster; that the threat is imminent; that only torture would lead to the disclosure of the information; and that torture is the fastest means of extracting valid, actionable information. Of course, this scenario also recasts the person who tortures as a principled, heroic figure who reluctantly uses torture to save innocent lives. While this scenario might provide a useful stimulus for discussion in college ethics courses, or an interesting plot device for a television drama, we can find no evidence that it has ever occurred and it appears highly improbable.

## 4. The Effects of Torture on Survivors and Perpetrators

Torture is one of the most extreme forms of human violence, resulting in both physical and psychological consequences. It is also widespread and occurs throughout much of the world. Despite potentially confounding variables, including related stressors (such as refugee experiences or traumatic bereavement), and comorbid conditions (such as anxiety, depression, or physical injury), torture itself has been shown to be directly linked to post-traumatic stress disorder (PTSD) and other symptoms and disabilities. The findings from both uncontrolled and controlled studies have produced substantial evidence that for some individuals, torture has serious and long-lasting psychological consequences.

Most trauma experts—including survivors of torture, mental health researchers, and therapists—agree that the psychiatric diagnosis of PTSD is relevant for torture survivors. However, these same experts emphasize that the consequences of torture go beyond psychiatric diagnoses. Turner and Gorst-Unsworth highlighted four common themes in the complex picture of torture and its consequences: (1) PTSD as a result of specific torture experiences; (2) depression as a result of multiple losses associated with torture; (3) physical symptoms resulting from the specific forms of torture; and (4) the "existential dilemma" of surviving in a world in which torture is a reality. The 10th revision of the *International Classification of Diseases* includes a diagnosis of "Enduring Personality Change after Catastrophic Experience" as one effort to capture the long-term existential consequences of the tearing up of a social world caused by torture. The profound psychological and physical consequences of torture are also evident in several carefully written personal accounts of the experience of torture.

Comprehensive reviews of the psychological effects of torture have systematically evaluated research with torture survivors, examining the unique consequences associated with torture and the complex interaction of social, environmental, and justice-related issues. As noted in these reviews, the psychological problems most commonly reported by torture survivors in research studies include (a) psychological symptoms (anxiety, depression, irritability or aggressiveness, emotional instability, self-isolation or social withdrawal); (b) cognitive symptoms (confusion or disorientation, impaired memory and concentration); and (c) neurovegetative symptoms (insomnia, nightmares, sexual dysfunction). Other findings reported in studies of torture survivors include abnormal sleep patterns, brain damage, and personality changes. The effects of torture can extend throughout the life of the survivor affecting his or her psychological, familial, and economic functioning. Such consequences have also been shown to be transmitted across generations in studies of various victim/survivor populations and across trauma types.

Studies conducted over the past 15 years strongly suggest that people who develop PTSD may also experience serious neurobiological changes, including changes in the body's ability to respond to stress (through alterations in stress hormones), and changes in the hippocampus, an area in the brain related to contextual memory. Thus, the development of PTSD has direct and long-term implications for the functioning of numerous biological systems essential to human functioning.

For survivors, having "healers" participating in their torture by supporting interrogators or providing medical treatment in order to prolong torture can erode future recovery by damaging the legitimate role that physicians or therapists could provide in offering treatment or social support, essential components in the recovery of trauma survivors. For these reasons, numerous medical associations, including the American Psychiatric Association and the World Medical Association, include as part of their ethical and professional standards a complete prohibition against participation of their members in interrogation, torture, or other forms of ill treatment. Similarly, the South African Truth and Reconciliation Commission documented how health providers were at times complicit in human rights abuses under apartheid, and through their report, hoped to shed light on this worldwide phenomenon and work toward an international effort to prevent such abuses from occurring.

Research that focuses directly on the participation of health professionals in torture and interrogation has documented important contextual issues for understanding how such participation can occur. Robert Lifton interviewed Nazi doctors who participated in human experimentation and killings, and found them to be "normal professionals" who offered medical justifications for their actions. In studies of physicians and other health providers who are involved in forms of military interrogation, Lifton elaborates on "atrocity-producing" environments in which normal individuals may forsake personal or professional values in an environment where torture is the norm. Furthermore, these same health care professionals may, through their actions, transfer legitimacy to a situation, supporting an illusion for all participants that some form of therapy or medical purpose is involved.

Other studies of those who torture have provided details about the step-by-step training that can transform ordinary people into people who can and will torture others, by systematically providing justifications for actions, professional or role authority, and secrecy. Participation in torture and other atrocities has been shown to have long-term negative psychological consequences for perpetrators, even in situations where professional or environmental justifications were offered to them in the context of their actions. . . .

Therefore, we urge APA and other scholarly and professional associations of psychologists to:

1. Unambiguously condemn the use of torture and other forms of cruel, inhuman, or degrading treatment as interrogation devices and call upon the U.S. government and its military to explicitly ban the use of such treatment and enforce all laws and regulations prohibiting its use.

2. Conduct an independent investigation of the extent to which psychologists have been involved in using torture or other cruel, inhuman, or degrading treatment as interrogation tools. If psychologists are found to have participated in the design or conduct of interrogations that have made use of torture, they should be appropriately sanctioned by APA and other professional organizations.
3. Expressly forbid psychologists from planning, designing, assisting, or participating in interrogations that involve the use of torture and any form of cruel, inhuman, or degrading treatment of human beings.
4. Develop specific guidelines and explicit codes of conduct for psychologists working in contexts of war and imprisonment. These guidelines should be consistent with international treaties and human rights covenants as well as guidelines developed for health professionals. Such guidelines should include meaningful enforcement, processes for the investigation of violations, and professional and legal consequences for violations.

**Kirk M. Hubbard**

# Psychologists and Interrogations: What's Torture Got to Do with It?

In an article that has been endorsed by SPSSI, Costanzo, Gerrity, and Lykes (2007) argue that "psychologists should not be involved in interrogations that make use of torture or other forms of cruel, inhumane, or degrading treatment" (doi: 10.1111/j.1530-2415.2007.00118.x). Their statement is ironic, for torture is illegal in the United States. But even more importantly, it seems to come from and apply to a world that no longer exists, and that simplifies issues so that they can be as one might like them to be. As recent events in England illustrate (August 2006), Islamic militants seek to kill us and undermine if not destroy our way of life. We have only to listen to what they say and watch their actions in order to know that regardless of how we would like things to be, they mean us harm. We also know from findings of the 9/11 commission that this problem did not start, nor will it likely finish, with the current presidential administration. An important point that is illustrated is that we no longer live in a world where people agree on what is ethical or even acceptable, and where concern for other humans transcends familial ties. When adolescents carry bombs on their bodies and plan suicides that will kill others, we know that shared values no longer exist. In the words of Scottish comedian Billy Connolly, "It seems to me that Islam and Christianity and Judaism all have the same god, and he's telling them all different things."

A prominent challenge for psychologists is determining how narrowly or broadly the field should prescribe what is acceptable behavior for professionals working with diverse populations, for increasingly psychologists come from differing backgrounds and hold varying beliefs. Effective practice with one population may be totally ineffective with another; we as a profession have not yet thoughtfully addressed how we balance what one culture defines as ethical against what another could view as necessary to be successful. The comment by Costanzo et al., and its rejoinders, provide a good illustration, namely, how does one balance standards of behaviors against results. What if, hypothetically, Middle Eastern psychologists told us that in order to successfully obtain information from suspected terrorists we would have to use approaches that we found inappropriate or unethical? I reject the idea that it is somehow unfair to use what we know about psychological science to protect our families and defend our lives and culture. Many areas of psychology owe their advancement in large

From *Analyses of Social Issues and Public Policy,* 7(1), December 2007, pp. 29–33. 

part to research conducted under the auspices of the military and supported by it. Clinical psychology has roots in the military and the OSS, and many psychologists have proudly defended their country with honor. In this context, the SPSSI policy statement by Costanzo et al. is both unnecessary and gratuitous. It is unnecessary because torture is already illegal in the United States. It is gratuitous because it feeds the egos of those who endorse it. It gives the illusion of possessing a higher moral ground, when in fact what is left unsaid and readable between the lines reveals it to be ideological and political. As parallels, SPSSI might put out policy statements against rape and murder, for those also are illegal, and we would not want our members participating in such behaviors. But murder and rape occur despite being illegal, and similarly, behaviors that are classified as torture may periodically occur. But that does not mean that torture is a government-sanctioned tool for conducting interrogations or even acceptable to use. There are specific and strict federal guidelines regarding what constitutes a legal and acceptable interrogation. I submit that there is no evidence that psychologists were involved in cases of torture—certainly not at Abu Ghraib prison.

A second issue of import is whether or not psychologists should be involved in legal interrogations. Again, the position of the authors is too simplistic. I take exception to the suggestion that all psychologists should be banned from assisting in legal interrogations. It is one thing to "ban" psychologists who are members of APA from engaging in torture, but quite another to prohibit them from consulting or advising during legal interrogations. First, there are many types of psychologists (social psychologist, industrial/organizational psychologists, and experimental psychologists, for example) who are not licensed mental health professionals and therefore should not be bound by the doctor/patient relationship code of ethics. Yet they bring information from their fields that help exert influence. Second, I object to the "psychocentric" and seemingly arrogant position that receiving training in psychology trumps all other roles a person may choose to pursue, or because of circumstances, are obliged to fulfill. Is it not possible for someone to receive training in psychology and then decide to pursue a career in law enforcement and engage in legal interrogations? Should being a psychologist as well as a law enforcement agent prohibit their participation if psychologists are prohibited? And, third, how is psychology accountable to society—should it withhold information about ways in which to protect our population or to influence terrorists to disclose information? What does psychology owe society? Should we focus exclusively on individuals with whom psychologists come in contact? What about helping to protect communities from terrorism? I simply do not believe that at a policy level we should decide that the "rights" of an individual count more than the rights and safety of society. APA and SPSSI should do something positive to fight terrorism rather than merely sit on the sidelines and criticize others who are trying to protect the United States from another senseless 9/11 attack. Honorable men and women are at war with those who seek to harm us, and the rest of us are at risk from terrorists. If psychology wants to make a positive contribution, the profession should accept that it is sometimes necessary to get information from those who would harm us and are intentionally withholding information that could stop attacks. If we as a profession do not like the use of coercion to obtain actionable information, then we as a profession should be willing to step up to the plate and suggest reliable and effective alternatives that do not rely on psychological or physical coercion. Have we as professional organizations of psychologists committed resources to develop ethical, non-punishing approaches that improve the quality of information that we can extract from individuals who are not willing to share it?

I also find it ironic that SPSSI can so readily become exercised about cruel and degrading treatment of suspected terrorists, yet conduct only limited research on similar behaviors that are manifested all too frequently in military boot camps, in legal police interrogations, in U.S. prisons, and government psychiatric hospitals. Indeed, even college fraternities and schoolyard bullies engage in cruel and degrading behavior. Why is it so easy for SPSSI to react so adamantly about illegal interrogations, yet do so little about domestic kinds of cruel and degrading treatment?

I also wonder how Costanzo et al. would feel if the "ticking time bomb scenario" that they attempt to render as "implausible" were to occur. Would they feel responsible for telling U.S. citizens that it won't ever happen? The "ticking bomb" scenario may be implausible for many APA members, but it was very real for those individuals interrogating Khalid Sheik Mohammed or Abu Zubayadh. Instead of focusing on decades old research that may no longer be relevant, Constanzo et al. might have cited the Jose Padilla case that was covered by the press. As readers may recall, Jose Padilla was a trained al Qaeda operative who was arrested as he tried to enter the United States in Chicago on May 8, 2002. He had accepted an assignment to destroy apartment buildings and had planned to detonate a radiological device commonly referred to as a "dirty bomb." As reported by CNN (June 11, 2002) and *Time* (June 16, 2002), Padilla was arrested directly as a result of an interrogation of captured senior al Qaeda member Abu Zubaydah. The Padilla case is a prime example of how a legal interrogation of a known terrorist led to the prevention of another terrorist attack.

Similarly, imagine that al Qaeda leader Abu Mussib al Zarqawri has been captured alive in Iraq rather than killed by bombings. Is there anyone who believes that he would have no potentially worthwhile knowledge of attacks planned to occur in the days following his capture? Costanzo et al. create a scenario that is not grounded in current knowledge of terrorism in general and terrorists in particular when they attempt to (mis)lead us into thinking legal interrogations do not yield actionable intelligence.

The prototypical "expert" on interrogation asserts that information is more reliable when voluntarily given rather than coerced. Well, of course it is. The expert then may assert that the way to elicit voluntary provision of information is to build a relationship with the terrorist so that the terrorist likes you or to appeal to common values so the terrorist sees your interests as converging with his/hers, and then the terrorist will tell you what you need to know. Such reasoning ignores the demand characteristics of both the prototypical law enforcement interrogation and the terrorist's values and operational intent. Are we to think the terrorist has the following thoughts: "You know, nobody has ever been as nice to me as these people—I'm going to turn my back on my

God and my life's work and tell them what they what to know." Alternatively, maybe the terrorist will think "What a clever way of asking that question. Now that they put it that way, I have no choice but to tell them what they need to know to disrupt my plans." Unfortunately, it is difficult to envision scenarios where useful information will be forthcoming.

For many Westerners caught after committing a crime, the psychological pressure of trying to influence whether or not they are charged, what they are charged with, and the kind of punishment they are likely to receive coerces them into working with the person who seems to understand them to make the best deal in a bad set of circumstances. The "experts'" assertion that rapport and liking are the keys to obtaining information, ignore the coercive pressures inherent in the circumstances. To pretend that these coercive pressures are not present does not make them go away. For terrorists who do not care if they live or die and have no fear of prison, there is little or no incentive to work with interrogators. And, to our discredit, we as psychologists have contributed little to increasing our understanding of circumstances like these and techniques of persuasion that might be effective.

Lastly, I found the call for an independent investigation of the extent to which psychologists have been involved in using torture or other cruel, inhuman, or degrading treatment during an interrogation unwarranted. Costanzo et al. present virtually no evidence that psychologists have been involved in even a single case. APA/SPSSI has no authority by which to sanction non-members. Many psychologists are choosing not to join APA or to allow their memberships to lapse, believing that as it does not represent their interests and values. In my opinion, APA and some of its divisions have drifted from a being a professional organization advancing the science of psychology and translating research to action and policy, to a point where they are promoting a social and political agenda.

I am opposed to torture. But I endorse the use of interrogation when used consistently with current federal law and conducted by trained interrogators. And I certainly see no reason why psychologists cannot assist in developing effective, lawful ways to obtain actionable intelligence in fighting terrorism. If the information can be obtained noncoercively, all the better. Social psychology taught us how to use social influence in getting people to do things they ordinarily would not do and buy things they often do not need or want. In my view, it is common sense that you would want psychologists involved in the interrogation of known terrorists. As psychologists, rather than decrying illegal use of cruel and inhumane treatment to obtain information, we should work to develop reliable noncoercive ways to get people to tell us about terrorist activity of which they have knowledge and are attempting to withhold. We need to take a proactive stance in saving lives and preventing acts of terror. The Costanzo et al. article does not appreciably help psychology to move forward, for it limits opportunities for psychologists to gain first-hand knowledge of the nature of the challenges interrogators face, and focuses on current approaches rather than on developing new ones that apply and improve current psychological knowledge.

# CHALLENGE QUESTIONS

## Should Psychologists Abstain from Involvement in Coercive Interrogations?

1. Costanzo, Gerrity, and Lykes argue that psychologists are acting harmfully by participating in coercive interrogations, whereas Hubbard argues that psychologists are potentially allowing harm to occur by not participating in interrogations. How do you think that psychologists should approach the issue of interrogation if they intend to "first do no harm"? Is it possible to do no harm in this scenario?
2. Hubbard seems to suggest that psychologists may be justified in causing enemy detainees a certain (legal) degree of harm if it produces life-saving information. Do you agree with this position? Why or why not?
3. Since, as both articles concede, torture is illegal and is officially condemned by the APA, why might it still be useful to expressly ban psychologists' involvement in coercive interrogations? Why might such a ban be problematic?
4. Is it possible for psychologists both to serve the interests of defending their country and to abstain from involvement in coercive interrogation? Why or why not?
5. Summarize the positions of the two articles on the "ticking time bomb scenario" and provide your own rationale for how you would act in this scenario.

# ISSUE 16

## Do Video Games Lead to Violence?

**YES: Douglas A. Gentile and Craig A. Anderson**, from "Violent Video Games: The Newest Media Violence Hazard," in Douglas A. Gentile, ed., *Media Violence and Children: A Complete Guide for Parents and Professionals* (Praeger, 2003)

**NO: Cheryl K. Olson**, from "The Electronic Friend? Video Games and Children's Friendships" Society for Interpersonal Theory and Research Newsletter (October 2008)

### ISSUE SUMMARY

**YES:** Developmental psychologist Douglas A. Gentile and department of psychology chair Craig A. Anderson assert that violent video games cause several physiological and psychological changes in children that lead to aggressive and violent behavior.

**NO:** Cheryl K. Olson, professor of psychiatry and co-author of a recent book on violent video games, suggests not only that there is insufficient research to say that such games lead to violence but also that they may even have pro-social consequences.

**W**idely publicized tragedies, such as campus shootings, have raised an important public question: what caused these events? Often violent media, such as first-person shooting games (or other games in which a player participates in violent actions), are suggested as important contributing factors to the assailant's mindset. As technology improves, video game graphics have become increasingly realistic, making depictions of violence extremely life-like. The government has even taken advantage of the life-like depiction to help train soldiers for the violence of war. This increasing realism raises understandable concerns about children who get heavily involved in such virtual violence in their video play.

On the other hand, does this video involvement *have* to mean real-life violence? Even virtual soldier training does not mean that soldiers commit such real-life violence. Indeed, it is extremely rare for those who play violent videos to become real-world killers. If violent video games are such strong influences, why are the vast majority of such gamers not affected? Can video games really be blamed for real world violence, or are there other factors that need to be taken into account? Seeking answers to these crucial questions is important to parenting and governmental policy-making. Consequently, psychologists have attempted to address them through rigorous research.

In the first article Douglas A. Gentile and Craig A. Anderson believe the research has made it clear that playing violent videogames leads to violent behavior. These researchers claim that several things happen when a child is playing violent games: an increase in physiological arousal, aggressive cognitions and emotions, aggressive behaviors, and decreased pro-social behaviors. These researchers also take on some of the more popular criticisms facing video game research, such as the claim that violent video games only affect those who are already abnormally aggressive. Gentile and Anderson argue that this criticism is not valid because no group has ever been discovered to be totally immune from the effects of violent video games.

Psychiatrist Cheryl K. Olson asserts that there is not a causal connection between violent video games and violent behavior. In the second article, she summarizes several of her relevant research studies, including multiple qualitative and quantitative projects, a survey of over 1,000 middle school-aged children, and in-depth conversations with 42 youths in focus groups. While she allows that some individuals may have bad experiences with video games, she reports that playing such games, even violent ones, is a normal part of adolescent development. Indeed, they may even have pro-social and relationship-building consequences.

**POINT**

- Experimental research shows that playing violent video games increases aggressive behavior
- No one is immune to the effects of video game violence
- There is empirical evidence that some populations are more affected then others
- Violent video games promote anti-social behavior

**COUNTER POINT**

- There is not sufficient evidence to hold that violent video games causes real world violence
- For most, playing violent video games does not have a significant impact
- More research is needed to draw conclusions for "at risk" populations
- Violent video games can have pro-social consequences

YES 

**Douglas A. Gentile and Craig A. Anderson**

# Violent Video Games: The Newest Media Violence Hazard

## . . . Time Spent with Video Games

Video games have become one of the dominant entertainment media for children in a very short time. In the mid-1980s, children averaged about four hours a week playing video games, including time spent playing at home and in arcades. By the early 1990s, home video game use had increased and arcade play had decreased. The average amount was still fairly low, averaging about two hours of home play per week for girls, and about four hours of home play per week for boys. By the mid-1990s, home use had increased for fourth grade girls to 4.5 hours per week, and to 7.1 hours per week for fourth grade boys. In recent national surveys of parents, school-age children (boys and girls combined) devote an average of about seven hours per week playing video games. In a recent survey of over 600 eighth and ninth grade students, children averaged 9 hours per week of video game play overall, with boys averaging 13 hours per week and girls averaging 5 hours per week. Thus, while sex-correlated differences in the amount of time committed to playing video games continue to exist, the rising tide has floated all boats.

Even very young children are playing video games. Gentile & Walsh found that children aged two to seven play an average of 43 minutes per day (by parent report), and Woodard and Gridina found that even preschoolers aged two to five average 28 minutes of video game play per day. Although few studies have documented how the amount of time devoted to playing video games changes with development, some studies have suggested that video game play may peak in early school-age children. Buchman & Funk found the amount of time was highest for fourth grade children and decreased steadily through eighth grade. Others have suggested that play is highest between ages 9 and 12, decreases between ages 12 and 14, and increases again between ages 15 and 18. Surprisingly, the amount of time children devote to television has remained remarkably stable even as the amount of time devoted to video and computer games has increased.

Although the research evidence is still limited, amount of video game play has been linked with a number of risk factors for maladaptive development, including smoking, obesity, and poorer academic performance. These results parallel those showing that greater use of television is correlated with poorer grades in school. . . .

### Preferences for Violent Video Games

Although video games are designed to be entertaining, challenging, and sometimes educational, most include violent content. Recent content analyses of video games show that as many as 89 percent of games contain some violent content, and that about half of the games include violent content toward other game characters that would result in serious injuries or death.

Many children prefer to play violent games. Of course, what constitutes a "violent" game varies depending upon who is classifying them. The video game industry and its ratings board (Entertainment Software Rating Board) claim to see much less violence in their games than do parents and other researchers. Even within the research community there is some inconsistency in definition of what constitutes a violent video game. Generally, however, researchers consider as "violent" those games in which the player can harm other characters in the game. In many popular video games, harming other characters is the main activity. It is these games, in which killing occurs at a high rate, that are of most concern to media violence researchers, child advocacy groups, and parents. . . . In studies of fourth through eighth grade children, more than half of the children state preferences for games in which the main action is predominantly human violence or fantasy violence. In surveys of children and their parents, about two-thirds of children named violent games as their favorites. Only about one-third of parents were able to correctly name their child's favorite game, and in 70 percent of the incorrect matches, children described their favorite game as violent. A preference for violent games has been linked with hostile attribution biases, increased arguments with teachers, lower self-perceptions of behavioral conduct, and increased physical fights. . . .

## Why Violent Video Games May Have a Greater Effect Than Violent TV

The public health community has concluded from the preponderance of evidence that violent television leads to "increases in aggressive attitudes, values, and behavior, particularly in children." Although the research on violent video games is still growing, there are at least six reasons why we should expect violent video games to have an even greater impact than violent television. These reasons are based on what we already know from the television and educational literatures.

1. *Identification with an aggressor increases imitation of the aggressor.* It is known from research on violent television that children will imitate aggressive actions more readily if they identify with an aggressive character in some way. On television, it is hard to predict with

which characters, if any, a person will identify. One might identify most closely with the victim, in which case the viewer would be less likely to be aggressive after watching. In many violent video games, however, one is required to take the point of view of one particular character. This is most noticeable in "first-person shooter" games, in which the players "see" what their character would see as if they were inside the video game. Thus, the player is forced to identify with a violent character. In fact, in many games, players have a choice of characters to play and can upload photographs of their faces onto their character. This identification with the aggressive character is likely to increase the likelihood of imitating the aggressive acts.

2. *Active participation increases learning.* Research on learning shows that when one becomes actively involved in something, one learns much more than if one only watches it. This is one reason computer technology in the classroom has been considered to be educationally beneficial. Educational video games are theorized to be effective partly because they require active participation. With regard to violent entertainment, viewers of violent content on television are passive observers of the aggressive acts. In contrast, violent video games by their very nature require active participation in the violent acts.
3. *Practicing an entire behavioral sequence is more effective than practicing only a part.* If one wanted to learn how to kill someone, one would quickly realize that there are many steps involved. At a minimum, one needs to decide whom to kill, get a weapon, get ammunition, load the weapon, stalk the victim, aim the weapon, and pull the trigger. It is rare for television shows or movies to display all of these steps. Yet, violent video games regularly require players to practice each of these steps repeatedly. This helps teach the necessary steps to commit a successful act of aggression. In fact, some video games are so successful at training whole sequences of aggressive behaviors that the U.S. Army has licensed them to train their forces. For example, the popular violent video game series *Rainbow Six* is so good at teaching all of the steps necessary to plan and conduct a successful special operations mission that the U.S. Army has licensed the game engine to train their special operations soldiers. Furthermore, the U.S. Army has created their own violent video game as a recruitment tool.
4. *Violence is continuous.* Research with violent television and movies has shown that the effects on viewers are greater if the violence is unrelieved and uninterrupted. However, in both television programs and movies, violent content is rarely sustained for more than a few minutes before changing pace, changing scenes, or going to commercials. In contrast, the violence in violent video games is often continuous. Players must constantly be alert for hostile enemies, and must constantly choose and enact aggressive behaviors. These behaviors expose players to a continual stream of violent (and often gory) scenes accompanied by screams of pain and suffering in a context that is incompatible with feelings of empathy or guilt.
5. *Repetition increases learning.* If one wishes to learn a new phone number by memory, one often will repeat it over and over to aid memory. This simple mnemonic device has been shown to be an effective learning technique. With few exceptions (e.g., *Blue's Clues*),

children rarely see the same television shows over and over. In a violent video game, however, players often spend a great deal of time doing the same aggressive actions (e.g., shooting things) over and over. Furthermore, the games are usually played repeatedly, thus giving a great deal of practice repeating the violent game actions. This increases the odds that not only will children learn from them, but they will make these actions habitual to the point of automaticity.

6. *Rewards increase imitation.* There are at least three different processes involved. First, rewarding aggressive behavior in a video game (e.g., winning extra points and lives) increases the frequency of behaving aggressively in that game (see number 5, above). Second, rewarding aggressive behavior in a video game teaches more positive attitudes toward the use of force as a means of solving conflicts. Television programs rarely provide a reward structure for the viewer, and it would be rarer still to have those rewards dependent on violent acts. In contrast, video games often reward players for participating. Third, the reward patterns involved in video games increase the player's motivation to persist at the game. Interestingly, all three of these processes help educational games be more effective. The last process can make the games somewhat addictive.

## The Effects of Violent Video Games

Over the past 20 years, a number of scholars have expressed concern over the potential negative impact of exposing youth to violent video games. . . .

## Meta-Analytic Summary of Violent Video Game Effects

Narrative reviews of a research literature, such as that by Dill and Dill, are very useful ways of examining prior studies. Typically, the researchers try to find an organizing scheme that makes sense of the varied results that typically occur in any research domain. However, as useful as such reviews of the literature are, meta-analyses (studies of studies) are a much more powerful technique to find the common effects of violent video games across multiple studies. Specifically, a meta-analysis uses statistical techniques to combine the results of various studies of the same basic hypothesis, and provides an objective answer to the questions of whether or not the key independent variable has a reliable effect on the key dependent variable, and if so, what the magnitude of that effect is. Only recently have there been enough studies on violent video games to make meta-analysis a useful technique. In 2001, the first comprehensive meta-analysis of the effects of violent video games was conducted. A more recent update to that meta-analysis produced the same basic findings. A consistent pattern of the effects of playing violent games was documented in five areas.

1. *Playing violent video games increases physiological arousal.* Studies measuring the effects of playing violent video games tend to show larger increases in heart rate and systolic and diastolic blood pressure compared to playing nonviolent video games. The average effect size

across studies between violent game play and physiological arousal was 0.22.[1] For example, Ballard and West showed that a violent game (*Mortal Kombat* with the blood "turned on") resulted in higher systolic blood pressure responses than either a nonviolent game or a less graphically violent game (*Mortal Kombat* with the blood "turned off"). . . .

2. *Playing violent video games increases aggressive cognitions.* Studies measuring cognitive responses to playing violent video games have shown that aggressive thoughts are increased compared to playing nonviolent video games. The average effect size across studies between violent game play and aggressive cognitions was 0.27. These effects have been found in children and adults, in males and females, and in experimental and nonexperimental studies. . . .
3. *Playing violent video games increases aggressive emotions.* Studies measuring emotional responses to playing violent video games have shown that aggressive emotions are increased compared to playing nonviolent video games. The average effect size across studies between violent game play and aggressive emotions was 0.18. These effects have been found in children and adults, in males and females, and in experimental and nonexperimental studies. In one study, adults' state hostility and anxiety levels were increased after playing a violent game compared to controls. In a study of third through fifth grade children, playing a violent game increased frustration levels more than playing a nonviolent game.
4. *Playing violent video games increases aggressive behaviors.* Studies measuring aggressive behaviors after playing violent video games have shown that aggressive behaviors are increased compared to playing nonviolent video games. The average effect size across studies between violent game play and aggressive behaviors was 0.19. These effects have been found in children and adults, in males and females, and in experimental and nonexperimental studies. . . .
5. *Playing violent video games decreases prosocial behaviors.* Studies measuring responses to playing violent video games have shown that prosocial behaviors are decreased compared to playing nonviolent video games. The average effect size across studies between violent game play and prosocial behaviors was –0.16. These effects have been found in both experimental and nonexperimental studies. In one study of 278 seventh and eighth graders, children who named violent games as their favorite games to play were rated by their peers as exhibiting fewer prosocial behaviors and more aggressive behaviors in the classroom. . . .

## Critiques of the Video Game Research Literature

Any new research domain has strengths and weaknesses. If all goes well, over time the researchers identify the weaknesses and address them in a variety of ways. When the new research domain appears to threaten the profits of some large industry, there is a tendency for that industry to deny the threatening research and to mount campaigns designed to highlight the weaknesses, obfuscate the legitimate findings, and cast doubt on the quality of the research. The history of the tobacco industry's attempt to ridicule, deny, and obfuscate research linking smoking to lung cancer is the prototype of such efforts. The TV and movie industries have had considerable success in their 40-year campaign against the media violence research community. The same type of effort has now been mounted by the video game industry. We do not claim that there are no weaknesses in the video game research literature. Indeed, we have highlighted some of them in our own prior writings. In this final section, we focus on two types of criticisms, legitimate ones (usually raised by researchers) and illegitimate ones (usually raised by the video game industry and their supporters in the scholarly community).

## Illegitimate Criticisms

1. *There are too few studies to warrant any conclusions about possible negative effects.*

This can be a legitimate concern if the small number of studies yields a lack of power to detect small effects. However, it is an illegitimate argument when it is used to claim that the current set of video game studies do not warrant serious concern about exposure to violent video games. If anything, it is remarkable that such reliable effects have emerged from such a relatively small number of studies (compared to TV and movie violence studies), and that the studies that vary so much in method, sample population, and video game stimuli.

2. *There are problems with the external validity of lab experiments due to demand characteristics, participant suspicion and compliance problems, trivial measures, artificial settings, and unrepresentative participants.*

These old arguments against laboratory studies in the behavioral sciences have been successfully debunked many times, in many contexts, and in several different ways. Both logical and empirical analyses of such broad-based attacks on lab experiments have found little cause for concern. Furthermore, more specific examination of these issues in the aggression domain have consistently found evidence of high external validity, and have done so in several very different ways.

3. *Complete dismissal of correlational studies: "Correlation is not causation."*

This is an overly simplistic view of how modern science is conducted. Psychology instructors teach this mantra to introductory psychology students, and hope that they will gain a much more sophisticated view of methods and scientific inference by the time they are seniors. Whole fields of science are based on correlational data (e.g., astronomy). Correlational studies are used to test causal theories, and thus provide falsification opportunities. A well-conducted correlational design, one which attempts to control for likely "third variable" factors, can provide much useful information. To be sure, correlational studies are generally (but not always) less informative about causality than experimental ones. What is most important is the whole pattern of results across studies that differ in design, procedure, and measures. And the existing research on violent video games yields consistent results.

4. *Arousal accounts for all video game effects on aggressive behavior.*

Physiological arousal dissipates fairly quickly. Therefore, the arousal claim does not apply to studies that measure aggressive behavior more than 30 minutes after game play has occurred, or studies in which aggression is measured by a retrospective report. For example, this criticism generally doesn't apply to correlational studies, but correlational studies show a significant link between violent video game exposure and aggression. Furthermore, there are a few experimental studies in which the violent and nonviolent game conditions were equated on arousal, and significant violent-content effects still occurred.

5. *There are no studies linking violent video game play to "serious" or actual aggression.*

This criticism is simply not true. A number of correlational studies have linked repeated violent video game play to serious aggression. For example, Anderson and Dill showed that college-student reports of violent video game play in prior years were positively related to aggression that would be considered criminal (e.g., assault, robbery) if known to police. Similarly, Gentile et al. found significant links between violent game play and physical fights.

6. *Violent media affect only a few who are already disturbed.*

As discussed earlier, there are reasons (some theoretical, some empirical) to believe that some populations will be more negatively affected than others. However, no totally "immune" population has ever been identified, and populations sometimes thought to be at low risk have nonetheless yielded significant violent video game exposure effects.

7. *Effects of media violence are trivially small.*

Once again, this is simply not true. Violent video game effects are bigger than: (a) effects of passive tobacco smoke and lung cancer; (b) exposure to lead and IQ scores in children; (c) calcium intake and bone mass.

Note that the critics use these seven illegitimate criticisms to basically dismiss all research on violent video games. Once one has dismissed all correlational studies (number 3, above) and all experiments that use laboratory or other "trivial" measures of aggression (number 2, above), the only potential type of study left is clearly unethical: an experimental field study in which violent crime is the measure of aggression. Such a study would require randomly assigning children to high versus low video game violence conditions for a period of years and then following up on their rates of violent criminal activity over the course of their lives. It is not an accident that all ethically feasible types of studies are dismissed by the industry and its supporters.

## Legitimate Criticisms

1. *Sample sizes tend to be too small in many studies.*

If the average effect size is about r = 0.20, then N (the number of study participants) should be at least 200 for 0.80 power (power is the likelihood of being able to find a legitimate difference between groups). When N is too small, individual studies will *appear* inconsistent even if they are all accurate samples of the true r = 0.20 effect. For this reason, the best way of summarizing the results of a set of too-small studies is to combine the results via meta-analysis, rather than using the more traditional narrative review. When this is done, we see that the video game studies yield consistent results.

2. *Some studies do not have "violent" and "nonviolent" games that are sufficiently different in actual violent content.*

This problem was noted earlier in this chapter in the discussion of how early studies might find weaker effects because the "violent" video games in the early years were not very violent by contemporary standards. . . . Future studies need to do a better job of assessing the violent content of the video games being compared.

3. *Some experimental studies have used a "control" or "nonviolent game" condition that was more boring, annoying, or frustrating than the violent game.*

The obvious solution for future studies is to do more pilot testing or manipulation checks on such aggression-relevant dimensions. In trying to summarize past research, one can sometimes find a more appropriate comparison condition within the same experiment.

4. *Some studies did not report sufficient results to enable calculation of an effect size for participants who actually played a video game.*

This problem arose in several cases in which half of the participants played a video game while the other half merely observed. Reported means then collapsed across this play versus observe dimension. Future reports should include the individual means.

5. *Some studies that purportedly study aggressive behavior have used dependent variables that are not true aggressive behavior.*

A surprising number of past studies have used trait or personality aggression scales as measures of aggressive behavior in short-term experiments.

This is a problem because there is no way that a short-term manipulation of exposure to violent versus nonviolent video games (e.g., 20 minutes) can influence one's past frequency of aggression. In this short-term context, such a trait measure might possibly be conceived as a measure of cognitive priming, but clearly it is not a measure of aggressive behavior.

A related problem is that some studies have included hitting an inanimate object as a measure of aggressive behavior. Most modern definitions of aggression restrict its application to behaviors that are intended to harm another person.

The obvious solution for future studies is to use better measures of aggression. In the analysis of past research one can sometimes disaggregate the reported composite measure to get a cleaner measure of aggression.

6. *There are no longitudinal studies.*

This is true. Major funding is needed to conduct a large-scale longitudinal study of video game effects. To date, such funding has not been forthcoming. Thus, one must rely on longitudinal studies in the TV/movie violence domain to get a reasonable guess as to the likely long-term effects. . . .

## Summary

Although there is less research on the effects of violent video games than there is on television and movies, the preponderance of evidence looks very similar to the research on violent television. In particular, violent video games appear to increase aggressive thoughts and feelings, physiological arousal, and aggressive behaviors, as well as to decrease prosocial behaviors. There are many theoretical reasons why one would expect violent video games to have a greater effect than violent television, and most of the reasons why one would expect them to have a lesser effect are no longer true because violent video games have become so realistic, particularly since the late 1990s. . . .

## Note

1. All effect sizes reported in the chapter are scaled as correlation coefficients, regardless of whether the study was experimental or correlational in design. . . .

**Cheryl K. Olson**

# NO

# The Electronic Friend? Video Games and Children's Friendships

A 2007 survey of teachers by the British charity Save the Children, widely reported by newspapers, concluded that children were spending more time on solitary pursuits such as computer games to the detriment of their social skills. This assumption that video games undermine friendships is widespread. When we talked to parents of teen boys in focus groups, one of the first concerns they raised—ahead of violent video game content—was that game play might be isolating or interfere with social functioning. As one mother said, "Five, six years from now, will they be able to socialize in a group amongst people who don't necessarily play these games?".

Based on surveys of arcade-gaming preteens, Selnow concluded that videogames were primarily a solitary activity, and that this "electronic friend" might substitute for human companionship. However, there is scant evidence that modern video and computer games promote social isolation.

In a set of qualitative and quantitative studies at Massachusetts General Hospital, we looked at the "epidemiology" of adolescent video game play: the who, what, where, when and how, as well as the why. We found that video and computer games are central to the social lives of many young teens, especially boys, and serve a number of social functions.

In this article, I'll draw on our school-based survey of 1,254 middle-school youth in South Carolina and Pennsylvania, as well as data from focus groups with 42 boys in the greater Boston area. We were struck by the ubiquity of electronic games in children's lives. Just 17 of our survey subjects had never played electronic games; 63 others had not played in the previous six months. (Their responses were excluded from our analyses.)

We asked children whether they agreed or disagreed (on a 4-point scale) with a series of possible reasons for electronic game play. Many agreed that social factors motivated their play, . . . including competition, joining friends in play, teaching others how to play, and (least frequently) making new friends. Boys were significantly more likely than girls to agree with the first two of these motivations.

"To compete and win" was particularly popular among boys; 57% "strongly agreed" that this motivated their video game play (second only to

From *Society for Interpersonal Theory and Research SITAR Newsletter,* vol. 9, no. 1, October 2008, pp. 2, 7–8. 

"it's just fun"). Focus group comments supported this finding. A typical example: "Usually me and my friends, when we're over at each others' houses, and they have a good game, [we'll play it]. They're like, 'Oh, I'll kill you in Madden 2005.' It's fun to beat them."

These results are in line with a recent large study by the British Board of Film Classification (which rates video games in the U.K.). Their report noted that "the social rewards of gaming—talking about how you are doing, playing together, helping or beating each other—are less a part of the attraction for females than males." It's important to note, however, that the urge to compete is not limited to boys. In our survey, 61% of girls who played games were motivated in part by the chance to compete and win.

We speculate that for boys, video games may serve some of the same purposes as "rough and tumble" play, in terms of jockeying for social status. Boys can gain status among peers by owning or mastering a popular game. In fact, a study of adolescent male social identity by Tarrant et al. found that "good at computer/video games" was one of the most desirable traits, ranking second only to being "fun" among one's "ingroup" members.

Along with friendly competition, boys and girls gain satisfaction from teaching others how to play. In focus groups, boys described sharing advice and tips: "'Oh, this guy is the best.' 'Where are you in this game?' 'Oh, I'm having a hard time in the queen's castle' or whatever." They direct each other to web sites for the latest "cheat" codes. In surveys of (mostly adult) online game players, Yee found that helping other players and being part of a group effort were important motivators for play.

Boys told us that games are a frequent focus for conversation among their peers. When I asked one boy what the kids at school would talk about if they weren't talking about games, he replied: "I don't know. Probably like girls, or something like that . . . I don't even know, 'cause the most they talk about is girls and games—the two Gs."

Although making new friends was not among the top motivations for video gaming in our survey, video games clearly create common ground that young people can use to make friends. As one boy explained in a focus group, start by asking "'Do you own a system, a game system?' If he says 'yes,' then, 'What kind?'"

Making friends was a higher-ranked motivator, however, for the 78 children we surveyed who were classified as mildly learning disabled. Children in this group were more likely to be victims of bullying, and to report being left out or excluded by their peers. Their overall top reasons for playing games reflect their needs to connect with friends: playing because their friends did, to make new friends, or to teach others. They were also significantly more likely to play to cope with feelings of loneliness.

Most children who play video games play alone at times, whether for fun, out of boredom, or to help them deal with stress. Boys are more likely than girls to report playing by themselves; 62.8% play "often" or "always" alone, compared to 45.6% of girls. However, boys are also more likely than girls to play often/always with multiple friends in the same room (33.4% vs. 12.5%). Children who are heavy game players (the 12.6% of boys and 1.5%

of girls who report playing more than 15 hours in a typical week) are more likely to play in groups, whether in person or over the Internet. . . . Playing video games alone almost all of the time is not typical, and may be a marker for social or emotional problems. More research is needed on healthy and unhealthy patterns of video game play, especially among children with emotional problems or developmental delays.

Much of the debate about video games, among both academics and the public, has focused on the potential influence of violent content. Despite the frequent media speculation, no link has been found between school shootings and violent video games. (It's important to note that it's the media coverage of school shootings, rather than the rate of violence, that has increased). Nevertheless, we dread the thought of a socially outcast child holed up in his bedroom, engrossed in practicing various methods of murder. Fortunately, this is by no means typical. Our survey found that children who play Mature-rated, violent games are not more likely than other children their age to play games alone. In fact, . . . compared to children who don't play M-rated games regularly, M-game players were significantly *more* likely to play games in social settings. The majority of boys in our sample (including the 12-year-olds) routinely played at least one M-rated title, along with 29% of female game players. Thought the thought may be discomforting, violent video game play has become a normal part of male childhood.

And it may not be all bad. Some researchers have questioned whether we worry too much about teens who play violent games in groups, and speculate on possible benefits. Jansz notes that "the gamer wants to experience particular emotions with his friends to intensify their mutual bonds." Goldstein takes a cultural/historical perspective, noting that "Violent entertainment appeals primarily to males, and it appeals to them mostly in groups. People rarely attend horror films or boxing matches alone, and boys do not often play war games by themselves. These are social occasions, particularly suitable for . . . communicating a masculine identity to your mates."

# CHALLENGE QUESTIONS

## Do Video Games Lead to Violence?

1. Gentile and Anderson list several reasons why children may be more affected by violent video games than by violent television. Which do you think has the greater effect? Defend your position.
2. Olson suggests that playing violent video games is now a normal experience for adolescent boys. How should society respond to such changing norms?
3. Based on these readings, what restrictions, if any, should parents place on their children's exposure to violent video games? Defend you answer with information from both articles.
4. Gentile and Anderson discuss differing definitions of violence. How do these differing definitions change the stance one might take on this issue?
5. Olson points to many positive effects of violent video games. Should policy decisions from the government take these into account? Do the possible pro-social benefits outweigh the alleged negative consequences?
6. How might the differing research methods used in these articles help shape the conclusions drawn by each set of researchers?

# ISSUE 17

## Can Sex Be Addictive?

**YES: Patrick Carnes**, from "Understanding Sexual Addiction," *SIECUS Report* (June/July 2003)

**NO: Lawrence A. Siegel and Richard M. Siegel**, from "Sex Addiction: Recovering from a Shady Concept," An Original Essay Written for *Taking Sides: Human Sexuality*, 10th edition (2007)

### ISSUE SUMMARY

**YES:** Sexual addiction expert Patrick J. Carnes argues not only that sex can be addictive but that sex can be as addictive as drugs, alcohol, or any other chemical substance.

**NO:** Sex therapists Lawrence A. Siegel and Richard M. Siegel believe that while some sexual behaviors might be dysfunctional, calling those behaviors "addictive" confuses a moralistic ideology with a scientific fact.

Addiction has become a pervasive feature of modern societies. Of the $666 billion spent for health care in the United States, 25% was spent on health-care problems related to addiction (Kinney, 2003; American Medical Association, 2003). Of the 11 million victims of the violent crimes that are committed each year in the United States, nearly 3 million reported that the offender had been drinking prior to the crime (Greenfield, 1998). Research also suggests that between 6 and 15 million Americans have compulsive shopping behaviors that result in unmanageable debt, bankruptcy, and damaged relationships (Stanford University, 2005). These varied examples demonstrate not only the damage addiction does but also the widely varying meanings it has—from drug addiction to shopping addiction.

Should we add "sex addiction" to the list? Few would dispute that certain chemicals, such as cocaine and even alcohol, merit the addiction label, but is it taking the label too far to consider sexual practices that lead to dysfunction an addiction? The term "addiction" is thought to be derived from the Latin word *addicere,* meaning to adore or to surrender oneself to a master (White, 1998). From this perspective, the term might seem to fit because some people appear to "surrender" themselves to the "master" of sexual games, sexual banter, and sexual intercourse. Indeed, sexuality seems to consume our popular culture. On the other hand, would not many adolescents (and even our popular culture itself) be considered "addicts" in this sense? What meaning does addiction have if everyone is addicted? Would not everyone be addicted to food in the same sense? Obviously, such questions have great importance for whether something should be treated in psychotherapy.

Widely regarded as an expert on sexual addiction, Patrick J. Carnes has been at the forefront of sexual addiction therapy. Carnes firmly believes that sex can be addictive and dysfunctional sexual practices ought to be treated in therapy. In fact, he promotes the use of a 12-step program, not unlike Alcoholics Anonymous, to help overcome sexual addiction on his Web site, www.sexhelp.com. He justifies this parallel with chemical dependency and treatment because sexual intercourse has a clear physiological component—sexual pleasure. Carnes claims that compulsively seeking sexual stimulation can lead to many negative consequences in an addict's life.

Sex therapists Lawrence A. Siegel and Richard M. Siegel disagree sharply with Carnes's position. In the second article they argue that those who want to call sex addictive have a hidden agenda. Their agenda is to extend society's fairly clear moral condemnation of drug abuse to sexual behaviors. The Siegels ask whether sexual behaviors are not in a different category altogether than drug abuse. If they are, then the unacceptability of drug-related abuse should not be extended to sexual behaviors, at least not in the same way. The Siegels go on to argue that the term "addiction" itself has difficulties. They contend that psychology cannot decide what it means, either to be addicted to something or to have an addictive nature. They conclude by reviewing some of Carnes's early work in sexual addiction, and then they respond to it by attempting to show his moral bias toward any sexual practice other than monogamous intimacy in marriage.

**POINT**

- Sex can be addictive.
- Sex addiction has physical and chemical components.
- Many deviant sexual behaviors fit the definition of what makes something addictive.
- Sex addicts, like those with eating disorders or alcoholism, cannot control their destructive behavior and need help.

**COUNTERPOINT**

- Addiction is merely a term for any behavior that falls outside of social norms.
- Chemical dependency should not be confused with mechanisms that drive sexual appetite.
- A consistent clinical definition of "addiction" has not been agreed upon.
- Sexual behavior is an issue of personal responsibility, not personal physiology.

# YES  Patrick Carnes

# Understanding Sexual Addiction

During the past three decades, professionals have acknowledged that some people use sex to manage their internal distress. These people are similar to compulsive gamblers, compulsive overeaters, or alcoholics in that they are not able to contain their impulses—and with destructive results.

## Definition

To facilitate classification and understanding of psychological disorders, mental health professionals rely on the *Diagnostic and Statistical Manual of Mental Disorders* (DSM) published by the American Psychiatric Association and now in its fourth edition.

Each edition of this book represents a consensus at the time of publication about what constitutes mental disorders. Each subsequent edition has reflected changes in understanding. The *DSM's* system is, therefore, best viewed as a "work in progress" rather than the "bible."

The term *sexual addiction* does not appear in *DSM-IV.* In fact, the word *addiction* itself does not appear. It condenses the criteria for addictive disorders—such as substance abuse and pathologic gambling—into three elements:

- *Loss of control (compulsivity).* "There is a persistent desire or unsuccessful efforts to cut down or control substance abuse." "Has persistent unsuccessful efforts to control, cut back, or stop gambling."
- *Continuation despite adverse consequences.* "The substance use is continued despite knowledge of having a persistent or recurrent physical or psychological problem that is likely to have been caused or exacerbated by the substance use." "Has committed illegal acts such as forgery, fraud, theft, or embezzlement to finance gambling."
- *Obsession or preoccupation.* "A great deal of time is spent in activities necessary to obtain the substance, use the substance, or recover from its effects." "Is preoccupied with gambling."[1]

## Complex Problem

Typically, individuals in trouble for their sexual behavior are not candid about whatever incident has come to light, nor are they likely to reveal that the specific behavior actually is a part of a consistent, self-destructive pattern. The nature of this illness causes patients to hide the severity of the problem from others, to delude themselves about their ability to control their behavior, and to minimize their impact on others.

Often some event will precipitate a visit to the primary care provider. Sexual excess of some type will create a physical problem. Sexually transmitted diseases, damage to genitals, unwanted pregnancies: all are among the reasons for such a visit. Most patients will say that the event is a unique situation.

The primary care provider will often treat the physical problem without probing for more information. If, however, there is sexual addiction, the problem will not disappear. A wide range of behaviors can be problematic, including compulsive masturbation, affairs, use of pornography, voyeurism, exhibitionism, sexual harassment, and sex offending.

Health care providers must understand that underneath what appears to be an isolated event may be a more complex pathologic problem with a host of related factors such as the following:

- A high incidence of depression and suicide
- The presence of high-risk and dangerous behaviors including self-harm designed to escalate sexual experiences
- The high probability of other addictive behaviors including alcoholism, drug abuse, and pathologic gambling
- Extreme disruption of the family, including battering, sexual abuse, and financial distress

## Behaviors

Clinicians should remember that the discovery of something sexual does not make an addictive illness. A long-term affair, for example, would be a problem for a spouse but would not be a compulsive pattern. Likewise, a person with exploitive or violent behavior does not necessarily have an addictive illness.

I have been gathering data on sexual addiction since 1985. In the process, I have found that sexually addictive behavior clusters into 10 distinct types. Patients often will be active in more than one cluster. That is one of the most important lessons of sexual addiction: Patterns exist among behaviors.

The 10 distinctive types of behaviors are:

- *Fantasy sex.* Arousal depends on sexual possibility. The individual neglects responsibilities to engage in fantasy and/or prepare for the next sexual episode.
- *Seductive role sex.* Arousal is based on conquest and diminishes rapidly after the initial contact. It can be heightened by increasing risk and/or number of partners.
- *Voyeuristic sex.* Visual stimulation is used to escape into an obsessive trance. Arousal may be heightened by masturbation or risk (peeping), or violation of boundaries (voyeuristic rape).
- *Exhibitionistic sex.* The individual attracts attention to the body or its sexual parts. Arousal stems from the shock or the interest of the viewer.

- *Paying for sex.* Arousal is connected to payment for sex and, with time, it actually becomes connected to money itself. Payment creates an entitlement and a sense of power over meeting needs. The arousal starts with "having money" and the search for someone in "the business."
- *Trading sex.* Arousal is based on gaining control of others by using sex as leverage.
- *Intrusive sex.* Arousal occurs by violating boundaries with no repercussions.
- *Anonymous sex.* Arousal involves no seduction or cost and is immediate. It has no entanglements or obligations associated with it and often is accelerated by unsafe or high-risk environments such as parks and restrooms.
- *Pain-exchange sex.* Arousal is built around specific scenarios or narratives of humiliation and shame.
- *Exploitive sex.* Arousal is based on target "types" of vulnerability. Certain types of vulnerable people (such as clients/patients) become the focus.

In addition, in recent years people have begun to use cybersex in unexpected numbers, and many are finding themselves accessing sex in problematic ways.

Individuals suffering from sexual addiction have found sex on the Internet a natural extension of what they are already doing. They can act out any of the previously mentioned 10 types of sexual behavior on the Internet. They can find sex partners, be voyeuristic, start affairs, and swap partners, among other things.

There are also many individuals who never would have experienced sexual compulsive behavior had it not been for the Internet. Consider this:

- About 200 sex-related Web sites are added each day, and there are more than 100,000 existing sites.
- Sex on the Internet constitutes the third largest economic sector on the Web (software and computers rank first and second), generating one billion dollars annually.
- A total of 65 million unique visitors use free porn sites, and 19 million unique visitors use pay porn sites each month.
- Approximately one percent of Internet users have a severe problem that focuses almost exclusively on cybersex, with major neglect of the rest of their life's activities.[2]

## Successful Treatment

A number of key factors are involved in successful recovery from sexual addition. They include:

- *A good addiction-oriented primary therapist.* Most successful recoveries involve a relationship with a therapist over a three- to five-year period, the first two years of which are very intense.

- *A 12-step sexual addiction group.* The probability of relapse is extremely high if the addict does not attend meetings.
- *A 12-step program for other addictions.* If the addict has other addictions, a 12-step program is necessary for those as well. A suggestion that makes things easier is to find a sponsor or sponsors who attends all of the same meetings your patient does. This way, there is a consolidation of relationships.
- *Program work, not just attendance.* Completing step work, finding a sponsor, and doing service are all key elements of recovery. Individuals should become actively involved in the program's activities. In a recent outcome study of an inpatient program for sexual addiction, researchers discovered that only 23 percent actually complete the first nine of the 12 steps in 18 months. However, of those who did, recidivism was rare.[3]
- *Early family involvement.* Family participation in the patient's therapy improves the chance for success.
- *Spiritual support.* Addicts report that the spiritual work started in their 12-step communities and continued in various spiritual communities was critical to the changes they needed to make.
- *Exercise along with good nutrition and a healthy lifestyle.* Addicts who reduce their stress, start an exercise program, and eat more healthfully do better in their recovery.

In discussing what had helped them in their recovery, over 190 sex addicts indicated that these treatments were the most helpful (in order from most to least): a higher power (87 percent); couples 12-step group based on sexual addiction (85 percent); a friend's support (69 percent); individual therapy (65 percent); a celibacy period (64 percent); a sponsor (61 percent); exercise/nutrition (58 percent); a 12-step group based on subjects other than sexual addiction (55 percent); partner support (36 percent); inpatient treatment (35 percent); outpatient group (27 percent); therapy (21 percent); family therapy (11 percent); and after care (hospital) (9 percent).[4]

## Healthy Sexuality

The goal of treatment is healthy sexuality. Some therapists insist on a period of celibacy, which does help to reduce chaos and make patients available for therapy. But recovery from sexual addiction does not mean sexual abstinence.

The objective of treatment is to help individuals develop a healthy, strong sexual life. One of the risks is that the patients may slip to a position of sexual aversion, in which they think all sex is bad. Sexual aversion, or "sexual anorexia," is simply another variant of sexual compulsive behavior.

Patients will sometimes bounce from one extreme to the other. True recovery involves a clear understanding about abstaining from certain sexual behaviors combined with an active plan for enhancing sexuality.

Recovery from sexual addiction is likened to recovery from eating disorders. Food is a necessary part of life, and recovery from eating disorders requires defining what is healthy eating and what is not. Similarly, the goal of recovery from sexual addiction is learning what is healthy sexuality for the individual.

Healthy sexuality for most sexually addicted individuals involves not only a change in behavior but also an avoidance of fantasizing about behaviors that are unhealthy. Sexual fantasizing can be healthy, particularly for a reasonably healthy couple that uses their increased excitement to move toward rather than away from the partner. However, sexual imagery that is not respectful of other human beings increases objectification, depersonalization, and destructive bonding based on hostility rather than affection. Asking patients about his or her "sobriety" definition and about the content of fantasies provides clues to help with treatment and recovery.

## Keeping Up

To determine how well the patient is doing in establishing a healthy lifestyle, clinicians can ask some simple questions. Does the patient have tools for avoiding relapse during times of hunger, anger, loneliness, and tiredness? Is the patient attending 12-step self-help meetings? If not, what are the obstacles preventing the patient from doing so? What are the patient's perceptions of what goes on at a meeting? Does he or she have a sponsor (a person longer in recovery who can guide the newer member)?

Is the patient seeking a counselor or therapist who is knowledgeable in addiction recovery? Is there balance between work and recreation? Is the patient exercising or engaging in any sports? Is the patient actively working to improve his or her relationship with a spouse or significant other? Is the spouse also attending a self-help meeting? These are all indicators to determine if the individual is fully engaged in building a healthier lifestyle.

## Conclusion

The treatment of sexual addiction has taken a long time to gain recognition and respect as an area of medical specialty.

As with other disorders, such as alcoholism or anorexia, clinicians face many challenges in learning about sexual addiction. Most who take time to learn find patients who are profoundly grateful.

In many ways, the field of sexual addiction lags behind both professional and lay awareness of alcoholism or anorexia. Yet, important strides are being made in both understanding and awareness.

Appreciating the issues and challenges of sexual addiction will help clinicians when their patients' behaviors cross the line from problems of judgment to symptoms of a clinical disorder.

## References

1. *Diagnostic and Statistical Manual of Mental Disorders* (Fourth Edition) (Washington, DC: American Psychiatric Association, 1994), pp. 181, 618.

2. P. Carnes et al, *In the Shadows of the Net* (Center City, MN: Hazelden Foundation, 2001), pp. 6–7.
3. P. Carnes, "Sexual Addiction and Compulsion: Recognition, Treatment, and Recovery," *CNS Spectrums*, Vol. 5, No. 10, October 2000, pp. 63–68.
4. Ibid.

**Lawrence A. Siegel and Richard M. Siegel**

# Sex Addiction: Recovering from a Shady Concept

It seems, more than ever, that many Americans are more comfortable keeping sex in the dark or, as sex addiction advocates might actually prefer, *in* the shadows. We seem to have gotten no further than the Puritan claims of sex being evil and pleasure being threatening. "The Devil made me do it" seems to be something of a battle cry, especially when someone gets caught cheating on their spouse, having inappropriate dalliances with congressional pages, or visiting prostitutes. Even those not in relationships are easily targeted. We constantly hear about the "dangers" of internet porn and how every internet chat room is just teeming with predators just waiting to devour our children. Daily masturbation is considered by these folks as being unhealthy and a marked pathology. As a society, we seem able to be comfortable with sex only as long as we make it uncomfortable. As one of the leading sexologists, Marty Klein, once wrote:

> "If mass murderer Ted Bundy had announced that watching Cosby Show reruns had motivated his awful crimes, he would have been dismissed as a deranged sociopath. Instead, Bundy proclaimed that his 'pornography addiction' made him do it, and many Right-wing feminists and conservatives treated this as the conclusion of a thoughtful social scientist. Why?"[1]

The whole idea of "sex addiction" is borne out of a moralistic ideology masquerading as science. It is a concept that seems to serve no other purpose than to relegate sexual expression to the level of shameful acts, except within the extremely narrow and myopic scope of a monogamous, heterosexual marriage. Sexual diversity? Interests in unusual forms or frequency of sexual expression? Choosing not to be monogamous? Advocates of "sex addiction" would likely see these as the uncontrollable acts of a sexually pathological individual; one who needs curing.

To be clear, we do not deny the fact that, for some people, sexual behavior can become problematic, even dysfunctional or unmanageable. Our objection is with the use of the term "sexual addiction" to describe a virtually unlimited array of—in fact, practically ANY—aspect of sexual expression that falls outside of the typically Christian view of marriage. We believe that the term contributes to a generally sex-negative, pleasure-phobic tone in American society, and it also tends to "pathologize" most forms of sexual expression that fall outside of a narrow view of what "normal" sex is supposed to look like. This is a point made clear by sex addiction advocates' own rhetoric. Three of the guiding principles of Sexaholics Anonymous include the notion that (1) sex is most healthy in the context of a monogamous, heterosexual relationship; (2) sexual expression has "obvious" limits; and (3) it is unhealthy to engage in any sexual activity for the sole purpose of feeling better, either emotionally or to escape one's problems. These principles do not represent either science or most people's experience. They, in fact, represent a restrictive and repressive view of sex and sexuality and reflect an arrogance that sex addiction proponents are the keepers of the scepter of morality and normalcy. Moreover, the concept of "sex addiction" comes out of a shame-based, arbitrarily judgmental addiction model and does not speak to the wide range of sexual diversity; both in and outside the context of a committed relationship.

A primary objection to the use of the term "sex addiction," an objection shared with regard to other supposed behavioral "addictions," is that the term *addiction* has long ago been discredited. Back in 1964, the World Health Organization (WHO) declared the term "addiction" to be clinically invalid and recommended in favor of dependence, which can exist in varying degrees of severity, as opposed to an all-or-nothing disease entity (as it is still commonly perceived).[2] This is when we began to see the terms *chemical dependency* and *substance abuse,* terms considered to be much more appropriate and clinically useful. This, however, did not sit well with the addiction industry. Another objection to the concept of "sex addiction" is that it is a misnomer whose very foundation as a clinically significant diagnosis is built on flawed and faulty premises. For example, a common assertion put forth by proponents of sex addiction states that the chemical actions in the brain during sexual activity are the same as the chemical activity involved in alcohol and drug use. They, therefore, claim that both sexual activity and substance abuse share reward and reinforcement mechanisms that produce the "craving" and "addictive" behaviors. This assertion is flawed on several levels, not the least of which is that it is based on drawing conclusions from brain scan imaging that are devoid of any real interpretive foundation; a "leap of faith," so to speak. Furthermore, it is somewhat of a stretch to equate the neurophysiological mechanisms which underlie chemical dependency, tolerance, and withdrawal with the underlying mechanisms of what is most often obsessive-compulsive or anxiety-reducing behaviors like gambling, shopping, and sex. Another example often cited by sex addiction proponents is the assertion that, like alcohol and drugs, the "sex addict" is completely incapable of controlling his or her self-destructive behavior. Of course, this begs the question of how, then, can one change behavior they are incapable of controlling? More importantly, however, is the unique excuse this "disease" model provides for abdicating personal responsibility. "It's not my fault, I have a disease." Finally, a major assertion put out by sex addiction advocates is that anyone who is hypersexual in any way (e.g., frequent masturbation, anonymous "hook ups," infidelity, and cybersex) must have been abused as children or adolescents. Again, the flaws here are obvious and serve to continue to relegate any type of frequent sexual engagement to the pathological and unseemly.

Every clinician knows that "addiction" is not a word that appears anywhere in the *Diagnostic and Statistical Manual,* or "DSM," the diagnostic guidebook used by psychiatrists and psychologists to make any psychopathological diagnosis. Nor does it appear in any of the International Classification of Diseases (ICD-10), codes used for classifying medical diagnoses. "Abuse" and "dependence" do appear in the DSM, relevant only to substance use patterns, but "addiction" does not. Similarly, there is an ICD-10 code for "substance dependence," but not addiction. Why? Perhaps because the word means different things to different people, especially when used in so many different contexts. Even without acknowledging the many trivial uses of the addiction concept, such as bumper stickers that proclaim, *"addicted to sports, not drugs,"* cookies that claim to be *"deliciously addicting,"* Garfield coffee mugs that warn *"don't talk to me until after my first cup,"* or T-shirts that say *"chocoholic,"* there aren't even consistent *clinical* definitions for the concept of addiction. A 1993 study, published in the *American Journal of Drug and Alcohol Abuse,* compared the diagnostic criteria for substance abuse and dependence between the DSM and ICD-10. The results showed very little agreement between the two.[3]

Pharmacologists, researchers who study the effects of drugs, define addiction primarily based on the presence of tolerance and withdrawal. Both of these phenomena are based on pharmacological and toxicological concepts of "cellular adaptation," wherein the body, at the very cellular level, becomes accustomed to the constant presence of a substance, and readjusts for "normal" function; in other words, whatever the "normal" response was before regular use of the substance began returns. This adaptation first accounts for tolerance, wherein an increasing dose of the substance to which the system has adapted is needed to maintain the same level of "normal." Then it results in withdrawal, wherein any discontinuation of the substance disrupts the "new" equilibrium the system has achieved and symptoms of "withdrawal sickness" ensue. This is probably most often attributed to addiction to opiates, such as heroin, because of its comparison to "having a monkey on one's back," with a constantly growing appetite, and its notorious "cold turkey" withdrawal. But perhaps it is most commonly observed with the chronic use of drugs with less sinister reputations, such as caffeine, nicotine or alcohol.

Traditional psychotherapists may typically define addiction as a faulty coping mechanism, or more accurately, the *result* of using a faulty coping mechanism to deal with some underlying issue. Another way to consider this is to see addiction as the symptom, rather than the disease, which is why the traditional therapist, of any theoretical orientation, is likely to want to find the causative issue or issues, and either teach the patient more effective coping mechanisms or resolve the unresolved issue(s) altogether.

Another definition of addiction has emerged, and seems to have taken center-stage, since the development of a pseudo-medical specialty known as "addictionology" within the last twenty or so years. Made up primarily of physicians, but including a variety of "addiction professionals," this field has helped to forge a treatment industry based on the disease model of addiction that is at the core of 12-Step "fellowships," such as Alcoholics Anonymous and Narcotics Anonymous. Ironically, despite the resistance to medical or psychiatric treatment historically expressed in AA or NA, their philosophy has become the mainstay of the addictionological paradigm.

If the concept of chemical addictions, which have a neurophysiological basis that can be measured and observed, yields no clinical consensus, how, then, can we legitimize the much vaguer notion that individuals can be "addicted" to behavior, people, emotions, or even one's own brain chemistry? Other than to undermine responsibility and self-determination, we really can't. It does a tremendous disservice to our clients and patients to brand them with a label so full of judgment, arbitrary opinion, and fatuous science. It robs individuals of the ability to find their own levels of comfort and, ultimately, be the determining force in directing their own lives. There is a significant and qualitative difference between the person who acts because he or she can't (not a choice, but a position of default) and the person who is empowered to choose not to. As clinicians, we should be loathe to send our clients and patients down such a fearful, shameful road.

In 1989, Patrick Carnes, founder of the sex addiction movement, wrote a book entitled "*Contrary to Love.*" The book is rife with rhetoric and personal ideology that reveals Carnes's lack of training, knowledge, and understanding of sexuality and sexual expression; not surprising for someone whose background is solely in the disease model of alcoholism. This, while seemingly a harsh judgment, is clearly reflected in his Sex Addiction Screening Test (SAST). Even a cursory glance at the items on the SAST show a deep-seeded bias against most forms of sexual expression. Unlike other legitimate screening and assessment tools, there is no scientific foundation that would show this tool to be credible (i.e., tests of reliability and validity). Instead, Carnes developed this "test" by simply culling his own ideas from his book. Annie Sprinkle, America's first adult-film-star-turned-PhD-Sexologist, has written a very good web article on the myth of sex addiction. In it, she also describes some of the shortcomings of the SAST. While not describing the complete test here, a listing of some of the assessment questions are listed below, along with commentary.[4]

1. *Have you subscribed to sexually explicit magazines like* Playboy *or* Penthouse? This question is based on the assumption that it is unhealthy to view images of naked bodies. Does that mean that the millions of people who subscribe to or buy adult magazines are sex addicts? Are adolescent boys who look at the *Sports Illustrated* Swim Suit edition budding sex addicts? By extension, if looking at Playboy or Penthouse is unhealthy and pathological, then those millions of people who look at hardcore magazines or Internet porn should be hospitalized!
2. *Do you often find yourself preoccupied with sexual thoughts?* This is totally nebulous. What does "preoccupied" mean? How often does one have to think about sex in order to constitute preoccupation? Research has shown that men, on average, think about sex every eight seconds; does that mean that men are inherently sex addicts?
3. *Do you feel that your sexual behavior is not normal?* What is normal? What do they use as a comparison? As sexologists, we can state unequivocally that the majority of people's sexual concerns relate, in one way or another, to the question "Am I normal?" This is incredibly vague, nebulous, and laughably unscientific.

4. *Are any of your sexual activities against the law?* This question is also steeped in a bias that there is only a narrowly acceptable realm of sexual expression. It assumes that any sexual behavior that is against the law is bad. Is being or engaging a prostitute a sign of pathology? What about the fact that oral sex, anal sex, and woman on top are illegal in several states?
5. *Have you ever felt degraded by your sexual behavior?* Again, there is a serious lack of quantification here. Does regretting a sexual encounter constitute feeling degraded? Does performing oral sex for your partner, even though you think it's degrading, constitute a pathology or compromise? What if one's partner does something during sex play that is unexpected and perceived as degrading (like ejaculating on someone's face or body)? What if someone enjoys feeling degraded? This question pathologizes at least half of the S/M and B/D communities. Moreover, anyone who has had a long and active sexual life may likely, at one point, have felt degraded. It is important to note that this question does not ask if one consistently puts oneself in a position of being degraded but, rather, have you ever felt degraded. We suspect that most people can lay claim to that.
6. *Has sex been a way for you to escape your problems?* Is there a better way to escape one's problems temporarily? This is a common bias used against both sex and alcohol use: using sex or alcohol to provide relief from anxieties or problems is inherently problematic. It also begs the question: why are things like sex and alcohol not appropriate to change how one is feeling but Zoloft, Paxil, Xanax, and Klonopin are? The truth of the matter is that sex is often an excellent and healthy way to occasionally experience relief from life's stressors and problems.
7. *When you have sex, do you feel depressed afterwards?* Sex is often a great way to get in touch with one's feelings. Oftentimes, people do feel depressed after a sexual experience, for any number of reasons. Furthermore, this doesn't mean that sex was the depressing part! Perhaps people feel depressed because they had dashed expectations of the person they were involved with. Unfulfilled expectations, lack of communication, and inattentiveness to one's needs and desires often result in post-coital feelings of sadness and disappointment. In addition, asking someone if they "feel depressed" is arbitrary, subjective, and clinically invalid.
8. *Do you feel controlled by your sexual desire?* Again, we are being asked to make an arbitrary, subjective, and clinically invalid assessment. There is an undercurrent here that seems to imply that a strong sexual desire is somehow not normal. Human beings are biologically programmed to strongly desire sex. Our clients and patients might be better served if we addressed not their desires, but how and when they act upon them.

Again, it needs noting that the concept of "sex addiction" is one with very little clinical relevance or usefulness, despite it's popularity. Healthy sexual expression encompasses a wide array of forms, functions, and frequency, as well as myriad emotional dynamics and personal experiences. Healthy behavior, in general, and sexual behavior, in particular, exists on a continuum rather than a quantifiable point. Using the addiction model to describe sexual behavior simply adds to the shame and stigma that is already too often attached to various forms of sexual expression. Can sexual behaviors become problematic? Most certainly. However, we must be careful to not overpathologize even problematic sexual behaviors because, most often, they are symptomatic expressions rather than primary problems.

For many years, sexologists have described compulsive sexual behavior, where sexual obsessions and compulsions are recurrent, distressing, and interfere with daily functioning. The actual number of people suffering from this type of sexual problem is relatively small. Compulsive sexual behaviors are generally divided into two broad categories: *paraphilic* and *non-paraphilic*.[5] Paraphilias are defined as recurrent, intensely arousing fantasies, sexual urges, or behaviors involving non-human objects, pain and humiliation, or children.[6] Paraphilic behaviors are usually non-conventional forms of sexual expression that, in the extreme, can be harmful to relationships and individuals. Some examples of paraphilias listed in the DSM are pedophilia (sexual attraction to children), exhibitionism (exposing one's genitals in public), voyeurism (sexual excitement from watching an unsuspecting person), sexual sadism (sexual excitement from dominating or inflicting pain), sexual masochism (sexual excitement from being dominated or receiving pain), transvestic fetishism (sexual excitement from wearing clothes of the other sex), and frotteurism (sexual excitement from rubbing up against or fondling an unsuspecting person). All of these behaviors exist on a continuum of healthy fantasy play to dangerous, abusive, and illegal acts. A sexologist is able to view these behaviors in varying degrees, knowing the difference between teacher-student fantasy role play and cruising a playground for victims; between provocative exhibitionist displays (including public displays of affection) and illegal, abusive public exposure. For those with a "sex addiction" perspective, simply having paraphilic thoughts or desires of any kind is reason to brand the individual a "sex addict."

The other category of compulsive sexual behavior is non-paraphilic, and generally involves more conventional sexual behaviors which, when taken to the extreme, cause marked distress and interference with daily functioning. This category includes a fixation on an unattainable partner, compulsive masturbation, compulsive love relationships, and compulsive sexuality in a relationship. The most vocal criticism of the idea of compulsive sexual behavior as a clinical disorder appears to center on the overpathologizing of these behaviors. Unless specifically trained in sexuality, most clinicians are either uncomfortable or unfamiliar with the wide range of "normal" sexual behavior and fail to distinguish between individuals who experience conflict between their values and sexual behavior, and those with obsessive sexual behavior.[7] When diagnosing compulsive sexual behavior overall, there is little consensus even among sexologists. However, it still provides a more useful clinical framework for the professional trained in sexuality and sexual health.

To recognize that sexual behavior can be problematic is not the same as labeling the behaviors as "sexually compulsive" or "sexual addiction." The reality is that sexual problems are quite common and are usually due to non-pathological factors. Quite simply, people make mistakes (some more than others). People also act impulsively. People don't always make good sexual choices. When people do make mistakes, act impulsively, and make bad decisions, it often negatively impacts their relationships; sometimes even their lives. Moreover, people do often use sex as a coping mechanism or, to borrow from addiction language, medicating behavior that can become problematic. However, this is qualitatively different from the concept that problematic sexual behavior means the individual is a "sexual addict" with uncontrollable urges and potentially dangerous intent. Most problematic sexual behavior can be effectively redirected (and cured) through psycho-sexual education, counseling, and experience. According to proponents of "sex addiction," problematic sexual behavior cannot be cured. Rather, the "sex addict" is destined for a life of maintaining a constant vigil to prevent the behavior from reoccurring, often to the point of obsession, and will be engaged in a lifelong process of recovery. Unfortunately, this view often causes people to live in fear of the "demon" lurking around every corner: themselves.

## References

1. Klein M. The myth of sex addiction. Sexual Intelligence: An Electronic Newsletter (Issue #1). March, 2000. . . .
2. Center for Substance Abuse Treatment (CSAT) and Substance Abuse and Mental Health Services Administration (SAMHSA). Substance use disorders: A guide to the use of language. 2004.
3. Rappaport M., Tipp J., Schuckit M. A comparison of ICD-10 and DSM-III criteria for substance abuse and dependence. American Journal of Drug and Alcohol Abuse. June, 1993.
4. Sprinkle, A. Sex addiction. Online article. . . .
5. Coleman E. What sexual scientists know about compulsive sexual behavior. Electronic series of the Society for the Scientific Study of Sexuality (SSSS). Vol 2(1). 1996. . . .
6. American Psychiatric Association. Diagnostic and Statistical Manual of Mental Disorders. 4th edition, TR. Washington: American Psychiatric Publishing. June, 2000.
7. Coleman E. What sexual scientists know about compulsive sexual behavior. Electronic series of the Society for the Scientific Study of Sexuality (SSSS). Vol 2(1). 1996. . . .

# CHALLENGE QUESTIONS

## Can Sex Be Addictive?

1. The Siegels see the "diagnosis" of sexual addiction as having a moral basis. Are there other, more conventional diagnoses in the *DSM-IV* that might also be viewed in this manner? If so, what implications would this have for those diagnoses?
2. Examine some of the addiction literature and see what other definitions of "addiction" there might be. What might those definitions imply about the possibility of a sexual addiction? Support your answer.
3. Imagine you are working with a couple in therapy and the husband frequently views pornography. What possible dangers could his behavior present? Should his habit be considered a sexual addiction? Support your answer.
4. What is involved in the process of a 12-step program? How well do these programs address the specific issues involved in sex addiction? What might the Siegels criticize about the application of the Alcoholics Anonymous model to sex?
5. Compare and contrast the physiological mechanisms underlying chemical addiction with the physiological mechanisms underlying sexual stimulation. Are they similar as Carnes seems to believe?
6. What is "healthy sex"? Who should get to define it? Would what is considered "healthy" sexual practices be different for a (recovering) sex addict?

# Contributors to This Volume

## EDITOR

**DR. BRENT SLIFE** is currently professor of psychology at Brigham Young University, where he chairs the doctoral program in theoretical and philosophical psychology and serves as a member of the doctoral program in clinical psychology. He has been honored recently with several awards for his scholarship and teaching, including the Eliza R. Snow Award (for research on the interface of science and religion), the Karl G. Maeser Award (top researcher at BYU), Circle of Honor Award (Student Honor Association), and both Teacher of the Year by the university and Most Outstanding Professor by the psychology student honorary, Psi Chi.

Professor Slife moved from Baylor University where he served as director of clinical training for many years and was honored there as Outstanding Research Professor. He also received the Circle of Achievement award for his teaching. The recipient of numerous grants (e.g., NSF, NEH), he is also listed in *Who's Who in the World, America, Science and Engineering,* and *Health and Medicine.* As a fellow of several professional organizations, including the American Psychological Association, he recently served as the president of the Society of Theoretical and Philosophical Psychology and serves currently on the editorial boards of six journals: *Journal of Mind and Behavior, Journal of Theoretical and Philosophical Psychology, Humanistic Psychologist, Qualitative Research in Psychology, International Journal of Existential Psychology and Psychotherapy,* and *Terrorism Research.*

He has authored over 120 articles and six books, including *Taking Sides: Clashing Views on Psychological Issues* (2008, McGraw-Hill), *Critical Thinking About Psychology: Hidden Assumptions and Plausible Alternatives* (2005, APA Books), *Critical Issues in Psychotherapy: Translating New Ideas into Practice* (2001, Sage Publications), *What's Behind the Research? Hidden Assumptions in the Behavioral Sciences* (1995, Sage Publications), and *Time and Psychological Explanation* (1993, SUNY Press). Dr. Slife also continues his psychotherapy practice of over 25 years, where he specializes in marital and family therapies. Please check his website, www.brentdslife.com, for downloadable articles and links to his books.

# AUTHORS

**CONSTANCE AHRONS** is professor emeritus from the Department of Sociology and former director of the Marriage and Family Therapy Doctoral Training Program at the University of Southern California. An internationally renowned lecturer, researcher, family therapist and consultant, she has received several prestigious awards and has published over 40 articles and books. Dr. Ahrons is the director of Divorce and Remarriage Consulting Associates.

**BRENDA J. ALLEN** is an Associate Dean in the College of Liberal Arts and Sciences, and a professor in the Department of Communication at the University of Colorado, Denver. Her research and teaching areas are organizational communication, diversity, group communication, and computer-mediated communication. Dr. Allen has received numerous awards and accolades, including the Francine Merritt Award for Outstanding Contributions to the Lives of Women in Communication from the National Communication Association.

**LOUANN BRIZENDINE** is a practicing clinician, author, and teacher who specializes in the relationship dynamics that result from the neurobiology of male and female brains. She completed her degree in neurobiology at UC Berkeley, graduated from Yale School of Medicine and did her internship and residency at Harvard Medical School. Dr. Brizendine founded the Women's Mood and Hormone Clinic.

**DAVID J. BULLER** is a professor in the department of philosophy at Northern Illinois University. He has published numerous articles and books on evolutionary psychology.

**BRAD BUSHMAN** is a research professor for the Institute for Social Research at the University of Michigan. He received his Ph.D. from the University of Missouri. His research interests focus on the causes and consequences of human aggression.

**DAVID BUSS** is a professor of psychology at The University of Texas at Austin and is well known for his evolutionary psychology research on human mating strategies. He is the author of over 200 scientific articles and has won several awards for his work such as the *APA Distinguished Scientific Award for Early Career Contribution to Psychology* and the *APA G. Stanley Hall Lectureship*.

**LISA D. BUTLER** is a research associate and professor in the School of Social Work at the University at Buffalo, SUNY. She received her Ph.D. from Stanford University. Her research interests include trauma, resilience, and dissociative processes.

**KEITH CAMPBELL** is a professor of social psychology at the University of Georgia. He received his Ph.D. from the University of North Carolina and has published numerous articles and books, chiefly on the topic of narcissism.

**MARK COSTANZO** is a professor of psychology and the co-director of the Center for Applied Psychological Research at Claremont McKenna College. He has published research on a variety of law related topics. He frequently serves as an expert witness and has appeared in the national media to discuss the applications of psychological science to the legal system.

**LAUREN DONCHI** has a bachelor's degree with honors from Swinburne University in Melbourne, Australia. She is a registered psychologist with a strong background in schools and education and is currently employed by the Department of Education & Training to provide psychology services within a network of schools in outer eastern Melbourne.

**BRENT DONNELLAN** is a professor of psychology at Michigan State University. He received his Ph.D. from the University of California, Davis. His research interests include personality development, self-esteem, and narcissism.

**JOSHUA D. FOSTER** is a professor of social psychology at the University of South Alabama. He received his Ph.D. from the University of Georgia and his primary research interests include narcissism, personality, and relationships.

**EDWIN GANTT** is a professor of psychology at Brigham Young University. He received his Ph.D. in from Duquesne University. Dr. Gantt is interested in theory and philosophy of psychology and co-edited *Psychology for the Other: Levinas, Ethics and the Practice of Psychology.*

**GLENN GEHER** is professor and Director of Evolutionary Studies in the Deparment of Psychology at SUNY New Paltz. He received his Ph.D. in social and personality psychology.

**ELLEN GERRITY** is the associate director of the UCLA-Duke University National Center for Child Traumatic Stress and is on the faculty of the Duke University Department of Psychiatry and the Duke University Sanford Institute of Policy Studies. She has worked in the field of trauma and violence for over 25 years and is the senior editor of *Mental Health Consequences of Torture.*

**DAVID H. GLEAVES** is a professor of psychology at University of Canterbury. His primary research interests include eating disorders and behaviors, body image, dissociative disorders, and taxometric methods.

**KIRK M. HUBBARD** received his doctorate from the University of Minnesota, Minneapolis and has served in both administrative and clinical positions in the Veterans Administration Medical Center in Hampton, VA. He has also held adjunct faculty positions at the Eastern Virginia Medical School and the College of William & Mary. Dr. Hubbard served as a psychologist supporting field operations for the Central Intelligence Agency for ten years and served as the Director of Behavioral Sciences Research at the CIA. Dr. Hubbard is now president of Porter Judson, LLC, a private consulting firm involved in the application of psychology to operational and field settings.

**STANTON JONES** is a professor of psychology and provost at Wheaton College. He received his Ph.D. in Clinical Psychology at Arizona State University and is the author of over 50 articles and book chapters.

**JOHN F. KIHLSTROM** is a professor of psychology and director of the Group Major in Cognitive Science at the University of California, Berkeley. He received his Ph.D. from the University of Pennsylvania.

**SARA H. KONRATH** works at the University of Michigan in the Research Center for Group Dynamics. Her research interests include narcissism and political psychology.

**ALEX W. KWEE** is a licensed clinical psychologist and co-founder and president of Harmony Pacific Clinical Consultants (HPCC). He has published and presented internationally on various facets of cross cultural psychology, values, and addiction.

**M. BRINTON LYKES** is a professor of community-cultural psychology in the Lynch School of Education and the associate director of the Boston College Center for Human Rights and International Justice. She has contributed chapters on participatory action research in the Handbooks of Feminist Research and Action Research II and a chapter on reparations and psychosocial interventions in the Handbook on Reparations, a project of the International Center of Transitional Justice. She is the 2007 recipient of the American Orthopsychiatric Association's Marion Langer Award for distinction in social advocacy and the pursuit of human rights.

**ELIZABETH MARQUARDT** is director of the Center for Marriage and Families at the Institute for American Values in New York City and is widely known for her work on the impact of divorce. Marquardt holds an M.Div. and an M.A. in international relations from the University of Chicago and a B.A. in history and women's studies from Wake Forest University.

**BRENT MELLING** is a doctoral candidate in theoretical and philosophical psychology at Brigham Young University. He holds a B.S. in Bioinformatics.

**SUSAN MOORE** is a professor in the department of life and social sciences at the University of Swinburne. She has over 30 years teaching and research experience in universities, in psychology and education as well as experience as a school psychologist.

**JOCHEN PETER** is an associate professor in the Amsterdam School of Communications Research at the University of Amsterdam. He received a Veni award for talented junior researchers from the Dutch National Science Foundation. His research focuses on the consequences of adolescents' internet use for their sexual socialization and psycho-social development.

**QAZI RAHMAN** is a cognitive biologist at Queen Mary, University of London. His research interests focus on the biological origin of sexual orientation in humans.

**RICHARD ROBINS** is a professor in the department of psychology at the University of California, Davis. He received his Ph.D. from the University of California, Berkeley. He has received the APA's Distinguished Scientific Award for Early Career Contribution and the Theoretical Innovation Prize from the Society for Personality and Social Psychology.

**STEVEN M. SMITH** obtained his B.A. in psychology from Bishop's University and his M.A. and Ph.D. from Queen's University in Kingston, Ontario. Dr. Smith currently serves as professor of psychology and associate dean of science at Saint Mary's University. His research interests include attitudes and persuasion, psychology and law, the role of human factors in decision making, and how this issues relate to specific health outcomes.

**DAVID SPIEGEL** is a professor of psychiatry & behavioral science at Stanford University. He currently directs the Center on Stress and Health. His research interests involve stress and health: cognitive control over somatic functions, the response to traumatic stress, and the perception of pain and anxiety.

**KALI TRZESNIEWSKI** is a professor of psychology at the University of Western Ontario. Receiving a Ph.D. from the University of California, Davis, Dr. Trzesniewski's research interests include self-esteem and academic achievement.

**JEAN TWENGE** is a professor of psychology at San Diego State University. She has published extensive research on narcissism and young people. She received her Ph.D. from the University of Michigan.

**PATTI M. VALKENBURG** is a professor in the Amsterdam School of Communications Research and director of the Center for Research on Children, Adolescents, and the Media. She received her Ph.D. from Leiden University, the Netherlands. She received a Vici award for top researchers from the Dutch National Science Foundation. Her research interests include children's and adolescents' likes and dislikes of entertainment, their development as consumers, and the cognitive, emotional, and social effects of media contents and technologies on young people.

**ROGERS H. WRIGHT** is a past president of Division 12 and founding president of Division 31 of the APA. He co-founded and was founding president of the Council for the Advancement of the Psychological Professions and Sciences.